Economic and Social History of Modern Europe

Edited by

Prof. Dr. Jan-Otmar Hesse
Prof. Dr. Christian Kleinschmidt
Dr. Alfred Reckendrees, Associate Professor
Prof. Ray Stokes, Ph.D.

Volume 8

Politics of Security

Edited by

Prof. Dr. Thorsten Bonacker
Prof. Dr. Horst Carl
Prof. Dr. Eckart Conze
Prof. Dr. Christoph Kampmann
Prof. Dr. Regina Kreide
Dr. Angela Marciniak

This volume is associated with the Nomos publication series "Politics of Security", which is edited and supported by the Collaborative Research Centre/Transregio 138 "Dynamics of Security" at the universities of Marburg and Gießen.

Mark Jakob | Nina Kleinöder
Christian Kleinschmidt [eds.]

Security and Insecurity in Business History

Case Studies in the Perception and Negotiation of Threats

Nomos

Published with support from the Deutsche Forschungsgemeinschaft (DFG) in the context of the Collaborative Research Centre 138 "Dynamics of Security. Processes of Securitization in Historical Perspective" at the universities of Marburg and Gießen.

The Deutsche Nationalbibliothek lists this publication in the Deutsche Nationalbibliografie; detailed bibliographic data are available on the Internet at http://dnb.d-nb.de

ISBN 978-3-8487-8071-6 (Print)
978-3-7489-2457-9 (ePDF)

British Library Cataloguing-in-Publication Data
A catalogue record for this book is available from the British Library.

ISBN 978-3-8487-8071-6 (Print)
978-3-7489-2457-9 (ePDF)

Library of Congress Cataloging-in-Publication Data
Jakob, Mark / Kleinöder, Nina / Kleinschmidt, Christian
Security and Insecurity in Business History
Case Studies in the Perception and Negotiation of Threats
Mark Jakob / Nina Kleinöder / Christian Kleinschmidt (eds.)
282 pp.
Includes bibliographic references.

ISBN 978-3-8487-8071-6 (Print)
978-3-7489-2457-9 (ePDF)

Onlineversion
Nomos eLibrary

1st Edition 2021

Acknowledgements

The editors want to thank the people who made this book possible despite the obstacles created by the COVID-19 pandemic. A conference that was planned for June 2020 had to be cancelled, and the contributions to this book were written in insecure times indeed. We are grateful to the authors for devoting their time and expertise to this venture in a difficult situation. The collaborative research group (*Sonderforschungsbereich/Transregio*) 138 "Dynamics of Security" at the universities of Marburg and Gießen provided us with the theoretical groundwork and inspiration as well as the material basis for this publication. The copy editor Chris Riley contributed innumerable valuable comments and suggestions, and we had reliable support by our student assistant Lars Eike. This book appears as part of two different series, one of which addresses economic historians and the other scholars in security studies and security history, thus reflecting its intended combination of the two disciplines. We are grateful for the opportunity to present our work to the reader in this form through the help and support of many. The mistakes, however, are all our own.

Mark Jakob, Nina Kleinöder, Christian Kleinschmidt
Marburg, December 2020

Table of Contents

The Security and Insecurity of Enterprises: Constructing and Negotiating Dangers, Hazards, and Threats in Business History

Mark Jakob & Nina Kleinöder

Introduction

By definition, business is risky, but only sometimes it is dangerous. In this volume, we set out to explore how enterprises conceived of the boundaries between risk and danger, security and insecurity, and what effect these observations had on their entrepreneurial decisions. In everyday business, enterprises make decisions based on their anticipation of their relative chances of loss or gain in the market. The risk of bankruptcy does not, in principle, endanger the security of the economic system. Business failure is an integral part of the capitalist economy, and not a fatal flaw that needs to be eliminated. However, war, revolution, terrorism, state failure, the breakdown of social order, pandemics, piracy, and so on create external perils that, as so-called *political risks* or *catastrophic risks*, go beyond the routine risk assessments of enterprises.[1] When, for instance, enterprises ponder events and changes that might very well not only put an end to their own existence, but to the very social and economic order that is a condition for the existence of enterprises *per se*, and attempt to persuade political leaders to take vigorous preventive action, then we no longer deal with business risks, but with security issues. Security from catastrophic threats usually cannot be provided by enterprises themselves. In the modern world, states are thus the first and primary, but not the only, addressee of security requests. At the time of writing, the world is undergoing a fundamental economic crisis that was deliberately caused by measures to counter a pandemic. Suddenly, economic security must be measured against the threat of the virus, and we observe highly diverse and controversial responses between the countries of the globe in weighing economic losses against the health and lives of citizens. Enterprises here are made the object of protec-

1 Cf. e.g. *Kobrak/Hansen*, European Business; *Forbes/Kurosawa/Wubs (eds.)*, Multinational Enterprise; *Donzé*, Advantage.

tive measures. Inversely, enterprises themselves can and often did pose serious threats to their social, political, and natural environment, either in collusion with or against state agencies. Lastly, enterprises (especially private security firms, IT providers, and insurance companies) commodify security and sell products and services promising safety from harm, or they use the language and images of security as a marketing tool. In these cases, business itself becomes an issue of and an agent for security.[2] It follows that the security and insecurity of enterprises is a variable rather than a constant, and business history must solve the question as to what the terms "security" and "insecurity" refer.

The idea for this edited volume came from the observation that phenomena of *security* and *safety* are ubiquitous in business history, but that there is no systematic study of the topic. The book project is meant as a first step in this direction. In the context of the transregional collaborative research centre "Dynamics of Security" (SFB/Transregio 138), an interdisciplinary research group of historians, social scientists, political scientists, art historians, and legal historians,[3] it was originally planned as the result of an international conference in the summer of 2020. However, personal exchange in the year of Corona became impossible for the project. Thanks to the commitment of the contributors, it was nevertheless possible to compile the different case studies in a digital workshop as a first contribution to this field. We therefore aim to address the rise of *security* as a topic in history, and how business history might be affected by the growing interest in historical security studies. Our involvement in the collaborative research group "Dynamics of Security" at the universities of Marburg and Gießen provides us with the theoretical background of historical Critical Security Studies (CSS) and hopefully enables us to make connections between the rising interest in the history of security and economic and business history.

The business world has been changing and evolving together with and in relation to the state, law, society, religion, and science since the Early Modern period. Its conceptions of what acceptable risks were and how peril should be coped with have changed accordingly. Security and insecurity therefore should be understood as bound in their historical context and as the construction of concrete situations by historical actors, not as abso-

2 Cf. e.g. *Daniels*, Landesverrat; *Daniels*, Brain Drain.

3 DFG Collaborative Research Centre/Transregio 138: "Dynamics of Security. Types of Securitization from a Historical Perspective", URL: <https://www.sfb138.de/en/> [08.12.2020].

lutes. Nevertheless, historical analysis requires at least an abstract definition of "security", "risk", "danger", and so forth. Generally speaking, "[c]hance, risk, and security make up a triad of interacting modes of handling uncertainty".[4] For our purposes, we start with the distinction between the concept of "risk", which is well-established in economics and business history, and the (in business history under-researched) concept of "security". Security studies provide inspiration: "Whereas risk describes an active stance of seeking out uncertainty for the possible gains contained in it, security designates a constellation in which the perception of a malevolent threat creates the necessity to act."[5] This constructivist perspective towards "security" does not suggest that threats are fictitious, but rather directs our attention to historical change in realising them and coping with them.

The first section of this introduction will explore the semantic field of "danger" and "security", and examine what these terms can mean for the interpretation of historical cases. The second section will discuss *security* as a topic in business history. By employing the approaches of historical security studies to business history, we assemble preliminary ideas of and approaches towards the nexus of *enterprise* and *security*. The case studies in this volume will be introduced in the third section, where we point out common themes and topics that connect the contributions and their diverse subject matters.

1. *The semantics of security and insecurity: risk, danger, and threats*

Security is not a sharply defined concept, and any treatment of security has to start with a few remarks on terminology. The term has normative connotations and can denote many things. "*Security*" has been a key political concept since the beginnings of modern statehood in the Early Modern period, reaching the same importance as other core concepts like *liberty* or *justice*. Originally meaning the security from aggression that states provided to their citizens or subjects, the nineteenth and twentieth centuries in particular saw an expansion of the realm of security to areas beyond the classic military and political sphere. Internal security looks back on the long tradition of policing cities and the countryside, but urbanisation, industrialisation, and social struggle led to new forms of policing in the

4 *Voelz*, Chance, 391.
5 *Voelz*, Chance, 398.

nineteenth century, and the dissolution of a clear-cut distinction between external and internal threats blurs the lines between internal and external security.[6] Social security, especially in the form of social insurance, emerged as the third pillar of classical security. Since the 1970s, security studies observed an expansion of the concept of security to more dimensions.[7] Global environmental security, for example, is a relatively young subject, which nevertheless shares the key elements of a security issue: the evocation of a threat against which swift and effective measures have to be taken at the peril of irreversible comprehensive damage and destruction. Although natural disasters are a constant in human history, and modern techniques, including insurance, were developed for coping with them in the late eighteenth century and contributed to the emergence of the modern welfare state,[8] the view that the natural environment itself has become a threatened object and that its security must have priority emerged only in the later twentieth century. If companies appear as actors in a history of environmental security, then as part of a larger history of modernity and its secularised language of security, for which *risk* has been identified as the key term.[9]

Although *risk* and *security/insecurity* are related concepts, we would like to emphasise a fundamental difference. *Risk* is understood as the driving force behind economic development and innovations because, in a Schumpeterian sense, it designates opportunities. Enterprises are rewarded with profits for taking risks in the market, and the costs of failure can be calculated and hedged, provided that prudency and capital are not in short supply. However, the overemphasis of a positively-connotated "entrepreneurial risk" neglects economic actors' fundamental desire for security and aversion to risk. Risk-taking is only made possible by a sufficient degree of stability and security. For example, the globalisation backlash of the 1930s was also the breakdown of certainty and confidence in economic institu-

6 Cf. *Conze*, Sicherheit; *Krüger*, Dienstethos. See also for an overview *de Graaf/Zwierlein*, Historicizing Security, 47–50.

7 For an overview, cf. *Conze*, Sicherheit, 47–68.

8 *Hannig*, Kalkulierte Gefahren.

9 *Zwierlein*, Prometheus; "Global Cultures of Risk. Insurance in Non-Western Contexts (1870–1980)", URL: <https://www.culturesofrisk.net/> [08.12.2020].

tions.[10] Business history needs only look to cartel history[11] to find plenty of examples for measures that were designed to eliminate risks. States guarantee investments and exports, or bail out companies in trouble. The elimination of risks is not necessarily a security measure, but we can observe a recourse to security in the dialogue of business and politics in these cases, as several contributions in this volume show. *Security* appears as a category of its own apart from business history's dominant perspective on risk.

For our purposes, *security* as an analytical category can be broken down into at least four dimensions. First, *security* in the classical sense refers to protection from threats provided in the first place by the political system. This dimension encompasses the range of dangers that are man-made and existential, and closest to what is rubricated as *security* in the context of International Relations.[12] Second, *safety* refers primarily to technical security, both of production facilities and employees. In the case of nuclear power plants, security would be concerned with protection from terrorist attacks, for instance, and safety would be concerned with preventing malfunctions and accidents, as well as protecting the health of the workforce, and is thus closely connected to the term *prevention* in the course of the twentieth century. Third, *certainty* refers to the ability to identify and assess threats, and to distinguish risks from dangers. The use of knowledge, experience, and science to project outcomes is captured within the concept of "heuristics" (see below). However, the concept of heuristics is not limited to intrinsic modes of risk assessment and danger projection of a given historical subject, but rather asks for the cognitive frames of reference to which actors revert when distinguishing between secure and insecure situations. Fourth, *confidence* refers to economic actors' trust in their ability to act successfully within the economic system and to trust in the stability of institutions. Security situations are marked by a sense of threat that challenges economic actors' confidence in the established routines and procedures of political, social, and economic systems to cope with shocks and crises.[13] Communi-

10 "Complex transactions and relations in a globalized society and economy require an element of certainty that is provided by a simple capacity to make equivalences. The most obvious form of this security is the stability provided by an unwavering monetary standard. ... Severe financial crises of the 1931 type do their damage by dramatically heightening monetary uncertainty, and eroding or destroying the idea of a common way of measuring": *James*, Creation, 233–234.

11 E.g. *Roelevink*, Intransparenz; *Schröter*, Cartelization.

12 Cf. *Buzan/Waever/de Wilde*, Security, 21–22.

13 Cf. *Siegenthaler*, Regelvertrauen, 149–177.

cating these concerns can be taken as evidence that a situation is assessed as a security problem, not a risk.

Most importantly, following CSS's constructivist approach, *security* as an analytical category should not be understood as a state of affairs or an end in itself. Rather, *security* refers to actions taken in the face of (real, imagined, actual, or anticipated) threats, and to communicating urgency. Security studies have coined the term "securitization"[14] for the act of successfully marking some issue as a security problem and thus legitimising extraordinary action that breaks the rules of political conduct, and "de-securitization" for the return from a securitised state of affairs to the normal political process.[15] Thus, when thinking about business companies and security using the *securitisation* concept, we seek to understand the role of companies in the making and unmaking of security issues and in the process of making "danger knowable and actionable".[16]

Critical Security Studies were developed in the social sciences and therefore as a concept for the analysis of the contemporary world without or with only a limited explicitly historical perspective. Nevertheless, its constructivist approach proved inspiring for historical security studies. Therefore, researchers in historical security studies as in the Collaborative Research Group 138 "Dynamics of Security" are working to historicise the concept and develop a theoretical framework that is more sensitive to historical dynamics. It follows the general idea that *security*" does not signify a constant state of affairs or object, but rather must be viewed as a social and communicative construct.[17] CSS asks how something – for example, a political party, immigration, foreign trade, economic policies, industrial espionage – is made into a security problem by persuading an audience of the existence of an existential threat requiring swift and extraordinary action. The term *securitisation* (homonymous with, but very different in meaning from the financial term) denotes the (communicative, political, social) act of declaring something as security-relevant and provoking a response to a given threat.[18] The concept originates from the Copenhagen School, which introduced a framework for analysing actions in Western democracies that circumvented the normal political, constitutional process by legitimising extraordinary actions with reference to *security*. CSS originally re-

14 "Securitisation" in this volume therefore does not refer to the financial meaning of the term, unless stated otherwise.

15 *Buzan/Waever/deWilde*, Security, 21–26.

16 *De Graaf/Zwierlein*, Historicizing Security, 49.

17 Cf. e.g. *Bonacker*, Sicherheit.

18 For a summary of "securitization" approaches, cf. *Conze*, Sicherheit, 82–101.

garded securitisation as primarily a speech act and explored who persuaded what audience with which communicative means that something was a security problem and thus made it the legitimate object of extraordinary measures by the state.[19] In contrast to Copenhagen's focus on political communication, the Paris School of CSS focuses on security apparatuses, experts, and their routines, e.g. in border control, and studies the bureaucratic process of constructing security issues. From its more sociological perspective, security experts (e.g. policemen, spies, IT specialists) – on the grounds of their professional expertise – define dominating areas of security at the expense of others and create atmospheres of insecurity beyond the exceptional circumstances which are central to the Copenhagen School's approach.[20]

Both the Copenhagen and Paris outlooks are not immediately applicable to historical situations: the Early Modern commonwealth certainly did not work in a manner akin to modern states, let alone Western democracies, and although *security* became a key concept in the political language of the Early Modern period, it hardly regarded the economy as a distinct sector–. Or, to use another example, CSS's focus on states as actors creates a blind spot for non-state actors of *securitisation*.[21] The SFB 138 develops a more comprehensive language and approach to securitisation by historicising *security* and *securitisation*, and its approach therefore acknowledges the dynamic historical development of "spaces of experience" and "horizons of expectations" towards security.[22] For empirical analysis it has developed three key terms: first, "heuristics" provides the cognitive and semantic framework in a given historical setting that guide actors' perception and identification of threats and responses; second, "repertoires" focuses on security measures based on, but also influencing heuristics that are created to counter perceived, usually future, threats; and third, "situations" encompasses the concrete instances when heuristics and repertoires can be identified to have created a security issue and/or are changed themselves by coping with a security issue. To sum up, in historical security research, situations can be a starting point for reconstructing and analysing the emer-

19 *Conze*, Sicherheit, 82–94.

20 For a summary, cf. *Conze*, Sicherheit, 94–98.

21 Cf. *Westermeier/Carl*, Einleitung.

22 However, it should be noted that the tension between historical experience and future expectations marking the distinction between the "pre-modern" and "modern" world view, as in Reinhart Koselleck's classical formulation, poses problems of its own when applied to contemporary history: see *Geulen*, Plädoyer, and *Graf*, Zeit.

gence and development of heuristics and repertoires. This starting point can also be the study of a repertoire (e.g. international law) or heuristics (e.g. the discourse marking minorities as a threat to society) themselves.

2. *Enterprises and security*

If the language and logic of security can be expanded to areas beyond the military and foreign relations, the denotation of a subject as a security problem should be regarded from a constructivist viewpoint as the result of complex social negotiations and the application of political power. On the one hand, we therefore aim to avoid anachronistic assumptions about security to the past, and ask what security meant in a given business historical instance. We have to trace the emergence, evolution, and in some cases disappearance of security concepts through history. On the other hand, *securitisation* as a perspective from which we approach the past might reveal observations about the relations of businesses with their social and political environment that have been overlooked so far. Overall, the relation of enterprises and security is varied and complicated, not least owing to the mostly blurry definition of *security*. As a starting point, we assume that *security* is broadly recognised as a relational term that only obtains its meaning in relation to *risk* or *safety* in specific situations.

While Critical Security Studies have touched upon the economic implications of politics of *catastrophe* and *security* (while focusing on the question of insurances), economic and business historians have almost never used *security*, *danger*, or *threat* as analytical concepts.[23] Predominantly, business history has been concerned with "risk", especially "entrepreneurial risk", "risk management", and "prevention". Recently, the "vulnerability" of businesses and their "resilience" have been brought into focus. Although this strand of research addresses questions that are immediately connected to security, like risks, preparedness, and the capability to adapt to threats, the concept of "resilience" is still underdeveloped as an analytical tool in business history.[24] Current research on the interplay between historical experience and the formation of economic expectations has clear implications for the history of business security. It shows that the

23 *Aradau/van Munster*, Politics of Catastrophe, 52–67; regarding insurance, see *Rohland*, Sharing the Risk; *Zwierlein*, Prometheus (although exceptions ought to be mentioned: cf. *Daniels*, Brain Drain; *Daniels*, Landesverrat).

24 Cf., however, *Köhler/Schulze*, Resilienz, for a successful and yielding operationalization of the resilience approach.

expected outcomes guiding the decisions of economic actors are deeply affected by historical situations and depend on immediate or remembered experiences.[25] Economic actors form "fictional expectations" to overcome fundamental uncertainty, and potential or actual security problems implicitly or explicitly enter the construction of "imagined futures".[26] *Expectation* appears not so much as an antagonist term of economic risk perception, but experience and expectations rather serve as the empirical foundation and analytical tool respectively to conquer future risks and to overcome the status of uncertainty.[27]

Entrepreneurial *risk* and *uncertainty* have been the object of economic study at least since Frank Knight in the 1920s, of course.[28] Nevertheless, this does not cover the whole spectrum of security, and only partially relates to the concepts of *security* and *securitisation* developed in the social sciences. These social science concepts enable us to write more well-rounded security history and assess the importance of security for entrepreneurial decisions. Moreover, enterprises' existence and prosperity rely on (legal, political, technological, etc.) security – covered at least in part by institutional economics. They have developed strategies and institutions to overcome, handle, and/or manage risks with the help of institutional and practical instruments from the type of the enterprise to organisational units (cartels, statistics and forecasting, etc.).[29]

Risk minimisation strategies of enterprises require a *de-securitised* environment. Economic history studies on the theoretical basis of New Institutional Economics have demonstrated the importance of legal security (such as property rights and contracts) as well as forms of social organisation (such as norms or trust) for economic development.[30] On the contrary, in an environment that enterprises perceive as unsafe, they have to cope with dangers and threats that might incite them to initiate or participate in *securitisation*. As the example of fortifications of the British East India Company in the seventeenth century has shown, security itself could

25 Cf. *Jakob/Nützenadel/Streb*, Erfahrung.

26 *Beckert*, Imagined Futures.

27 Cf. *Lenel*, Mapping.

28 Cf. e.g. *Knight*, Risk, Uncertainty, Profit; *Keynes*, Theory, esp. chapters 5 and 12; *Taleb*, Swan; for a concise discussion of the treatment of uncertainty cf. *Boeckelmann/Mildner*, Unsicherheit.

29 See the closely-related collaborative research network, Priority Program 1859 "Experience & Expectation. Historical Foundations of Economic Behaviour", URL: <https://www.experience-expectation.de/> [08.12.2020]; Jahrbuch für Wirtschaftsgeschichte 59 (2018), no. 2, special issue: Experience and Expectation.

30 Cf. e.g. *Demsetz*, Theory; *North*, Process; *Wischermann/Nieberding*, Revolution.

become a marketable service: "The company began to regard security of the modest kind which its major settlements could offer as not just essential, but also as a marketable commodity."[31] In the end, the Company transformed "from a trading company to a territorial sovereignty".[32] At the same time, enterprises themselves can and have become *securitised*, or enterprises were included in more encompassing securitisation moves. One must only look to the discrimination and destruction of Jewish enterprise and businesspeople in Nazi Germany for a complex and brutal example. The *securitisation* approach can prove useful for the examination of less drastic cases as well. The contributions of this volume present historical situations in which enterprises' heuristics, by which they mark observations as dangerous and the repertoire that companies could bring to bear on them, can be exemplified. Moreover, in the methodological attempt to historicise security dynamics – such as continuity, change, simultaneousness in different organisational units in different regions in different times – the underlying processes rather than outcomes are relevant. Who are the "securitising actors" and which subjects are addressed? Can we identify peaks or patterns in security communication?[33]

Inspirations for business history in particular are derived from the broadened perspective on *threat*, *risk*, *danger*, etc. assembled in the semantic field of *security*, as shown above. Inversely, business history can contribute to the empirical horizon of dynamics of security: modern enterprises as non-state actors also ought to be considered as agents of securitisation. They construct their environment according to opportunities for turnover/profit, but how do they construct security in that process? Whose security is defined as relevant? Where and when do they perceive threats? Who do they address when demanding security? Why are certain issues marked as highly security-relevant while others are de-securitised? Is there a competition between securities (security of supply, legal security, financial security, etc.) in entrepreneurial discourse?

Research on an enterprise-security- nexus must take into account that the economy underlies political and military abilities to provide security, but that – at least in liberal market economies – business and the economy follow their own intrinsic logics. Accordingly, there is no consensus on the meaning of "economic security". The Copenhagen School points out that

31 *Bruce P. Lenman*, Britains Colonial Wars 1688–1783, *Harlow* 2001, 90, cited in *Füssel*, Politik der Unsicherheit, 304.

32 *Füssel*, Politik der Unsicherheit, 306.

33 Cf. *de Graaf/Zwierlein*, Historicizing Security, 50, 59.

matters negotiated under the rubric of *economic security* really refer to other sectors of security – the political, military, or social, for example.[34] What is meant by economic security in historical situations and in different economic orders? How do security expectations of enterprises change over time, affecting their attitudes towards risk? How and why do perceptions of security change, for example in times of crisis? Or is economic security merely a rhetorical figure that is applied when economic gains are at stake and contested?

What sources and methods promise to yield insights into enterprises' security and securitisation? The case studies in this volume show that the selection of sources must be a highly individual task. Mostly, the authors reconstruct "dialogues" or "conversations" between enterprises and other actors (state agencies, other enterprises, trade associations, etc.) about security issues on the basis of diverse archival material from corporate and non-corporate sources. In business records, the historian will only seldom find direct references to *security*, but abundant references to *risks*, *hazards*, or *threats* arising in certain situations. The Copenhagen School's approach would direct us to extraordinary situations and let us observe the ensuing communication between an enterprise and its environment for indicators of *securitisation*. The Paris School's approach would direct us to corporate organisation as an object of study and let us observe the preparedness and coping apparatus of enterprises for the management of crises and security breaches. In both cases, the decision to employ a certain approach already limits the perspective on what security refers to in a given historical context, with direct consequences for the selection and assessment of source material that might further exclude security aspects or actors. If we accept that what security means in a given situation is constructed, depending on the perceptions and frames of mind of the actors, the selection of sources cannot follow a general rule. Apart from the focus on the written record, two contributions in this volume (*Brünig* and *Schäffler*) use images not only to illustrate their argument, but show how these images worked as communicative tools in instances of securitisation. Studying entrepreneurial action in given security situations as well might tell us much about the role of security for business decisions and the function of enterprises for the demand and supply of security. How do enterprises participate in the construction and running of repertoires? How do state and private busi-

34 *Buzan/Waever/de Wilde*, Security, 95.

ness perceptions negotiate security in such cases?[35] How do enterprises participate in the formation of heuristics, especially media enterprises?

So far, there are only tentative answers to these manifold questions. For a preliminary conclusion, we argue that enterprises have multiple connections to security and can play various roles in securitisation. In the most familiar case, enterprises become victims of external threats like revolution, war, or nationalisation, and the states that normatively are to provide security become a risk or danger themselves. The economic system itself and the natural environment contain their own threats in the form of extreme financial crises or "natural"[36] disasters like floods and earthquakes. Additionally, enterprises themselves become a danger or risk to their social and natural environment, for example through negligence of the safety regulations that ought to protect their employees, massive industrial accidents like the Seveso or Bhopal incidents, dangerous products like Contergan, participation in human rights violations,[37] or endemic criminal behavior.

However, it is not the task of this volume simply to identify different categories of risk and danger for and from enterprises.[38] Rather, it is to generate insights into the historically variable ways in which enterprises understood dangers, risk, and security. We assume that the observably different transformations of dangers into risks, enterprises' perception and negotiation of threats, and their attitudes towards security and risk reveal the historicity of (in)security concepts. Historical security studies so far have used the history of insurance as a platform from which to show the emergence of "modern" perceptions of risk and danger in Western societies since the late seventeenth and eighteenth centuries.[39] But there is more to it: in this volume, we turn to the microcosm of enterprises themselves and enquire into the impact of security concepts and risk assessment upon entrepreneurial decisions and strategies. As de Graaf and Zwierlein describe it, "Security is not just the outcome of physical or political cir-

35 Mario Daniels did pioneering work on these questions in two recent articles: *Daniels*, Landesverrat; *Daniels*, Brain Drain.

36 For a discussion of the distinction between "natural" and "man-made" disasters, cf. e.g. *Rohland*, Sharing the Risk.

37 Cf. e.g. *Kopper*, Verantwortung.

38 Especially since there are studies which attempt that already, for example the risk management literature that *Kristin Bårnås* draws upon in her contribution to this volume.

39 *Zwierlein*, Prometheus; Daase, Historisierung; *Rohland*, Sharing the Risk; see also the Research Netwerk "Global Cultures of Risk. Insurance in Non-Western Contexts (1870–1980)", URL: <https://www.culturesofrisk.net/> [08.12.2020].

cumstances and incidents. People and organisations have to attribute meaning to those circumstances and incidents. They have to be incorporated into political, administrative and bureaucratic decision-making-processes and procedures."[40] Thus, the connected research question of the contributions assembled in this volume is: how did enterprises perceive and negotiate layers and statuses of (in)security?

Overall, the relationship between the modern business enterprise and security remains ambiguous. We have indicated that the enterprise-security nexus may be constituted by enterprises being the subject as well as the object of situations of securitisation. Enterprises can protect or harm, provide relief or cause distress to their employees, their customers, and populations in their vicinity. At the same time, businesses are consumers and providers of security. Enterprises are vulnerable to natural, political, and technological threats and require secure environments for their existence and profitable operation. Goods and services are sold by enterprises to private and public customers with the promise directly or indirectly to provide a measure of security. Moreover, enterprises themselves can become veritable sources of risks and dangers to society and the environment. Their products and production processes can cause extreme pollution, cause disease and injuries, or fuel violent conflicts, thus making enterprises the object of preventive security regulations. In the past and present, enterprises collaborated with dictatorial regimes or were directly involved in crimes. Security has thus been a constant factor in the relation between enterprise and society.

Among the case studies, we will find situations that were created by business action themselves – e.g. foreign direct investment in insecure markets – and situations in which enterprises reacted to external action. In both cases, we have to ask what specifically stands out as a business perspective on security and insecurity, distinguishing a genuine entrepreneurial perspective from, for instance, a political one that just happens to be found in a business environment. In the following section, building on the terms and concepts laid down above, we would like to point out some common themes and subject matters which connect the individual contributions in this volume.

40 *de Graaf/Zwierlein*, Historicizing Security, 46.

3. Themes and subject matters in this volume

Most importantly, the contributions shed light on the dynamics of security from a business history perspective. They all reconstruct historical examples that highlight security as a phenomenon hinging on interaction, mostly among businesses and state actors. The fundamental question when looking for an enterprise-security nexus is the question respecting its origins: when and why do what actors perform *securitisations*? Closely connected to this question is the performative character of security: when does it change, and what are its dynamics and driving forces? Whether businesses become the subject or object of processes of securitisation in a given situation, the question arises how a particular distribution of security and insecurity is realized, and with what consequences for all actors and stakeholders involved? Finally, what are the policy consequences of securitisation, that is, how does the recourse to security shape the conduct of an organisation and affects the parties involved? Again, from a business perspective as well, this is a question of applied repertoires, for example the erection of insurance regimes or the PR strategies identifying and countering challenges by anti-nuclear movements, but also the basis for enquiries into inclusion, exclusion, and intersectionality.

The table of contents already hints at the variety of contributions according to the different types of threats that are addressed and analysed: four chapters deal with business risks and safeguards against them (*Pitteloud, Jakob, Barnas, Schäffler*), two with security of supply (*Kleinschmidt, Sparenberg*), two with identity (*Marx, Brünig*), and one with the commodification of security (*Böick*). It is striking, and neither unexpected nor unwanted, that each has chosen a different approach to "security" and selected a certain meaning and topic from the broad semantic field and range of subject matters. *Marcus Böick* writes about security firms that treat security as a commodity and might challenge the state monopoly on violence. *Mark Jakob* tries to disentangle the convergence of state and business security interests embodied in export credit insurance schemes. Similarly, *Sabine Pitteloud* analyses the security choices of Swiss industrialists when seeking investment guarantees. *Kristin Bårnås* typifies risk management strategies of MNEs, while *Eva Schäffler* picks liquidity risks caused by, among other things, misconduct during the transition to a market economy. *Ole Sparenberg* writes a history of economic policy securing access to essential raw materials and *Christian Kleinschmidt* explores the security of food during the German Empire. Finally, *Christian Marx* describes the discussions about the danger posed by the acquisition of shares by undesirable foreigners, and *Sascha Brünig* shows us how the German nuclear industry drew on images of German diligence to create a positive form of safety-related public relations.

Some articles have chosen to stress reference objects explicitly: what object exactly is marked as threatened in a securitisation move? Whereas in *Christian Marx's* contribution, it is the rather fluid concept of the "nationality" of German firms in question, *Eva Schäffler* deals with threats to the essential ability of companies to generate revenue flows. Others deal primarily with what we would call heuristics, that is, the knowledge systems developed to recognise threats and repertoires, which are the standardised paradigms to fall back on when dealing with risks and threats. Contributions identifying different *heuristics* cover different cognitive and communicative frames for threats. Explicitly addressed are risk management as part of business administration (*Bårnås*), the securitisation of foreign competition (*Jakob, Marx*), work ethic versus the critical stance of public opinion (*Brünig*) or competing "securities" concerning food safety (*Kleinschmidt*). Moreover, some *repertoires* of business action in questions of "security" have been identified: the call for state guarantees (*Pitteloud, Jakob*), the interaction with media (*Brünig*) as well as the reference to corporate law (*Marx*). As one preliminary result of this book project, the decisive relation between state and private actors seems to be a promising question for future research: the state plays an important role in most of the contributions. Agents of security have been identified while the question of the source remains open and bound to individual situations. Which idea arose from what source? How can the relationship and the dynamics between states and the economy be characterised?

The modern state and the modern business company co-evolved in the recent centuries. This results in a peculiar observation problem: unlike research in political security, we can hardly refer to "pre-modern" social arrangements (for want of a better term) and study corporate security actors in a diachronically comparative way.[41] The modern enterprise cannot be observed outside its relation with the modern state, it seems. For that reason, studies like *Eva Schäffler's* contribution that observe transitions from one political and economic system into another from a business perspective are especially valuable. In that liminal state marked by fundamental uncertainty about and sometimes virtual absence of state institutions, en-

41 Unless one subscribes to the view that equivalents of the modern business enterprise existed in antiquity, which we do not. We can, of course, study the security-relevant behaviour of individual economic actors over a long time period: cf. *Kleinschmidt*, Eigeninitiative (but not regarding business organisations and corporate institutions).

terprises must rewrite their heuristics completely. What happens when the state as the primary audience of securitisation moves ceases to exist?

Lastly, the chapters also contribute to the idea of security *situations*, when for example *Ole Sparenberg* identifies historical moments of precarious dependence on foreign supply that incite corporate actors to regard security as being at stake in business actions. These circumstances and situations vary between countries and over time: security was in the end an agreement defined and developed through communication between actors as well as a normative precept, which has historically been changeable. Accordingly, the different contributions cover different explorations of national settings. At some time in the future, one might hope for more and elaborate inter-temporal and international comparisons of enterprises' expectations towards security.

Bibliography

Aradau, Claudia/van Munster, Rens: Politics of catastrophe. Genealogies of the unknown. New York/Abingdon 2013

Beckert, Jens: Imagined Futures. Fictional Expectations and Capitalist Dynamics. Cambridge (MA) 2016

Boeckelmann, Lukas/Mildner, Stormy Annika: Unsicherheit, Ungewissheit, Risiko, in: SWP Zeitschriftenschau 2001/ZS02, September 2011

Bonacker, Thorsten: Situierte Sicherheit. Für einen methodologischen Situationismus in den Critical Security Studies, in: Zeitschrift für Internationale Beziehungen 28 (2021), forthcoming

Buzan, Waever, de Wilde: Security: A New Framework for Analysis. London 1997

Conze, Eckart: Geschichte der Sicherheit. Entwicklung, Themen, Perspektivem. Göttingen 2018

Daase, Christopher: Die Historisierung der Sicherheit. Anmerkungen zur historischen Sicherheitsforschung aus politikwissenschaftlicher Sicht, in: Geschichte und Gesellschaft 38 (2012), p. 387–405

Daniels, Mario: Brain Drain, innerwestliche Weltmarktkonkurrenz und nationale Sicherheit. Die Kampagne der westdeutschen Chemieindustrie gegen Wissenstransfers in die USA in den 1950er Jahren, in: Vierteljahreshefte für Zeitgeschichte 64 (2016), 3, p. 1–25

Daniels, Mario: „Wirtschaftlicher Landesverrat" im „Wirtschaftskampf gegen Deutschland". Die deutsche Chemieindustrie und die Bekämpfung ausländischer Industriespionage in den 1920er Jahren, in: Historische Zeitschrift 299 (2015), 2, p. 352–383

de Graaf, Beatrice/Zwierlein, Cornel: „Historicizing Security – Entering the Conspiracy Dispositive", in: Historical Social Research 38 (2013), p. 46–64

Demsetz, Harold: Towards a theory of property rights, in: The American Economic Review 57 (1967), 2, p. 347–359

Donzé, Pierre-Yves: The Advantage of Being Swiss: Nestlé and Political Risk in Asia during the Early Cold War, 1945–1970, in: Business History Review 94 (2020), 2, p. 373–397

Forbes, Neil/Kurosawa, Takafumi/Wubs, Ben (eds.): Multinational Enterprise, Political Risk and Organisational Change. From Total War to Cold War. New York/Abingdon 2019

Füssel, Marian: Die Politik der Unsicherheit. Versicherheitlichung, Gewalt und Expansion in den britischen Kolonien im Siebenjährigen Krieg, in: Kampmann, Christoph/ Niggemann, Ulrich (eds.): Sicherheit in der Frühen Neuzeit (=Frühneuzeit Impulse 2). Köln et. al. 2013, p. 299–312

Geulen, Christian: Plädoyer für eine Geschichte der Grundbegriffe des 20. Jahrhunderts, in: Zeithistorische Forschungen/Studies in Contemporary History, Online Edition, 7 (2010), 1, URL: https://zeithistorische-forschungen.de/1-2010/4488, DOI: https://doi.org/10.14765/zzf.dok-1790, (printed edition: p. 79–97)

Graf, Rüdiger: Zeit und Zeitkonzeptionen in der Zeitgeschichte, Version: 2.0, in: Docupedia-Zeitgeschichte, 22.10.2012, http://docupedia.de/zg/graf_zeit_und_zeitkonzeptionen_v2_de_2012, DOI: http://dx.doi.org/10.14765/zzf.dok.2.266.v2

Hannig, Nicolai: Kalkulierte Gefahren. Naturkatastrophen und Vorsorge seit 1800. Göttingen 2019

Jakob, Mark/Nützenadel, Alexander/Streb, Jochen: Erfahrung und Erwartung. Eine vernachlässigte wirtschaftshistorische Perspektive?, in: Jakob, Mark/Nützenadel, Alexander/Streb, Jochen (eds.): Erfahrung und Erwartung/Experience and Expectation. Jahrbuch für Wirtschaftsgeschichte/Economic History Yearbook 59 (2018), 2, p. 329–341

James, Harold: The Creation and Destruction of Value. The Globalization Cycle. Harvard 2009

Keynes, John M.: The general Theory of Employment, Interest, and Money. New York 1936

Kleinschmidt, Christian: Zwischen Eigeninitiative, Vergemeinschaftung und herrschaftlich-staatlichem Schutz. Aushandlungsprozesse kaufmännischer Sicherheit vom Frühmittelalter bis ins 20. Jahrhundert, in: Westermeier, Carola/ Carl, Horst (eds.): Sicherheitsakteure. Epochenübergreifende Perspektiven zu Praxisformen und Versicherheitlichung. Baden-Baden 2018, p. 197–210

Knight, Frank H.: Risk, Uncertainty, and Profit. Boston/New York 1921

Kobrak, Christopher/Hansen, Per (eds.): European Business, Dictatorship, and Political Risk, 1920–1945. New York 2004

Kopper, Christopher: Unternehmerische Verantwortung in Militärdiktaturen und ihre historische Aufarbeitung: das Beispiel VW do Brasil, in: Zeitschrift für Unternehmensgeschichte 63 (2018), 1, p. 153–164

Köhler, Ingo/Schulze, Benjamin W.: Resilienz. Unternehmenshistorische Dimensionen der Krisenrobustheit am Beispiel deutscher Brauereien in den 1970er Jahren, in: Jahrbuch für Wirtschaftsgeschichte/Economic History Yearbook 57 (2016), 2, p. 455–491

Krüger, Christine: Dienstethos, Abenteuerlust, Bürgerpflicht. Jugendfreiwilligendienste in Deutschland und Großbritannien im 20. Jahrhundert (Kritische Studien zur Geschichtswissenschaft, Bd. 219), Göttingen 2016

Lenel, Laetitia: Mapping the Future. Business Forecasting and the Dynamics of Capitalism in the Interwar period, in: JWG 59 (2018), 2, p. 377–413

North, Douglass C.: Understanding the process of economic change. Princeton/ Oxford 2005

Roelevink, Eva-Maria: Organisierte Intransparenz. Das Kohlensyndikat und der niederländische Markt, 1915–1932. München 2015

Rohland, Eleonora: Sharing the Risk. Fire, Climate and Disaster. Swiss Re, 1864–1906. Lancashire 2011.

Schröter, Harm G.: Cartelization and decartelization in Europe, 1870–1995: rise and decline of an economic institution, in: The Journal of Economic History 25 (1996), 1, p. 129–153

Siegenthaler, Hansjörg: Regelvertrauen, Prosperität und Krisen. Die Ungleichmäßigkeit wirtschaftlicher und sozialer Entwicklung als Ergebnis individuellen Handelns und sozialen Lernens. Tübingen 1993

Taleb, Nassim Nicholas: The Black Swan. The Impact of the Highly Improbable. New York 2007

Voelz, Johannes: Chance, Risk, Security in American Literature. An Introduction, in: Amerikastudien/American Studies 60 (2015), 4, p. 385–402

Westermeier, Carola/Carl, Horst: Einleitung: Sicherheitsakteure, in: Westermeier, Carola/Carl, Horst (eds.): Sicherheitsakteure. Epochenübergreifende Perspektiven zu Praxisformen und Versicherheitlichung. Baden-Baden 2018, p. 11–27

Wischermann, Clemens/Nieberding, Anne: Die institutionelle Revolution. Eine Einführung in die deutsche Wirtschaftsgeschichte des 19. und frühen 20. Jahrhunderts. Stuttgart 2004

Zwierlein, Cornel: Der gezähmte Prometheus. Feuer und Sicherheit zwischen Früher Neuzeit und Moderne. Göttingen 2011

Weak States, Strong Businesses? The History of Private Security Firms in Twentieth-Century Germany

Marcus Böick

Introduction: Security beyond the State?

In 2017, the US Department of Labor published occupational statistics referring to domestic security. While 666,000 police officers were performing their duty, the number of private security guards in the US reached almost 1.1 million. In Germany, the ratio between public and private security forces was quite different: 256,000 people worked in the private security sector compared to 274,000 policemen. The numerical proportion between public and private forces has been an often-debated question within the public, political, and scientific spheres in Germany, especially since the 1990s. Is the growing number of private security staff – mostly visible at airports, at mass events, in public buildings, supermarkets or squares – a dramatic warning sign of a 'weakening' or even 'retreat' of the state and the loss of its monopoly on the legitimate use of violence, as mostly leftist and some conservative critics point out?[1] Or is it, *vice versa*, a beneficial form of collaboration in the shape of Public Private Security Partnerships (PPSPs), which efficiently raises security levels against the growing risks of big-city crime and transnational terrorism, as liberal commentators and many politicians assert? Will the rapidly increasing 'security market' provide security for all citizens, or just for the wealthier parts of society that can afford the costs of maintaining their own 'self-security', with private guards using smart security technologies in gated communities?[2]

While scientists, politicians, lawyers as well as a growing number of security experts have been struggling with these highly political questions, especially since the 1970s and 1990s, this paper aims to provide a long-term perspective on the establishment and the transformations of the modern commercial security business in Germany during the twentieth centu-

1 *Eppler*, Gewaltmonopol.
2 *Abrahamsen*, Security.

ry. The question as to which protagonists, organisations, or groups provide or 'produce' security within pre-, high- or post-modern societies has been crucial for political philosophy and theory in the Western world for centuries. After 1648 and especially in the eighteenth and nineteenth centuries, the bureaucratic European nation state was able to claim a (in fact never entirely established) monopoly on power enacted through its newly-formed administrative bodies and its increasingly professionalised officials: soldiers, police officers, judges and other public servants. They seemed to be the only legitimate guarantors of public security – in sharp contrast to vigilante groups, mercenaries, or other traditional and mostly rural forms of nefarious 'vigilantism'. After all, non-state, societal or private security measures were increasingly depicted as suspicious or even dangerous by politicians, lawyers, and scientists, indicating the limitations of and restrictions to this ultimate claim of state monopoly. In fact, however, non-state forms of societal, corporate or individual security production never completely vanished, as Les Johnston has convincingly argued.[3] Quite the contrary, as I want to show, the twentieth century saw an astonishing rise of a specific mode of commercial corporate security production and distribution. This new 'security capitalism' originated from the US frontier settings and class-conflict struggles in the middle of the nineteenth century and spread to Europe some decades later, and it gradually started to transform the way security was produced and perceived all over the Western world. As we will see, it was mainly the task of guarding and patrolling private properties and estates by uniformed watchmen at night that formed the core of the new private security business model, at least until the 1970s. Especially richer citizens from the middle- or upper-classes as well as smaller or medium-sized companies felt the urgent need to 'buy' some extra security services to protect their property in times of crisis, conflicts, revolutions or wars; these groups became the customers, or perhaps more accurately the subscribers, of new private security firms.

This overall development happened within the context of different national 'security cultures', thus fueling controversial debates and provoking fierce criticism, but also slowly transforming them into more 'hybrid' ways of thinking about security production and its cultural framings and interpretations. By focusing on the rise of the German security business and its firms during the twentieth century, this paper explores a new historical perspective on the transformations of security and statehood into a vast field of negotiations and interactions between state, economy, society, and

3 *Johnston*, Rebirth.

individual citizens. The analysis of different conceptions of security production centres around one of the key questions about the "limits of the sovereign state", as David Garland has put it.[4] Additionally, Charles Maier prominently underlined the need to analyse the "transformations" of the state in terms of territoriality.[5] Such perspectives can challenge the often clear cut distinctions between state, economy, society, and citizens, especially when it comes to security as a core matter of modern statehood. With a focus on a broad conception of "private policing", Mark Button identified this field as a mixed zone with a considerable amount of varieties and shapes that challenges simple ideas like the public sector (of state/police) versus the private sector (of economy/society): "Publicness and privateness [are] best considered as a continuum, rather than as a black and white concept."[6]

In debating the changing role of private security business during the eventful twentieth century and the rise of a new mode of security capitalism, these hybrid relationships and their different interpretations and often conflicting perceptions of publicness and privateness are the main focus of this paper. Since the provision of domestic security is situated at the conceptional core of the modern nation state, with its ideological foundations and its claim for legitimacy, it is necessary to analyse what Wilber R. Miller has described as the "national contexts for private policing".[7] At the same time, such a national perspective needs to be extended to transnational processes of mutual observations, connections, entanglements and transfers, as David Churchill, Dolores Janiewski, and Pieter Leloup convincingly argued recently.[8]

This applies particularly to the case of modern private security firms: in *fin-de-siècle* Germany, the private security sector emerged in line with contemporary developments in the United States with its soaring number of private security companies, most notably those such as the notorious Pinkerton National Detective Agency (PNDA). German entrepreneurs thus imported from across the Atlantic the idea of commercially-fashioned 'self-protection' in terms of professional security services with staff and technology beyond those of the state and its regular police force. Since 1900, a new (and always sceptically-viewed) German security business sector and its mainly small- or medium-sized, frequently family-owned com-

4 *Garland*, Limits.
5 *Maier*, Borders.
6 *Button*, Private, 12.
7 *Miller*, History.
8 *Churchill/Janiewski/Leloup*, State.

panies steadily made their way through eventful times of two World Wars, abrupt political regime changes, economic crises and reconstructions, as well as dramatic technological and multimedia changes and social transformations. Exploring the changing history of the German security business in the twentieth century within a transnational context will result in a clearer understanding of the changing perspectives of different actors and modes of security production beyond the nation state.

Do 'weak' states really lead to 'strong' businesses (or *vice versa*)? This highly debated question is one that has haunted many politicians, police officers and other security experts for around a century. Since 'strength' and 'weakness' are not viable categories for proper historical analysis, one should focus more on the role of these categories in contemporary mindsets. This is especially necessary because the private security business is simply not another service industry – its mere existence leads to the crucial question of modern statehood itself: who has the legitimate right to provide security (and safety) to whom and by what means? The present paper thus intends to highlight the highly ambiguous role of private security companies in general: on the one hand, they aim to capitalise and commodify their business as professional providers of security services to their corporate or individual customers; on the other hand, this business model was often seen (especially in times of political upheaval and social unrest like in the 1920s or 1970s) as a symptom of decline or even a dangerous threat to modern statehood itself.[9]

First, I will outline why private security companies were not centre stage in the field of contemporary history by taking a closer look at the emergence of the paradigm of 'securitisation' in recent historical research. Second, I will present a brief history of private security firms in Germany from 1900 onwards, describing the changing political, economic, social, and cultural contexts of this often precarious business model. Third, I will discuss the matter of 'national security cultures' to develop some overarching historical perspectives and answer some possible questions that could enrich further discussions in the field of contemporary as well as economic and business history. Finally, in a brief conclusion, I will discuss the transforming perceptions of danger and security at a crucial cultural intersection between states, markets, and societies.

9 *Churchill/Janieweski/Leloup*, State.

1. State of the Art: Bringing Security back to Contemporary History

Over the last couple of years, the nation state as well as 'classical' questions of security have made a significant comeback in German historical research. This happened only after a long absence: during the 1970s and 1980s, influential scholars of social history like Jürgen Kocka and Hans-Ulrich Wehler challenged more old-fashioned political historians and their emphasis on international political security with the notion of 'great men' waging wars and negotiating peace treaties. With a focus on social science theories and methods, this new generation of historians turned their attention to social processes and structures and to a macro level of class or milieu.[10] Since the late 1980s, a series of cultural turns has shifted the main lines of historical debate even further away from traditional questions of political or state history to a micro or meta level; in radical culturalist terms the state seemed to be a powerful producer of 'discourses' while trying to control its subjects on a micro-level, as Michel Foucault prominently put it.[11] The blossoming subfield of the history of crime, criminology, state police, and policing might be the exception to this rule.[12]

After the widely unexpected collapse of European State Socialism in 1989–91, a powerful push towards market-oriented globalisation, supranational Europeanisation, as well as the dawn of transnational digitalisation, rendered the traditional nation state a somewhat obsolescent and overburdened model: global dynamics, European integration and local ambitions for self-rule seemed to mark the ultimate end of the autonomous 'Westphalian' state as the core actor of political power and security production.[13] The comeback of the state as a field of research in German contemporary history only happened after the turn of the millennium, however. With the 9/11 terrorist attacks in 2001, the global financial crisis in 2008, the crisis of the Euro currency system after 2010, the fierce state orchestrated responses to the recent COVID-19 pandemic in 2020, as well as the overall rapid rise of anti-globalist and anti-migrant populism in the Western world, the crucial role of nation states, and the long-neglected questions of security production suddenly resurfaced with renewed force. In Germany, Eckart Conze tried to revive the historical debate by combining political and cultural approaches in his essay 'Security as Culture' in 2005

---

10 *Hitzer/Welskopp*, Sozialgeschichte.

11 *Foucault*, Überwachen.

12 *Lüdtke/Reinke/Sturm*, Polizei; *Evans*, Politik.

13 *Bislev*, Globalization.

and his book *In Search for Security* in 2009, describing the history of the Federal Republic as a long struggle for political, economic as well as cultural stabilisation of a post-national nation state.[14] Conze and other historians like Cornel Zwierlein and Achim Saupe have suggested putting questions of "extended security" back on the research agenda.[15] Recently, Alexandra Schwell and Katharina Eisch-Angus have also tried to reconcile traditional top-down and bottom-up perspectives by suggesting a helpful distinction of "security" in discourses on a state or macro-level and "safety" in everyday practices on a micro or individual level.[16]

Traditional topics like the state and its different protagonists and its strategies of security production have thus been reassessed through the lens of cultural history, with a focus on changing perceptions, discourses and practices regarding security and danger. This recent development is useful not only in bridging the longstanding gap between older and newer cultural approaches in historical theory, but also between the nowadays quite distanced disciplinary fields of history and the social sciences.[17] Especially the concept of 'securitisation' of the so-called Copenhagen school, which focuses on cultural perceptions and social interpretations of external as well as internal insecurities, was and is being discussed through a methodological recourse to sophisticated concepts of political sciences and international relations.[18]

Furthermore, the concept of "security cultures", put forward by Christopher Daase, prominently raised the critical question of the increasingly precarious "interplay between a growing demand for security in liberal societies and the willingly given promises of security given by the states" – a process often referred to as an emerging "security paradox" that describes how increasing levels of provided security (i.e. falling crime rates) lead to a significant rise in individual perceptions of personal insecurity especially fueled by extended media coverage and scandalisation.[19]

The eclectic as well as pragmatic adoption of different approaches and theories from the social sciences led to a flourishing debate in German contemporary history that tried to shed new light in this area: The research on 'securitisation' in emerging modern metropolitan areas like Hamburg

14 *Conze*, Suche.
15 *Zwierlein*, Sicherheitsgeschichte; *Saupe*, Dispositive.
16 *Schwell/Eisch-Angus*, Sicherheitsgesellschaft.
17 *Kühl*, Organisationen.
18 *Conze*, Entwicklung.
19 *Daase*, Sicherheitskultur.

and London, done by Christine Krüger[20], for instance, or other case studies concerned with changing or even transforming conceptions of future securities (and insecurities), brought forward by Steffen Henne, Wencke Meteling and others, broadened and deepened our understanding of the production, distribution, perception and reflection on security matters from a historical perspective in underlining that even modern security always had and has a very changing history.[21]

Despite this remarkable comeback of security matters in an 'extended' perspective, security production beyond the modern nation state still seems to be a noteworthy desideratum, especially in the case of Germany.[22] Non-state actors of 'securitisation' like commercial companies, municipal organisations as well as political or social groups are often disregarded as second-rate topics in current historical research. This gap also seems to be a consequence of a more traditional, state-centred focus on official archival sources from state entities in German contemporary history.[23] The same is true for many economic or business historians who tend to focus mainly on big industry and their often well-established archives, although some historians have recently tried to establish new approaches especially by focusing on small- or medium-sized companies.[24] Furthermore, the vast amount of publications on private security firms in the political sciences or in legal studies are mostly centred around the astonishing rise of this new form of enterprise, especially since the 1990s and 2000s in the context of PPSPs all over the Western world. Many writers have criticised this shift as a neoliberal trend towards an increasingly individualised "risk policy" of "responsibilisation".[25]

All in all, apart from some singular case studies or popular publications,[26] no comprehensive analysis of the history of private security firms in Germany has yet been carried out. This is different to the United States, the United Kingdom and even Belgium, where Wilbur R. Miller, Mark Button, Rita Abrahamsen, and Pieter Leloup have recently published extensive contributions to the history of private policing and the emerging private security businesses in these countries in the course of the late nine-

---

20 *Krüger,* Slums.
21 *Henne/Kampmann/Marciniak/Meteling,* Security.
22 *Churchill/Janieweski/Leloup,* State.
23 *Patel,* Zeitgeschichte.
24 *Berghoff/Vogel,* Perspektivenwechsel.
25 *Klimke,* Sicherheitsmentalitäten; *Garland,* Limits.
26 *Kupferschmidt/Menzel,* Geschichten.

teenth and early twentieth centuries.[27] A historical analysis of the establishment and development of this new security service branch and its political, social and cultural frameworks in Germany should also be embedded in its transnational connections especially with the United States. In attempting to do so, this paper aims to shed new light on the transformations of state-economy-society relations in the field of domestic security production. By adopting a long-term perspective, I will address the underlying implications for the understanding of 'publicness' and 'privateness' in Germany during the twentieth century – ranging from the beginnings of commercial security business after 1900 until the recent debates on PPSPs at the end of the century. An empirical analysis of the German 'special case' might also prove to be fruitful when discussing comparative perspectives on the (re-)emergence of private security production and various modes of 'securitisation' and different national 'security cultures' in states, economies, and societies, especially in the wider contexts of the transformations and varieties of statehood, capitalism or modernism in general. This development will be discussed in terms of the establishment over time of a new business model which serves as the foundation of a new form of transnational security capitalism.

2. *Rise and Fall, and Rise again? A brief History of the Security Industry in Twentieth-century Germany*

In a professional sense, profit-oriented and privately-owned security firms began to develop in the German Reich only after 1900, when several, often German-Jewish, entrepreneurs returned from extensive trips to the US where they studied an already booming and increasingly professionalised private security branch, with the hotly debated PNDA leading the way. These US security firms were engaged in violent class conflicts (including strike-breaking and industrial espionage in east coast areas) or in guarding services protecting private properties (mostly owned by the rapidly expanding mining or railway companies in the frontier areas of the midwest).[28] But in recently unified imperial Germany, new forms of non-state security production emerged in the last quarter of the nineteenth century – for instance, private colonial security guards were established to protect private properties in the time just before the formal acquisition of the

27 *Leloup,* Antwerp.
28 *O'Hara,* Pinkertons.

African and Asian colonies in the 1870s, and the new and highly police-regulated private security militias operated by mining and coal companies in the Ruhr area since the 1880s controlled the working classes and prevented strikes. But in both cases, these new modes of private security production were limited and did not establish a corporate business model; they were just auxiliary modes of private security production run by colonial entrepreneurs and coal and steel companies with the aim of protecting their own property rights in the absence of a strong state police force. In contrast, at the same time the US saw the spectacular rise of a new and highly visible market of private security firms, often run by former soldiers or experienced police officers, offering a whole range of guarding, investigating or even spying services to state agencies, private companies, or wealthy individuals.[29]

On the other side of the Atlantic, however, this development seemed to begin some decades later and with a slightly different scope. In Hanover, the merchant Lachmann Jacob founded the first German security company on 15 July 1901 after he had visited the US and studied the remarkable but not undisputed success story of the Pinkertons. Some months later, in December 1901, Benno Koßmann started his own security firm in Cologne with twelve guards. In Munich in April 1902, brothers Joseph and Hermann Sternefeld started by hiring twenty-eight watchmen and one district inspector (as a night watch officer). Despite suspicious remarks appearing in the public newspapers and some distrust and scepticism articulated by Bavarian police forces, the Munich-based company grew quickly, promoting their new security services with a lot of advertisements in the public press. Six months later, the Sternefeld brothers already employed sixty-one night watchmen patrolling private properties for well-off customers and companies. In 1908 they were able to obtain their first public assignments when their watchmen started to guard high-profile events like *Oktoberfest*. In 1914, shortly before the outbreak of the First World War, the Bavarian security firm's staff had risen to 180 men.[30]

Only five years after the turn of the century, in nearly every big city and medium-sized town in Germany, one or several private security firms had been founded, offering mainly professional guarding and night patrolling services for private, corporate, and industrial properties. These newly-established security firms were often labelled as *Wach- und Schließgesellschaften*

---

29 *Bührer,* Schutztruppe; *Caruso,* Forces; *Moyd,* Intermediaries; *Zollmann,* Kolonialpolizei.

30 *Kupferschmidt/Menzel,* Geschichten, Vol. 1, 179; *Nelken* Bewachungsgewerbe.

(Guarding and Locking Societies), with quickly growing companies in Hamburg, Leipzig and Berlin leading the way, each recruiting several hundred uniformed guards (mostly elderly men) to their ranks in only a few years. These new security firms advertised their new services in public newspapers as a much needed filling of a 'security gap' that opened after an extensive reform of state police in Prussia in the early 1890s, when the existing system of night watchmen organised at a municipal level was abolished. On the one hand, this professionalisation and centralisation of the state police forces seemed to strengthen the state monopoly of force in the field of domestic security; on the other hand, rising costs for well-trained and well-equipped police officers led to a significant reduction of visible patrolling duties and guarding services in rapidly growing towns and cities, especially at nighttime. This in fact led to an increasing demand for commercial security services to protect private or corporate properties from thieves or burglars, especially in the rapidly developing and industrialising cities of the German Empire.[31]

The first years after 1900, the astonishing boom of private security firms led to fierce competition, but also to the founding of national interest groups to fight for a political acknowledgement of this new service branch that was suspiciously observed by police authorities. In 1904, Benno Koßmann, head of the *Kölner Wach- und Schließgesellschaft*, founded the first national interest group with eighteen other security companies, which joined together in an effort not only to improve their somewhat shady public image, but also to lobby politicians and police officials to acknowledge and also regulate their new business model to fight off 'dirty' or even criminal competitors. This initial commercial boom came to an abrupt end with the sudden outbreak of the First World War, however, something which endangered the private security branch with its mass conscriptions and strict military rulings on the right to private patrolling, carrying arms, and wearing uniforms in public – with all of these measures and strategies being the core symbolic and practical elements of the private security business model that was not authorised with special policing rights. Especially in the first years of their existence, many smaller companies were literally wiped out by a lack of staff, with only older watchmen remaining as a last resort for filling their ranks. This led to fierce reactions in the field of recruitments: in 1917, the *Berliner Wach- und Schließgesellschaft* even started to hire women (most of them wives of recently enlisted guards) for unarmed guarding and patrolling services, something which

31 *Jessen*, Industrierevier.

provoked debate about the end of 'femininity' in local newspapers. With soaring crime rates in the second half of the war – with many cases of burglary or theft in bigger German cities that suffered from allied blockades and a crippling war economy – the private as well as public demand for private security services rose again. This trend accelerated during the crisis-ridden history of the Weimar Republic after 1919, when an eruption of political violence and severe economic setbacks like in 1922–3 and 1929–31 led to growing fears of exploding crime rates in bigger cities. Private security firms tried to fill the gap, presenting themselves to their mostly well-off corporate customers as a professionalised alternative between a 'weak' state police force and the 'extreme' vigilante forces of the political right and left.[32] In 1927, the national lobby group finally achieved their long-term goal when the German government in Berlin introduced a new license requirement for private security firms to set some (quite humble) standards regarding the qualifications of staff and the liability of the owners of companies. Additionally, the efforts for a democratically reformed and republican state police force also led to new forms of cooperation between police forces and security firms to prevent burglary in private homes with the help of newly established anti-crime advice centres (*kriminalpolizeiliche Beratungsstellen*).[33]

In the turbulent interwar years, the German private security business was oscillating between boom and crisis. From a commercial perspective, shop, business and property owners who had lost their faith in the state now seemed to be the main subscribers of private security firms and tried to present themselves as highly-professional service companies by using modern security technologies (like alarms) as well as psychologically and physically trained staff. In 1927, for example, the *Münchner Wach- und Schließgesellschaft* published an account of their activities in the previous twenty-five years further to advertise their services, containing a huge amount of statistics that give us an indication as to what the private guards were doing for their customers from day to day (or maybe even better: from night to night). They locked 615,195 open doors, extinguished 71,211 candles, rescued 2,401 horses from danger, reported 311 cases of water main breaks and 244 open gas pipes, extinguished 362 small fires and also alarmed firefighters in a further 183 instances. Moreover, the Munich guards deterred 780 burglars and detained 378 of them before transferring them to the police. 219 safe boxes of shops and business were also

32 *Nelken*, Bewachungsgewerbe; *Kupferschmidt/Menzel*, Geschichten, Vol. 1.
33 *Götting*, Kriminalberatungsstellen.

found open and secured. Data concerning the security technologies that they utilised are also available: in 1927, the watchmen used 139 watchmen's clocks, served 573 control stations and administrated 2,906 keys for their customers – checking on thousands of storerooms, cellars, shop floors and factory buildings every night. Additionally, some public spaces like market halls and train maintenance facilities were guarded by the security company, as well as the *Deutsches Museum* and the Ministry of Public Transport.[34]

The rise to power of National Socialism in 1933 proved to be another tough challenge especially for many Jewish-owned security companies that also had to struggle with the new regime's favour for a 'strong' and centralised police force in contrast to the allegedly 'weak' republican Weimar state. In the early 1930s many security firms thus faced the heavy-handedness of the new regime and its own guarding activities, with an astonishingly intense and nearly fetish-like focus on black uniforms worn by private security guards. All over Nazi Germany, private security firms were closely monitored and controlled by the police, trade inspectors, and Nazi party officials. Jewish companies were quickly forced off the market or hastily 'aryanised' after 1935–6, apparently because they were thought to pose a double threat to renewed state sovereignty in the eyes of the Nazi regime by treacherously commercialising or even exploiting social fears of 'asocial' crime and a weak state. According to this line of thinking, the new National Socialist state would not need private security services any longer because it would simply wipe out any crimes threatening the *Volksgemeinschaft* with extreme racial measures of criminal biology and preventive policing.[35] This initial trend reversed again during war time, however, when the remaining private security firms became deeply involved in the overall war effort by guarding thousands of forced labourers for the German industry as a kind of tightly state-observed reserve army force.[36]

The post-war period abruptly ended the activities of nearly all private security firms. While this hiatus only lasted for a relatively short time in West Germany, it lasted much longer in the Soviet-occupied Eastern part of the country, because the Russian-backed German Democratic Republic (GDR) nationalised the whole security sector and integrated it as *Betriebsschutz* into the state police forces. In contrast, after 1946 the Western-allied occupation governments lessened their strict restrictions on private securi-

34 *Kupferschmidt/Menzel*, Geschichten, Vol. 1, 181f.
35 *Wagner*, Maßnahmenstaates.
36 *Kapinos*, Entwicklung.

ty businesses, especially on uniforms and on the military and police backgrounds of their staff. Their initial fears of uniformed and armed former Nazis patrolling the ruined cities was replaced by a social and public demand for reducing property crime rates that were soaring, especially during the 'hunger years' of 1946–7. After the foundation of the Federal Republic in 1949, a quickly reestablished private security sector steadily grew in the context of the *Wirtschaftswunder* of the 1950s and 1960s. Whereas this commercial expansion was mostly related to more traditional guarding activities on behalf of industrial corporations, the 1970s and 1980s saw a remarkable transformation of private security and especially in public perceptions and political discussions. Many firms were now visibly entering the public sphere in the context of a growing public concern with new forms of terrorism as well as drug- and gang-related organised crime in bigger cities. Again drawing on US models, a newly founded security company in Munich, the *Ziviler Sicherheitsdienst* (ZSD), became particularly notorious as the 'black sheriffs' of Bavaria – hinting at their allegedly Americanized style of black uniforms and intimidating appearances, with martial arts-trained staff which guarded the Munich subway system (mostly against drunken youths, homeless people, and so forth).[37]

Despite a lot of concerns and criticisms, the 1980s and 1990s were to see a dramatic takeoff of private security businesses, not only in West Germany, but also nearly all over the Western world. Private security firms like the quickly expanding family-owned company *Kötter* in Essen, the traditional *Niedersächsische Wach- und Schließgesellschaft* (NWSG) in Hanover, and the Swedish security company *Securitas* in Berlin (that only entered the West German market in the 1990s through a series of corporate takeovers) were now transforming themselves into bigger and increasingly professionalised as well as transnational security providers, also adding a lot of new security technologies and high-profile surveillance services to their commercial portfolio. In this period, other services companies forcefully started to enter the new security market. In 1986, for example, *Raab Karcher*, a traditional service and construction company, took over *Gesellschaft für Eigentumschutz*, a security technology firm founded in 1902 with a focus on alarm technologies, and started to develop its own security branch with several thousands of guards. Another example of the rapid transformation and professionalisation on a corporate level is *DSW Security* from Düsseldorf. Originally founded by Alfred Oppermann in 1925 in Berlin, the company was re-established by him and his son Hans-Joachim

37 *Böick*, Gewaltmonopol.

in 1946 after he came back from being a prisoner of war. After another visit to the US in the mid-1960s, the younger Oppermann decided to merge the company with Dutch security firm *Nederlands Veiligheits Dienst* (NVD), owned by Ernst van der Lee. The new *DSW* group established its headquarters in Frankfurt and tried to adapt to 'modern' styles of management there, but soon moved to Düsseldorf. Now it was the new professional manager Reinhard W. Ottens that tried to transform this group into a transnational and highly professional security company by developing new forms of organisation, introducing new security technologies (like security centres) and implementing new qualification requirements for DSW guards.[38]

Additionally, these quickly expanding and professionalising security firms started systematically to guard airports, trains, nuclear power plants, and mass events, as well as public buildings and spaces in general, drawing a lot of attention in the political arena as well as the public sphere, with concerns raised about the emergence of 'private armies' beyond the state. This first big wave of the privatisation of security services led to a heated political debate in West Germany on the decline of the state monopoly in favour of profit-oriented security businesses – with the US as an example of a 'weak' or even 'sold-off' state as a threatening and dangerous future scenario looming in the background. Furthermore, the reputation, qualification and payment of the rank-and-file guarding staff was (and still is) a pressing question in these discussions.[39]

Finally, the fall of the Berlin Wall in 1989 and the 9/11 terrorist attacks in 2001 led to other staggering booms in the private security sector. In East Germany after the fall of the GDR, many laid-off military officers and state security agents tried to enter the mostly unregulated security market by founding private companies like *Preußen-Wacht* in Potsdam near Berlin, which was criticised for the use of extensive violence by former Stasi officers in its ranks. With growing fears of crime (coming from Eastern Europe) or terrorism (coming from the Near or Middle East), politicians in reunified Germany also started to establish a wide range of PPSPs, in the belief that cooperative arrangements between state police forces and private security firms could raise security levels with a higher amount of efficiency while simultaneously reducing public expenditures. This remarkable trend again fueled an intense political debate and prompted new scientific research to be conducted into the 'economisation' of public security produc-

38 *Kupferschmidt/Menzel*, Geschichten, Vol. 2, 60–103.

39 *Böick*, Gewaltmonopol.

tion. However, the general boom of the security sector in Germany still goes on today. While critics are interpreting the rapid quantitative and qualitative growth of private security firms as a 'neoliberal' shift of security paradigms from overall state guarantees to individual self-responsibilities, other authors tend to underline the normality and efficiency of non-state as well as commercial security production and evaluate this recent development as yet another transformation of state sovereignty in a (post-)modern age.[40]

3. *Perspectives: From 'National Security Cultures' to global 'Security Capitalism'?*

In general, this brief sketch of the history of the private security business in Germany also raises questions about the national specifics of its development. Despite the abovementioned transnational entanglements and references, however, there seem to be astonishing differences regarding national '(private) security cultures' and the underlying concepts of state sovereignty and economic activities, as well as the social and individual organisation of security matters, especially regarding different conceptions of publicness and privateness in the field of domestic security and policing. In the early 2000s, when many scholars were nervously talking about a decline of statehood due to a quickly advancing trend towards privatisation in nearly all fields, German political scientist Rainer Eisfeld conceptualised the US, the UK and Germany as three different ideal types concerning the different conceptions of the state's monopoly of force, state-society relations, and overall political culture.[41]

In Eisfeld's view, the UK represented an example of a long-term and evolutionary development of state structures as a result of negotiations between elites and class society. According to him, this led to a distinctive and evolving liberal model of 'civic (security) culture', where an unarmed police force operated cooperatively with private, social or 'mixed' actors, with an emphasis on non-violent strategies of domestic security. Eisfeld contrasts this 'moderate' or mixed UK model with two other cases: Germany and the US. In continental Germany, a conservative and top-down model of a 'strong' nation state, following the Prussian militaristic tradition after 1871, seemed to render any decline of its power in a material or

40 *Fratzky*, Gefahrenabwehr; *Kirsch*, Sicherheitsdienste.
41 *Eisfeld*, Vigilantes.

even symbolic way as a dangerous loss of national sovereignty, something that was already considered to be at risk from the threat of public enemies both within and outside the country. The emphasis on a 'strong' and powerful state and its police force made the relations between public and private security producers a very delicate and complicated matter. Among other things, the newly established security firms were not allowed to carry arms or to wear official uniforms. In contrast to the glorification of an omnipotent "*Machtstaat*", Eisfeld argued, the United States never developed a 'strong' centralised state along strict European lines. Within the remote areas of the vast and quickly expanding country, statehood was established only gradually and in a bottom-up way in a process of conflicts and negotiations undertaken by different local elite groups long after the successful revolution at the end of the eighteenth century. With a new and dynamic capitalist society of competing individualists and immigrant groups, he argued, the implementation of the monopoly of force was a highly utopian vision, especially within the chaotic context of a 'frontier setting' in the middle of the nineteenth century. Here, following Eisfeld, in the eyes of many settlers and entrepreneurs, most state officials seemed to be remote, corrupt or even dangerous; especially with the new capitalist elites of this emerging 'frontier' society relying upon private and heavily-armed security forces to protect their new wealth and property.[42]

But is Eisfeld's notion of the long-term evolution of unique 'national security cultures' and their different conceptions of statehood, the markets, society, and security production really the final stage? Opposite to this national approach, a historical as well as transnational perspective could also shed a new light on the history of the modern security business in general. One could also argue that the twentieth century in particular saw the non-linear development of a new business model of private security firms emerging from the US in a way which was closely connected to a form of capitalist commodification of security services in order to protect private properties and, later, public spaces. The establishment of commercial private security companies all over the Western world during the twentieth century may thus be described as a mixture of different processes and transformations of the state, the market, and society. By analysing the contemporary discourses regarding public-private relations between the state, the economy, and society, we can make four key observations.

First, that the discourse surrounding the potential Americanization of security politics was one of the main themes of political debate, as politi-

42 *Eisfeld*, Vigilantes.

cians, lawyers, security experts and police officials in Germany intensively debated the transformations of statehood from 'strong' to 'weak' (or *vice versa*). Second, that this debate is closely connected to the notion of marketisation (or economisation) in contemporary discourses on domestic security production and its impact on social inequality via commercial and capitalist 'profit-taking' or efficiency orientation in emerging security markets, for example in terms of lower-class security officials guarding the property of their upper-class customers within gated communities. Third, that notions of privatisation (or individualisation) raise questions surrounding the relationship between public or private security producers and individual citizens or customers on a micro level (for example issues related to the connections between collective or corporative security and individual safety in everyday situations of a growing 'responsibilisation' or 'personal risk management'). Fourth, and finally, that the debate surrounding securitisation ought to be framed within a broader context of transformations in national 'security cultures', namely by analysing the transatlantic relations and political and cultural frameworks regarding domestic security in public discourse as well as in practice, both strategic and technological.

I argue that the overall intermingling of these distinct processes of Americanization, marketisation, privatisation and securitisation eventually led to the establishment of a new model of public-private security production during the twentieth century. This I want to conceptualise and describe as a transnational, post-modern and hybrid form of security capitalism that has to be distinguished from pre-modern modes of traditional self-defense, as well as highly modern forms of monopolised state policing. This new, market-driven, and highly competitive business model of offering commercial security services to private or public customers originated from the US, but came to Europe after the turn of the century where it confronted and slowly transformed different national 'security cultures' throughout the twentieth century – from its early beginnings after 1900 to the recent boom of PPSPs, especially during the 1990s and 2000s.[43]

After all, the rise of security capitalism has never been limited to the Western world. In Latin America and Asia, private security firms are even more present in the field of domestic security production, with India having 7 million private security workers in 2017, China having 5 million, and Brazil having 1.7 million – even exceeding those of the advanced and heavily-armed security businesses in the US (1.1 million), itself just in

43 *Plumpe*, Kapitalismus.

front of Russia (800,000). When comparing these absolute numbers (that are surely different in relative terms), the simple opposition of 'weak' states and 'strong' businesses seems rather unhelpful, with 'strong' states like China and 'weak' states like Brazil leading the charts. This notion becomes even more blurry if attention is paid to the rising number of transnationally operating security firms. These include organisations such as US company Blackwater (renamed Academi in 2009 after public criticism of its role in the post-9/11 wars in the Middle East), which sells a broad range of security, surveillance, and logistical services all over the world to very different states and private customers, and in so doing blurs the established boundaries between internal and external security worldwide. But a truly global history of these private security firms is yet to be written.

Conclusion: 'Weak' States, 'Strong' Businesses?

By focusing on the mostly disregarded German private security firms in the period in question, this article has briefly highlighted some changes and transformations of security production beyond the state. After arguing that this field of research has often remained in the shadows even after the renaissance of new security studies in historical research in the wake of securitisation theory, I have outlined the main lines of its diverse development throughout the eventful twentieth century. Whether this is being seen as a special evolution along the lines of 'national security cultures' or whether it should be interpreted as part of a broader and even global trend of the emergence of a new form of security capitalism is something which should be debated in the future. The national developments mentioned above, including those which took place in Germany, were always influenced by broader international or even transnational trends (concerning organisation, technology, management, and qualifications) – with many innovations spreading to Europe from the bigger US security market some years later. This transfer of a new form of 'security capitalism' to the continent was especially evident during the 1900s (with the introduction of the new business model), the 1920s (with the cooperation with the state police), and the 1970s (with the 'professionalisation' of corporate models), when German entrepreneurs and managers tried to introduce new Americanized strategies into the domestic security market, thus fueling fierce competition in that field. But these new commercial strategies, mostly copied from US security companies, were readily scrutinised in national and local settings – by the media, but also by politicians and police officials, who always kept a close eye on the transforming and expanding security branch and occasionally tried to regulate it.

However, a new historical perspective should not just reproduce rather simplistic narratives of a criticisable replacement of the state and its police forces by private firms and its guards. On the contrary, these developments should be seen as a transformation of the complicated relationships between the state, the market, and society, leading to hybridisation (and mostly growth) in the field of domestic security production, as David Churchill, Dolores Janiewski and Pieter Leloup convincingly described it very recently. They argue that these relations between private security and the modern state

> highlight wide disparities in the claims of specific states to maintain a monopoly of legitimate force, the dynamics of cooperation and conflict between state policing systems and private security provision, the development of public-private security partnerships and the recognition of individual rights and responsibilities to protect oneself.[44]

This multi-layered understanding of security production and provision in (post-)modern societies becomes particularly interesting when considering changing understandings of 'publicness' and 'privateness' (and also of 'strength' and 'weakness') in the area of statehood and domestic (in)security. Has the picture of a strong and omnipotent nation state, which claims the full monopoly of force, been transformed into a more pluralistic model of decentralised and commercial security production in vast social or economic networks? And is this also leading towards a post-modern or hybrid form of statehood that resembles pre-modern strategies of security production beyond the state primarily provided by competitive and commercial markets, independently acting social or political groups, or self-responsible individuals?

To address these questions, future research should methodologically combine different approaches of political, economic, social and cultural history, as Hartmut Berghoff and Jakob Vogel suggested some years ago. In doing so, the study of modern security business should not only focus on the 'hard' facts of the economic history of the security industry, but it should unearth the wider ranging political, scientific and cultural discourses and debates, as well as the social contexts of these developments in terms of the rise of a new form of security capitalism. This should be also done with a special focus on its transatlantic dynamics and implications by

---

44 *Churchill/Janiewski/Leloup*, State, 10.

analysing political debates and negotiations, economic strategies and corporate self-representations, scientific discourses and analysis, technological developments as well as cultural framings and reflections on private security on different levels throughout the twentieth century.[45] The emergence and transformations of the security business model could then be seen as genuinely capitalist way of 'securitisation' by way of 'commercialisation'. By quickly introducing and broadly advertising new security services or technologies to ward off the dangers of crime, terrorism or disasters, this business model could be seen as a commercial strategy to transform publicly-debated fears and dangers into a successful business model by not only pointing out the possible dangers to their mostly well-off corporate or public customers, but also presenting the perfect private security solution to these possible threats.

The notion of 'selling security'[46] thus seems to provide us with a very promising historical perspective into the methods of commercial securitisation beyond the state. The new business model of private security companies was established after 1900 in Germany and had an eventful history in the twentieth century. As a very sensitive sector close to the core of modern statehood, wars, economic crises, social upheavals, and political changes could pose significant challenges but also provide fruitful opportunities for the mostly small- and medium-sized and family-owned security firms that sold guarding or patrolling services to corporate or private customers, as well as to state agencies themselves. In the case of Germany, their unclear legal status underlines this balancing act in the shadows of the state monopoly. Since the early 1900s, established security companies and their national lobbying associations tried to convince very different German governments to pass a national security law in order to regulate the domestic security market – a very interesting case of a business sector pushing hard for more regulation. But the different attempts to set clear rules for basic regulative standards for admission, recruitment, equipment, qualifications, payments and special policing powers were unsuccessful – neither in the 1900s nor in the 1920s, 1970s or 1990s. These attempts should not just control or set entry barriers to the market (especially for 'Black Sheep' or 'Black Sheriffs'), but they were also meant to secure an official acknowledgement of the private security business model to be accepted by the state not just as a threat to its monopoly or a competitor to its police forces, but as a reputable and reliable partner in domestic securi-

45 *Berghoff/Vogel*, Perspektivenwechsel.
46 *Wakefield*, Security.

ty production. Interestingly, in early 2020, with the COVID-19 pandemic overwhelming a lot of nation states and cities with a broad range of new public health security tasks the Federal Government announced another attempt to regulate (and this way officially recognise) the private security sector in Germany – with the results remaining to be seen.

Bibliography

Abrahamsen, Rita: Security Beyond the State: Private Security in International Politics, Cambridge 2010

Berghoff, Hartmut/Vogel, Jakob (eds.): Wirtschaftsgeschichte als Kulturgeschichte. Dimensionen eines Perspektivenwechsels, Frankfurt/M 2004

Bislev, Sven: Globalization, State Transformation and Public Security, in: International Political Science Review 25 (2004), 3, p. 281–296

Böick, Marcus: Ökonomisierung des Gewaltmonopols? Die Sicherheitswirtschaft und die Privatisierung öffentlicher Sicherheitsaufgaben seit den 1970er Jahren, in: Rüdiger Graf (eds.): Ökonomisierung. Debatten und Praktiken in der Zeitgeschichte, Göttingen 2019, p. 139–165

Bührer, Tanja: Die Kaiserliche Schutztruppe für Deutsch-Ostafrika. Koloniale Sicherheitspolitik und transkulturelle Kriegführung, 1885 bis 1918, München 2011

Button, Mark: Private Policing, London 2019

Caruso, Amerigo: Joining Forces against 'Strike Terrorism': The Public-Private Interplay in Policing Strikes in Imperial Germany, 1890–1914, in: European History Quarterly 49 (2019), 4, p. 597–624

Churchill, David/Janiewski, Dolores/Leloup, Peter (eds.): Private Security and the Modern State. Historical and Comparative Perspectives, London/New York 2020

Conze, Eckart: Geschichte der Sicherheit. Entwicklung – Themen – Perspektiven, Göttingen 2018Conze, Eckart: Die Suche nach Sicherheit: Eine Geschichte der Bundesrepublik Deutschland von 1949 bis in die Gegenwart, Berlin 2009

Daase, Christopher: Wandel der Sicherheitskultur, in: Aus Politik und Zeitgeschichte 58 (2010), 50, p. 9–16

Eisfeld, Rainer: Die organisierte Gewalt „selbstloser Männer": Vigilantes in den Vereinigten Staaten, in: van Elsbergen, Gisbert(eds.): Wachen, kontrollieren, patrouillieren. Kustodialisierung der Inneren Sicherheit, Wiesbaden 2004, p. 101–118

Eppler, Erhard: Vom Gewaltmonopol zum Gewaltmarkt? Die Privatisierung und Kommerzialisierung der Gewalt, Frankfurt/M 2002

Evans, Richard J.: Polizei, Politik und Gesellschaft in Deutschland 1700–1933, in: Geschichte & Gesellschaft 22 (1996), 4, p. 609–628

Fratzky, Karl-Uwe: Ökonomisierung der polizeilichen Gefahrenabwehr, Hamburg 2013

Foucault, Michel: Überwachen und Strafen: Die Geburt des Gefängnisses, Frankfurt 1993

Garland, David: The Limits of the Sovereign State. Strategies of Crime Control in Contemporary Society, in: The British Journal of Criminology 36 (1996), 4, p. 445–471.

Götting, Dirk: 90 Jahre Kriminalberatungsstellen in Deutschland – Wegbereiter einer bürgerorientierten Polizeiarbeit, in: Kriminalistik13 (2011) 4, p. 213–216

Henne, Steffen/Kampmann, Christoph/Marciniak, Angela/Meteling, Wencke: "Security turns its eye exclusively to the future". Zum Verhältnis von Sicherheit und Zukunft in der Geschichte, in: Kampmann, Christoph/Marciniak, Angela/Meteling, Wencke (eds.): „Security turns its eye exclusively to the future". Zum Verhältnis von Sicherheit und Zukunft in der Geschichte. Baden-Baden 2017, p. 9–36

Hitzer, Bettina/Welskopp, Thomas (eds.): Die Bielefelder Sozialgeschichte: Klassische Texte zu einem geschichtswissenschaftlichen Programm und seinen Kontroversen, Bielefeld 2010

Jessen, Ralph: Polizei im Industrierevier. Modernisierung und Herrschaftspraxis im westfälischen Ruhrgebiet 1848–1914, Göttingen 1991

Johnston, Les: The Rebirth of Private Policing, London 1992

Kapinos, Klaus: Entwicklung des Bewachungsgewerbes unter den Nationalsozialisten von 1933–1945, Hamburg 2018

Kirsch, Benno: Private Sicherheitsdienste im öffentlichen Raum, Wiesbaden 2003

Klimke, Daniela: Wach- & Schließgesellschaft. Sicherheitsmentalitäten in der Spätmoderne, Wiesbaden 2008

Krüger, Christine G.: Slums und Villenviertel. Städtische Grenzziehungen und Sicherheitsentwürfe in London und Hamburg im ausgehenden 19. Jahrhundert, in: Saeculum 68 (2018), 1, p. 37–60

Kühl, Stefan: Ganz normale Organisationen. Zur Soziologie des Holocaust, Frankfurt/M 2014

Kupferschmidt, Erich/Menzel, Thomas: Geschichten eines Sicherheitsunternehmens, Vol. 1: Von den Anfängen bis zum Beginn des 20. Jahrhunderts. Berlin 2013

Kupferschmidt, Erich/Menzel, Thomas: Geschichten eines Sicherheitsunternehmens, Vol. 2: Besetzung. Spaltung. Einheit. Vom Kriegsende bis zur Gegenwart. Berlin 2016

Leloup, Pieter: The private security industry in Antwerp (1907–1934). A historical-criminological analysis of its modus operandi and growth, in: Crime, History & Societies 19 (2015), 1, p. 119–147

Lüdtke, Alf/Reinke, Herbert/Sturm, Michael (eds.): Polizei, Gewalt und Staat im 20. Jahrhundert. Wiesbaden 2011

Maier, Charles: Once within Borders. Territories of Power, Wealth, and Belonging since 1500, Cambridge/M 2016

Miller, Wilbur R.: A History of Private Policing in the United States, London 2019

Moyd, Michelle R.: Violent Intermediaries. African Soldiers, Conquest, and Everyday Colonialism in German East Africa, Ohio 2014

Nelken, Sigmund: Das Bewachungsgewerbe. Ein Beitrag zur Geschichte des Selbstschutzes, Berlin 1926

O'Hara, S. Paul: Inventing the Pinkertons. Or Spies, Sleuths, Mercenaries, and Thugs, Baltimore 2016

Patel, Kiran Klaus: Zeitgeschichte im digitalen Zeitalter. Neue und alte Herausforderungen, in: Vierteljahrshefte für Zeitgeschichte 59 (2011), 3, p. 331–351

Plumpe, Werner: Das Kalte Herz. Kapitalismus: die Geschichte einer andauernden Revolution, Berlin 2019

Saupe, Achim: Von „Ruhe und Ordnung" zur „inneren Sicherheit". Eine Historisierung gesellschaftlicher Dispositive, in: Zeithistorische Forschungen 7 (2010), 2, p. 170–187

Schwell, Alexandra/Eisch-Angus, Katharina (eds.): Der Alltag der (Un-)Sicherheit. Ethnografisch-kulturwissenschaftliche Perspektiven auf die Sicherheitsgesellschaft. Berlin 2018

Wakefield, Alison: Selling Security. The Private Policing of Public Space, London 2015

Wagner, Patrick: Der Kern des völkischen Maßnahmenstaates – Rolle, Macht und Selbstverständnis der Polizei im Nationalsozialismus, in: Wolfgang Schulte (eds.): Die Polizei im NS-Staat, Frankfurt/M 2009, p. 23–48

Zollmann, Jakob: Koloniale Herrschaft und ihre Grenzen. Die Kolonialpolizei in Deutsch-Südwestafrika 1894–1915, Göttingen 2020

Zwierlein, Cornel: Sicherheitsgeschichte. Ein neues Feld der Geschichtswissenschaften, in: Geschichte und Gesellschaft 38 (2012), 2, p. 365–386

Food and Supply Security in the first Phase of Globalisation: the Role of Producers, Consumers, and the State in the German Empire

Christian Kleinschmidt

1. *Introduction*

The period between the middle of the nineteenth century and the First World War is regarded as the first phase of globalisation, which was characterised by the growing interdependence of trade, capital and labour markets, with the free trade movement, the emergence of the gold standard, and the transport and communications revolutions providing important foundations.[1] This also applied to the production and distribution of food,[2] which took on global dimensions from the middle of the nineteenth century onwards – no longer just for luxury goods such as coffee, cocoa and other colonial produce, but increasingly for everyday foodstuffs such as cereals, meat, and fruit. This can be seen in a contemporary description by the national economist Paul Arndt from 1908:

> World traffic extends to the smallest German hut. Today, the most modest household contains products from almost every country in the world. If you look around in your everyday surroundings, you will come across objects everywhere that originate in whole or in part from abroad. You will find – even in the home of the less well-off – bread made from Russian, Romanian, North American, Argentinean or Indian grain, eggs from Italy or Russia, fish from the Norwegian or Scottish coast, meat, bacon and lard from the United States, cheese from Holland or Switzerland, tropical fruits from Spain, Italy or Turkey, rice from the East Indies, coffee from Central or South America. ... There is probably hardly a product in Germany whose producer would not have any relations to foreign market conditions.[3]

1 *Pfister*, Globalisierung, 282–294.
2 *Nützenadel*, Green, 153–171; *Trentmann*, Herrschaft, 217–234.
3 *Arndt*, Weltwirtschaft, 14f. (translation from the original German version).

The globalisation of the coffee trade, for example – its professionalisation in the form of futures trading, the improvement of infrastructure, and the development of information and transport facilities – led to the "popularisation" of coffee consumption, making it possible for coffee to be consumed throughout Germany and by all social classes.[4] Grain, which was grown in large quantities in the German Reich, became an import product, not least because of its growing population, while on the other hand surplus producers such as the US, and increasingly Canada, Argentina, Russia, India, and Australia, exported large quantities. In 1907, the German Empire imported more than one-fifth of the total world grain exports, equating to 1.8 million tons of wheat and around one-third of German consumption between 1909 and 1914.[5] The globalisation of the grain trade in turn led to a corresponding globalisation of the meat trade, so that, between the 1870s and the First World War, beef became "the most important globally traded agricultural product after grain", with the German Empire as one of its most important importers.[6]

In addition to the globalisation of the food supply, three other phenomena are mentioned here which are characteristic of the period in question. First, the emergence of the mass consumption society, which was closely linked to the food supply, as pointed out by economic historian Hans Jürgen Teuteberg in the mid-1980s when he spoke of the "breakthrough to modern mass consumption", especially with regard to the supply of food and the question of nutrition.[7] Second, the democratisation of consumption (even if this did not remove the social barriers within society), with ever broader social classes being able to enjoy food and beverages that were once produced only for a minority. Third, the increased security of food supply (the last crisis of the "*typ ancien*" with its corresponding famine in Europe occured in 1846–47). Afterwards, the consumption of higher-quality food, such as meat, continued to increase. At the same time, there was an increase in choice and thus in the freedom of consumption.

In Europe in this period, a growing number of international contracts were concluded on the question of food, something which was complemented with an increase in European communication in the form of congresses, exhibitions and institutions, such as the first International Congress of Agriculture in Paris in 1889, and further congresses in Bu-

---

4 *Rischbieter*, Globalisierungsprozesse, 31–37.

5 *Pfister*, Globalisierung, 290; *Rita*, Agrarpolitik, 174.

6 *Loheide*, Beef, 48.

7 *Teuteberg*, Durchbruch.

dapest, Lausanne, Paris and Rome, Vienna and Madrid. These were followed by the establishment of an International Agricultural Institute in Rome, the founding of the Commission Internationale d'Agriculture (with members from eighteen mainly European states), and the development of the first supranational organisations, for example in the sugar industry. In addition, increasingly interwoven European labour markets, especially for seasonal agricultural activities, also emerged.[8]

Taken together, these factors show growing levels of security and stability of food supplies worldwide, including in Europe and therefore in the German Reich. Paul Arndt's promise of a comprehensive and global supply of food via the world market stood in stark contrast to the negative side effects of globalisation in reality, however. Thus, in various fields, great potential for uncertainty arose in the form of new crises, new risks, threats and challenges to the food supply, as well as different settings of securitisation for different groups of actors such as consumers, producers, and the state. The crisis in European agriculture in the 1870s brought uncertainty and problems regarding prices and sales for producers. For consumers, as will be shown below, uncertainties arose due to food adulteration, disease, and rising prices. A fundamental improvement in the food supply in the context of the first wave of globalisation was thus diluted by new risks, uncertainties, abuses, and dangers. In this respect, the globalisation of the food supply also led to its securitisation – that is, global food supply chains were made the object of a discourse that stressed its dangerous potential and aimed at political intervention.

Wolfgang Sofsky claims that "freedom creates insecurity" in his book *The Principle of Security*.[9] This can be seen very clearly in the example of free trade, because free trade, globalisation, and the market economy were closely interlinked and harboured new uncertainties and risks for those who were involved. On the one hand, agricultural producers, farmers and their interest groups, but also industrial food producers, saw free trade as an opportunity to open up new markets. On the other hand, many market participants feared increasing international competition and food imports as a threat, which in their view would lead to dependency on the world market, falling prices, growing indebtedness on farms and, from the 1870s at the latest, the call for state protection in the form of protective tariffs.[10] In addition, protection against American competition and its supposedly

8 *Aldenhoff-Hübinger*, Agrarpolitik, 42–70; *Ambrosius*, Wettbewerb, 30.
9 *Sofsky*, Sicherheit, 149.
10 *Aldenhoff-Hübinger*, Agrarpolitik, 12–20; *Torp*, Herausforderung, 97–101.

destructive effect on European agriculture also played a role. In 1883, the government of the Reich commissioned the political scientist Max Sering to travel to North America with the aim of "reporting on the causes and probable course of North American agricultural competition",[11] with a view to comparing not only German conditions but also those in Europe more generally. In view of American agricultural competition, the European perspective on the protection of European agriculture even led to considerations regarding a potential customs union between Germany, Austria-Hungary, France, and Italy, with the aim of high common external and low internal tariffs.[12] The question of customs protection was in turn linked to the demand for the "protection of national labour", which, although not exclusively with regard to agriculture (and in contrast to a market-liberal understanding of labour), was intended to protect "German labour" and workers from foreign competition and also to secure the threatened existence of farmers.[13]

In the context of an increasingly globalised food supply, new risks and dangers for consumers became apparent, because food adulterations, pathogens in food, quality defects, lack of controls and hygiene standards, price increases as well as the food scandals publicised in the press also caused further uncertainty at this time – leading to a clear discrepancy between the security promises of sufficient globalised food production and distribution on the one hand and the new dangers for consumers and producers on the other.

These specific new challenges and insecurities as a result of globalisation were a major trigger for the securitisation of food, which met with different reactions, perceptions and interpretations among the actors involved (heuristics), which then led to different concrete patterns of action (repertoires). These will be examined in more detail below as different settings for the securitisation of food, with particular attention paid to the triad of consumers, producers, and the state. It will be shown that consumers and producers perceived different threats, dangers, and risks and adressed them to the state or public authorities as security problems. At the same time, state actors took the initiative to advance the protection and security of citizens, in some areas comparable with the initiatives to establish and expand welfare state security measures which had been taken from the 1880s onwards. After all, Bismarck's social policy was intended to provide protec-

---

11 *Sering*, Konkurrenz, V; s.a. *Aldenhoff-Hübinger*, Agrarpolitik, 60.

12 *Aldenhoff-Hübinger*, Agrarpolitik, 59f.

13 *Wehler*, Kaiserreich, 46; *Conrad*, Globalisierung, 282–293.

tion against the risks of old age, illness, and accidents. In critical security research, the state is not the only addressee of securitisation attempts.[14] However, although the present contribution also focuses on the securitisation of food by the collective action of producers and consumers it will show that in this specific triangular constellation in the phase after the emergence of the German Empire, consumers and producers addressed the state or state actors as a superior protective power or security guarantor.

The question thus arises as to how the actors involved dealt with the new challenges, threats and uncertainties of globalisation with regard to food security. Which perceptions and interpretations of the actors involved (heuristics) can be observed, what were the concrete actions that resulted from them, and, finally, who were the winners and who were the losers of this process?

Recently, numerous publications have appeared on the subject of food. Their focus has been on certain aspects of the food supply, the development of industrial and consumer society, agricultural policy, questions of marketing, globalisation, the relationship between market and state, and food quality.[15] The last of these ties in with questions of food controls, consumer protections and thus also questions of food safety, which are the focus of the present paper. It is not so much a matter of presenting new, source-based research results as one of looking at the existing literature insofar as it relates to the safety paradigm and securitisation and making it useful for economic and business history.

2. *The consumers*

In contrast to pre-industrial agriculture, increasingly mechanised, industrialised, global and market-based agriculture and food production provided the basis for an adequate food supply, but also increased dependencies, uncertainties, and risks for consumers. Until the middle of the nineteenth century, the supply of consumer goods and food was largely based on subsistence farming. In a small town in Thuringia around 1820, for example, approximately 40% of all cattle and pigs were still slaughtered at home. Otherwise, food was purchased at local markets by direct visual and tactile

14 *Conze*, Sicherheit, 82.

15 Cf., amongst others, *Nützenadel/Trentmann (eds.)*, Food; *Epple*, Unternehmen; *Rischbieter*, Mikro-Ökonomie; *Hierholzer*, Nahrung; *Aldenhoff-Hübinger*, Agrarpolitik.

inspection of the goods, based on personal trust and the integrity of the trader.[16] With the transition to mass production and mass sales as well as the distribution of food via the market and longer distribution chains between producers and consumers, the supply situation improved on the one hand, while personal relationships were increasingly lost and replaced by anonymous market processes on the other. Information about the origin and quality of products became less and less obtainable, most notably regarding the production methods of industrially produced food such as canned food, "artificial flour" and "artificial butter", sugar, and beer. From Holland, for example, came adulterated flour, so-called "artificial flour", which was lengthened with, among other things, gypsum, lime, and barytes. In order to be able to reuse adulterated flour, alum, sulphuric alumina, copper or zinc vitriol were then used. This flour was often added to sausages, boiled with water to form a paste, mixed with meat waste and fat, and mixed with fuchsin to improve the colour. Even contemporaries noticed that such a sausage ceased to be "what it is called".[17] Colours and preservatives allowed consumers to be deceived, and also increased the health risks for consumers. This led to discussions about declarations, limit values, and bans – such as the ban on copper greening, which is hazardous to health, but this was often circumvented or ignored.[18] There was also international competition, for example from Holland, for "artificial butter", which had been developed as margarine in France around 1870. As margarine consumption increased, so did butter falsification, for example by adding water, potato flour, tallow and fats, although, as mentioned above, foreign products could not easily be checked.[19] Meat, which was increasingly being imported from other European countries such as Austria-Hungary or Russia, or from the US, was often produced from animals infected with parasites and trichinae. In his novel *The Jungle*, Upton Sinclair gave a high-profile account of the rotten meat scandals of the early twentieth century, including cases involving meat from waste and from tuberculous-ridden cattle, and the criminal methods used by Chicago-based slaughterhouses.[20]

All this created new health challenges, risks and dangers for consumers, which individual markets and collective players had little to avert. Individual consumers in private households did not have access to sufficient prod-

16 *Wischermann/Nieberding*, Revolution, 120ff.
17 *Grüne*, Anfänge, 37; *Grüne*, Staatliche, 188.
18 *Spiekermann*, Kehrseite, 118f. See also in detail *Spiekermann*, Künstliche Kost.
19 *Grüne*, Anfänge, 59.
20 *Sinclair*, Sumpf, 69ff.

uct information due to the lack of mandatory food labelling requirements, so that price was usually the decisive factor in purchasing. The lack of consumer interest in the nature and quality of food was also frequently noted by contemporaries, specifically with regard to the price argument. For example, one of the leading food chemists, Joseph König, who regarded himself as a "representative" of consumers and who might be considered a "pioneer of modern consumer protection",[21] complained as early as 1878 that the public

> still has little interest in the quality of the goods; if for little money they only get a large measure and a large heap that looks good on the outside, then they are satisfied. This indifferentism goes so far, especially in Westphalia, that some people could not even decide to send in samples of suspicious food, even though I promised them free examinations. But as long as the consumer does not make any demands on the goods, the merchant and manufacturer certainly has no reason to do so.[22]

In addition to the reference to the lacking interest of consumers and the "indifference of the masses" with regard to food quality, the quote refers to two further phenomena of the time: first, an increasing public discussion about the risks and dangers of food in the context of its industrialised and globalised supply, and second, the fact that these dangers were neither perceived by a large proportion of those affected (i.e. consumers with low incomes and low educational prerequisites) themselves nor led to self-help initiatives. Rather, the problem was adressed through intermediaries and "lawyers" of the consumers, who wanted to compensate for the consumers' lack of information with the help of appropriate institutions, media presentation and education. Aside from the (food) reform movement at the turn of the century – which was primarily concerned with the consumption of healthy and natural food – a consumer movement of its own, with food quality as its focus, had not yet crystallised in the empire.[23] The reform movement was a minority, while a large part of the population attached less importance to these issues. In most households, housewives alone were still responsible for food preparation and therefore nutritional value, but they often lacked the appropriate education.[24]

---

21 *Ellerbrock*, Lebensmittelqualität, 184; *Hierholzer*, Arbeitsteilige Regulierung.
22 Cit. Joseph König, from: *Grüne*, Anfänge, 34.
23 *Baumgartner*, Ernährungsreform.
24 *Hierholzer*, Nahrung, 276–283.

Moreover, paternalistic authoritarian state thinking is likely to have seen the responsibilities here as resting primarily upon the sciences. As Vera Hierholzer shows, it was, for example, medical doctors and chemists who, from the 1880s onwards, wrote layman's manuals on the subjects of food, hygiene standards, preservation methods, and food adulteration as "instructions for self-protection", and who tried to address housewives and mothers.[25] In addition to specialist scientists, local associations and consumer groups, such as the *Allgemeine deutsche Verein gegen Verfälschung der Lebensmittel* (General German Association against Food Adulteration) also played a part. Its members and board members were mostly from the upper-middle classes (including chemists, pharmacists, doctors, and food manufacturers) and assumed – as did the food chemist König – that consumers were partly to blame for the threats to the food supply, as they themselves were hardly committed to improving the situation. In the spirit of the image of a responsible consumer, they pleaded for more personal responsibility and initiative, to which the associations sought to contribute through education – for example in the form of magazines, exhibitions, and cooperation with authorities.[26] Through these means a process of food securitisation was set in motion and thus the public awareness of the quality of food increased.

Other actors in this process of securitisation included consumer cooperatives as well as the Social Democratic Party, which, as the advocate of the consumer, especially during the time of dramatic price increases, fought against a "meat shortage" in food at the turn of the century. Between 1873 and 1913, meat prices rose by about 50% and consumption by about 67%,[27] leading to consumer protests and boycotts, which were often initiated by the SPD and the trade unions. These were not so much about food safety and food quality, however, but rather about the security of meat supply due to high prices, about inflation, and about "justice" and "fairness", so that boycotts, for example, were seen as "tools of great importance" in wage struggles.[28]

25 *Hierholzer*, Nahrung, 275.

26 *Hierholzer*, Nahrung, 289–303.

27 *Nonn*, Verbraucherprotest, 13f; *Loheide*, Beef, 65.

28 *Gerth*, Verbraucher, 221–226.

3. *The producers*

The term "food producers" does not only cover the agricultural sector but also the food industry more generally, which had risen to become the second largest industrial sector in terms of employees during the "take off" of industrialisation.[29] Against the background of international competition on the German market for food over the course of globalisation, the "suffering farmers" and their interest groups had increased the pressure on Reich Chancellor Bismarck to protect agriculture, entirely in the sense of the "common good". The implementation of the customs laws of 1879, which were met with fierce controversy, put an end to a short phase of free trade that had begun with the abolition of the British Corn Laws (1846) and the Cobden-Chevalier Treaty (1860), and was the beginning of a longer phase of protectionism which affected not only agriculture but also industry more generally. On the occasion of the first reading of the laws, Bismarck also invoked the "protection of national labour", as mentioned above, which served the goal of securing income in agriculture.[30] Terms such as "protection" and "protectionism" were now increasingly used in debates by producers and were part of a semantic turnaround in economic policy, which now was directed at the state in the form of demands for support, whereas in the decades before, the aim had been to minimise state interference in economic affairs.[31]

The food industry faced a double challenge: the transition to a market economy and mass production on the one hand, and increasing national and international competition on the other. Here too, safety and security played an important role. A central issue in this context was food safety. Individual players in the industry had been subject to public criticism for some years, which in turn was due to the food adulterations that had become increasingly known since the 1870s. Food law norms and standards were characterised by a "jungle" of confusing authorities and regulations. Producers increasingly attempted to interpret, undermine or circumvent the regulations in their favour, or in the words of institutional economics, to display opportunistic behaviour, and in this respect there were no limits to the imagination. One of the more harmless examples of food adulteration was the stretching of beer with water, which some producers consid-

29 *Ellerbrock*, Geschichte, 162f.

30 *Wehler*, Gesellschaftsgeschichte, 163–175.

31 It is not a question here of a detailed description of the customs protection problem, but rather of pointing out the associated semantic turnaround of the actors involved.

ered to be a benefit to the "lower classes", because the beer merchants in question were "useful members of the human community, working to ensure that even the less well-off could enjoy beer, albeit not in its original strength, which was not even beneficial to everyone".[32] Significantly more drastic cases of the increasingly publicised food adulterations and scandals – around 1910, for example, several hundred people fell ill and four people died from margarine poisoning[33] – forced the food industry to react, to distance itself from the criminal machinations of some producers, and to win back lost consumer confidence. This happened in a period which can certainly be interpreted as a paradigm shift in corporate strategy from production to sales orientation in which, in addition to classic advertising methods and questions of "advertising for public trust", the development of the branded article and thus early forms of marketing orientation can be observed.[34] Here the new methods of market communication as part of the "institutional revolution" of the nineteenth century became apparent.[35] This was certainly part of the globalisation-induced securitisation of the food industry. "Advertising for public trust" is a formulation that was only to become established after the Second World War under the American term "Public Relations",[36] but in view of food scandals, some manufacturers already practised this in the Empire in order to counteract the loss of consumer confidence and (re)establish the credibility of their own companies in the face of considerable potential for uncertainty.

For example, the margarine manufacturer Schlinck & Cie. responded with advertisements for its product "Palmin" with references to the high quality and, indirectly, to the safety of margarine, which had previously been called into question by repeated scandals. In these advertisements a caring housewife stated: "My husband has a weak stomach and can only tolerate the best fat! Since I introduced Palmin, he hasn't felt any discomfort!"[37] Sometimes nationalistic tones also played a role, for after all, the good reputation of "Made in Germany" was at stake for many products. Numerous actors and stakeholders took part in the food safety discourse,

---

32 Stenogr. Berichte über die Verhandlungen des Deutschen Reichstages 1878, cit. from *Schmauderer*, Beziehungen, 168.

33 *Ellerbrock*, Lebensmittelqualität, 173.

34 *Rossfeld*, Markenherrschaft, 35–62.

35 *Wischermann/Nieberding*, Revolution, 124.

36 *Kleinschmidt*, Blick, 204–213.

37 Berliner Illustrirte Zeitung No 9, 02.03.1913; see also URL: https://commons.wikimedia.org/wiki/File:Mein_Mann_hat_einen_schwachen_Magen_-_Palmin,_1913.jpg (08.02.2021).

with a captivating and original example of this coming in the form of a parody on Schiller's "Bell" which featured in the *Tierärztliche Rundschau* (Veterinary Review) of 1906:

> *‚Das Lied vom Schlachthaus'.*[38]
> *Eingeschlachtet zum Verpöckeln*
> *Liegt das Schwein in langer Reih';*
> *Keiner darf davor sich ekeln,*
> *Frisch, Gesellen kommt herbei!*
> *Stopft in Darm und Büchs'*
> *Unbesehn und fix!*
> *Soll das Werk den Meister loben,*
> *Darf man den Geschmack nicht proben.*
> *Das Werk, das schweinisch wir bereiten,*
> *Man nennt's ein Schweinefleisch-Produkt,*
> *Doch niemand ahnt auch nur von weitem,*
> *Was er mit ihm noch sonst verschluckt ...*
>
> *Nur für Deutschland sei die Ware säuberlicher zum Export,*
> *Und das gar zu Schauderbare*
> *Lasst aus deutschen Waren fort!*
> *Nehmt die Katz heraus und die tote Maus,*
> *Dass der Deutsche mit Behagen*
> *„Made in Germany" kann sagen!*

Food impurities, so the warning went, endangered the good reputation of German goods, because even the label "Made in Germany" was after all a call for trust in German products at home and abroad.

Manufacturers of chocolate, such as the Stollwerk company, also used advertising as early as the 1870s to distinguish themselves as quality producers from their national and international competitors by introducing the term "purity brand", whereby Stollwerck explicitly positioned itself against the "adulteration of cocoa products" and for the safety of food. To this end, the company also used the tradition and image of cocoa as a medicinal product, which suggested a close connection to the subject of health and food safety. Angelika Epple points out that Stollwerk not only relied on market-compatible advertising and marketing measures, but also took advantage of state customs protections and legally-provided reim-

38 cit. after Tierärztliche Rundschau, XII (1906), 27, 210 (extract from original version).

bursement schemes in order to differentiate itself from foreign competitors.[39] Within Stollwerk's advertising strategy, which covered a wide range of topics and also focused on aspects such as gourmetism, a sense of family or global presence, the question of food safety and the promotion of consumer confidence played a central role.

As the example of the margarine manufacturer Schlinck&Cie. shows, the branded article was of great importance. Here, too, we are dealing – in a double sense – with security issues. "Palmin", for example, was a trademark which was also explicitly referred to in the advertisement. In 1874 the first trademark protection law was passed, which was reformed again twenty years later and guaranteed companies appropriate protection of their respective brands and trademarks. During this time, numerous brands were created, some of which are still in use today, such as Odol (1893), Dr. Oetker (1899), Kaffee Hag (1906), Persil (1907), and Nivea (1912). In terms of brand or product communication, it is not just a matter of protecting the brand for the respective company, but also of signs and signals for the consumers,[40] which, for example, also refer to the reliability of the product, to orientation and recognition, to the consistent quality and features of the product, and thus also to trust and safety.

A third safety aspect from the point of view of the producers concerned the question of mergers, the formation of associations, agreements and cooperations to secure the market or to protect against domestic and foreign competition. In meat marketing, for example, mergers in cooperatives and farmers' associations served to counter the tendency towards cartel-like agreements observed by producers in the meat trade. Such agreements or cartels, which were not prohibited in the German Empire, were also an expression of the suppliers' desire for security. Even if cartels were not very successful in the meat trade – unlike in heavy industry, for example – efforts to circumvent the market and competitive conditions in the age of globalisation, which were increasingly uncertain from the point of view of the individuals involved, are also evident here. And in the meat industry, too, there have been strong tendencies since the 1880s towards state protective measures in the form of tariff protection and non-tariff trade barriers, as described in the following section.[41]

The transition from an association to a cartel was often fluid, as Vera Hierholzer points out with reference to the Chocolate Association, which she

39 *Epple*, Unternehmen, 132–136, 147–149.

40 *Hellmann*, Soziologie, 51–53; *Gries*, Produkte, 71–84.

41 *Nonn*, Fleischvermarktung, 68–75; *Wehler*, Gesellschaftsgeschichte, 651f.

refers to as a "quality cartel", since it aimed at close cooperation between chocolate manufacturers and was thus one of the first quality mark associations in German industry. In this case the question of quality standards and food safety was less connected with demands for protection from the state. On the contrary, the chocolate producers and their representatives of interests sharply criticised the growing state food controls and relied more on their own initiatives.[42]

In principle, however, it is clear that in questions of food safety, state or public institutions – which can be understood as agents of welfare state intervention – gained in importance and influence since the foundation of the Reich.

4. *The State*

As was shown in the previous sections, both farmers and actors in the food industry, or their representatives or intermediaries, demanded protective measures from the state or public authorities against the perceived threat posed by globalisation. The customs laws of 1879, which are described in detail in the literature, are an expression of this successful lobbying, which resulted in extensive measures of protectionism not only for agriculture but also for heavy industry.[43] So far, the fact that the Food Act was also passed in the same year has been less of a focus, so that through this parallelism of events the intentions of state policy become very clear: it was about consumer and producer protection through new institutions. The Food Act came in response to the demands for stronger food regulations and enabled, among other things, stricter state supervision, analytical controls, and preventative measures, while at the same time tightening the criminal laws which were to be fundamental for its implementation.[44] Three years earlier the Imperial Health Office had been established as a central and special technical authority. It served to control food and above all to mediate and balance the interests of science, the state, producers and consumers, and it saw itself as part of state health policy.[45] It was implemented not only at the level of empire, but also at state and municipal levels, where the health authorities and food testing institutes, with the help

---

42 *Hierholzer*, Nahrung, 233–239.
43 *Wehler*, Gesellschaftsgeschichte, 637–661; *Torp*, Herausforderung, 147–177.
44 *Schmauderer*, Beziehung, 173–174; *Hierholzer*, Nahrung, 80–85.
45 *Ellerbrock*, Lebensmittelqualität, 129f.

of experts (including chemists and food technicians), established an increasingly professionalised food monitoring system. After the founding of the empire, a federal and complex multi-level system emerged, which communicated the new food standards at state and municipal levels and which included both state and non-state actors. The aforementioned Joseph König is regarded as the "father of food chemistry",[46] who not only acted as a scientist but as such also contributed to food securitisation. According to Paul Hähnel, this was the "beginning of coordinated consumer protection in Germany". In addition to the Food Law of 1879, the Reichstag also passed its own Margarine Law in 1887, which was a reaction to the adulteration of artificial butter and margarine and which aimed at implementing clear labelling requirements to distinguish between butter and margarine.[47]

The close connection between producer and consumer protections became apparent in further state regulatory measures, whereby it became clear that in the interests of producer protection, regulations were increasingly being instrumentalised by producers which were initially intended to protect consumers. This was the case, for example, with the Cattle Pest Act of 1872, which was part of a veterinary policy designed to protect consumers from meat that was harmful to their health, but in the stricter version of 1880 it increasingly developed into a "blanket power" for import bans.[48] The Prussian slaughterhouse obligation had been introduced in 1868, but only for local butchers. It was only after several petitions, and in particular following pressure from local authorities and the Association for Public Healthcare, however, that the compulsory slaughtering of all animals became widespread in 1881.[49] The Meat Inspection Act of 1900 extended meat inspection to imports of foreign meat. Cattle, sheep, goats, horses, and so forth, were subject to official inspection before and after slaughter, and the import of canned meat was prohibited. German agriculture criticised the nature and quality of foreign imports. Producers were to be protected from unfair competition and consumers from inferior meat – with the welcome side-effect for producers being that, after the Meat Inspection Act of 1900, European and American meat products were almost completely squeezed out of the German market.[50] "The demand of the agricultural lobby to improve meat inspection", said Gerold Ambrosius,

46 *Grüne*, Staatliche, 190–192.
47 *Hierholzer*, Nahrung, 151–153.
48 *Wottawa*, Protektionismus, 52.
49 *Herten*, Schlacht- und Viehhof, 122.
50 *Teichmann*, Politik, 79–81.

"was ultimately a cover-up of agricultural interests which had been pressing for years to supplement customs protection with non-tariff trade barriers".[51] However, it should be stressed that the state reacted to the demands of both producers and consumers with regard to controls on meat consumption. Similar discussions can be observed with regard to other foodstuffs such as beer, sugar, and wine – and this also in a European context and with regard to other phenomena such as occupational health and safety and patent protection.[52] In the course of growing world economic integration, globalisation and international competition, states were increasingly called upon as protecting powers, which were supposed to protect and safeguard individual interest groups (including those which represented agriculture, industry, and consumers) against specific threats.

5. *Conclusion*

The first phase of globalisation before the First World War presented consumers, producers, and the state with new challenges, which affected individual players in different ways with regard to food supply and food safety. Greater freedom and choice in food supply and consumption introduced new threats and dangers in the form of food adulteration, which led to the spread of diseases and cases of poisonings that were in some instances fatal. The promise of a globally-based, increasingly safe and stable food supply, from which in fact the majority of the population benefited, was not always consistently fulfilled, and these shortcomings, uncertainties, and dangers led to securitisation through public discourse and political debates on food safety. With regard to research on securitisation, it should be noted at this point, using food safety as an example, that there were diverging and competing interests and concepts of security, which in turn led to different securitisation activities and strategies that were characterised by considerable imbalances. Even though the consumers who were affected the most hardly spoke out themselves owing to a lack of representation of their interests, professional actors articulated their requirements on their behalf in publications and exhibitions and through political parties and trade unions, which demanded more security in the food supply from the state.

Producers, farmers, and representatives of the food industry behaved in a similar way, pointing out in public discourse the threat to their liveli-

51 *Ambrosius*, Wettbewerb, 81.

52 See the appropriate chapters in *Ambrosius*, Wettbewerb.

hoods and, beyond that, to the "common good" in the face of growing global competition. To solve the security problem, the actors relied on self-regulation through the formation of associations, market agreements, and "solicitation of public trust" on the one hand, but also on state protectionism and security measures, targeted aid and support through customs duties, laws and non-tariff trade barriers on the other. The state was thus not the only but the central actor in the cause of food safety.

The Imperial Government met these demands for protection and requests for help by actively protecting producers and consumers, not least on the basis of new institutions at empire, country, and local level (including laws, regulations, and organisations). This can certainly be understood as a supplement to the welfare state model and services of general interest. If consumers, producers, and the state all benefited from these measures, this appears at first glance to be a "win-win" situation. However, if consumer protection was increasingly instrumentalised for producer protection, and if consumer protection was understood as what Gerold Ambrosius called a "supplement to customs protection", a certain imbalance in favour of producer interests becomes evident. This imbalance was particularly evident in the asymmetrical distribution of knowledge and information in favour of producers and the state, which was characterised until well into the twentieth century by a low level of transparency and a lack of consumer sovereignty in the sense of an involuntary immaturity. In the triad of consumers, producers and the state, the latter remained predominant. Until the 1960s, consumers played only a secondary role: they were the object of state and corporate initiatives, and they found it difficult to abandon this role in favour of their own activities and organisations in the field of consumer protection. In the Federal Republic of Germany, as in other European countries, this was only to change with the implementation of institutionalised consumer protections, which, however, were often the product of strong state influence.[53]

Bibliography

Aldenhoff-Hübinger, Rita: Agrarpolitik und Protektionsimus. Deutschland und Frankreich im Vergleich 1879-1914. Göttingen 2002

---

53 *Rick*, Verbraucherpolitik.

Ambrosius, Gerold: Regulativer Wettbewerb und koordinative Standardisierung zwischen Staaten. Theoretische Annahmen und historische Beispiele. Stuttgart 2005

Arndt, Paul: Deutschlands Stellung in der Weltwirtschaft, Leipzig 1908

Baumgartner, Judith: Ernährungsreform, in: Kerbs, Diethard/Reulecke, Jürgen (eds.): Handbuch der deutschen Reformbewegungen 1880–1933. Wuppertal 1998, p. 115–126

Conrad, Sebastian: Globalisierung und Nation im Deutschen Kaiserreich, München 2006

Conze, Eckart: Geschichte der Sicherheit. Entwicklung – Themen – Perspektiven, Göttingen 2018

Ellerbrock, Karl-Peter: Lebensmittelqualität vor dem Ersten Weltkrieg: Industrielle Produktion und staatliche Gesundheitspolitik, in: Teuteberg, Hans Jürgen (ed.): Durchbruch zum modernen Massenkonsum. Lebensmittelmärkte und Lebensmittelqualität im Städtewachstum des Industriezeitalters. Münster 1987, p.127–188

Ellerbrock, Karl-Peter: Geschichte der deutschen Nahrungs- und Genussmittelindustrie 1750–1914. Stuttgart 1993

Epple, Angelika: Das Unternehmen Stollwerck. Eine Mikrogeschichte der Globalisierung. Frankfurt 2010

Gerth, Martin: Wenn Verbraucher streiken. Ein Überblick über Rahmenbedingungen moralisierten Verbraucherverhaltens am Beispiel des Konsumentenboykotts zur Zeit des Deutschen Kaiserreichs, in: Bala, Christian et al. (eds.): Verbrauch in Geschichte und Gegenwart. Wandel und Konfliktfelder der Verbraucherpolitik. Düsseldorf 2017, p. 85–103

Gries, Rainer: Produkte als Medien. Kulturgeschichte der Produktkommunikation in der Bundesrepublik und der DDR. Leipzig 2003

Grüne, Jutta: Anfänge staatlicher Lebensmittelüberwachung in Deutschland. Stuttgart 1994

Grüne, Jutta: Staatliche Lebensmittelüberwachung in Deutschland, in: Der Bürger im Staat 52 (2002), 4, p. 188–192

Herten, Josef: „Eine durchaus wünschenswerte Kontrolle über die Gesundheit des geschlachteten Viehs“. Der Schlacht- und Viehhof der Stadt Essen, in: Wisotzky, Klaus/Zimmermann, Michael (eds.): Selbstverständlichkeiten. Strom, Wasser, Gas und andere Versorgungseinrichtungen. Die Vernetzung der Stadt um die Jahrhundertwende. Essen 1997, p.172–184

Hierholzer, Vera: Arbeitsteilige Regulierung: die Nahrungsmittelüberwachung im Deutschen Kaiserreich als Zusammenspiel staatlicher Institutionen und wissenschaftlicher Expertise, in: Jahrbuch für europäische Verwaltungsgeschichte 20 (2008), p. 33–56

Hierholzer, Vera: Nahrung nach Norm. Regulierung von Nahrungsmittelqualität in der Industrialisierung 1871-1914. Göttingen 2010

Kleinschmidt, Christian: Der produktive Blick. Wahrnehmung amerikanischer und japanischer management- und Produktionsmethoden durch deutsche Unternehmer 1950-1985. Berlin 2002

Loheide, Boris: Beef around the World – Die Globalisierung des Rindfleischhandels bis 1914, in: Comparativ, 17 (2007), 3, p. 46–67

Nonn, Christoph; Verbraucherprotest und Parteiensystem im wilhelminischen Deutschland. Düsseldorf 1996

Nonn, Christoph: Fleischvermarktung in Deutschland im 19. und 20. Jahrhundert, in: Jahrbuch für Wirtschaftsgeschichte 1996/1, p. 53–75

Nonn, Christoph: Die Entdeckung der Konsumenten im Kaiserreich, in: Haupt, Heinz-Gerhard/Torp, Claudius (eds.): Die Konsumgesellschaft in Deutschland 1890-1990. Frankfurt/New York 2009, p. 221–231

Nützenadel, Alexander: A Green International? Food Markets and Transnationale Politics, c. 1850-1914, in: Nützenadel, Alexander/Trentmann, Frank (eds.): Food and Globalization. Consumption, Markets and Politics in the Modern World. Oxford/New York 2008, p. 153–171

Nützenadel, Alexander/Trentmann, Frank (eds.): Food and Globalization. Consumption, Markets and Politics in the Modern World. Oxford/New York 2008

Pfister, Ulrich: Globalisierung der Weltwirtschaft, in: Thamer, Hans-Ulrich (ed.): Globalisierung 1880 bis heute. Darmstadt 2010, p. 277–336

Rick, Kevin: Verbraucherpolitik in der Bundesrepublik Deutschland. Eine Geschichte des Konsumtionsregimes, 1945–1975. Baden-Baden 2018

Rischbieter, Laura: Globalisierungsprozesse vor Ort. Die Interdepenedenz von Produktion, Handel und Konsum am Beispiel „Kaffee“ zur Zeit des Kaiserreichs, in: Comparativ, 17 (2007), 3, p. 31–37

Rischbieter, Laura: Mikro-Ökonomie der Globalisierung. Kaffee, Konsumenten und Kaufleute im Kaiserreich 1870–1914. Köln 2011

Rossfeld, Roman: Markenherrschaft und Reklameschwung. Die Schweizerische Schokoladenindustrie zwischen Produktions- und Marketingorientierung, 1860-1914. Frankfurt a. M. 2007

Schmauderer, Eberhard: Die Beziehungen zwischen Lebensmittelwissenschaft, Lebensmittelrecht und Lebensmittelversorgung im 19. Jahrhundert, problemgeschichtlich betrachtet, in: Artelt, Walter/Heischkel, Edith (eds.): Ernährung und Ernährungslehre im 19. Jahrhundert. Vorträge eines Symposiums am 5. und 6. Januar 1973 in Frankfurt am Main. Göttingen 1976

Sering, Max: Die landwirtschaftliche Konkurrenz Nordamerikas in Gegenwart und Zukunft. Leipzig 1887

Sofsky, Wolfgangy: Das Prinzip Sicherheit. Frankfurt 2005

Spiekermann, Uwe: Die Kehrseite des Fortschritts. Kritik an Zusatzstoffen und „Veredelungsindustrie“ in der Zwischenkriegszeit, in: Bala, Christian et al. (eds.): Verbrauch in Geschichte und Gegenwart. Wandel und Konfliktfelder der Verbraucherpolitik. Düsseldorf 2017, p. 105–128

Spiekermann, Uwe: Künstliche Kost: Ernährung in Deutschland, 1840 bis heute. Göttingen 2018

Sinclair, Upton: Der Sumpf. Berlin 1949

Teichmann,U.: Die Politik der Agrarpreisstützung. Köln 1955

Teuteberg, Hans Jürgen (ed.): Durchbruch zum modernen Massenkonsum. Lebensmittelmärkte und Lebensmittelqualität im Städtewachstum des Industriezeitalters. Münster 1987

Torp, Cornelius: Die Herausforderung der Globalisierung. Wirtschaft und Politik in Deutschland 1860–1914. Göttingen 2005

Trentmann, Frank: Herrschaft der Dinge. Die Geschichte des Konsums vom 15. Jahrhundert bis heute. München 2017

Wehler, Hans-Ulrich: Das Deutsche Kaiserreich 1871–1918. Göttingen, 5. Aufl. 1983

Wehler, Hans-Ulrich: Deutsche Gesellschaftsgeschichte 1849–1914. Frankfurt/Main 1995

Wischermann, Clemens/Nieberding, Anne: Die institutionelle Revolution. Eine Einführung in die deutsche Wirtschaftsgeschichte des 19. und frühen 20. Jahrhunderts. Stuttgart 2002

Wottawa, Dietmar: Protektionismus im Außenhandel Deutschlands mit Vieh und Fleisch zwischen Reichsgründung und Beginn des Zweiten Weltkrieges. Frankfurt a. M. et al. 1985

Between Entrepreneurial Risk-Taking and Reason of State: Export Credit Insurance in Germany and Britain during the Interwar Period

Mark Jakob

One of the measures taken by European Union (EU) governments to counter the detrimental economic effects of the COVID-19 pandemic (which, of course, were partly self-inflicted by the same governments' decision to bring large parts of the economy to a halt), was to alleviate the rules for state-backed export credit insurance, specifically allowing exporters to obtain credit guarantees for transactions within the European Union.[1] In general, EU national governments are prohibited from guaranteeing export credits for sales to other EU countries because that would give certain exporters a competitive advantage and violate EU competition rules. However, the extraordinary situation created by the economic lockdown was regarded as sufficient legitimation for the suspension of these specific rules of competition in favour of state export promotion.[2] In an historical perspective, this might be called one of the latest instances of the "securitisation" of foreign trade: a continuous negotiation of security issues between exporting private business, insurers, and the state has been the constitutive element of state-backed trade credit insurance since its invention about a century ago and reflects changing perceptions of security in the sphere of the international economy.

In this article, we attempt to relate the concepts of historical security studies to the subject matter of state-backed trade credit insurance (TCI)[3] and explore the potential of an international comparison. State-backed TCI schemes appear to be well suited for that task because in their creation and development, they tied together state agencies, private industrial and trading companies, trade associations, banks, and insurance companies. Different actors representing these entities brought differing views on risk and insurability into the negotiations, so that concepts of danger and secu-

1 *Nikolaeva et al*, EU states.
2 *Jakob*, Exportsicherheit.
3 "Trade credit insurance" and "export credit insurance" are used synonymously in the sources and in this article.

rity were verbalised and became accessible in the sources. Britain and Germany are compared not only because they were the major European exporters nor because of their positions as winner and loser of the First World War respectively, but also because of the different British and German systems of TCI which were adapted by other industrial nations. Although geopolitical strategies, constitutional and legal limitations, ideologies, and economic performance all play an important part in the relationship between state and business,[4] for this article we will have to employ a much more limited comparative perspective that focuses on the solutions found for the problem of securing foreign trade through state-backed credit insurance.

The concept of "securitisation"[5] that was developed by Critical Security Studies expresses a constructivist view on security issues. Security there is understood as a social act in which issues are selected, marked and treated as threats to a given state of affairs in order to create a consensus and mobilise extraordinary political action. Within this common constructivist approach, distinctive schools of thought have emerged, among which the so-called Copenhagen and Paris schools seem most influential and inspiring for historical research. The Copenhagen School of Security Studies stresses that the public construction of security problems legitimises extraordinary measures which bypass the ordinary legislative process of liberal democracies,[6] whereas the Paris School emphasises the role of experts and bureaucratic routines for the distinction between "security" and "insecurity".[7] Their focus on the present and their claims that their respective object of study represents the key to understanding security makes them not directly applicable for historical research, even if their fundamental constructivist perspective and the questions it provokes may guide historians to fresh perspectives on the security problems of the past.[8]

Economic and business historians encounter security issues throughout their objects of study, be it in the form of wars that inflict shocks on economies, predatory states that hinder or prevent business development, corporate crime, or a myriad of other phenomena that are described as threats, dangers, or risks in the sources. Although enterprises do communi-

4 *Cf. Millward*, Business, esp. 530–535.

5 *Buzan/Wæver/de Wilde*, Security, 23-26. This concept of "securitisation" is not to be confused with the homonymous financial term denoting the creation of securuities from a company's assets or loans.

6 As outlined in *Buzan/Wæver/de Wilde*, Security.

7 *Bigo/Tsoukala*, Understanding (in)security.

8 For an overview of historical security studies cf. *Conze*, Geschichte, 69–106.

cate about their security concerns, the sources much more often speak of risks, dangers, threats, and uncertainties. This, however, seems little more than a different way of speaking about security. Although the Copenhagen School, within its international relations context, found it difficult to conceptualise the securitisation of enterprises and stressed supranational economic orders as the referent object of securitisation,[9] enterprises nevertheless should be considered as possible agents of securitisation rather than dismissed on theoretical grounds. This seems especially true for enterprises dealing on international markets, with their increased uncertainty in legal, financial, and political respects.

International trade has been an especially risky or even dangerous enterprise throughout history, and safeguards against the loss of ships and cargo, against piracy, war, fraud, and other perils accordingly emerged early. Insurance against the hazards at sea go back to the Middle Ages, mostly in the form of mutual aid corporations and individual rulers' initiatives, whereas the first commercial insurance societies emerged in the late eighteenth century, and a fully-fledged insurance industry based on scientific risk calculations had developed by the late nineteenth century.[10] The expansion and internationalisation of the private insurance industry up to 1914 has been described as a co-evolution driven by the intensification of world trade and the first wave of globalisation.[11] The study of the beginnings of TCI, however, directs our view to the interaction of exporting businesses, insurers, and state agencies in the creation and practice of a security measure for foreign trade at a time of heightened uncertainty, risk, and danger.

The First World War not only disrupted the international economic structures and division of labour that had evolved in the so-called "first wave of globalisation",[12] but also resulted in a more pronounced politicisation of the economy in general and international trade in particular. Both the structure and semantics of world trade and the international division of labour changed to such a degree that a return to the *status quo ante bellum* became impossible. In the decades before the First World War, politics and business viewed economic pursuits as a predominantly private affair that was to be separated from political intervention as far as possible; during and after the war, this separation was dissolved at an increasing

9 *Buzan/Wæver/de Wilde*, Security, 22.
10 *Borscheid*, Introduction, 2–4.
11 *Borscheid/Haueter*, World Insurance.
12 *Findlay/O'Rourke*, Power, 429–436; *Torp*, Weltwirtschaft.

speed.[13] The war also changed the meaning of security: rather than the traditional protection of people, property, and territory against war, the capitalist order itself had become endangered by revolution and the wave of violence that ensued in the years after the armistice of 1918.[14]

This article explores the effects of the German and British state-backed trade credit insurance schemes on the relation between state agencies and enterprises before the Second World War. First, it introduces the workings of trade credit insurance. Second, state and business interests in the creation of the TCI schemes are discussed. Third, the influence of TCI schemes on business decisions are examined. Due to the COVID-19 pandemic, however, no British archives could be visited before writing this article, so for the British case we rely mostly on the literature and sources that are available in print or online. The exploration of British cases based on archival sources must be left for a later date. We ask if security gained a new quality and importance for the economic decisions of state, industry, trade and finance and changed the character of foreign trade after the First World War. However, from a business history perspective, there has not been much systematic research into the changing conception and importance of security. Although after 1918, businessmen had to cope with a radically changed world (in particular, new states and borders and a profoundly different international division of labour) and faced numerous new risks (in particular, currency risks after the collapse of the gold standard, political intervention into the flow of capital and goods, and the rise of working-class parties to political power), we do not know much about how this changed the way in which businesses formed security expectations. We hypothesise that for the formation of business expectations, security attained a status as important as market observation. The study of export credit insurance seems especially suitable as a test for this assumption since the effects of First World War motivated the creation of a new instrument for securing international trade.

1. Principles and the beginnings of trade credit insurance

Today, TCI is an established, if somewhat overlooked, feature of international commerce. It provides exporting companies with cover against default on trade credits by their clients abroad. The risks that are covered are

13 *Lojko*, Age of Illusion.
14 *Clavin*, International organisation, 170.

usually distinguished by the cause of the default into "normal" or "commercial" risks, like the bankruptcy of a trade partner, which are insured by private means of insurance companies, and into "catastrophe" or "political" risks, like war, revolutions, or earthquakes, which are deemed uninsurable by private means and covered by state schemes. Although the trade covered by TCI schemes usually only amounts to a small percentage of a country's total trade volume, state insurance and guarantees remain an important tool for the promotion of exports and the stabilisation of foreign trade within high-risk markets. TCI schemes are therefore intended to provide a measure of financial security against risks that would otherwise prevent exporters from engaging in trade with particular customers or countries.

The system of state-backed TCI we know today was founded immediately after the First World War. Contemporary economists in Germany and Britain felt that the new state-backed TCI schemes were not so much a continuation of older developments,[15] but part of an unprecedented intrusion of the state into the economic sphere[16] that had been brought about by the extreme politicisation of international trade during the war. Debates on state-backed TCI included arguments from before the war against government intervention,[17] but the new insurance model was not just another method of subsidising export trade.[18] Rather, by combining the principles of credit insurance that had been developed before the war with state reinsurance, a new safety measure for international trade was created which transformed catastrophic and political dangers into manageable commercial risks and promised to multiply the effect of the state funds employed. For exporting business companies, they became a new instrument for coping with increased insecurity and uncertainty in international trade after the First World War. Yet, at least in some cases, TCI also created conflicts between diverging state trade policies, entrepreneurial interests, and the logic of insurers. The shifting of risks from private enterprise to the state and/or its agents in private insurance was intended to create incen-

15 The First World War "disrupted the budding development. The export credit insurance schemes of the present are something genuinely new. ... The war turned export credit insurance into an instrument of trade policy." Translation by MJ from: *Goldschmidt*, Exportkreditversicherung, 54.

16 "We feel ... justified in stating that ... government intervention has grown into an organic necessity, if international trade is to be conducted on a safe basis and on a wide scale": *Shenkman*, Insurance, 345.

17 *Hauffler*, Commerce, 61.

18 For the various German export subsidies cf. *Ebi*, Export.

tives for exporters to undertake commercial operations which they otherwise would have shunned. This, however, inevitably also changed entrepreneurial expectations and could create the opportunity for hazardous behaviour.

The risk that a customer in a foreign country, after purchasing goods on a supplier's credit, defaults on the payment of his obligations is as old as foreign trade on the basis of credit itself. When world trade expanded and intensified during the so-called first wave of globalisation in the latter half of the nineteenth century, merchants and exporting manufacturers developed new safety measures that complemented the existing safeguards of foreign trade. Information on customers was essential to assess credit risks. Whereas the older mercantile world had relied mainly on networks of family and trusted long-standing business relations, the rise of credit agencies in the later nineteenth century promised to provide a world-wide source of reliable and up-to-date knowledge about the financial stability and commercial character of customers.[19] The formalisation and homogenisation of commercial law was an ongoing project when WWI broke out.[20] Self-insurance by exporters in the form of adding a certain percentage to sales prices that should compensate for the expected usual default of some customers was a recognised practice which nevertheless could not protect the exporter from widespread defaults during economic crises or political upheaval. Accordingly, the idea of credit insurance emerged early in the nineteenth century, yet all early attempts to establish credit insurance companies failed. Only shortly before the turn of the century had the requirements of this particular branch of insurance been understood sufficiently to enable the operation of viable private credit insurance businesses.

In the late nineteenth century, modern credit insurance was developed on the London insurance market, which had become the global centre for maritime insurance and other forms of insurance against trade risks since the beginning of the century. In particular, Lloyd's underwriters proved creative in finding new contract solutions for the evolving risks that co-developed with modern trade and warfare at that time.[21] However, the early export credit insurance policies offered by British underwriters and private companies since the 1890s never attained much commercial significance.[22]

---

19 *Berghoff*, Markterschließung

20 *Petersson*, Anarchie.

21 Cf. *Haufler*, Commerce, 28–59, for an overview.

22 *Goldschmidt*, Exportkreditversicherung, 53; *Brown*, Cuthbert Heath, 134–136; *Shenkman*, Insurance, 128–129.

German credit insurance companies had failed until late in the nineteenth century when a more viable business model was found. In 1898, Hanseatische See- und Allgemeine Versicherungs-Gesellschaft, founded in 1885 in Hamburg as a marine insurance company, took over the business of the Hamburg branch of British Ocean Accident and Guarantee Corporation Limited and offered credit insurance successfully.[23]

The theoretical groundwork for German credit insurance was laid by Emil Herzfelder in his 1903 legal dissertation on its history and practice, which he published in an expanded form in 1904.[24] Herzfelder explored the legal problems of credit insurance and stressed the economic and moral limits of insurance against bankruptcy: total insurance against losses would remove all restraints and disrupt entrepreneurial prudence.[25] The problem of credit insurance companies was to find the right balance between the exclusion and inclusion of risks. Herzfelder argued against the general exclusion of export credits from insurance, because for the insurer, this would result in the loss of a large share of German companies' business. The constant observation of market developments, firms' creditworthiness, and country-specific risks was as necessary as cautious insurance contracts. Herzfelder justified the suspension of insurance for exports to certain high-risk countries, yet only as a temporary measure.[26] Credit insurance was only to cover extraordinary losses that threatened the merchant's existence, not the average losses every merchant could expect and self-insure against by placing surcharges on the sales price.[27] He stressed the importance of credit information on the insured and believed that a significant share of the risk should be borne by the insured exporter himself. He identified insufficient information and unclear or incomplete contract regulations in the terms and conditions of existing credit insurers as the most frequent and gravest risks for the insurance companies, especially with regard to determining the veracity of claims.[28] Herzfelder remarked that the quality and availability of credit information outside the US, the UK and Germany left much to be desired and advised the opening of branches of

23 *Herzfelder*, Problem, 71–72.

24 *Herzfelder*, Problem. For earlier approaches to credit insurance see *Koch*, Versicherungswissenschaft, 70, 271.

25 *Herzfelder*, Problem, 93–94.

26 *Herzfelder*, Problem, 97.

27 Herzfelder estimated a surcharge of 2% on average, which could be significantly higher if the merchant traded to countries with unfavourable credit laws or a lax administration of debts: *Herzfelder*, Problem, 98–100.

28 *Herzfelder*, Problem, 106–111.

international credit agencies, which to the merchant sometimes would make the difference in deciding whether or not to trade with a country.[29] In summary, Herzfelder had identified the careful construction of legal requirements to pay in the insurance contract and information on creditworthiness as the crucial problems in credit insurance. As an insurance manager, he would implement and further develop the principles outlined in his dissertation in the context of the dynamic German insurance business before and after the First World War.

The German insurance industry had internationalised successfully from the last decades of the nineteenth century and became part of the global web of insurance and reinsurance that counterbalanced the increased risks stemming from industrialisation and urbanisation.[30] However, the First World War led to a sharp decline of international business, and during the inflation period, the frequent default of insurance companies on their foreign customers vaporised the considerable trust German insurers had enjoyed abroad. The global insurance market became increasingly nationalised after 1914, and German insurers themselves were now seen as security risks abroad.[31] Münchener Rück, the leading German international reinsurer, lost its lucrative international markets during the war without hope of returning to them after hostilities ceased. Anticipating that the German economy would be in need of large sums of capital after the war, but that credits would bear a greater risk, Münchener Rück founded Hermes credit insurance bank in 1917, together with Globus insurance company and the Austrian Kompass credit insurance bank.[32] Emil Herzfelder, who had been member of the board of Globus insurance company in Hamburg, was appointed director of Hermes, which took over Globus's business and acquired the German branch of R.G. Dun & Co. credit rating agency, thus gaining access to a comprehensive collection of business information.[33]

Theory and practice of trade credit insurance thus emerged in the first wave of globalisation before 1914 as a purely commercial innovation. Yet only with the further politization of foreign trade brought about by the First World War did the problem of trade credit insurance leave the sphere of business risks and become part of an economic policy security repertoire. Apart from the economic rationales for its existence, the literature as-

29 *Herzfelder*, Problem, 125–127.
30 *Borscheid*, Systemwettbewerb.
31 *Borscheid*, Vertrauensgewinn.
32 *Bähr/Kopper*, Munich Re, 102.
33 *Habicht*, 50 Jahre, 17–22.

cribes the use of export credit insurance to political motivations.[34] In a political atmosphere marked by international conflict and not co-operation, states stepped in where private insurers would no longer provide cover against political risks.[35] The origins of the state-backed trade credit insurance systems still in existence today thus lie in the economic nationalism of the 1920s and 1930s.

2. *The creation and operation of the British and German TCI schemes*

Britain

During the latter half of the First World War, the British government was concerned that it would take considerable time until Britain's international trade resumed its pre-war level, and in 1919 decided to adopt a scheme providing a £26 million credit guarantee against abnormal commercial risks via the newly-founded Export Credit Department (ECD).[36] The Overseas Trade (Credit and Insurance) Act of 1920 retrospectively empowered the Board of Trade from 21 June 1919 onwards to grant credits and undertake insurances for the re-establishment of overseas trade.[37] However, during the first two years, the ECD acted as a *de facto* state bank, making direct cash advances to cover between 50% and 80% of the costs of exports.[38] As in the German case, the British government pursued several aims: to promote employment by stimulating exports and thus manufacturing; to secure export markets; and to assist in the economic restoration of the Central European and South-Eastern European states that had been devastated by the war.[39] The failure of this new scheme to stimulate exports led to a complete re-organisation of the ECD, turning it from a *de facto* state credit bank into a state credit insurance scheme in 1921.[40]

---

34 For a discussion of market failure due to informational asymmetries, employment policies, and the balancing of chances on foreign markets as justifications of trade credit insurance, cf. *Mildner*, Handeln.

35 *Hauffler*, Commerce, 60–62.

36 *Aldcroft*, History, 69; *Dietrich*, Export Credit Insurance, 236–237.

37 *Sun*, History, 86–87.

38 *Aldcroft*, History, 70.

39 The Schedule to the Act specifically limited the countries for which guarantees could be grated to Finland, Latvia, Estonia, Lithuania, Poland, Czechoslovakia, the Serb-Croat-Slovene State, Romania, Georgia and Armenia, although other countries were added later: *Sun*, History, 87.

40 *Aldcroft*, History, 70.

After the reform of 1921, the ECD no longer advanced cash, but guaranteed bills drawn by British exporters. The ECD's liability varied depending on what amount of recourse was agreed on.[41] This scheme operated until 1926 but discontinued when it failed to meet expectations – less than 10% of the scheme's funds were utilised at any given time during its operation, and demand came mainly from only three industries, which exported to only around twenty countries. The rules were deemed overly complicated, the private banking sector did not cooperate with the department, and the premiums were too high to attract many customers, but too low to cover the department's own expenses.[42]

The reforms that were implemented on 1 July 1926 made the newly-named Export Credit Guarantee Department (ECGD) practically an independent subdepartment of the Overseas Trade Department and again changed its operations. The former system of "Advances" and "First Guarantee" was discontinued and instead the so-called "Second Guarantee Scheme" became operational and ran until 1930. The ECDG could offer different contracts: Contract A covered bills of exchange given by the importer up to 75% and Contract B covered a bank providing credit to an exporter against default of the exporter up to 100%, thus facilitating the obtainment of credit.[43] However, the high premium rates again led to disappointing results. Although the acceptance of the new scheme again fell behind expectations, it was continued after 1930 following a report by a committee chaired by Sir Otto Niemeyer. Aldcroft supposes that political reasons guided the decision to continue the scheme, namely its usefulness for supporting certain industries and in signalling the government's goodwill to influential entrepreneurial circles.[44]

A 1930 reorganisation based on the Niemeyer committee's recommendations brought relief for the overworked Advisory Committee through the installation of an Executive Committee composed of businessmen that were entrusted with the management of the scheme.[45] The ECDG was made an independent department within the Department of Overseas Trade, receiving its own allocation of funds, and was now to operate on a

---

41 *Sun*, History, 88, and *Aldcroft*, History, 70–71 give slightly different descriptions of the first guarantee scheme. The maximum coverage was either 85% according to *Aldcroft* or up to 100% according to *Sun*.

42 *Aldcroft*, History, 71–72.

43 *Sun*, History, 90.

44 *Aldcroft*, History, 73–75.

45 *Aldcroft*, History, 76.

commercial basis and draw up annual commercial accounts.[46] Most importantly, from 1930 onwards the ECGD made several changes that reduced its extensive losses in previous years and attracted more customers. Whereas the earlier schemes had insured the exporter against the failure to pay on the maturity of bills, the ECDG switched to make payment conditional on the proof of insolvency of the foreign buyer.[47] The department also no longer insured against transfer risks caused by exchange restrictions between 1931 and 1934 in reaction to the difficult situation created by the banking crisis of 1931.[48] With the conclusion of the Anglo-German Payments Agreement of 1934, this decision was reversed and the ECGD guaranteed the transfer of debts paid by German importers in sterling.[49] In November 1932, the ECGD introduced the Comprehensive Credit Guarantee Policy (the German equivalent was the so-called *Bündelvertrag*, literally "bundle contract") that insured all of an exporter's business with a certain market, allowing for wide distribution of risks and low premiums.[50] Holders of Comprehensive Credit Guarantee Policies trading with Germany were insured against transfer risks in case of a breakdown of the Anglo-German Payment Agreement in 1934, and in 1935 holders of Comprehensive Policies in general were given the opportunity to insure against transfer risks.[51] Whereas these measures were aimed at short-term credits for consumer goods with a duration of up to twelve months (which was a considerably longer payment period than the Germans usually offered to insure), the ECGD also developed new insurance contracts for long-term credits. Between 1933 and 1938, it guaranteed several ventures of British firms building infrastructure and manufacturing plants abroad.[52]

As mentioned above, at first the British TCI scheme was limited to certain countries, and its scope later extended. Trade with the Soviet Union (SU), however, was a special case for British and German export credit insurers, although both countries had signed trade treaties with the SU in 1921 and 1925 respectively. Both at first excluded the SU from the scheme. The Soviet trade partners were the state trade delegations in the respective countries and trade organisations for specific products. Trust played an es-

46 *Sun*, History, 92.
47 *Sun*, History, 91.
48 *Aldcroft*, History, 77.
49 *Aldcroft*, History, 78.
50 *Aldcroft*, History, 77; *Sun*, History, 92–94 in more detail.
51 *Sun*, History, 94–96.
52 *Sun*, History, 97–98; *Aldcroft*, 78.

pecially important role for the establishment of business relations between private firms and communist officials.[53]

Germany

Like the British, the German government hoped to create further employment by stimulating exports of goods manufactured or refined in Germany, but also was much more pressed to achieve export surpluses because of its obligation to make reparation payments.[54] In contrast to the British case, the construction of the German state-backed trade credit insurance schemes was shaped by private enterprise from the beginning. In view of the numerous problems that had plagued the first years of the ECD/ECGD, the British TCI scheme was taken as a model from which the German one was to be different. German state and business actors were well aware of the British system, and made frequent references to it in their discussions.

Apart from their second-mover advantage in being able to observe the results of the first years of the British experiment, the German creators of the TCI scheme of 1926 operated under the far more limited financial and organisational capabilities of the Reich government.[55] The Reich government did not, and would probably simply not have been able to, create a ministerial department like the ECGD, but instead chose to offer TCI through and together with private insurance companies. The construction of a public-private partnership was not a new form of economic organisation. For example, an institution that combined private and state representatives had been created and widely implemented in the German *Kriegsrohstoffgesellschaften* (war raw materials companies).[56] German businessmen and state officials had not only become used to working together in times of crisis in a previously unknown manner,[57] but their close cooperation had contributed to a shared trust in each other's capability to find

53 *Lutz*, Siemens und die Anfänge.

54 Niederschrift einer Besprechung am 19.12.1925 über die Einrichtung einer EKV, Bundesarchiv Berlin (BArch) 3101/19304.

55 Guarantees were also given by the individual states of the German Reich, e.g. Saxony, which were often offered in conjunction with Reich guarantees. In this article, we will focus on the Reich level.

56 Cf. *Rathenau*, Organisation; *Michalka*, Kriegsrohstoffbewirtschaftung; *van de Kerkhof*, Partnership.

57 *Boldorf*, Ordnungspolitik, 41.

an organisational compromise. Nevertheless, the creation of the German TCI scheme required intensive and controversial negotiations between the Reich ministry for Economic Affairs, insurers, and the business companies that were the intended object of the new measure.

The idea to use public money for the creation of an insurance fund became tangible for the first time during the German Bankers' Congress in September 1925, when Hermann Hecht, co-owner of a major Berlin export firm, put it forward in a statement.[58] Hecht, who also lectured at Berlin's commercial school, was well-connected with insurance and politics, being a member of the supervisory board of Hermes credit insurance company, a member and former chairman of the association of German exporters, and member of the provisional Reich economic council (*Reichswirtschaftsrat*).

Negotiations between Hecht, Emil Herzfelder, director of Hermes Credit Insurance Bank, and ministerial director Hans Schäffer of the Reich Ministry for Economic Affairs (RWM) began at the same time. Hecht drafted a proposition for a credit insurance scheme that already contained many features of the government plan realised a few months later.[59] In his draft, Hecht argued that high wages in Germany, import substitution in former export markets, and protectionist measures had led to a sharp decline of exports, so that export promotion had become a necessity. He wrote that German merchants possessed the necessary knowledge about markets in the periphery and could outperform their foreign competitors, but lacked the necessary capital to cover the higher risks and compensate for the greater difficulties in obtaining payments. Hecht proposed a 10 million Reichsmark fund for a trade credit insurance scheme in which coverage of the insured risk was divided between government, insurance companies, and exporters, and which would enable exporters to obtain bank credits by covering the bank's potential loss fully. Hecht pointed out what he regarded as a crucial flaw in the British model, namely that political risks leading to default such as war, revolution, or riots were not covered. The German scheme, in contrast, had to provide full coverage of political risks if exports to high-risk countries were to be stimulated. Hecht expected that the first fund of 10 million Reichsmarks would put in motion exports amounting to 100 million Reichsmarks per year, and suggested expanding the sum if the first experiment proved successful.

58 Verhandlungen des 6. Allgemeinen Deutschen Bankiertages, 175–177.
59 Letter from Hermann Hecht to MinDir Hans Schäffer, 01.10.1925, and attached proposal, BArch R 3101/19304.

Hecht's first draft and further specifications were not completely acceptable to the Reich Ministry for Economic Affairs,[60] mainly because the Reich would have to bear too large a share of the risk and receive no compensation, but the basic idea of this export credit insurance scheme was fully compatible with the Ministry's line of thought and developed in subsequent negotiations. Hermann Hecht, Emil Herzfelder, and Geheimrat Heimann of the state-owned Reich Credit Bank (*Reichskreditgesellschaft*) explored the possibilities of insured credits further, and the Reich Ministry for Labour was asked to provide the first 10 million Reichsmarks from its budget for productive unemployed relief.[61] In December 1925, the refined plan was discussed within an expanded circle, now also including members of the Foreign Office, Reich Ministry of Finance, Prussian Ministry of Trade, Reich Chancery, and trade associations representing industry, export trade, and the chambers of industry and commerce.[62]

The influential *Reichsverband der Deutschen Industrie* (RDI, German Industrial Association), which represented in particular the interests of smaller and medium-sized industrial companies, was in favour of the German TCI scheme, and its representatives were involved in negotiations with the Reich Ministry for Economic Affairs from an early stage. After debating the scheme in its committee for banking and credit, the RDI's board announced its unanimous support in its meeting of 11 February 1926.[63]

The insurance scheme provided that the state would cover a part of the export trade risks only for "additional" exports that otherwise could not be transacted, and which created or secured employment, that is, only goods with a high share of "German" labour were to be considered. One third of the default risk would be borne respectively by the exporter, the insurer, and the Reich in the case of normal commercial risks, and two-thirds by the Reich in the case of political risks. The Reich was to receive part of the insurance premium and increase the original 10 million RM fund from these revenues. Any liabilities that exceeded the fund were to be borne fully by the re-insurers of the credit insurance companies. A central trade credit insurance office for the processing of applications, staffed by insurance clerks and government officials, was to be set up in the headquarters

60 Annotation by MinDir Hans Schäffer of a letter addressed at him by Geheimrat Heimann, Reichskreditgesellschaft, 06.10.1925, BArch R 3101/19304.

61 Vermerk in der Angelegenheit Förderung der Ausfuhr durch Kreditversicherung, 13.10.1925, BArch R 3101/19304.

62 Besprechung am 19.12.1925 über die Einrichtung einer Exportkreditversicherung, BArch R 3101/19304.

63 *Reichsverband der Deutschen Industrie*, Exportkreditversicherung, 7.

of Hermes credit insurance company in Berlin. Representatives of export trade and industry were provided for only in an advisory role for fear of competition and exploitation of insider knowledge. For each insured transaction, exporters had to file an application, and the office was thoroughly to investigate the creditworthiness of importers and the risk on the basis of information not older than two or three months.[64]

During the meetings in December 1925, the first fundamental criticism of the scheme was formulated by representatives of the Hamburg export trade. The established merchant houses and export firms of the Hanseatic cities had had a strained relationship with the Reich Ministry for Economic Affairs since the beginning of the Weimar Republic, when ideas of *Gemeinwirtschaft* (public economy) and state intervention developed in the context of the war economy were regarded as a model for the organisation of the post-war economy by Moellendorf and other leading politicians. Foreign exchange controls introduced during the war had been kept and were renewed in 1919, and in 1923 the Hanseatic traders complained of bureaucratic obstructions and, what was worse, that the system of foreign trade control created incentives for immoral business practices.[65] Given this experience, Hanseatic merchants at first regarded the export credit insurance scheme as an attempt to reinstate a comprehensive control of all foreign trade by way of a mandatory insurance.[66] But even if the state was not aiming at further controls, the Hanseatic merchants predicted that the export credit insurance scheme would do more harm than good: an insurance would draw traders onto the foreign markets who did not possess the necessary experience for exporting to remote areas in Africa or South America, and the insurance premium would ruin the already low margins. The Hanseatic trade did not, according to Petersen and Wagner, suffer from excessive risks, but from too high wages and too expensive credits in Germany. The Berlin exporters represented by Hermann Hecht, on the other hand, claimed that Hamburg possessed unique sources of credit that were closed to the export circles in Berlin, and that export credit insurance was a necessary means not only to facilitate other exporters' access to trade credits, but to enable exports into regions where German traders had no

64 Vermerk „Einrichtung einer Exportkreditversicherungsstelle", 08.12.1925, BArch R 3101/19304.

65 *James*, Reichswirtschaftsministerium, 526–527.

66 Rudolf H. Petersen, representing Hamburg's chamber of commerce, and Wagner of the Association of German Exporters were the most ardent critics, cf. Besprechung am 19.12.1925 über die Einrichtung einer Exportkreditversicherung, BArch R 3101/19304.

experience and ran higher risks.[67] These debates showed that German export trade was highly differentiated concerning goods, regions, and finance, and that a government scheme had to consider these interests if additional exports were to be generated. In the following weeks, Ministerial director Schäffer was able to dispel the gravest concerns of the sceptical Hanseatic faction and invited them to join to a greater extent in the development of the scheme so that their needs would be catered for. Schäffer probably felt that their objections – although they certainly were at least in part tactical arguments used for protecting Hamburg's trade – could not be dismissed, as the danger of moral hazard was real; and that additional exports could at best be realised by securing the co-operation of Germany's major seaports Hamburg and Bremen, which were at the same time self-governed city-states.

So, somewhat ironically, the very trade credit insurance scheme intended to be a safeguard for export risks was perceived as a source of uncertainty and hazards itself. Three aspects turned out to be especially controversial during the negotiations in late 1925 and early 1926: first, the definition of "additional exports" that were to be achieved and were originally to be made a condition for granting an export credit insurance; second, the definition of "political risk" or "catastrophe risk" (in general, the terms were used synonymously), which were considered non-insurable by private enterprise and therefore were to be covered completely by the state as re-insurer; and third, the moral hazards created by the scheme itself.

The definition of "additional exports" was unproblematic only at first glance. Herzfelder and the Ministry defined them as exports "which could not be made otherwise and create additional employment of German labour".[68] This was further specified also to include imported and re-exported goods which were refined or processed using a substantial amount of labour in Germany at the request of the Hamburg traders, who specialised in peeling and polishing imported rice for re-export.[69] This focus on added labour did not, however, remove the uncertainty created by the counter-factual meaning of "additional exports" that otherwise would not have been made. An expert critique of the insurance scheme written by a

67 Niederschrift einer Besprechung am 19.12.1925 über die Einrichtung einer Exportkreditversicherung, BArch R 3101/19304.

68 Emil Herzfelder, Vermerk betr. Einrichtung einer Exportkreditversicherungsstelle, 08.12.1925, BArch R 3101/19304.

69 Niederschrift über das Ergebnis der Besprechung vom 28.12.1925 über die Errichtung einer EKV-Stelle, BArch R 3101/19304. For the Hamburg rice trade, cf. *Lindner*, Schiffbau.

member of the association of the German chambers of industry and commerce asked explicitly on what grounds the decision whether insured exports were "additional" should be made, and presumed that fixing an export contingent and calculating excess exports on that basis would only encourage "parasitic intermediary trade".[70] The word "additional" was dropped from further drafts, and the problem was suspended and shifted to the future, when practical experience was expected to clear up what could be understood as "additional export".[71] "Additional" exports were only mentioned for fiscal reasons in correspondence with the Reich Ministry of Labour, which provided the original 10 million RM from its budget for productive unemployment relief.[72] By pointing out the ambiguity of the term "additional exports", business representatives had effectively eliminated a possible source of uncertainty in the application process for trade credit insurance. Exporters still had to prove that the goods were manufactured using mainly German labour, but the application could not be rejected on the grounds that the export would have occurred without credit insurance.

The distinction of political and commercial risks and coverage for each determined the responsibilities of state and private actors, and a risk distribution that was acceptable to both of them was crucial for the success of the scheme. Political risks that led to default in export trade comprised war, revolution, riots, and moratoriums, and for the German export trade in the 1920s, markets like Yugoslavia, China, and Mexico were considered to be as risky as they were promising.[73] Catastrophic risks usually meant natural disasters, especially earthquakes, which potentially destroyed the ability of the customer abroad to pay.[74] During the negotiations leading to the establishment of trade credit insurance, political risks were treated as a new area. The actors saw that the post-war world held new insecurities which were beyond their experience, but which had to be calculated and covered if export trade was to be stimulated. Hecht, in his original draft,

---

70 Deutscher Industrie- und Handelstag to RWM, 16.01.1926: Gutachtliche Äusserung zum Plane der Errichtung einer Exportkreditversicherung in Deutschland, January 1926, BArch R 3101/19304. The arguments in the expertise were very similar to the position of the skeptical Hanseatic representatives.

71 Niederschrift über die Besprechung in der Münchner Rück, 19.01.1926, BArch R 3101/19304.

72 Niederschrift über die Besprechung des Generalvertrages am 10.06.1926, BArch R 3101/19395.

73 *Gross*, Export Empire, 27–28.

74 *Goldschmidt*, Exportkreditversicherung, 21–32.

stressed that so far, British trade credit insurance had failed to stimulate exports to risky markets because the insurance companies could only cover commercial risks, whereas the new German scheme had to find a way for the state to cover political risks fully.[75] Ministry officials, insurers, and exporters agreed that if political risks were covered, exports might be financed that otherwise would not be made.[76] Formulating insurance conditions proved to be more difficult. Ministry Director Schäffer argued in a meeting in December 1925 that the Reich, like other governments, had to cover the disaster and political risks fully even without having experience, but that too low a premium would lead to a run on the insurance by all exporters and an accumulation of bad risks. Somewhat optimistically, he added that the significance of disaster risks was overestimated, since one could expect that political developments would calm down in the coming years, and that insurance would have to get used to handling political risks.[77] Herzfelder reminded him that disaster risks had been excluded from private credit insurance on principle. There was the precedent of earthquake coverage in fire insurance, which had caused Hermes's mother company Münchener Rückversicherungs AG heavy costs in 1906. During the First World War, the *Deutsche See-Versicherungsgesellschaft von 1914* (German Marine Insurance Company of 1914) had insured maritime transports against war risks, but other experience was not available. Yet they agreed that export credits required a new basis of security if trade with countries like Romania were to be made possible, since Romania in late 1925 had not yet renounced its right to confiscate German goods guaranteed by the Treaty of Versailles.[78] Critics of the scheme regarded political risks as a certain cause of failure, and warned against wasting financial resources on securing deals in countries with a volatile political situation like Poland, the Baltic States, or in the Balkans.[79] However, the consensus dur-

75 Hermann Hecht, Ausfuhrförderung, Oktober 1925, BArch R 3101/19304.

76 Niederschrift einer Besprechung am 19.12.1925 über die Einrichtung einer Exportkreditversicherung, BArch R 3101/19304.

77 Niederschrift über das Ergebnis der Besprechung vom 28.12.1925 über die Errichtung einer Exportkreditversicherungs-Stelle, BArch R 3101/19304.

78 Ibid. Romania was one of the most interesting markets in South-East Europe. In March 1927, the German government authorised credit guarantees of 238 million Reichsmarks for its trade with Romania that was to stimulate growth in the German industries and open the Romanian market for German trade. *James*, Reichswirtschaftsministerium, 546.

79 Letter of member of parliament Walther Dauch to Reich Chancellor Luther, 22.12.1925, BArch R 3101/19304. Dauch argued along the line of the Hanseatic

ing the negotiations was that the political risks had to be covered if foreign markets were to be developed for German exporters.

The debate highlighted a fundamental dilemma of trade credit insurance. The usual commercial risks (default of individual customers because of business failure, bad luck, incompetence, and so forth) were known and considered calculable. Traders and exporting manufacturers could attempt to protect themselves by gathering information, imposing payment conditions, or through self-insurance and securities. Insurance companies would only insure trade credits if the risks seemed acceptable, i.e. if the foreign customer was a firm in good standing, with sufficient capital, and competent owners without a single default in the past. This made the insurance of such "good" commercial risks almost superfluous, and the insurance of "bad" commercial risks was rejected because that would lead to an accumulation of claims and raise insurance premiums to prohibitive heights. The actual range of insurable commercial credit risks therefore was only a narrow section of credit-based exports.

Political and disaster "risks", on the other hand, affected all export trade with a country and a much higher number of claims were generated in case of such events. Individual exporters with capital reserves and enough trust in their information might still be willing to take a chance, but neither private insurers nor credit banks would provide coverage against the fundamental uncertainty and the danger of accumulating claims. The German government, Hermes credit insurance company, and the re-insurers therefore found a contract solution that limited potential losses, but at the same time reduced the scope of the scheme. The insurers Hermes and (until 1929) *Frankfurter Allgemeine Versicherungs-Aktiengesellschaft* (FAVAG)[80] insured two-thirds of credits granted by banks to exporters in case of default, and the exporter bore one third of the loss. The German state provided an original fund of 10 million RM from which claims were to be settled. The insurers and the state each paid half of the claims from commercial risks, and the state paid the full claims from catastrophe risks (political events and earthquakes) until the fund, which in turn was increased by revenue from premiums, was used up. In case the fund was exceeded, the

---

export circles in favour of cheapening export credits through better discount rates at the Golddiskontbank

80 The FAVAG went bankrupt in 1929 because of mismanagement, cf. *Eggenkämper/Modert/Pretzlik,* Frankfurter, 11–19. The ministry of economic affairs did not wish for a monopoly, but failed to win over another insurance company to take over part of the TCI business, and Hermes became the only provider of state-backed TCI in Germany until after the Second World War.

re-insurers of the insurance companies covered the remaining claims from catastrophe risks.[81] This arrangement was seen as a satisfying solution for all involved. With a fund of 10 million RM, insurers and ministry officials expected to be able to insure about 100-150 million RM of export credits per year. This sum represented only a small percentage of German foreign trade,[82] and certainly was not enough to solve Germany's balance-of-payment problems. However, additional funds were not available, and given the lack of experience with trade credit insurance schemes, a potential loss in the first experiment was limited. For the following year, the fund was increased from the Reich Ministry for Economic Affairs budget as part of the Reich's export stimulation programme.[83] In effect, the German government acted as a re-insurer for the insurance companies, and received part of the premiums as compensation. Schäffer presented the scheme as a means to provide a protected area for the time it took the insurance companies to gather experience with trade credit insurance, and preferred that the companies would be able to act without state support after a learning period.[84] It seems improbable, however, that TCI without state backing would have been realised.

The general agreement between the German government and the insurance companies defined an additional catastrophe risk apart from the usual ones such as war: namely a catastrophe concerning the liabilities of the Reich and insurance companies if gross claims payments exceeded 125% of gross premium revenues,[85] so that excessive losses were to be borne by the state. The realisation of the German credit insurance scheme as a private-public partnership meant that risk-averse private business interests and political aims to overcome incalculable dangers in foreign trade had to be reconciled. The general agreement between the Reich and the insurance companies achieved a distribution of the political and catastrophe risks that was considered adequate by both parties in addressing the relative stakes of both. But if the contract fixing the relation between the Reich

81 Generalvertrag zwischen dem Deutschen Reich, vertreten durch den Reichswirtschaftsminister, und der Hermes Kreditversichungs AG, 23.04.1926, Corporate Archive MunichRE AA 791; Vermerk 24.04.1926, BArch R 3101/19306.

82 In 1926, German imports amounted to 9.951 billion RM, and exports to 9.783 billion RM. Statistisches Jahrbuch für das Deutsche Reich vol. 1928.

83 Verhandlungen des Deutschen Reichstages vol. 391, III. Wahlperiode 1924, 260. Sitzung vom 14.12.1926, 83330-8333.

84 Niederschrift über die Banken-Besprechung, 22.04.1926, BArch R 3101/19306.

85 Generalvertrag zwischen dem Deutschen Reich und Frankfurter Allgemeine Versicherungs AG/Hermes Krediversicherungs AG, 23.04.1926, BArch R 3101/19305.

and insurance companies managed to create predictable options for the behaviour of the partners, it could create only a limited solution for the potentially hazardous behaviour of exporters, their customers, and other parties involved in the export trade.

A number of moral hazards were anticipated during the negotiations to create the trade credit insurance scheme. The Hanseatic faction's concerns that the covering of risks would create incentives for inexperienced or even fraudulent traders, and lead to price dumping and the loss of trust in German traders' reliability abroad, have already been mentioned above.[86] As much as these objections can be regarded as tactical arguments by Hamburg exporters to protect their market areas, the danger of attracting highly speculative businesspeople and bad risks was considered real enough. The insurance conditions therefore initially not only limited the insurance coverage for credit risks to two-thirds and left one-third to be borne by the exporter at his own risk, but also included a clause that explicitly forbade the exporter to seek additional insurance for his remaining own risk.[87] This regulation was considered a sufficient incentive for the exporter to thoroughly examine the creditworthiness of his customer and not to engage in highly speculative transactions. Another danger was that an exporter would increase the declared value of his exports by including an excessively high profit margin, thus effectively lowering his own risk and gaining coverage for the whole transaction.[88] Schäffer proposed to have the exporter bear the full loss of his first transaction to ensure his participation, although this could have deterred potential customers. The exploitation of insider information was another concern: the knowledge of exporters like Petersen was considered indispensable to detect fraudulent calculations, and the exporters therefore were to be included in the committee deciding about applications, although this could lead to conflicts since an exporter would gain insight into potential competitors' businesses.

---

86 Cf. Rudolf Petersen's statements during a meeting in December 1925: Niederschrift einer Besprechung am 19.12.1925 über die Einrichtung einer Exportkreditversicherung, BArch R 3101/19304.

87 The percentage of the exporter's own risk was made negotiable in a revision of the trade credit insurance scheme in September 1928, and then was between 12.5% and 50% for commercial risks, and a maximum of 33% for catastrophe risks. Cf. *Goldschmidt*, Exportkreditversicherung, 77, and *Geschäftsführung des Reichsverbandes der Deutschen Industrie*, Exportkreditversicherung, 23–24, 42.

88 Niederschrift über das Ergebnis der Besprechung vom 28.12.1925 über die Errichtung einer Exportkreditversicherungs.-Stelle, BArch R 3101/19304.

In a similar manner, another hazard that originated from the insurers themselves was pointed out by ministry officials: although the Hermes company specialised in credit insurance, it was part of Allianz-Müchener Rück insurance group, and the FAVAG offered a wide range of insurance services. The insurance companies were thus in a position to make the conclusion of a trade credit insurance policy dependent on the exporter buying additional insurance (e.g. transport insurance) from them or a company of the same business group.[89] Accordingly, the general agreement between the Reich and the insurance companies explicitly forbade this practice. Along similar lines, Petersen as spokesman of the Hamburg exporters expressed concerns that, in the future, banks would make trade credits dependent on them being insured. This would create a mandatory insurance even for exports that were considered safe and would raise prices, when in fact the rationale behind the trade insurance scheme was to provide exporters with guarantees enabling them to obtain bank credits in the first place. Lastly, and perhaps most importantly, the practice of approving applications was prone to another hazard, namely that political aspects could outweigh economic considerations and lead to a high share of bad risks from politically desirable, but economically unsound exports. In anticipation, the general agreement gave the re-insurers the possibility to exclude certain countries from the scheme that they considered too risky because of political instability, economic crisis, or other reasons. The export credit insurance committees handling the applications were located in the insurance companies' offices, and insurance clerks inspected the applications first before ministry officials evaluated them.

The negotiations between the German government, insurers, exporters, banks, and trade associations therefore created a complex institutional solution for a large number of different risks and dangers. Experiences from before the First World War were applicable only in part, and all parties involved underwent a readjustment of their expectations. That a contractual solution was found for the conflicting interests and most hazards anticipated can be attributed to a general consensus that a new tool for stimulating exports was necessary, and also to the personality of Ministry Director

89 Niederschrift über das Ergebnis der Besprechung vom 28.12.1925 über die Errichtung einer Exportkreditversicherungs.-Stelle, BAB R 3101/19304; cf. also the letter from Walther Dauch to Chancellor Luther warning against the creation of an insurance monopoly, 22.12.1925, BArch R 3101/19304.

Hans Schäffer, who managed to integrate the sceptical Hanseatic faction into the creation of the trade credit insurance scheme.[90]

However, as all contracts are incomplete, the solutions found could not provide for all conceivable hazards. The trade credit insurance scheme was created as a political instrument with clear-cut rules designed in large part by Emil Herzfelder and other insurance experts. However, after it had begun to work in April 1926, it proved astonishingly flexible despite its contractual fixings.[91] By 1937, the German scheme had not only undergone a similar evolution in response to experiences from its operation and demands from business customers as the British one, but also had been made a tool of Nazi autarky and armament policy. Weimar Germany had already used TCI as a means for covert financing of armament projects, whereas the British explicitly forbade the ECGD to engage in arms deals until 1937.[92] Although neither the German nor the British[93] TCI schemes were able to insure a significant share of the respective country's foreign trade, it could prove useful for entry into certain markets or business transactions that were deemed in the interest of the state. In a memorandum written in 1937, a British Foreign Office official concluded that the German system "may well continue indefinitely – at least for certain markets. There is, therefore, a danger that German exporters will entrench themselves so firmly in such markets that our own exporters may find themselves seriously handicapped".[94] In the following and final section, an attempt to entrench German business in such a market with the help of trade credit insurance will be examined more closely.

90 The original government plan, insuring exporting manufacturers against default of their customers abroad, was put in practice as plan A, whereas the proposal of the Hamburg traders was put into practice as plan B, which insured the crediting bank against default of the exporter. Plan C insured exports to the Soviet Union and resembled plan A, but with different payment periods and conditions.

91 For example, export credit insurance was used to secure imports of furs from the Soviet Union in order to restore Leipzig's position as a European furrier centre lost in the First World War.

92 *Kaiser*, Economic Diplomacy, 176–180.

93 *Aldcroft*, History, 79–80.

94 German Export Credits: Memorandum by J. W. Nicholls, 14.04.1937, in: D. Cameron Watt (ed.): British Documents on Foreign Affairs, Part II, Series K, vol. 3, Document 103, 293.

3. *The state-backed high hopes of Gutehoffnungshütte in Colombia*

The case presented here is not a typical application of the German trade credit insurance scheme in the interwar period. It was chosen, however, because it shows the room for manoeuvre that this instrument allowed, and demonstrates how the co-operation of business, insurers, and the government created risk expectations and a notion of security that set a major business operation in motion despite warnings against it from the very beginning. As in the creation of the export credit insurance scheme, personal networks played an important part in creating reciprocal trust.

In autumn 1928, Gutehoffnungshütte (GHH), one of the major German steel, engineering, and shipbuilding corporations,[95] began to plan a substantial investment in Colombia after the market chances in Latin America had been explored by its director Olaf Sommerstad. GHH had struggled with insufficient sales and excess capacities since 1924, and was seeking a further expansion of its already substantial exports.[96] GHH Oberhausen's technical expertise had been undisputed since before the First World War. In the 1920s, it constructed some of the world's largest bridges, including the bridge over the river Dulce in Argentina in 1924–25, and its new shipyard at Walsum on the Rhine had built the first fully electrified Diesel river tugboat.[97] With many Latin American countries investing in their infrastructure, the region was a promising market for GHH's products and expertise.

Between November 1927 and May 1928, Sommerstad travelled through the Americas. The report on the Latin American countries that he wrote for GHH mixed business opportunities with a larger political outlook. Sommerstad depicted the engagement of German firms on that continent as part of a larger political struggle for influence. He wrote:

> The countries of Tropical America wish for German industrial products, German expertise, and German immigration. They expect benefits for their countries from a co-operation with Europe, and hope to be able to resist effectively North American attempts to encircle them.

---

95 GHH had been founded in 1758 as an ironworks. After the First World War, its director Paul Reusch built a vertically integrated and diversified corporation, with the takeover of MAN as the most important step. Cf. *Bähr/Banken/Flemming*, MAN; *Marx*, Paul Reusch.

96 In the 1920s, exports comprised about one third–of GHH Oberhausen AG's turnover. *Bähr/Banken/Flemming*, MAN, 254.

97 *Bähr/Banken/Flemming*, MAN, 525.

> ... Leading men of Colombia thought that the near future will decide whether Tropical America will succumb to the pan-American power politics of the United States, or if Tropical America manages to keep its economic and political independence through strengthening its relations to Europe.[98]

Sommerstad's report focused on Colombia. He pointed out that the country had increased its imports from Germany since the First World War again, so that German imports came third in rank of Colombia's import countries.[99] He argued that Colombian investments in its infrastructure enabled it to absorb more German imports. In particular, he pointed out that "at present, there is a unique opportunity for Germany to gain a lasting influence on Colombia's most important traffic artery, the river Magadalena, and gain a firm foothold in Colombia".[100] The report went on to say that although roads and railway lines were being constructed, the river Magdalena would remain the most important transport route for heavy goods for the foreseeable future. Sommerstad stressed that Germany had an opportunity here to intervene and increase the effectiveness of transport, and in consequence Colombian sympathies for Germany would be reinforced to great economic effect.[101] At the mouth of the river Magdalena, work was in progress to deepen the river bed and connect the river port of Barranquilla directly to the Atlantic Ocean, whereas so far, goods were landed in Puerto Colombia and brought to Barranquilla by rail for shipment upriver. GHH at the time assembled tugboats and lighters for the Colombian Ministry of Public Works at Barranquilla and was familiar with the area. Sommerstad wrote that a shipyard and freight terminal at Barranquilla would be very profitable, and that a suitable plot of land was available.[102]

---

98 Amerikareise Sommerstad November 1927-Mai 1928, Teilbericht Tropicalamerika, p. 1, BArch R 3101/19399. Translation MJ.

99 According to Sommerstad, in 1926, imports from the US amounted to $53 million, from Britain $17 million, and from Germany £13 million. More than 90% of Colombian exports (mostly coffee) in the same year went to the US, and only about 1% to Germany. Cf. Amerikareise Sommerstad November 1927-Mai 1928, Teilbericht Tropicalamerika, BArch R 3101/19399, 2–3.

100 Amerikareise Sommerstad November 1927-Mai 1928, Teilbericht Tropicalamerika, BArch R 3101/19399, 3.

101 Amerikareise Sommerstad November 1927-Mai 1928, Teilbericht Tropicalamerika, BArch R 3101/19399, 6.

102 Amerikareise Sommerstad November 1927-Mai 1928, Teilbericht Tropicalamerika, BArch R 3101/19399, 7.

River transport on the Magdalena, however, was not an easy task. The river's water level varied greatly with the seasons, and on the upper part, the sharp bend and strong currents near Honda required that freight was unloaded from the barges, transported by railway to Beltran, loaded on barges again, and shipped further upriver to Girardot, from where the state railway brought the goods to the capital Bogotá. The frequent loading and unloading resulted in heavy damage to the goods, and the complicated method slowed the flow of goods so much that large piles of freight accumulated in the harbours.[103] Sommerstad had projected a technical solution that would make transshipping freight at Honda unnecessary, and the engineering firm Sigllechner&Hugo from Bogotá had made a profitability study that was to prove the economic viability of the project. Sommerstad's solution had been patented, and on the basis of the patents the Colombian government had granted an exclusive twenty-five-year concession for the direct shipment of goods from Barranquilla to Girardot to the newly-founded *Compania de Navegacion sin Transbordos* (*Nasintrans*).[104] Nasintrans had been founded by Colombian investors and was looking for the necessary capital to realise the project. Sommerstad warned that US banks were keen on investing in the project, and that talks with G.M. Forman&Co. of Chicago were progressing. Sommerstad warned that this would make the Honda project "a tool of US power politics", and advised that Germany should not allow that, but invest and secure its influence over the Colombian transport sector, complementing the already existing German air transport company Scadta, whose planes flew between Barranquilla and Girardot.[105] In conclusion, Sommerstad's report promised that yearly profits could amount to about 50% of the necessary investment capital of $2 million (about 8 million Reichsmarks), and that German banks should be interested in the venture.

Sommerstad's imperialistic outlook and repeated references to the competition posed by the US do not come as a surprise given the mostly conservative or right-wing attitudes among business leaders of the German iron and steel industry in the Weimar Republic. Yet how far were they the

103 Amerikareise Sommerstad November 1927-Mai 1928, Teilbericht Tropicalamerika, BArch R 3101/19399, 7–8.

104 Amerikareise Sommerstad November 1927–Mai 1928, Teilbericht Tropicalamerika, BArch R 3101/19399, 8–9. The company's name can be translated as „steamship company without transshipment", referring to its through service from Barranquilla to Girardot.

105 Amerikareise Sommerstad November 1927-Mai 1928, Teilbericht Tropicalamerika, BArch R 3101/19399, 9–10.

expression of genuine sentiment, and how far were they a rhetorical tool for gaining attention of the German government to garner support for the costly investment? Sommerstad's report was sent to the Reich Ministry for Economic Affairs together with the profitability study by Sigllechner & Hugo, but it seems to have been written for internal use by GHH in the first place. Nevertheless, Sommerstad could have had an official use of his report in mind. In any case, the reference to wider political implications of the business venture lent force to the urgency of his argument. But how serious could his depiction of the threat of US control over the project be when GHH itself had placed a bond of $10 million for twenty years on the American capital market in 1925 through the US banks W.A. Harriman & Co. and Lee, Higginson & Co. to finance its need for short-term capital?[106] In my view, it appears more plausible that GHH tried to win over German banks for the investment because it did not wish to or could not expand its liabilities on the US capital market. The GHH corporation's head manager Paul Reusch in general could mobilise credit from German banks in the second half of the 1920s,[107] yet the Colombian investment required a different degree of security than domestic ventures. Export credit insurance offered that degree of security, but required to convince the German government that its conditions for granting substantial insurance coverage could be met and that the risk was manageable.

Negotiations with the Reich Ministry for Economic Affairs began in September 1928. GHH had favourable relations with Deutsche Bank und Disconto-Gesellschaft, which offered to finance the venture. For a first meeting with representatives of GHH, the Reich Ministry for Economic Affairs invited an employee of the Hamburg trading firm Schlubach, Thiemer & Co. to write an expertise on the project.[108] This advisor pointed out that, although direct shipments from Barranquilla to Girardot navigating the currents at Honda would be a welcome alleviation for trading in Colombia, there was a number of risks involved. First, the profitability of the enterprise depended on the costs of the operation and the amount of freight passing through the installation at Honda. If Nasintrans operated its own lighters, the question arose if it would and could tug lighters of the

---

106 Cf. *Bähr/Banken/Flemming*, MAN, 255; *Marx*, Paul Reusch, 304–305.

107 *Marx*, Paul Reusch, 306–308.

108 Bericht über Reise Berlin – Besprechung im Reichswirtschaftsministerium am 23.09.1928, 24.09.1928, BArch R 3101/19399. One of the directors of Schlubach, Thiemer & Co. was Walther Dauch, member of the Reichstag for the DVP, who had been an outspoken critic of the export credit scheme in 1925 and 1926, see above.

other numerous shipping companies active on the Magdalena through the Honda currents. Second, although it might be possible to make an agreement with other shipping companies, the British-owned railway that so far handled the freight transport circumventing the Honda currents meant fierce competition. Third, two new railway lines were being built by British firms that would pick up freight downriver from the Honda currents and transport it directly to Bogotá, thus rendering the Honda installation largely superfluous in the foreseeable future. The GHH representatives dismissed the objections. In their opinion, the new railway lines would take several more years to be built, and even if they were finished, GHH expected sufficient demand for freight transports from riparian plantations and the Colombian government. It was only during this meeting that the Reich Ministry for Economic Affairs became aware that GHH planned not only to deliver equipment and build the installation but to operate its own shipping line. The representative of Schlubach, Thiemer & Co. concluded in his report for the Reich Ministry for Economic Affairs that GHH was promoting its own interests, and that the project would not advance German industry and trade in Colombia. He regarded it as a very risky venture because of Colombia's dependence on coffee exports and resulting vulnerability to fluctuations of the world market price and demand that would immediately affect its imports.[109]

The Reich Ministry for Economic Affairs regarded GHH's request as highly irregular, and pointed out that the trade credit insurance scheme had not been designed to cover more than 70% of potential losses, whereas GHH required that not only its own investment of $1,237,000 (with $250,000 provided by GHH, $1 million bank credit, and up to $500,000 raised in Colombia from emissions) would be covered, but also interest payments amounting to about $200,000, so that 86% of the invested sum would be insured. Even if the Ministry made an exception, it would not cover more than 70% and only if the Foreign Office provided a favourable report on the Colombian investors of the Nasintrans.[110] The German ambassador in Colombia, Podewils, reported that the Nasintrans had existed for three years, that the shareholders were morally impeccable (but lacked capital), and that it was doubtful if the $500,000 could be raised in Colombia because the completion of the new railways would diminish the importance of transport on the Magdalena river, so that the investment of Ger-

109 Bericht über Reise Berlin – Besprechung im Reichswirtschaftsministerium am 23.09.1928, 24.09.1928, BArch R 3101/19399.

110 Aufzeichnung, 29.09.1928, BArch R 3101/19399.

man capital in a project without good future prospects appeared hazardous.[111] Before the next meeting with the Reich Ministry for Economic Affairs, GHH was informed of Podewil's negative assessment by an official of the Foreign Office.[112] In the following days, the Ministry received more favourable reports from the Foreign Office,[113] and GHH submitted a statement offering to take a greater part of the risk and pointing out that the delivery contract with Nasintrans had been finalised,[114] so that time was pressing for a decision about the credit risk.

The Hermes credit insurance company, however, took the position that a trade credit insurance could not be granted because Nasintrans did not possess sufficient capital to provide securities for the credit, and that the plan for the operation of a shipping line was not profitable because of the large supply of freight space on the Magdalena. In effect, Hermes concluded, GHH was seeking a guarantee for the profitability of its business venture.[115] In the meantime, GHH mustered political support for the Nasintrans credit. A railway engineer named Wendland working for the German state railway (Reichsbahn) had been recruited by GHH to lead a construction project in Cali, Colombia. Wendland recommended an expert, *Regierungsbaumeister* (Government Construction Engineer) Randzio, to write a favourable evaluation of the Honda project.[116] Randzio's expertise was commissioned by GHH, and heargued that the completion of the new railway lines that would make navigating the Honda currents almost superfluous would probably occur several years later than the completion of

111 Telegram from Podewils to the Foreign Office, 06./07.10.1928, BArch R 3101/19399.

112 Krüger an Sommerstad, 09.10.1928, Rheinisch-Westfälisches Wirtschaftsarchiv zu Köln (RWWA) 130-404163/8.

113 These reports were written by the same Foreign Office official, von Löhneysen, who had received the GHH representative, and who also informed the RWM that he had sent GHH a copy of the more favourable report from Colombia, cf. the letter of the Foreign Office to Reich Ministry for Economic Affairs, 12.10.1928, BArch R 3101/19399.

114 Cf. Abschrift/Vermerk Landrichter Daniel, 11.10.1928, and the letter from GHH Oberhausen to RWM betr. Columbianische Binnenschiffahrt, 10.10.1928, BArch R 3101/19399.

115 Hermes to RWM, 15.10.1928, BArch R 3101/19399.

116 Cf. the letters from Wendland to Baumann, 13.10.1928, Wendland to von Rheinbaben, 14.10.1928, Wendland to Sommerstad, 14.10.1928, RWWA 130-404163/8.

Honda installation, and that even after completion, a large portion of freights would be continued to be shipped on the Magdalena.[117]

In view of these favourable evaluations which stressed that the risks of the project were manageable and its expected profits high, the Reich Ministry for Economic Affairs agreed to provide GHH with trade credit insurance. GHH was aware that it could probably cope with the commercial risk posed by the Nasintrans enterprise, but that political and catastrophe risks could scupper it and required insurance.[118] Deutsche Bank financed the venture with a credit to GHH, which in turn was used by GHH for Nasintrans. This arrangement, where the insured credit was taken by GHH and not Nasintrans, made it considerably easier for Hermes to conclude a contract.

The insurance with Hermes Kreditversicherung was made according to plan B of the trade credit insurance scheme, which meant that the bank financing exports was insured against default of the exporter, in this case Deutsche Bank against GHH Oberhausen AG. The object of the insurance was a credit sum of $900,000 and $180,000 interest (10% *per annum* for two years) which was used as an advance payment of GHH to Nasintrans. The insurance began at the date of the advance payment or, in the case of catastrophe risk, at the day of the first shipments from GHH to Nasintrans and ended one month after payments were due. Hermes received a premium of 4% for the credit sum and 1.6% for interest, which was a comparatively high premium reflecting a perceived high risk. With fees and taxes included, GHH had to pay a total premium of $41,364 (173,728.80 RM).[119]

The insurance conditions were tailored to fit the needs of this special transaction. To the usual definition of the catastrophe risk, whose occurrence would make the German state liable for 100% of the insured sum according to its general agreement with Hermes, a special condition was added: a catastrophe was assumed to have happened if two events coincided: 1.) the total amount of goods shipped on the Magdalena in one year fell below 60% of the average of the preceding five years, for which official statistics had to be presented as proof; and 2.) the whole import

117 Cf. Dr. ing. Dr. jur. Ernst Randzio, Gutachten, 20.10.1928, BArch R 3101/19399, 12–13.

118 Cf. the letter from Sommerstad to Blank, 20.10.1928: ‚Die Hütte leistet Gewähr für die Selbstkosten der Compania und somit für die Rentabilität unter normalen Verhältnissen. Gegen politische und wirtschaftliche Gewitter müssen wir voll versichert sein.‘ RWWA 130-404163/8.

119 Cf. insurance policy Nr. 26B, 25.03.1929, and General Insurance Conditions, RWWA 130-4001160/14.

and export of Colombia in the same year became less than 75% in value and quantity than the average of the preceding five years, for which official statistics had to be presented as proof. In the case that one of the parties doubted the claims of the other, a court of arbitration would decide.[120]

GHH delivered four Diesel tugboats, including one purpose-built for the Honda currents, along with twenty lighters, and completed the Honda installation. By September 1930, Nasintrans was fully operational. Two tugboats operated between Barranquilla and Honda, and another upriver of Honda to Girardot. Lighters loaded in Barranquilla were tugged to Girardot without transshipping.[121] From a technical and engineering standpoint, GHH had mastered the task satisfactorily.

However, Nasintrans never made a profit. Colombian imports dropped dramatically in 1930, and the large supply of freight space on the Magdalena let freight rates plummet. The railway lines providing a direct connection to Bogotá had been completed and provided fierce competition.[122] In the first half of 1931 alone, Nasintrans manager Mahler reported that the company had made a loss of $142,848.11. Mahler explained that the original expectations towards freight volume and rates on the upper Magdalena had been far too optimistic, and that the purpose-built tugboat Salto had cost $22,000 in maintenance, but only generated $9,600 in revenue.[123] In April 1931, it was clear that Nasintrans would not be able to meet its obligations with GHH, and it dawned on the GHH management that the very specific conditions laid down for the catastrophe risk might render the insurance worthless.[124] Sommerstad at that time reflected that, in retrospect, the insurance and the whole venture had been laid on weak foundations.[125] In July 1931, GHH notified Hermes that the insured catastrophe had indeed occurred, after negotiations between GHH, the Reich Ministry for Economic Affairs, and Hermes that resulted in an attempt to keep Nas-

120 Cf. Anlage zum Versicherungsschein Nr 26 B, RWWA 130-4001160/14.

121 For the completion and operation, cf. the correspondence in RWWA 130-404163/48.

122 Cf. the report of Hermann Lustig to GHH, 21.03.1932, RWWA 130-4041160/11.

123 Mahler, Barranquilla, to GHH, 01.08.1931, RWWA 130-4041160/11.

124 Cf. Schreiben von Hilbert an Wedemeyer, 24.04.1931, Besprechung betr. Hermes-Versicherung Nasintrans am 04.05.1931, Niederschrift vom 05.05.1931, RWWA 130-4001160/36. GHH attempted to achieve a dissolution of the contract with Hermes or to re-negotiate.

125 Sommerstad wrote in an internal memorandum what amounted to a confession that GHH had failed to understand what really was necessary for operating a successful transport business, but nevertheless regarded the trade credit insurance claim as GHH's rightful due: RWWA 130-4001160/36.

intrans afloat and try to salvage its operations after the economic crisis had run its course.[126]

However, the Great Depression was longer and deeper than anyone had expected. By the end of 1931, Nasintrans owed GHH $1.4 million, and since an end of the crisis was not in sight, GHH sought ways to minimise losses by selling, forming a cartel with other shipping companies, or mothballing the fleet.[127] Talks with the US firm Grace, who had shown interest in buying some parts of the fleet, were considered the best option, but came to no conclusion.[128] By September 1932, Nasintrans had been liquidated, and Hermes had paid GHH a first instalment of 1.8 million Reichsmarks from insurance claims.[129] Until December 1932, GHH had received 3,104,589.19 RM from Hermes insurance claims, and had relinquished its property in the fleet, which went over to Hermes and was in turn acquired by the Reich Ministry for Economic Affairs.[130] The RWM now was the proprietor of a practically worthless fleet of river tugboats and lighters from the Nasintrans liquidation, which were mothballed at Barranquilla and were practically unsaleable. In autumn 1934, the Colombian Association of Coffee Traders expressed interest in buying boats for about 250,000–300,000 RM, which was a small fraction of their original value. Ministerialrat Soltau of the RWM vented his frustration by saying that to sell at this price would mean to squander German values, and that it would be better to sink the fleet right away (although he reminded himself that technical and fiscal reasons spoke against that option).[131] Left without better options, the RWM accepted to sell at the offered price, but the sale was not concluded.[132]

The Nasintrans debacle also had repercussions for the relationship between the RWM and Hermes credit insurance company and its re-insurer Münchener Rückversicherung. Claims from the GHH venture used up almost the whole funds for plan B of the trade credit insurance scheme of 5

126 Cf. Besprechung bei Hermes wegen der Versicherung für Nasintrans in Berlin am 29. Juni 1931, 30.06.1931, and the following correspondence, RWWA 130-4001160/36.

127 Unterlagen für Hüttenentscheid, Barranquilla, 18.01.1932, RWWA 130-4001160/36.

128 Letter from R. Lustig to director O. Wedemeyer, 24.03.1932, RWWA 130-4001160/36.

129 Letter from GHH to Lustig in Barranquilla, 28.09.1932, RWWA 130-404163/10.

130 Hermes to RWM, 24.02.1933, BArch R 3101/19401.

131 Besprechung zum Verkauf am 05.11.1934 im RWM, Niederschrift, BArch R 3101/19402.

132 GHH to Hermes, 04.01.1935, BArch R 3101/19402.

million Reichsmarks. Münchener Rückversicherung instructed Hermes not to accept any more liabilities or new credit insurances for exports to the Soviet Union under plan B because of the high claims resulting from the GHH venture.[133] The RWM reminded them of their agreement to insure transactions worth multiple times the fund provided by the state, and that this agreement was the reason why Hermes and its re-insurers received part of the premium for catastrophe risks. Even though the fund was used up almost entirely and did not allow for risk distribution through other policies, the excesses of other exporters provided a certain risk compensation for the insurers. Therefore, the RWM advocated the granting of further credit insurance for firms that did not run the risk of bankruptcy in case a bill was not honoured.[134] Hermes let its parent company pursue further negotiations with the RWM. Münchener Rückversicherung argued that the Reich had changed the export credit insurance's character by using the fund for a few massive risks and effectively turned it into a state guarantee, and that therefore the conditions laid down in the general agreement between the Reich and the insurers, especially the guideline stipulating that insurance sums of up to twenty-five times the fund should be taken out, were not applicable any more. Münchener Rückversicherung asked the RWM not to take on more major risks and not be too generous with guarantees for exports to the Soviet Union until the general agreement had been re-negotiated. Münchener Rückversicherung also reminded the RWM of the re-insurer's right to exclude certain countries from insurance coverage.[135] In the following months, a new version the general agreement for plan B was negotiated.

Gutehoffnungshütte's investment in the Nasintrans shipping company in Colombia illustrates the implemented insurance mechanics and the use of political arguments in strictly economic contexts. The German firm not only built and delivered specialised diesel-powered tugboats to Nasintrans, but became a partner in its risky enterprise that depended on a constant flow of imported goods into Colombia and their distribution along the river Magdalena, eventually acquiring a majority of shares. GHH directors considered business in Colombia as part of the competition between the US and Germany for influence in the region. This argument was brought forth when applying for trade credit insurance against political and catas-

133 Hermes to RWM, 10.09.1930, BArch R 3101/19395.

134 Letter from RWM to Hermes, 29.09.1930, BArch R 3101/19395.

135 Münchner Rückversicherungsgesellschaft an RWM, 04.10.1930, BArch R 3101/19395.

trophic risks. Despite reports from the Foreign Office and other sources that a new railway line would make river transport unprofitable soon, GHH decided to enter a joint venture. When Nasintrans began operations in September 1930 (and demonstrated that it could solve the technical difficulties of river navigation satisfactorily), the Great Depression had already begun to affect Colombian imports. Predictably, the venture failed, and resulted in the payment of several million Reichsmarks of insurance from public funds. It would be wrong, however, simply to ascribe GHH's overly optimistic outlook to the availability of insurance. Financial losses were not compensated for fully, and the loss of reputation affected future business opportunities in Colombia and Germany. Personal networks had created trust between decision-makers in private business and government, so that arguments founded on entrepreneurial optimism and a politicised view on foreign investment overcame risk-averse business evaluations, which, however, in the end turned out to be right.

4. Summary and conclusion

In the interwar period, state-backed trade credit insurance was created as a measure to compensate for the effects of the First World War on trade and the international division of labour, as well as out of domestic political concerns, especially employment. Contemporary observers seemed to be correct in pointing out that foreign trade had been politicised to an unprecedented degree, and that TCI was an integral tool of new foreign trade policies. However, as much as foreign trade was regarded as an issue that required security measures against foreign competition, or was (in the case of German autarky politics) regarded as a security problem itself, state and private business interests seldom converged.

In contrast to the British model, German export credit insurance was realised as a public-private partnership, with two private insurance companies (Hermes and FAVAG, and Hermes alone when FAVAG went bankrupt in 1929) acting as insurers of commercial risks at their own expense, and the German state acting as re-insurer together with private reinsurance companies (Münchener Rück for Hermes and Frankona for the FAVAG). The Reich Ministry for Economic Affairs provided the original fund, co-ordinated negotiations and was involved in all decisions about applications for trade credit insurance. Although the Ministry always acted in consideration of business arguments, trade credit insurance was created as and used as a political tool for a variety of purposes: alleviating the scarcity of capital, directing trade flows, supporting employment, and regional aid among them. In practice, being a political, state-backed and state-funded insurance scheme, business and political considerations became inseparably mixed in risk assessments and decisions.

From the beginning, the scheme met with heavy opposition from the Hanseatic export trade and a part of German chambers of industry and commerce, whereas the powerful Reichsverband der Deutschen Industrie, representing the interests of smaller and medium-sized industrial companies, and other industrial associations greeted the scheme as a means to generate new export opportunities for its members.[136] A central argument of the critics was the anticipation that state-backed credit would lead to reckless risk-taking by inexperienced companies and disrupt existing trade relations. The Hanseatic trade circles favoured measures that would allow exporters easier access to bank credits. Their criticism was taken up and in addition to the original government scheme which insured the exporter, a second scheme was introduced that provided the lending bank with insurance against default of exporters. Whereas the Soviet Union was originally excluded from coverage, a third scheme was introduced especially for German-Soviet trade along with large trade credits granted by the state, which was used by medium and major companies.[137]

The negotiations to construct a working institutional framework for trade credit insurance thus highlight the diversified structure and attitudes of German export trade and export-oriented industry as well as credit banks. Expectations of moral hazard and unwanted encouragement of risky ventures were built into the construction of the trade credit insurance scheme. The nature of a private-public partnership, however, also implied the possibility of fundamentally differing views on the desirable uses of export credit insurance. Hermes usually applied a matter-of-fact, risk-averse approach, while the RWM soon exploited the export credit schemes' potential as a versatile tool to use foreign trade for political purposes.

In the case of GHH in Colombia, personal networks created an environment that overemphasised profit chances and neglected risks. The close connections of business and politics in Weimar Germany created trust in a system of risk management that promised security for national players in the international economy. Greater state intervention in the economy was

136 This divergence of interests and attitudes towards state export propagation could already be found in Imperial Germany, cf. *Ullmann*, Exportförderung.

137 See *Lutz*, Siemens, for a case study; *Pohl*, Geschäft, for a comprehensive overview.

not necessarily perceived as a danger for business, although GHH's general director Paul Reusch himself propagated entrepreneurial liberty and a minimum of intervention. However, security for international business transactions in the interwar period meant no longer only the companies' ability to enforce agreements and gather information, but guarantees were becoming an institutionalised feature of nation states in an environment which was perceived as a zero-sum game in which gains of security were only possible by inflicting losses on the other players.[138]

Bibliography

Aldcroft, Derek: The Early History and Development of Export Credit Insurance in Great Britain, 1919–1939, in: The Manchester School of Economic and Social Studies 30 (1962), p. 69–85

Bähr, Johannes/Banken, Ralf/Flemming, Thomas: Die MAN. Eine deutsche Industriegeschichte. München 2008

Bähr, Johannes/Kopper, Christopher: Munich Re. Die Geschichte der Münchener Rück 1880–1980. München 2015

Berghoff, Hartmut: Markterschließung und Risikomanagement. Die Rolle der Kreditauskunfteien und Rating-Agenturen im Industrialisierungs- und Globalisierungsprozess des 19. Jahrhunderts, in: Vierteljahrsschrift für Sozial- und Wirtschaftsgeschichte 92 (2005), 2, p. 141–162

Bigo, Didier/Tsoukala, Anastassia: Understanding (In)security, in: Bigo, Didier/ Tsoukala, Anastassia (eds.): Terror, Insecurity and Liberty. Illiberal practices of liberal regimes after 9/11. London/New York 2008, p. 1–9

Boldorf, Marcel: Ordnungspolitik und kriegswirtschaftliche Lenkung, in: Boldorf, Marcel (ed.): Deutsche Wirtschaft im Ersten Weltkrieg. Berlin/Boston 2020, p. 23–65

Borscheid, Peter: Vertrauensgewinn und Vertrauensverlust. Das Auslandsgeschäft der deutschen Versicherungswirtschaft 1870–1945, in: Vierteljahrsschrift für Sozial- und Wirtschaftsgeschichte 88 (2001), p. 311–345

Borscheid, Peter: Systemwettbewerb, Institutionenexport und Homogenisierung. Der Internationalisierungsprozess der Versicherungswirtschaft im 19. Jahrhundert, in: Zeitschrift für Unternehmensgeschichte 51 (2006), 1, p. 26–53

Borscheid, Peter/Haueter, Niels Viggo (eds.): World insurance. The evolution of a global risk network. Oxford 2012

Brown, Antony: Cuthbert Heath. Maker of the Modern Lloyd's of London. London 1980

138 *James*, Reichswirtschaftsministerium, 518.

Buzan, Barry/Wæver, Ole/De Wilde, Japp: Security. A New Framework for Analysis. Boulder (Col.)/London 1998

Clavin, Patricia: International Organisation and World War I, in: Broadberry, Stephen/Harrison, Mark (eds): The Economics of the Great War. A Centennial Perspective. London 2018, p. 169–173

Conze, Eckart: Geschichte der Sicherheit. Entwicklung – Themen – Perspektiven. Göttingen 2018

Dietrich, Ethel B.: British Export Credit Insurance, in: The American Economic Review 25 (1935), 2, p. 236–249

Ebi, Michael: Export um jeden Preis. Die Deutsche Exportförderung von 1932–1938. Stuttgart 2004

Eggenkämper, Barbara/Modert, Gerd/Pretzlik, Stefan: Die Frankfurter Versicherungs-AG 1865–2004. München 2004

Findlay, Ronald/O'Rourke, Kevin H.: Power and plenty. Trade, war, and the world economy in the second millennium. Princeton/Oxford 2007

Geschäftsführung des Reichsverbandes der Deutschen Industrie (ed.): Die Exportkreditversicherung mit Unterstützung des Reiches. Berlin 1929

Goldschmidt, Erich: Die Exportkreditversicherung. Ein kritischer Beitrag zum Problem der Exportförderung. (Diss. Freiburg 1928) Grünberg (Schlesien) 1928

Gross, Stephen G.: Export Empire. German Soft Power in Southeastern Europe, 1890-1945 (New studies in European history). Cambridge (UK) 2015

Habicht, Hermann: 50 Jahre Hermes Kreditversicherungs-Aktiengesellschaft. Ein Beitrag zur Geschichte der Kreditversicherung in Deutschland. Hamburg 1967

Haufler, Virginia: Dangerous Commerce. Insurance and the Management of International Risk. Ithaca/London 1997

Herzfelder, Emil: Das Problem der Kreditversicherung mit besonderer Berücksichtigung der berufsmäßigen Auskunftserteilung und des außergerichtlichen Vergleichs. Leipzig 1904

Jakob, Mark: Exportsicherheit in Zeiten der Pandemie. 2 July 2020, URL: https://soziopolis.de/beobachten/gesellschaft/artikel/exportsicherheit-in-zeiten-der-pandemie/

James, Harold: Das Reichswirtschaftsministerium und die Außenwirtschaftspolitik, in: Holtfrerich, Carl-Ludwig (ed.): Das Reichswirtschaftsminsterium der Weimarer Republik und seine Vorläufer. Strukturen, Akteure Handlungsfelder. Berlin/Boston 2016, p. 517–578

Kaiser, David E.: Economic Diplomacy and the Origins of the Second World War. Germany, Britain, France, and Eastern Europe 1930-1939. Princeton 1980

Koch, Peter: Geschichte der Versicherungswissenschaft in Deutschland. Karlsruhe 1998

Lindner, Jörn: Schiffbau und Schifffahrt in einer Hand. Die Unternehmen der Familie Rickmers 1918–2000. Bremen 2009

Lojko, Miklos: The Age of Illusion? The Department of Overseas Trade between the two World Wars: Three case studies, in: Fisher, John et.al. (eds.): The Foreign Office, Commerce and British foreign policy in the Twentieth Century. London 2016, p. 115–140

Lutz, Martin: Siemens und die Anfänge des Sowjetgeschäfts: zur Bedeutung von Vertrauen für ökonomisches Handeln, in: Zeitschrift für Unternehmensgeschichte 52 (2007), 1, p. 135–155

Lutz, Martin: Siemens im Sowjetgeschäft. Eine Institutionengeschichte der deutsch-sowjetischen Beziehungen 1917–1933. Stuttgart 2011

Marx, Christian: Paul Reusch und die Gutehoffnungshütte. Göttingen 2013

Michalka, Wolfgang: Kriegsrohstoffbewirtschaftung, Walther Rathenau und die 'kommende Wirtschaft', in: Michalka, Wolfgang (ed.): Der Erste Weltkrieg. Wirkung - Wahrnehmung - Analyse. München 1994, p. 485–505.

Mildner, Stormy: Staatliches Handeln in der Exportkreditversicherung. Die US-amerikanische Export-Import Bank. Frankfurt a. M 2007

Millward, Robert: Business and the State, in: Jones, Geoffrey/Zeitlin, Jonathan (eds.): The Oxford handbook of business history. Oxford 2008, p. 529–557

Nikolaeva, Maya/Sterling, Toby/Hübner, Alexander: EU states step in where trade credit insurers fear to tread. Reuters, 31 March 2020, URL: https://de.reuters.com/article/us-health-coronavirus-credit-insurance/eu-states-step-in-where-trade-credit-insurers-fear-to-tread-idUSKBN21I2FR, 30.09.2020

Petersson, Niels: Anarchie und Weltrecht. Das Deutsche Reich und die Institutionen der Weltwirtschaft 1890–1930. Göttingen 2009

Pohl, Manfred: Geschäft und Politik. Deutsch-russisch/sowjetische Wirtschaftsbeziehungen 1850–1988. Mainz 1988

Rathenau, Walther: Die Organisation der Rohstoffversorgung. Vortrag gehalten in der Deutschen Gesellschaft 1914 am 20. Dezember 1915. S. l. [1915]

Reichsverband der Deutschen Industrie: Die Exportkreditversicherung mit Unterstützung des Reiches. Darstellung und Erläuterung der Bedingungen und des Verfahrens. (Veröffentlichungen des Reichsverbandes der Deutschen Industrie 31, April 1926). Berlin 1926

Shenkman, Elia M: Insurance against Credit Risks in International Trade. London 1935

Sun, Yuyu: A History of Britain's Export Credits Guarantee Department, 1919–1979. PhD thesis, University of the West of Scotland 2017

Torp, Cornelius: Weltwirtschaft vor dem Weltkrieg. Die erste Welle ökonomischer Globalisierung vor 1914, in: Historische Zeitschrift 279 (2004), p. 561–609

Ullmann, Hans-Peter: Staatliche Exportförderung und private Exportinitiative. Probleme des Staatsinterventionismus im Deutschen Kaiserreich am Beispiel der staatlichen Außenhandelsförderung (1880–1919), in: Vierteljahrsschrift für Sozial- und Wirtschaftsgeschichte 65 (1978), p. 157–216

Van de Kerkhof, Stefanie: Public-Private Partnership im Ersten Weltkrieg? Kriegsgesellschaften in der schwerindustriellen Kriegswirtschaft des Deutschen Reiches, in: Berghoff, Hartmut/Kocka, Jürgen/Ziegler, Dieter (eds.): Wirtschaft im Zeitalter der Extreme. Beiträge zur Unternehmensgeschichte Deutschlands und Österreichs. Im Gedenken an Gerald D. Feldman. München 2010, p. 106–132

Verhandlungen des 6. Allgemeinen Deutschen Bankiertages zu Berlin in der 'Oper am Königsplatz' (Kroll) am 14., 15. u. 16. Sept. 1925. Auf Grund der stenographischen Niederschrift. Berlin 1925

Multinationals' Need for State Protection: the Creation of the Swiss Investment Risk Guarantee in the 1960s

Sabine Pitteloud

Political Risk in Host States versus Political Assistance from Home States: two Sides of the same Coin

The ability of multinational enterprises (MNEs) to secure foreign direct investment (FDI) constitutes one of the cornerstones of their global economic expansion. Indeed, the holding of investments abroad does not only require a calculus of future profitability, but also an assessment of potential political risks and of the strategies required to deal with them. Therefore, as Forbes, Kurosawa, and Wubs point out in their book *Multinational Enterprise, Political Risk and Organisational Change*, "non-market elements and historical context are key to understanding the way international business has been organised".[1] The impact on MNEs' operations of the recent trade war between China and the Trump administration or of the drastic political measures taken in response to the COVID-19 pandemic are just the latest examples of this simple truth.

Following this observation, several business historians made important contributions by showing how MNEs secured their investment in times of war, decolonisation, or nationalist uprisings. They underlined the wide range of organisational strategies that MNEs pursued over time, such as moving or duplicating their headquarters,[2] cloaking the nationality of the owners by using front men,[3] establishing joint ventures with local producers,[4] using bribes,[5] developing personal networks,[6] and adapting corporate discourse and guarding the firm's reputation.[7] While this growing body of

---

1 *Wubs/Forbes/Kurosawa*, Multinational, book cover.
2 *Lüpold*, Globalisierung, 211; *Kurosawa/Wubs*, Swiss and (Anglo)-Dutch.
3 *Donzé/Takafumi Kurosawa*, Nestlé, 1327; *Kobrak/Wüstenhagen*, International investment, 401; *Jones/Lubinski*, Managing Political Risk, 113.
4 *Donzé/ Kurosawa*, Nestlé, 1319.
5 *Bucheli*, Multinational Corporations, 438–443; *Donzé*, Siemens and the Construction of Hospitals, 475–502.
6 *Boon/Wubs*, Property, 481; *Lubinski/Giacomin/Schnitzer*, Internment, 19.
7 *Decker*, Corporate Legitimacy, 59–86; *Smith*, A LBV perspective, 27.

literature has significantly improved our understanding of firms' individual organisational strategies in response to host states' hostile political provisions, business historians have largely overlooked the existence of coordinated political strategies developed by groups of MNEs as well as the assistance that their home state might provide in securing FDI by developing new institutional tools.[8]

Indeed, in a historical perspective, it appears that for many governments, promoting the expansion of their national MNEs, despite all the ambiguities related to their nationality,[9] was of great concern. For this reason, following the Second World War, several MNEs' home states developed specific instruments and policies to foster and secure their FDI. For instance, Mira Wilkins underscores the enforcement of the Mutual Security Act of 1951, which allowed for the protection of US foreign direct investments against political risks.[10] In a similar fashion, the Federal Republic of Germany introduced the *Hermes* Cover in 1949 to offer protection to German exports and FDI. In his latest book, Quinn Slobodian also mentions the creation of several bilateral investment protection agreements in the 1950s.[11] Those instruments aimed at granting security to private assets against political risks endured over time, so that in 2008, about 30% of FDI inflows to developing countries were covered by such investment guarantees.[12] It therefore seems relevant to examine more closely the times in which such institutional provisions were created and what role politicians and civil servants played in fostering them.

---

8 In the Swiss case, historians of international relations have documented how Swiss foreign diplomacy usually tried to protect Swiss business interests with respect to third States or within international forums. See for the French case: *Schaufelbuel*, La France et la Suisse; for South-Africa: *Bott*, La Suisse et L'Afrique du Sud; for Argentina: *Lucas*, Tango de Neutres; for the GATT negotiations: *Dirlewanger/Guex/Pordenone*, La politique commerciale de la Suisse; for international fiscal negotiations: *Farquet*, Tax Avoidance. In their 2020 articles, Donzé has shown how the Swiss Confederation helped Nestlé in Asia during the Early Cold War while Pitteloud has uncovered how Swiss civil servants helped Swiss multinationals to prevent the implementation of mandatory corporate guidelines in international organization in the 1970s, see *Donzé*, The Advantage of Being Swiss; *Pitteloud*, Unwanted Attention.

9 *Jones*, The End, 151.

10 *Wilkins*, The Maturing, 288. See also the contribution of Kristin Stanwick Bårnås in this volume for the role of the Norwegian Guarantee Institute for Export Credits (GIEK) in securing FDI.

11 *Slobodian*, Globalists, 142–143.

12 *Gordon*, Investment Guarantees, 93. This number also includes private risk guarantee insurance.

What is more, since MNEs were the main beneficiaries of such institutional tools, it seems likely that MNEs' representatives would have been consulted or would have attempted to give their input during the formulation process. Therefore, analysing the creation of investment guarantee schemes also contributes to the historical studies dealing with the role of entrepreneurs and their organisations in influencing politics and building new institutions.[13] Within this developing body of literature, few studies focus specifically upon the coordinated political activities of groups of MNEs, especially during the post-war period. Indeed, most studies focus on MNEs' collective lobbying during the second wave of globalisation, from the mid-1970s onwards. For instance, Phillips-Fein and Waterhouse give insights into the Business Roundtable created in 1972, which gathered together the biggest US multinationals.[14] Cowles focuses on the role of big business in shaping European politics through her study of the European Committee of the American Chamber of Commerce which brought together representatives of US MNEs active in Europe[15] and of the Round Table of Industrialists (ERT), a prominent group of CEOs of European MNEs.[16] As Rollings underlined regarding the state of the art in 2008, "it is well known that multinational enterprises are market makers but relatively little study has been given to the extent to which they are not 'institution-takers' but have 'actively constructed new environments, including institutional infrastructures'".[17] His observation certainly remains true regarding MNEs' collective institutional action in securing FDI free from political risks.

To fill these gaps, this chapter focuses on the role of the Swiss government and of the Federation of Swiss Industrial Holding Companies — commonly known as "Industrie-Holding" — in the introduction of an investment risk guarantee (*Investitionsrisikogarantie*, hereafter IRG) during the 1960s. The Swiss IRG has received little academic attention so far, with the exception of two law studies which describe its legal characteristics[18] and two books in which the IRG is addressed within the broader context

13 For a literature review on this topic, see: *Lanzalaco*, Business Interest.
14 *Phillips-Fein*, Invisible Hands, 190; *Waterhouse*, Lobbying America, 78.
15 *Cowles*, The EU Committee of AmCham, 339.
16 *Cowles*, Setting the Agenda, 501; *Van Apeldoorn*, Transnational Class, 157.
17 *Rollings*, British Business, 266. For a similar call, see also: *Iversen*, 665.
18 *Schmidheiny*, Die Investitionsrisikogarantie. Stephan Schmidheiny is the son of Max Schmidheiny, one of the promoters of the IRG. See also: *Laviec*, Protection, 215-240.

of Swiss development assistance.[19] The only contribution that offers a historical record on the IRG is a 2013 memoir analysing several economic policies pursued during the 1960s and 1970s to foster the internationalisation process.[20] Therefore, it appears from the existing literature that the role of MNEs and their relationship to the rest of the business community and the Swiss government still need to be studied in order to understand what was at stake and what lay behind the creation of the IRG. Drawing on a wide variety of sources — from the archives of individual companies, those of the Swiss Union of Commerce and Industry and the Swiss Federal Archives — this chapter traces the political process through which the IRG was created, from its first iteration in the mid-1950s to its implementation in 1972.[21] Internal documents, such as correspondence, meeting minutes and records of the rounds of consultation facilitate the portrayal of the actors' perceptions of their historical context and of the need for a new institutional tool in securing FDI. A qualitative reading of these sources also sheds light on the presence of divergent interests and power relations, which ultimately explains the institutional outcome.

This chapter is structured as follows. The first section reveals which elements of the post-war context motivated a small group of Swiss MNEs to advocate for the assistance of the Swiss Federal State despite their usual strong aversion to state interventionism. The second section analyses the debates and controversies that the creation of a state guarantee provoked within the business community and the existence of a trade-off between short-term versus long-term political goals. The third section details the implementation of the IRG and provides a preliminary overview of its practical reach.

Swiss MNEs, Political Risks and Institutional Activism

Swiss companies, like many firms from other small European states, have a long experience of dealing with political risks to secure their economic expansion. During the nineteenth century, the political decisions of several European states to increase tariffs and to introduce quotas or other trade barriers constituted powerful drivers of Swiss firms' early and rapid inter-

19 *Dardel*, L'évolution. *Berweger Gottfried*, Investition und Legitimation.
20 *Meister*, Les Trente Glorieuses, 76–90.
21 This chapter and its empirical material stem from a dissertation project, see *Pitteloud*, Les invisibles, 196–228.

nationalisation.[22] Indeed, since exporting from Switzerland was no longer an option, many firms created subsidiaries abroad in order to avoid protectionist measures and to secure or even increase their market share in foreign markets. Furthermore, in the early stages of their internationalisation process, Swiss MNEs proved creative in adapting their corporate strategy and organisational structure to cope with adverse political decisions from host states. For instance, Donzé and Kurosawa showed how Nestlé — a Swiss food-processing MNE — dealt with Japanese nationalism and the strong opposition of local condensed milk producers between 1913 and World War II by establishing an incorporated company whose shareholders were Japanese nationals working for Nestlé.[23] To safeguard their operations in case of war, Nestlé as well as Roche — a Swiss pharmaceutical company — also adopted a dual structure with two headquarters based in different countries.[24]

Besides individual corporate strategies, Swiss MNEs also developed coordinated political strategies to provide security to their foreign assets through the creation of a related business interests association. It was during the turbulent context of World War II, in the last month of 1942, that four Swiss MNEs — Nestlé, Aluminium Industrie Aktien Gesellschaft, Elektrobank, and Bally — created the Federation of Swiss Holding Companies, commonly called Industrie-Holding.[25] In 1943, the association had eight members from diverse industrial sectors, ranging from shoemaking and food processing to heavy industry as well as the paper and electric industries. Its purpose was to sensitise the Swiss government and high-ranking civil servants to the specific challenges that the hostilities were generating for Swiss firms with foreign operations. For instance, Swiss MNEs needed political authorisations to repatriate their foreign revenues through the clearing system that the Swiss authorities had established.[26] Industrie-Holding's members also required the Swiss diplomatic service to work on their behalf in case of nationalisation and to comply with Roosevelt's deci-

---

22 *Schröter*, Swiss Multinational, 50; *Müller*, From Protectionism, 123–124.

23 *Donzé/Kurosawa*, Nestlé, 1319.

24 *Lüpold*, Globalisierung, 211; *Kurosawa/Wubs*, Swiss and (Anglo)-Dutch.

25 For the genesis of this association during the war see: *Pitteloud*, Industrie-Holding, 404–406.

26 The purpose of the bilateral and multilateral clearing agreements was to prevent trade imbalance and to secure the imports of raw materials for the export sector producing on Swiss soil and therefore fostering employment within the country, see *Perrenoud*, Banquiers, 140.

sion of June 1942 to freeze foreign assets in the US.[27] The US viewed Switzerland's declared status of neutrality with some scepticism, since the country maintained its economic relations with the belligerents during the war, and it was used by German enterprises as a hub to hide the company's nationality and to reinvest capital abroad.[28] Industrie-Holding therefore had to insist on the Swiss nationality of its members, i.e. they had to be constituted under Swiss jurisdiction and to have mainly Swiss nationals as shareholders,[29] since being recognised as a Swiss firm was the *sine qua non* condition to benefit from state assistance and to have US economic sanctions lifted. Recalling this particular context of its creation, Industrie-Holding often presented itself as a business interest association "born out of necessity" (*Kind der Not*).[30]

After 1945, Industrie-Holding continued, and the association even expanded, thanks to the inclusion before 1950 of the main multinationals from the chemical industry such as Geigy, Ciba, Sandoz and Hoffman-la Roche, followed by two giants of the machine industry, BBC and Sulzer. The organisation was based at Nestlé until 1949, when the secretariat was moved to the capital city of Bern in order to facilitate access to civil servants for the member firms' representatives.[31] Industrie-Holding focused primarily on issues directly related to the multinational character of its members while the Swiss Federation of Commerce and Industry, commonly called the "Vorort", was in charge of defending the general interest of Swiss outward-oriented industries and to ensure that Swiss politics kept a business-friendly orientation.[32] It is with good reason that the prevailing Swiss capitalist system is often presented in the literature as a form of liberal conservative corporatism, in which business interest associations played a crucial political role thanks to formal consultation rights, the weakness

27 *Wilkins*, Swiss Investments, 134–135.

28 *Uhlig/ König/Barthelmess/Pfaffenroth/Zeugin*, Tarnung, Transfer, Transit.

29 For the importance of provisions protecting the Swiss nationality of the companies, see *David et al.*, De la Forteresse des Alpes, 184, 243, 389; *Lüpold*, Festung Schweiz, 740. Regarding the debates about firms' nationality in Germany and the need to preserve it against foreign influence, see Christian Marx's contribution to this volume.

30 *SwissHoldings*, Jahresbericht 2017, 12.

31 J.L. Le Fort, (Secretary), Industrie-Holding, Procès-verbal de la 24ème séance du Comité, 07.11.1950, 5-; Schweizerisches Wirtschaftsarchiv [hereafter: SWA] PA 600a 37–12.

32 For the division of labour with other Swiss business interest associations, see: *Pitteloud*, Industrie-Holding, 411412. For the role and origin of the Vorort, see *Humair*, Du libéralisme, 133–142.

of the central state, and the porous boundaries between economic and political elites.[33] Within this system, Swiss MNEs were usually well represented, especially when their interest coincided with the broader business interests defended by the Vorort.[34]

With the new economic and political post-war conditions, Industrie-Holding's political activities were slightly reoriented. The association no longer focused only upon defensive political activities related to immediate war-related negative consequences, but also started to promote new institutional tools that would facilitate economic expansion. MNEs wanted a quick return to normalcy, namely the restoration of European currency convertibility and the reestablishment of freedom of trade and capital flows. For such a liberal international order to be realised, international private investors needed assurances from governments that they would respect private property rights in the future, even those of foreign firms. The memories of the two World Wars and the Russian Revolution were indeed still very vivid and though, if only retrospectively, one knows that the Cold War never became hot, historical actors feared that a new conflict could erupt on European soil. In addition, the decolonisation process and the hostility of some new states to their former colonising power was perceived as potentially problematic since this could lead to new waves of nationalisation or discriminatory measures against foreign investors.

For this reason, Swiss MNEs, as well as many of their foreign counterparts, tried to promote multilateral agreements to provide security for their foreign assets. In 1949, for instance, the International Chamber of Commerce (ICC) adopted a *Code of Fair Treatment for Foreign Investments*, which included provisions against discrimination, nationalisation, and currency restriction.[35] The International Association for the Promotion and Protection of Private Foreign Investments (APPI) – with its headquarters in Geneva – was also pushing for an international convention.[36] The proposal to create a multilateral agreement to secure FDI was advanced at the Organisation for European Economic Co-operation (OEEC) and at the United Nations, but the discussions did not produce any immediate results in the 1950s. On an individual basis, governments such as the US, Germany, the United Kingdom and Japan started to build their own networks of bilateral protection agreements with Third World countries and to develop state

33 *Eichenberger/Mach*, Organized Capital, 53-81; *Mach/David/Ginalski/Bühlmann*, Les élites économiques suisses.

34 *Pitteloud*, Les invisibles, 400–401.

35 *Snyder*, Protection, 480.

36 *Snyder*, Protection, 481.

guarantees or forms of public-private insurance to help their MNEs deal with political risks.

Swiss private investors were carefully following these international developments. After the US Mutual Security Agency (MSA) introduced a guarantee for US FDI in 1951, Industrie-Holding's committee suggested studying the relevance of establishing a Swiss equivalent.[37] The multinationals' association therefore consulted its members about the possibility of gathering a group of experts to work on the creation of a Swiss Investment guarantee.[38] Six out of eight responses were clearly negative, so Industrie-Holding's committee decided not to inaugurate this idea in the political arena.[39] MNEs' reluctance to move forward with the guarantee was related to "the state interference in private business that it might entail".[40] This anti-interventionist sentiment was in line with the usual liberal principles that the outward-oriented Swiss industries were promoting.[41] Indeed, while measures of selective protectionism were sometimes granted to secure the political alliance with the Swiss Federation of Arts and Crafts and the Swiss Farmer's Federation,[42] the Swiss variant of the liberal conservative corporatist regime usually allowed the Swiss Federation of Commerce and Industry to prevent state intervention in the economy.[43] Its main goal was to preserve the notion of 'freedom of trade and industry' entrenched in the Swiss Constitution and to avoid any policies that could interfere with entrepreneurs' investment decisions. Therefore, the MNEs feared that the IRG project might go against such liberal principles, and consequently, the IRG project lay dormant for several years.

---

37 Industrie-Holding, Procès-verbal de la 30e séance du Comité, 09.12.1952, 10. SWA PA 600a 37-12.

38 Industrie-Holding, Procès-verbal de la 32e séance du Comité, 12.06.1953, 9. SWA PA 600a 37-12.

39 Industrie-Holding, 10.

40 M. Oppikofer, Hoffman-La Roche, Industrie-Holding, Procès-verbal de la 30e séance du Comité, 09.12.1952, 10. SWA PA 600a 37–12.

41 Liberal principles might entail slightly different meanings regarding the context and their concrete applications might differ, see *Eichenberger*, The Eternal Rebirth.

42 For instance, some measures of selective protectionism had been granted to sectors producing for the domestic economy such as tariffs protection and subsidies for agriculture, see *David/Mach/Straumann*, The Questioning of Selective Protectionism, 451. For the classification as liberal conservative, see: *Mach*, La Suisse entre internationalisation, 97.

43 Switzerland did not experience Keynesian or ambitious industrial policies, see: *Foreman-Peck*, European Industrial Policies, 30; *Longchamp*, La politique financière fédérale, 24.

A shift occurred in MNEs' views after the mid-1950s. Nasser's decision to occupy the Suez Canal was a worrisome warning to occidental powers, but also to foreign investors. Moreover, with the passing years, it was clear that a multilateral solution granting security to FDI was not on the horizon, while other states such as the US and Japan, whose national MNEs were in competition with Swiss MNEs, were clearly forging ahead in the development of their own protection tools. Swiss-based enterprises might therefore suffer from a competitive disadvantage when it came to penetrating new markets. Thanks to their long experience of internationalisation, their managers were indeed very aware of the importance of being among the first movers to ensure satisfactory market share and to secure future development.[44] In addition, Swiss MNEs, unlike their US and German competitors, could not rely on a significant internal market and their expansion therefore depended greatly on foreign growth.

In 1958, because of these trends, Industrie-Holding again raised the question among its members of promoting the creation of a Swiss guarantee and started to contact some specific divisions within the federal administration to address the topic. The legislative process was officially launched in March 1960 when the parliamentarian Max Schmidheiny proposed asking the Federal Council to study various options for providing security to Swiss FDI and, specifically, the creation of a Swiss Investistionsrisikogarantie (IRG) and such an instrument's potential role in the broader issue of Swiss development assistance to Third World countries.[45] Outside of his political mandate, Schmidheiny was the CEO of Holderbank, an MNE that was a member of Industrie-Holding, and also served on the boards of directors of BBC and Landis & Gyr, two other large multinationals from the machine tool industry.[46] His profile is therefore representative of the interconnections between the political and economic spheres that are often underlined in the literature about Swiss capitalism,[47] and his proposal is also emblematic of the proactive political role that MNEs played in fostering the IRG. In September 1960, after some exchanges between MNEs' representatives and high-ranking civil servants of the federal administra-

44 Donzé and Kurosawa showed for instance how Nestlé stayed in Japan at severe costs during the war in order to take advantage of its position at the end of the hostilities: *Donzé/ Kurosawa*, Nestlé.

45 Nationalrat Dr Max Schmidheiny, Postulat, 08.03.1960. Archiv für Zeitgeschichte [hereafter: AfZ], IB-Vorort-Archiv, 463.1.3.

46 Base de données „élites suisses au XXe siècle", Université de Lausanne, URL: https://www2.unil.ch/elitessuisses/index.php.

47 *Mach/David/Ginalski/Bühlmann*, Les élites.

tion, the Federal Council announced that the introduction of the IRG would be further studied.[48] As we shall see in the next section, this federal decision initiated a long and labourious political process that was about to create a great deal of debate within the Swiss business community.

The Debates within the Business Community

In accordance with established Swiss procedures of interest consultation, those in its economic circles were invited to make a stand on the creation of the IRG during the pre-parliamentary phase — i.e. when a smaller commission composed of parliamentarians and experts was studying the subject in depth before submitting a legislation proposal to the whole parliament. Some representatives of business circles were also appointed as experts in this commission. Since the Swiss political system allows the launch of a referendum to prevent the implementation of new laws designed by the parliament, including interest groups in the early stages of the legislative process to avoid such deadlock was a common practice.[49] The concretisation of the IRG depended on a consensus formation process that would be spread over several years and be comprised of three rounds of consultation. As the association representing Swiss industries and particularly the interests of the outward-oriented sectors, the Vorort was at the forefront in producing common viewpoints by consolidating the individual statements of its members. The IRG was also discussed on several occasions during meetings of the Swiss Chamber of Commerce. Although the majority of the business representatives declared themselves as being generally in favour of the IRG, the deliberations were not free of tensions.

The principal controversy that emerged from the deliberations within business circles did not concern the practical aspects of the implementation of such a new institutional tool but was about its underlying economic philosophy. In their written answers, several sections of the Vorort suggested that the IRG might represent a dangerous precedent of state interventionism. Even the Vorort committee expressed many reservations. For instance, in an internal note, one of its members stated that with such

48 Theodor Faist, Sekretär der Vereinigung der industriellen Holdinggesellschaften, Der Schutz schweizerischer Investitionen in Entwicklungsländern durch Investitionsrisikogarantie (IRG) und Schutzabkommen, Separatabzug aus dem Dokumentations-und Pressedienst der Wirtschaftsförderung, Januar/Februar 1961, 3. AfZ, IB-Vorort-Archiv, 463.2.2.

49 *Lehmbruch*, Consociational Democracy, 51.

a guarantee, "the state would have to involve itself in matters ... which deeply interfere with entrepreneur's private economic spheres and financial decisions".[50] A matter of great concern was that the implementation would require a decision by experts from the federal administration as to which entrepreneurial projects would be granted the guarantee and, consequently, these civil servants would be influencing the investment decisions of the firm.[51]

The Vorort was also concerned with the adverse political consequences that such a tool could have on the promotion and valorisation of the free enterprise system in Switzerland, since the IRG seemed to contradict this principle. In one of the circulars sent to its members sections and firms, the Vorort even stated that the IRG might be considered as a "socialization of risks".[52] The economic circles therefore feared being attacked by their political opponents for this inconsistency and, moreover, that the left and the unions could use this as a pretext for requesting an extension of state interventionism in other domains. This could ultimately lead to an escalation of public spending and the economy would have to defray the cost by tax increases. As the Swiss Chemical Society stated in a letter to the Vorort, a trade-off therefore existed between the immediate benefit the IRG might provide to multinationals and the long-term political goal of limiting state intervention in the economy:

> Economically, i.e. from the selfish point of view of the investor, an IRG would be welcome because it would allow a balanced risk division between the state and entrepreneurs and would make it possible for the latter to undertake certain investments. On the other hand, if we consider the general principle of free enterprise and other aspects of domestic policies in the assessment, the establishment of such an institution is somewhat problematic.[53]

This quotation from the Swiss Chemical Society therefore shows how even the most internationalised sectors of the Swiss economy experienced

---

50 Dr. Aebi, Vorort, Notiz an Herrn Generalsekretär Kohli, Risikogarantie für Kapitalexporte, 12. AfZ, IB-Vorort-Archiv, 463.2.3.

51 Chambre de commercer de Genève, Garantie des risques d'investissements, au Vorort de l'Union suisse du commerce et de l'industrie, 01.11.1963, 5. AfZ, IB-Vorort-Archiv, 463.2.9.

52 Vorort des SHIV, Betrifft: Investitions-Risikogarantie, an die Sektionen, 31.12.1960, 3, AfZ, IBVorort-Archiv, 463.2.3.

53 Schweizerische Gesellschaft für chemische Industrie, Investitionsrisikogarantie (IRG), an der Vorort des SHIV, 30.10.1963, 4. AFZ, IB-Vorort-Archiv, 463.2.9.

mixed feelings regarding the IRG. Although the Swiss entrepreneurs might be depicted as rational actors seeking the prosperity of their businesses, it is interesting to note that it was not always easy for them to determine where their best interests lay, especially when they had to choose between short-term economic goals and long-term political strategy. The trade-off that would ultimately be adopted would therefore be a function of firms' subjectivity of risk assessment.

In the face of such reluctance, Industrie-Holding presented several counterarguments to plead its case. Its interventions took the form of memoranda, press articles and letters written to the Vorort and to the federal civil servants and politicians in charge of implementing the project. The first argument was that it was inaccurate to speak of state interventionism in the economic sphere, since the IRG was only covering political risks and leaving the economic risk assessments to entrepreneurs. In its memorandum, Industrie-Holding also stated that such logic had been commonplace in Switzerland since the 1930s with the introduction of an export risk guarantee (*Exportrisikogarantie*, hereafter ERG) and that this precedent had not endangered free enterprise principles.[54] Back then, the Vorort had easily found a consensus about the need to introduce such an instrument because of the precarious economic situation of the Swiss machine tool industry, the rising unemployment within Switzerland and the existence of various sorts of dumping introduced by foreign states to favour their own export industries.[55] The Swiss ERG provided a state guarantee to private exports against political risks such as wars and social unrest, and it was also used after 1958 to insure exporters against the government insolvency of third world countries. The ERG was granted by a commission equally composed of federal civil servants and representatives of business associations.[56] According to Industrie-Holding, the IRG could therefore be implemented on similar grounds as the ERG. Furthermore, the Association used the German and American examples to show that such institutional

---

54 Theodor Faist, Sekretär der Vereinigung der industriellen Holdinggesellschaften, Der Schutz schweizerischer Investitionen in Entwicklungsländern durch Investitionsrisikogarantie (IRG) und Schutzabkommen, Separatabzug aus dem Dokumentations-und Pressedienst der Wirtschaftsförderung, Januar/Februar 1961, 23.

55 SHIV, Protokoll der 7. Sitzung des Vororts im Vereinsjahr 1933/34, 01.12.1933, 4. AfZ, IB-Vorort-Archiv, 1.5.3.8.

56 *Meister*, Swiss Economic and Political Relations, 119.

tools were perfectly suited for countries in which a liberal economic order (*mit liberaler Wirtschaftsordnung*) was prevalent.[57]

According to Industrie-Holding, another positive effect of introducing the IRG was that the amount allocated to insure Swiss FDI in developing countries could be presented as a form of Swiss development assistance by the Swiss government:

> The introduction of the suggested IRG secure the largest practical effects with a relatively low state expenditure. The Federal state would not act as a capital provider, but would limit its action to improving conditions for private investment. ... This system will remain grounded in the free market. The private investor will have to safeguard profitability because commercial risks are not covered. From the point of view of the state, the IRG appears to be a form of development assistance that upholds market principles.[58]

At the time, Switzerland was pressured by international organisations, such as the Organisation for Economic Co-operation and Development (OECD), to increase its financial support to Third World countries. To avoid committing additional public funds, the Swiss government and Swiss business elite were therefore presenting private investments as a specific Swiss form of development assistance,[59] and the IRG might be considered as part of this strategy. In 1959, Swiss FDI stock in developing countries was estimated at 1.6 billion Swiss francs, i.e. 215 francs per inhabitant.[60] With their early experience of internationalisation, Swiss-based MNEs were well-positioned to gain ground in these newly emerging markets and could benefit from the fact that Switzerland, thanks to its small size and its neutrality, was "free of colonial past and of any suspicions".[61] As Donzé indicates, there was a strategic advantage for MNEs "of being

57 Vereinigung der Industriellen Holdinggesellschaften, an Herrn Minister Dr. Edwin Stopper, EVD, 31.05.1960, 2. AfZ, IB-Vorort-Archiv, 463.2.2.

58 Vereinigung der Industriellen Holdinggesellschaften, an Herrn Minister Dr. Edwin Stopper, EVD, 31.05.1960, 2. AfZ, IB-Vorort-Archiv, 463.2.2.

59 *Berweger*, Investition und Legitimation.

60 Max Schmidheiny, Schweizerische Handelskammer, Errichtung einer Investitionsrisikogarantie in der Schweiz, Protokoll der 219. Sitzung, 30.06.1961, 9. AfZ, IB-Vorort-Archiv, 463.2.5.

61 Theodor Faist, Sekretär der Vereinigung der industriellen Holdinggesellschaften, Der Schutz schweizerischer Investitionen in Entwicklungsländern durch Investitionsrisikogarantie (IRG) und Schutzabkommen, Separatabzug aus dem Dokumentations-und Pressedienst der Wirtschaftsförderung, Januar/Februar 1961, 25-6. AfZ, IB-Vorort-Archiv, 463.2.2.

Swiss" – in contrast to the liability of foreignness that MNEs from past colonial countries had to suffer – since developing governments did not suspect Switzerland of any imperialist intentions.[62] The political justifications for the introduction of the IRG were therefore twofold: on the one hand, the IRG was conceived as an instrument promoting Swiss MNEs' expansion; on the other hand, it was presented as an institutional tool at the service of poor countries.

Despite this dual rhetoric, it is clear that the business community was only considering this tool in terms of the opportunities it offered to the Swiss economy. Almost no standpoint that came back to the Vorort's survey attempted to address its potential economic impact on developing countries. In a discussion at a Chamber of Commerce meeting, a business representative only mentioned that helping developing countries was "vital for the West" in order to prevent the spread of communism.[63] Regarding IRG's potential effects on the Swiss economy, different scenarios were plausible. On the one hand, facilitating the implementation of production abroad might foster a relocation process and induce some restructuring within Switzerland. During the 1950s and 1960s, this was not an issue since Switzerland enjoyed a booming economy and suffered from a chronic labour shortage.[64] Nevertheless, it was clear that relocations might become very problematic if the economic climate were to be reversed. In addition, some representatives of the textile industry underlined that their sector was already suffering from restructurings and competition from low-wage countries and that the IRG was about to strengthen those trends.[65] On the other hand, the additional investments abroad fostered by the IRG might stimulate the Swiss domestic economy since the newly created subsidiaries required licensing agreements as well as technical and commercial assistance, which were high value-added tasks usually carried out within Switzerland. It would therefore provide more employment within the country. Because of such positive externalities, Industrie-Holding stated that the IRG was not only useful for MNEs, but ultimately for

62 *Donzé*, The Advantage of Being Swiss, 395.

63 Weber, Schweizerische Handelskammer, Zur Frage der Errichtung einer Investitionsrisikogarantie, Protokoll der 225. Sitzung, 12.07.1963, 28. IB-Vorort-Archiv, 463.2.8.

64 *Pitteloud*, The Social Desirability, 261.

65 Fritz Honegger, Schweizerische Handelskammer, Zur Frage der Errichtung einer Investitionsrisikogarantie, Protokoll der 225. Sitzung, 12.07.1963, 27. AfZ, IB-Vorort-Archiv, 463.2.8.

the Swiss economy as a whole.[66] It is therefore interesting to note that the IRG debate illustrates that there was no consensus on the effect of FDI on the home economy, a controversy that is still very active today.

The numerous controversies that the IRG induced within the business community – issues about state interventionism, IRG's political externalities, and its effects on the Swiss economy – led to the postponement of a legislative solution for almost a decade. In 1966, on the occasion of the third round of consultation, Industrie-Holding, a bit exasperated by the still ongoing discussions, stated:

> Swiss private investments abroad have never been abandoned to their fate by the Swiss state. ... The protection of private foreign investments belongs to the essential duty of any state. The forms of protection have evolved. It has been a long road from the 'Battle Ship Diplomacy' of the superpowers to protect their people and property in the 19th and early 20th century up to the investment protection agreements, the investment guarantee scheme and the 1965 arbitration convention of the World Bank.[67]

According to Industrie-Holding, the IRG was therefore a suitable institutional tool to provide security to foreign investments and, consequently, should be incorporated in the Swiss state apparatus.

The Implementation of the IRG

Industrie-Holding's efforts finally paid off at the end of 1960. While the Vorort committee remained unenthusiastic and did not use its influence to accelerate the political process, it ultimately supported the IRG. Among the other major interest groups, the Swiss Federation of Trade Unions (SGB) was the main opponent of the project, stating that an increasing share of public money was being dedicated to supporting outward-oriented sectors of the Swiss economy, which, at the same time, were paying a decreasing share of taxes thanks to fiscal privileges.[68] The Swiss Farmers Unions (SBV), the Swiss Union of Arts and Crafts (SVG), and the Swiss

66 Vereinigung der industriellen Holdinggesellschaften, Investitonsrisikogarantie (IRG), an der Vorort des SHIV, 09.10.1963, 3. AfZ, IB-Vorort-Archiv, 463.2.2.

67 Industrie-Holding, Investitionsrisikogarantie (IRG), an den Vorort des SHIV, Bern, 23.12.1966, 3. AfZ, IB-Vorort-Archiv, 463.2.12.

68 Gewerkschaftskorrespondenz, Pressedienst des schweizerischen Gewerkschaftsbundes.

Bankers' Association (SBV) were not *per se* opposed to the introduction of the IRG, but they questioned the timing as the federal finances were deteriorating at the end of the 1960s while business circles and right-wing political parties were calling for budgetary restraint.[69] Within the federal administration, diverging views were also prevalent: while the Division of Commerce and the Political Department supported the project, the Department of Finance considered unfavourably the additional expense the IRG might incur.[70] These budgetary concerns were ultimately dismissed owing to the fact that the IRG could be presented as the cheapest form of development assistance that the Swiss state could provide and therefore the law was transmitted to the parliament for approval.[71]

The two chambers largely approved the introduction of the IRG and did so without much debate. For the right, it was seen as a tool to foster the Swiss economy, and it was welcomed by the Swiss socialist party because of the assistance it provided to developing countries. A parliamentarian from the Labour Party (*Parti du Travail*) regarded the IRG as a "privilege granted to big business" disguised as "a generous aid to developing countries",[72] but its opinion was in the minority. The law was finally adopted in March 1970 and Industrie-Holding celebrated its introduction, stating that it had played the role of "promoter of this idea within Switzerland".[73]

Investitionsrisikogarantie inopportun, Jahresgang 1967, N° 3, Bern, 19.01.1967, 33. AfZ, VSM-Archiv, 2840.

69 J. Weber der Präsident & R. Juri der Direktor, Schweiz. Bauernverband, Betrifft: Entwurf eines Bundesgesetzes über die Investitionsrisikogarantie, an Bundespräsident Dr. H. Schaffner, Vorsteher desEidg. Volkswirtschaftsdepartementes, 15.11.1966. AfZ, IB-Vorort-Archiv, 463.2.12; Schweizerischer Gewerbeverband (SGV), Betrifft Entwurf eines Bundesgesetz über die Investitionsrisikogarantie, an das EVD, Zürich, 27.12.1966, 4. AfZ, VSM-Archiv, 2840; Schweizerische Bankiervereinigung (SBV), Entwurf eines Bundesgesetzes über die Investitionsrisikogarantie, an Herrn Bundespräsident Dr. Hans Schaffner, Vorsteher des EVD, 23.11.1966, 2. AfZ, IB-Vorort-Archiv, 463.2.12.

70 Industrie-Holding, Protokoll der 23. Generalversammlung, vom 14.04.1966, 6. SWA PA 540 a M 2-5-2 I.

71 Hans Schaffner, EVD, Investitionsrisikogarantie, an den Bundesrat, 27.08.1969, p. 2. Archives fédérales [hereafter: AF], E2005A#1980/82# 6*.

72 Garantie contre les risques de l'investissement. Loi, BOAF, CN, Vol. I, (1970), 147-148, quoted in *Meister*, Les Trente Glorieuses, 85.

73 Industrie-Holding, 27. Jahresbericht 1969 zuhanden der Generalversammlung, 20.03.1970, 1–2. SWA PA 540 a M 2-5-2 II.

The maximum commitment by the Swiss government was settled at 500 million Swiss francs.[74] The insurance coverage represented 70% of the invested amount and it was valid for fifteen years. The office in charge of evaluating firms' insurance requests (*Geschäftsstelle für die Investitionsrisikogarantie*) was composed of three civil servants as well as three representatives from the Vorort, from the chemical industry, and from the machine tool industry. Business representatives were therefore also crucial in implementing the IRG. According to IRG's established rules, in order to be eligible, the investment had to be directed to a developing country, and should, in principle, be made by a Swiss company, i.e. one headquartered in the country.[75] This provision is important since the investments were guaranteed with taxpayer money and, in case of political dispute with the government of a developing country, the affected firm would benefit from the assistance of Swiss diplomacy. The risk covered comprised the confiscation of, or damage to, private property while risk related to currency fluctuations was eliminated from the coverage.[76]

The insurance's granting was linked to the existence of an investment protection agreement with the host country. The Swiss government started to develop such bilateral investment protection agreement networks at the beginning of the 1960s, when the legislative process of the IRG was launched. Such diplomatic activity in favour of private interest was in line with the usual foreign economic policy of the Swiss authorities. In contrast to the IRG, protection agreements were not expected to interfere with private affairs, but were seen as a desirable improvement of the general investment environment. After 1963, thanks to a federal decree, the government could conclude such conventions without parliamentarian approval, which facilitated and accelerated the procedures. In 1970, when the IRG came into force, twenty-six bilateral protection agreements had been concluded.[77] The IRG and the investment protection agreements network

74 Arrêté fédéral concernant le maximum des engagements totaux pouvant être pris au titre de la garantie contre les risques de l'investissement, 09.10.1970. AfZ, IB-Vorort-Archiv, 463.2.16.

75 If a foreign company was able to prove an important embeddedness in the Swiss economy, it might be eligible. Loi fédérale sur la garantie contre les risques à l'investissement, 20.03.1970. AfZ, IB-Vorort-Archiv, 463.2.16.

76 Loi fédérale sur la garantie contre les risques à l'investissement, 20.03.1970. AfZ, IB-Vorort-Archiv, 463.2.16.

77 Industrie-Holding, Vereinigung der industriellen Holdinggesellschaften, 31. Jahresbericht 1973, zuhanden der Generalversammlung, 15.031974, 5–6.

were therefore considered as complementary devices to provide security to FDI.

During the decade after the IRG came into effect, its scope remained quite limited, with around ten to fifteen requests per year. In 1971, thirteen investment proposals were submitted, many of which came from Industrie-Holding's members. For instance, Nestlé submitted one request for the creation of a condensed and powdered milk production subsidiary in South Vietnam[78] and another to build a factory in South Korea. Nestlé justified its request on the basis of the "unstable political regime and the vulnerable economic situation".[79] It is also worth noting that the coverage which the pharmaceutical company Ciba-Geigy – now Novartis – sought for a new investment aimed at expanding its subsidiary in Karachi, while Amiantus made a request for an investment in Saudi Arabia.[80] Its CEO was Max Schmidheiny, the very same person who, as a parliamentarian, initiated the political process leading to the introduction of the IRG. These investments were usually planned as joint ventures with local capital and benefited from advantages granted by the host states such as tax exemptions, loans with attractive interest rates or tariff preferences for the importation of machines.

The majority of requests — eight out of thirteen — were denied for various reasons such as being too high risk or having too few links to, or benefits for, the Swiss economy. For instance, Nestlé's request in South Vietnam was declared too risky because of the troubled political situation and the absence of an existing investment protection agreement.[81] In the following years, this scenario repeated itself, with few firms' coverage demands and very few guarantees granted.[82] Between 1971 and 1980, sixty-one new investments were covered, to a total of 196.8 million Swiss

78 Geschäftsstelle für die Investitionsrisikogarantie, Gesuchsteller Nestlé Alimentana SA, Land: Sud Vietnam, 02.03.1971. AfZ, IB-Vorort-Archiv, 463.3.1.

79 Geschäftsstelle für die Investitionsrisikogarantie, Gesuchsteller Nestlé Alimentana SA, Land: Corée du Sud, 20.12.1971. AfZ, IB-Vorort-Archiv, 463.3.1.

80 Landis & Gyr, Nouvelle fabrique et compteurs d'électricité, Note à Monsieur le Ministre Bühler, 30.12.1971. AfZ, IB-Vorort-Archiv, 463.3.1. Geschäftsstelle für die Investitionsrisikogarantie, Gesuchsteller Amiantus AG, Land: Saudiarabien, 12.05.1971, 3. AfZ, IB-Vorort-Archiv, 463.3.1.

81 H. Bühler, Geschäftsstelle für die Investitionsrisikogarantie, Protokoll der 3. Sitzung der Kommission für die Investitionsrisikogarantie, 03.05.1971, 4. AF, E9500.217#1990/152# 1*.

82 H. Brunner, H. Bohren und W. Suter, Geschäftsstelle für die Investitionsrisikogarantie, 4. Jahresbericht über das Jahr 1972 an die Kommission für die Investitionsrisikogarantie, 06.02.1974. AfZ, IB-Vorort-Archiv, 463.3.3.2.

francs,[83] a modest amount in comparison to the funds committed to the export risk guarantee. At the beginning of the 1980s, in the context of a budget deficit, the possibility of dismantling the guarantee was discussed, but the Vorort opposed it.[84] Over the years, some voices expressed critical judgments about the IRG. For instance, Robert Jecker, CEO of the Bank *Crédit Suisse*, stated that it was "technically inadequate and useless".[85] At the end of the 1980s, Industrie-Holding also lobbied for Swiss participation in the Multilateral Investment Guarantee Agency (MIGA), since the association deplored the fact that the scope of the Swiss IRG was too limited.[86]

According to actors' perceptions and because of the limited financial resources of the IRG, it seems that, retrospectively, this institutional tool did not prove critical in explaining the expansion of Swiss FDI in developing countries and in providing security against political risks. This being said, its concrete results should be further investigated. Indeed, the global amount involved gives no information about the strategic importance of the investments covered by the IRG, which may, in the long run, have been crucial in the opening of new markets and the granting of monopolistic advantages. In addition, since the IRG was combined with bilateral protection agreements, it might have provided a symbolic protection that is difficult to quantify. Indeed, some firms might have carried out investments in risky business environments only because these institutional tools provided them a sufficient feeling of security. Finally, the IRG was also used by the Swiss government as proof of its goodwill in helping developing countries and therefore prevented the expenditure of more public money for development assistance.

A State Insurance Designed by and for Swiss MNEs

First, this case study on the development of the Swiss *Investitionsrisikogarantie* shows how securing FDI against political risks was a strategic consid-

---

83 Industrie-Holding, Jahresbericht 1980, 3.

84 SHIV, Protokoll der 2. Sitzung des Vororts im Vereinsjahr 1980–1981, 30.06.1980, 9. AfZ, IB Vorort-Archiv 1.5.3.28.

85 Robert Jecker, SHIV, Protokoll der 1. Sitzung des Vororts im Vereinsjahr 1984–1985, 28.05.1984, 4-5. AfZ, IB Vorort-Archiv 1.5.3.30.

86 Industrie-Holding, Dr. Arnold Knechtle Sekretär der Industrie-Holding, Multilaterale Investitionsrisikogarantie Agentur (MIGA) Informationstagung 13. Juni 1989 Zürich, an alle Mitglieder. SWA PA 540 a m 2-5-3 V.

eration for MNEs during the post-war period. Various motivations existed behind its implementation. On the one hand, the IRG was aimed at providing security against confiscation or discriminatory practices by host states. On the other hand, the IRG was an answer to the institutional instruments developed by other industrialised countries such as the US or Japan for their national MNEs, which might have resulted in a competitive disadvantage for Swiss MNEs.

Second, the IRG example demonstrates the importance of considering MNEs' collective political tactics in securing FDIs while the literature in business history usually focuses on firms' individual corporate strategies. Indeed, Industrie-Holding — the association representing several major Swiss industrial MNEs — played a crucial role in the political process that led to IRG's concretisation. A CEO of one its member firm launched the legislative procedure while the association provided the arguments in its favour during the multiple rounds of discussions. The business circle was also ultimately important for its implementation, with three of their representatives being responsible for evaluating firms' requests.

Third, the intense discussions within the business sector illustrate how difficult it might be for entrepreneurs to choose between different types of security. While Industrie-Holding was pushing for the IRG to secure MNEs' short-term economic expansion abroad, other segments of the business circle believed it to be a dangerous form of state intervention that could, in the long run, weaken the Swiss liberal political order. Granting political security in host states might therefore be detrimental to political stability in MNEs' home country. Such hesitations and disagreements within the business circles explain why the political process took more than a decade and why the IRG's scope was rather limited once it was introduced. Industrie-Holding's argument that it constituted the cheapest form of development assistance was certainly crucial to its acceptance.

Finally, the introduction of the IRG exemplifies how political risk in host states and political assistance from a home state can be understood as two sides of the same coin. The nationality of the firms therefore appears essential in understanding the global patterns of political protection and political risks. As a matter of fact, the Swiss government recognises that granting security to economic activities carried out by Swiss firms, even outside Swiss territory, was part of its mandate. It therefore developed the IRG as part of a dense network of investment protection agreements. Since such a governmental attitude is not exclusively Swiss and since such institutional tools are still commonly used today, their strategic importance in a historical perspective should be further investigated.

Bibliography

Boon, Marten/Wubs, Ben: Property Control and Room for Manoeuvre: Royal Dutch Shell and Nazi Germany, 1933–1945, in: Business History 58 (2016), 1, p. 1–20

Bott, Sandra: La Suisse et l'Afrique du Sud, 1945–1990: Marché de l'or, finance et commerce durant l'Apartheid. Zürich 2013

Berweger, Gottfried: Investition und Legitimation: Privatinvestitionen in Entwicklungsländern als Teil der schweizerischen Legitimationsproblematik. St-Gallen 1977

Bucheli Marcelo: Multinational Corporations, Totalitarian Regimes and Economic Nationalism: United Fruit Company in Central America, 1899–1975, Business History 50 (2008), 4, p. 433–454

Cowles, Maria Green: Setting the Agenda for a New Europe: The ERT and EC 1992, in: JCMS: Journal of Common Market Studies 33 (1995), 4, p. 501–526

Cowles, Maria Green: The EU Committee of AmCham: The Powerful Voice of American Firms in Brussels, in: Journal of European Public Policy 3 (1996), 3, p. 339–58

Dardel, Jean-Jacques: L'évolution en Suisse de la conception de la coopération au développement: de 1950 à nos jours. Genève 1980

David, Thomas/ Mach, André/ Straumann, Tobias: The Questioning of Selective Protectionism in Switzerland during the 1990s: Cartel Law Reform and Corporate Governance Changes, in Müller Margrit/Myllyntaus, Timo (eds.), Pathbreakers. Small European Countries responding to Globalisation and Deglobalisation, Berne 2008, p. 449–476.

David, Thomas et al: De la "Forteresse des Alpes" à la valeur actionnariale: histoire de la gouvernance d'entreprise suisse (1880–2010). Zürich 2015

Decker, Stephanie: Corporate Legitimacy and Advertising: British Companies and the Rhetoric of Development in West Africa, 1950–1970, in: Business History Review, 81 (2007), 1, p. 59–86

Dirlewanger, Dominique/Guex, Sébastien/Pordenone, Gian Franco: La Politique Commerciale de la Suisse de la Seconde Guerre mondiale à l'entrée au GATT (1945–1966). Zürich 2004

Donzé, Pierre-Yves/Kurosawa, Takafumi: Nestlé Coping with Japanese Nationalism: Political Risk and the Strategy of a Foreign Multinational Enterprise in Japan, 1913–45, in: Business History 55 (2013), 8, p. 1318–38

Donzé, Pierre-Yves: Siemens and the Construction of Hospitals in Latin America, 1949–1964, in: Business History Review 89 (2015), 3, p. 475–502

Donzé, Pierre-Yves: The Advantage of Being Swiss: Nestlé and Political Risk in Asia during the Early Cold War (1945–1970), in: Business History Review 94 (2020), 2, p. 373–397.

Eichenberger, Pierre/Mach, André: Organized Capital and Coordinated Market Economy: Swiss Business Interest Associations between Socio-Economic Regulation and Political Influence, in: Trampusch, Christine/Mach, André (eds.): Switzerland in Europe: Continuity and change in the Swiss political economy, London 2011, p. 53–81.

Eichenberger, Pierre: The Eternal Rebirth of the Liberal Creed: Alternative Temporalities of Swiss Neoliberalism, in: Journal of Modern European History, 17 (2019), 4, p. 390–395

Farquet, Christophe: Tax Avoidance, Collective Resistance, and International Negotiations: Foreign Tax Refusal by Swiss Banks and Industries Between the Two World Wars, in: Journal of Policy History 25 (2013), 3, p. 334–53

Forbes, Neil/Kurosawa, Takafumi/Wubs, Ben (eds.): Multinational Enterprise, Political Risk and Organisational Change: From Total War to Cold War. London 2018Foreman-Peck, James S.: European industrial policies in the post-war boom: 'planning the economic miracle', in: Grabas, Christian/Nützenadel, Alexander (eds.): Industrial Policy in Europe after 1945: Wealth, Power and Economic Development in the Cold War, Basingstoke 2014, 13–47.

Gordon, Kathryn: Investment Guarantees and Political Risk Insurance: Institutions, Incentives and Development, OECD 2008, p. 91–122

Humair, Cédric: Du libéralisme manchestérien au capitalisme organisé: genèse, structuration et spécificités de l'organisation patronale suisse (1860–1914), in: Rousselier-Fraboulet Danièle (ed.): Genèse des organisations patronales en Europe: XIXe-XXe siècles, Rennes 2012, p. 133–142.

Iversen, Martin Jes: The "Varieties of Capitalism" Approach as an Analytical Tool for Business Historians, in: The Business History Review 84 (2010), 4, p. 664–666

Jones, Geoffrey: The End of Nationality? Global Firms and "Borderless Worlds", in: Zeitschrift für Unternehmensgeschichte 51 (2006), 2, p. 149–165

Jones, Geoffrey/Lubinski, Christina: Managing political risk in global business: Beiersdorf 1914–1990, in: Enterprise & Society, 13 (2012), 1, p. 85–119

Kobrak, Christopher/Wüstenhagen, Jana: International investment and Nazi Politics: The cloaking of German assets abroad: 1936–1945, in: Business History, 48 (2006), 3, p.399–427

Kurosawa, Takafumi/Wubs, Ben: Swiss and (Anglo)-Dutch Multinationals and Organisational Change in the Era of Total War, in: Forbes, Neil/Wubs, Ben/ Forbes, Neil/Kurosawa, Takafumi/Wubs, Ben (eds.): Multinational Enterprise, Political Risk and Organisational Change: From Total War to Cold War. London 2018, p. 23–54

Lanzalaco, Luca: Business Interest Associations, in: Jones, Geoffrey/Zeitlin, Jonathan (eds.): The Oxford Handbook of Business History. Oxford 2009, p. 293–318

Laviec, Jean-Pierre: Protection et promotion des investissements: Étude de droit économique international. Geneva 1985

Lehmbruch Gerhard: Consociational Democracy and Corporatism in Switzerland, in: The Journal of Federalism 23 (1993), 43–60.

Longchamp, Olivier: La Politique Financière Fédérale (1945-1958), Lausanne 2014

Lubinski, Christina/Giacomin, Valeria/Schnitzer, Klara: Internment as a business challenge: Political risk management and German multinationals in Colonial India (1914–1947), in: Business History (2018)

Lucas, Isabelle: Tango de Neutres sur fond de guerre: les relations économiques entre la Suisse et l'Argentine (1938–1945), in: Relations Internationales 150 (2012), 2, p. 37–52

Lüpold, Martin: Globalisierung als Krisenreaktionsstrategie. Dezentralisierung und Renationalisierung bei Nestlé 1920–1950, in: Gilomen, Hans-Jörg/Müller, Margrit/Veyrassat, Béatrice (eds): Globalisierung-Chancen und Risiken. Die Schweiz in der Weltwirtschaft 18.–20. Jahrhundert, Zürich 2003, p. 211–234

Lüpold, Martin: Der Ausbau der "Festung Schweiz": Aktienrecht und Corporate Governance in der Schweiz, 1881–1961, Zürich 2010

Mach, André: La Suisse entre internationalisation et changements politiques internes : la législation sur les cartels et les relations industrielles dans les années 1990. Zürich 2006

Mach, andré/ David, Thomas/ Ginalski, Stéphanie/ Bühlmann Felix: Les élites économiques suisses au XXe siècle. Neuchâtel 2016

Meister, Magnus: Les Trente Glorieuses et la crise des années 1970 en Suisse. Une politique conjoncturelle et économique au service de l'internationalisation de l'économie suisse. Genève 2013

Meister, Magnus: Swiss economic and political relations with Israel, Egypt and Syria during the Arab-Israeli conflicts (1967-1983), Lausanne 2019

Müller, Margrit: From Protectionism to Market Liberalisation: Patterns of Internationalisation in the Main Swiss Export Sectors, in: Müller, Margrit/Myllyntaus Timo (eds.): Pathbreakers: small European countries responding to globalisation and deglobalisation. Bern 2008, p. 113–150

Müller, Margrit: Die Schweiz in der internationalen Arbeitsteilung, in: Halbeisen, Patrick/ Müller, Margrit/Veyrassat, Béatrice (eds.), Wirtschaftsgeschichte Der Schweiz Im 20. Jahrhundert. Basel 2012, p. 319–466

Perrenoud, Marc: Banquiers et Diplomates Suisses: 1938–1946, Lausanne 2011

Phillips-Fein, Kim: Invisible Hands: The Making of the Conservative Movement from the New Deal to Reagan. New York 2009

Pitteloud, Sabine: "Les invisibles deviennent visibles": le rôle politique des multinationales et les débats sur l'internationalisation en Suisse [1942–1993]. Genève 2019

Pitteloud, Sabine: Industrie-Holding: Creating a Community of Interest among Swiss "Multinationals", in: Revue suisse d'histoire SZG/RSH, 69 (2019), 3, p. 400–417

Pitteloud, Sabine: The social desirability of offshoring: a Swiss consensus [1945–1975], in: Zeitschrift für Unternehmensgeschichte (ZUG)/Journal of Business History 64 (2019), 2, p. 255–273

Pitteloud, Sabine: Unwanted Attention: Swiss Multinationals and the Creation of International Corporate Guidelines in the 1970s, in: Business and Politics, (2020), p. 1–25.

Rollings, Neil: British Business in the Formative Years of European Integration, 1945–1973. New York 2008

Schaufelbuehl, Janick Marina: La France et la Suisse, ou, la force du petit: évasion fiscale, relations commerciales et financières (1940–1954). Paris 2009

Schmidheiny, Stephan: Die Investitionsrisikogarantie. Zürich 1972

Schröter, Harm G.: Swiss Multinational Enterprise in Historical Perspective, in: Jones Geoffrey/Schröter, Harm G. (eds.): The Rise of Multinationals in Continental Europe. Aldershot 1993, p.49–64

Slobodian, Quinn: Globalists: The End of Empire and the Birth of Neoliberalism. Cambridge Mass 2018

Smith, Andrew: A LBV Perspective on Political Risk Management in a Multinational Bank during the First World War, in: Multinational Business Review, 24 (2016), 1, p.25–46

Snyder Earl: Protection of Private Foreign Investment: Examination and Appraisal, in: International &Comparative Law Quarterly, 10 (1961), 3, p. 469–494

Uhlig, Christiane/König, Mario/Barthelmess, Petra/Pfaffenroth, Peter/Zeugin, Bettina: Tarnung, Transfer, Transit: die Schweiz als Drehscheibe verdeckter deutscher Operationen (1938–1952), Zürich 2001.

Van Apeldoorn, Bastiaan: Transnational Class Agency and European Governance: The Case of the European Round Table of Industrialists, in: New Political Economy 5(2000), 2, p. 157–181

Waterhouse, Benjamin C.: Lobbying America: The Politics of Business from Nixon to NAFTA. Princeton, New Jersey 2014

Wilkins, Mira: The Maturing of Multinational Enterprise: American Business Abroad from 1914 to 1970. Cambridge Mass 1975

Wilkins, Mira: Swiss Investments in the United States, in: Guex, Sébastien (ed.), La Suisse et les Grandes Puissances, 1914–1945. Genève 1999, p. 91–139

The Management of Foreign Direct Investment Risk by two Norwegian Firms in the 1960s and 1970s

Kristin Stanwick Bårnås

The present paper will investigate the risk management strategies related to the foreign direct investment (FDI) decisions of two Norwegian manufacturing firms in the late 1960s and early 1970s. The two firms are: Dyno Industrier, which produced explosives and industrial adhesives, and invested in West Germany, England, Singapore, Denmark, and Finland; and Norcem, which produced cement, and invested in Ghana, Liberia, the Philippines, and Ras al-Khaimah in the United Arab Emirates.

Risks, in relation to FDI, are often defined as, "the dangers firms face in terms of limitations, restrictions or even losses when engaging in international business".[1] Security is a relational term closely connected to the meaning of risk, thus security in relation to FDI is the avoidance of such risk. This paper will examine, compare and discuss the strategies the two firms implemented to ensure the success of their investments and manage risks in their FDIs. The primary focus is on the firms' investments, which risks they were most concerned with when they invested abroad, and how they chose to manage them.

In the last thirty to forty years, research on risk and risk management has increased in scope and scale.[2] Although risk management and the security of investment was an important element of international investment prior to the increase in interest in the topic, there has thus far been only limited research conducted on how firms chose to manage risks related to international investments in business history. An article published by Casson and Lopes in 2013 is one of the few studies that takes an historical perspective and focuses specifically on how firms manage risk when they invest in high-risk environments. This is also one of few studies that compares responses to risk across firms.[3] However, Casson and Lopes's paper only presents examples of certain risk management strategies, and the reasoning behind the firms' management of risks is not discussed.

---

1 *Eduardsen/Marinova*, Decision-makers', 12.
2 *Inhaber/Norman*, Risk Interest, 119– 120.
3 *Casson/Da Silva Lopes*, High-Risk environments, 375–404.

The two firms in this paper are selected because they had FDIs both near and far, in unstable and insecure countries as well as in stable and secure countries. Their investments abroad coincided with an increase in FDIs by other Norwegian firms, and with an increase in interest in risk and risk management research. The two firms thus invested abroad in a period when there was some, though still limited, Norwegian experience on which to base investment decisions, and when there only was limited research available on how to manage the risks involved with such investments. The research below is primarily based on company archives, supplemented by company magazines, government archives and various governmental publications, primarily from the 1960s and 1970s. Oral history interviews were conducted with two former senior managers and decision-makers in the firms: Ragnar Halvorsen from Dyno and Gerhard Heiberg from Norcem.

The paper will first give a short introduction to the risk management strategies that are commonly used to manage risks involved with FDIs. Thereafter, the paper will describe the Norwegian context the two firms invested within. By doing so, the chapter will provide context and background for the firms' investments and help to contextualise the options that were available to the decision-makers. The two firms and their investments will thereafter shortly be described, before the risk management strategies employed by the two firms are discussed.

Definitions: Risk and risk management

Originally, Frank Knight defined risk as a situation in which possible outcomes are unknown but where their probabilities are calculable, and uncertainty as a situation in which even their probabilities are unknown.[4] Several researchers have since pointed out, however, that the proposed distinction between risk and uncertainty is not compatible with most uses of risk in modern society, nor with how risk is used in daily language.[5] The two firms did not make a distinction between uncertainty and risk, nor did they find risk to be a quantifiable construct. More recently, there has been an argument for defining risk in a way that includes both negative and positive outcomes. Rosa, for example, defined risk as: "A situation or event in which something of human value (including humans themselves) has

4 *Knight*, Risk, Uncertainty and Profit.
5 *Aven*, Risk Concept, 33–44.

been put at stake and where the outcome is uncertain".[6] Rosa's definition of risk has inspired several other commentators to devise definitions of their own. Renn, for instance, defined risk as "The possibility that human actions or events lead to consequences that affect aspects of what humans value".[7] Within the data collected about Dyno and Norcem, there is no evidence that any of them defined what they considered the concept of risk to mean. It is therefore likely that the decision-makers involved in the FDI decision had somewhat different perspectives on what exactly constituted risk and security, as evident from the oral history interviews.

Perceptions and conceptions of risk and security have an impact on decisions taken and the ways in which these decisions are reached.[8] The characteristics of individual managers and decision-makers, such as personal experience, risk appetite, and knowledge each impact their decision-making. The impact of risk on a decision is greater in respect to losses than it is to gains.[9] As such, decision-makers and managers may be more focused on security when the issue is framed as a potential loss with severe implications for the firm than when it is framed as a potential gain. Directly related to FDI, managers' perceptions can have an impact on the timing of internationalisation, the willingness to internationalise, and the selected entry mode. Eduardsen and Marinova found that managers' international orientation impacts how likely a firm is proactively to identify, create, and capture international opportunities.[10] Managers base their decisions on whether to invest abroad on a variety of aspects. Buckley found that decision-makers emphasise production costs, access to resources, market growth, trade barriers, and country-specific factors such as languages, when considering a foreign investment.[11] All these issues can create risks for a firm considering an FDI. Risk may also arise from other sources including the market and the political or socio-cultural environment in the host country.[12] Political risk includes some of the primary risks that can be faced by firms when they invest abroad; as such, it is a significant determinant of FDI decisions and it continues to be of importance even when the FDI is in place.[13] Political risk is often defined as the risk that the govern-

6 *Rosa*, Metatheoretical, 28.
7 *Renn*, Accomplishments, 51.
8 *Cohrssen/Covello*, Principles.
9 *Aharoni/Tihanyi/Connelly*, Managerial, 135–142
10 *Eduardsen/Marinova*, Decision-makers',4–26.
11 *Buckley/Devinney/Louviere*, Managers, 1069–1094.
12 *Heidenreich/Mohr/Puck*, Strategies, 793–803.
13 *John/Lawton*, Perspectives, 847–879.

ment will "unexpectedly change the 'rules of the game' under which business operate".[14] It is usually associated with changes in political regimes and can result from wars, revolutions, *coup d'états*, or political turmoil.

How the managers and decision-makers in Dyno and Norcem viewed risk and the need for keeping their firms and their investment secure could thus have influenced their investment decisions and the ways in which the two firms chose to manage risks.

Once a firm that is seeking to invest abroad has identified and assessed the risks associated with the investment, the next step is to decide whether and how to manage them. This can be done by implementing risk-management strategies. A risk-management strategy aims to reduce the impact a potential risk can have on the investment and the firm,[15] thus securing the investment and the firm itself. A firm can manage or mitigate risk through financial methods, such as insurance policies; it can also divide the risk between several partners in a joint venture; and networks and trust can be used to mitigate risks. Furthermore, risk can be managed strategically through, for example, avoidance, control, and cooperation. Avoidance occurs when the firm and its managers consider the risk to be at an unacceptable level. In this situation, the manager can respond either by postponing the investment or withdrawing altogether, if the firm is already involved.[16]

Insurance is one of the oldest strategies for coping with risk, and it can be traced back to Mesopotamia. Insurance is an effective risk-mitigation strategy because firms can secure against risk for a fixed cost. Insurance firms usually divide political risk into three categories: war and political violence; expropriation/breach of contract; and, transfer risk.[17] However, insurance, when it is available, is not always affordable. Commercial risk, changes in government regulation, and discrimination against foreign firms are examples of risks that are typically costly to insure against.[18]

When a company invests abroad, its management must decide on which entry mode they want to utilise and how the ownership structure should be organised. There are three main types of entry mode: contracts, joint ventures, and wholly owned subsidiaries. Entry modes can also be analysed as green field investment versus acquisitions. The choice of entry mode ultimately depends on how much risk the company is willing to take in return for the anticipated greater level of control and potentially higher re-

14 *Busse/Hefeker*, Political Risk, 397–415.

15 *Kobrin*, Political Risk: A Review, 67–80.

16 *Miller*, Framework, 311–331.

17 *Jensen*, Political Risk, 1040–1052.

18 *Casson/Da Silva Lopes*, High-risk Environments, 375–404.

turns.[19] A joint venture gives medium-level control, while a wholly owned subsidiary gives the most control but is less secure. However, a cooperative strategy such as a joint venture involves increased exposure to opportunistic behaviours by the cooperating parties.[20]

Networks, relationships, and trust can help in the mitigation of cross-border risks.[21] Relationships and networks are an important resource for firms as they can grant access to further knowledge and markets, together with benefits such as access to other relationships, resources, and organisations. Networks are particularly important in the early phases of internationalisation. And research has shown that networks have been particularly important in the internationalisation process for medium and small firms.[22] Cooperation and strategic alliances can, however, also create risks. For instance, conflicts can arise due to the opportunistic behaviour of the participants or through the expression of their individual interests. This is known as 'relational risk', which can be managed through control or trust, where control refers to the process of influencing the behaviour of the partner or participants.[23] Trust is an important aspect of any network and can be defined as the willingness to be vulnerable under conditions of risk and interdependence.[24] Trust is seen as a measure that firms can use to mitigate any opportunistic behaviour of partners, for example in a joint venture.

Background and context

> The decision to establish production in other countries is especially demanding and risky.[25]

The two firms serving as examples in this paper were both Norwegian-based companies founded, headquartered, and operated out of Norway, and owned and controlled by Norwegian interests. This means that the Norwegian socio-historical context was important for their investment de-

19 *Brouthers/Hennart*, Entry Mode, 395-425.
20 *Miller, framework*, 311–331.
21 *Doh/Lawton/Rajwani*, Nonmarket Strategy, 22–39.
22 *Björkman/Forsgren*, International Business, 6–25.
23 *Das/Teng*, Strategic Alliances, 251–283.
24 *Rousseau/Sitkin/Burt/Camerer*, Trust, 393–404.
25 NOU 1981: 47, 57.

cisions, the options available to them, their risk management strategies, and how they came to invest abroad.

Norwegian firms were generally slow to embark in FDIs, and it was only from the 1960s that there was any significant increase in FDIs by Norwegian firms. However, the 1970s marked a turning point: in this decade, both the number of FDIs and the value of investments abroad increased. Changing political views in Norway, the decision to not pursue EEC membership, the increasing importance of the oil industry, and growing investment and labour costs at home all contributed to the increase in FDIs from the 1970s onwards.[26] Consequently, the majority of Norway's largest manufacturing firms became multinationals during the 1970s, and between 1978 and 1986, the number of Norwegian FDIs quadrupled.[27] The major exception was the shipping industry, which had made several investments abroad somewhat earlier.

Regulations affecting Norwegian outward FDIs were limited, the most important of which being the currency licence. All FDIs by Norwegian firms had to obtain a currency licence from the Norwegian Central Bank (Norges Bank) before any capital could be transferred abroad and investments could be carried out. The exception to this rule was again the shipping industry, which needed approval from the Ministry of Trade and Shipping instead of from the Central Bank.[28] Norwegian investments abroad were otherwise not regulated under Norwegian law, and it was usually easy to obtain the licence. Applications were only rejected in the rare cases in which Norwegian industry would have had little involvement in the proposed project.[29]

One of the main institutions that supported Norwegian firms seeking either to export abroad or invest in foreign countries was the Norwegian Guarantee Institute for Export Credits (GIEK). The Institute helped to promote the export of Norwegian goods, the export of services, and Norwegian FDIs. It also gave special guarantees for export and investments in developing countries as a part of Norwegian developmental aid. This guarantee scheme was established in 1963 and provided guarantees for exports to and for investments in developing countries. This guarantee covered Norwegian investors for the political risks they might encounter while investing in a developing country, thus helping to make the investment more se-

26 NOU 1979: 35.
27 *Amdam*, Internationalisation Process, 445–461.
28 NOU 1983: 54, 61–63.
29 NOU 1981: 47, 27.

cure for the Norwegian firm. The political risks the scheme covered were divided into three main categories:

1. Expropriation, confiscation, or similar interventions from local governments.
2. War, rebellion, or similar conditions.
3. Obstacles to the conversion and transfer of funds from the host country to Norway.[30]

A strike was not covered by the insurance, nor were the commercial risks or expenses arising from mistakes or negligence by the investors. Guarantees would not be granted to already existing investments, unless the investment was a part of an expansion, modernisation, or rationalisation, or otherwise contributed to the further economic development of the business. The investments presented in this paper that received guarantees from the GIEK covered up to 90% of their investments.[31] Besides the guarantees for exports and investments in developing countries, firms could also receive financial support for feasibility studies in advance of a potential investment in a developing country. This support could cover up to 50% of the cost of a feasibility study,[32] representing a major state-financed contribution towards ensuring the security of FDIs for Norwegian firms.

Dyno Industrier

Dyno Industrier was established in 1972 after a merger between the only two civil explosive producers in Norway: Grubernes Sprængstoffabriker (Grubernes) and Norsk Sprængstofindustri (NSI). Their core activity was the production of explosives, but they also produced chemical products such as plastic sprayers and industrial adhesives.

Both Grubernes and NSI made independent FDIs in the years before they merged. The earliest FDI was in 1966 by NSI in a joint venture in West Germany with the local chemical producer E.H Worlée &Co. m.b.H. The joint venture produced amino resins and NSI contributed the production know-how. NSI's next investment was in Singapore in 1970 where

30 Særlige garantier ved eksport til utviklingsland og garantier for private investeringer i utviklingsland. 1967. (Riksarkivet, Oslo (RA). Garantiinstituttet for eksportkreditt (GIEK): Da-0005).

31 Utkast for protokoll for møtet i det utvidete styret den 1/2-68. 1968. (RA, GIEK: Da-0005).

32 NOU 1981: 47, 37.

they started an industrial adhesives factory in a joint venture with the local development bank. Grubernes, the other merging partner, made its first FDI in 1970 when it acquired a producer of plastic sprayers in the United Kingdom. After the merger of Grubernes and NSI to become Dyno, the company invested in industrial adhesives factories in Denmark and Finland in 1972, both of which were joint ventures with local plywood factories as participants. Most of these investments were financially successful, although the first, in West Germany in 1966–67, was in many ways a failure as it was never profitable and closed just a few years after opening.

Internationalisation through both exports and FDIs was seen as essential for the survival of the firm in the long run, a view which made Dyno especially willing to take risks when it came to investing abroad.[33] Dyno's monopolisation of explosives on its home market following the merger of Grubernes and NSI was one of the major driving factors behind its attempts to enter the international stage. Inflation in Norway and the increasing costs of labour and production were also important factors. The manager of the firm stated in 1973 that

> The expansion possibilities on the Norwegian market are limited for both the chemical and the explosive sectors. ... It is therefore natural to seek expansion abroad; partly through exports of products that can stand transportation costs and potential customs charges, and partly through the establishment of local production or acquisition of already existing firms.[34]

Norcem

Norcem was a producer of cement and related building materials, such as lightweight concrete and asbestos cement. They were also involved in plastic boat production. Norcem was established after a merger between three cement producers in Norway in 1968. Norcem's focus on exports, primarily of cement and clinker, gave it international experience and contacts. In the early 1970s, its focus on the export of cement was complemented with an emphasis on the export of industrial know-how and management ser-

---

33 Protokoll fra styremøtet 28.9.1971 i Norsk Sprængstofindustri A/S. 1971. (RA, Dyno: Styrende organ etter nøkkel nr. 34, 114 Styret).

34 Adm. direktørs redegjørelse på generalforsamlingen onsdag 9. mai 1973. (RA, Dyno: nr 1, 110.4-9433).

vices. The knowledge and contacts that the company gained through this contributed to Norcem's later involvement in FDIs.

Exports played a significant role in Norcem's development. For a short period, between 1965 and 1970, Norway was Western Europe's largest exporter of cement.[35] Norcem's primary export markets were outside of Europe. The decision primarily to export to markets outside of Europe was likely connected to the strength of its European competition. Several of the European countries were already producing cement and had no need to import it from abroad.[36] Norcem's recognition that its future markets would be those found abroad continued to be reaffirmed. The CEO stated that "it has become one of our long-term goals to use the strong reputation we have gained as a result of our know-how, our technology, and our competent people, on different projects in several places around the world".[37] Norcem saw the Norwegian market as too small for future growth, and export and internationalisation were therefore seen as necessary if the firm was to survive in the long term.[38]

The cement producers' first FDI was through a mutual sales company in 1967, the year before the merger, when it became the minority owner of two cement mills in Ghana. The Ghanaian state owned the majority share, and the main income for Norcem came from the export of cement clinker produced in Norway. It took nine years from Norcem's first investment abroad before it made its next and Norcem made two FDIs in 1976. One of these was a joint venture in plastic boat production in the Philippines; this investment only lasted for a few years and was largely unsuccessful. The second investment was in a block factory in Ras al-Khaimah. This was a joint venture with Sheikh Saqr bin Mohammed al-Qasimi, the ruler of Ras al-Khaimah. In 1977, Norcem also invested in cement mills in Liberia. This investment had many similarities to the earlier investment in Ghana, but this time with Norcem as the majority owner and the local government a minority owner. Norcem's FDIs in the 1960s and the 1970s were in distant countries with few cultural similarities to Norway, and in which few other Norwegian firms had invested. Furthermore, Norcem was more exposed to risks due to the nature of the industry in which it was involved.

35 *Gartmann*, Sement, 33.
36 "Norcem eksporterer", *Nytt i Norcem:* 1–69.
37 "Internasjonalisering", *Nytt i Norcem:* 3–76.
38 *Aftenposten*, "Norcem vokser internasjonalt".

Risk management strategies

One of the first steps in the risk management process is to identify and assess relevant risks. Both firms conducted research on the market, and on the potential risks involved with the investment. Norcem and Dyno both focused on risks that they could prepare mitigation plans for, and the two firms considered themselves to be well prepared for the investment and its accompanying risks. For instance, Heiberg from Norcem reported that he felt the company was "thorough" when evaluating and assessing the risks before the investment decision was taken.[39]

There are, however, marked differences in how much risk the managers of the two firms were willing to take, and how much they focused on keeping the firms' investments secure. Norcem, under Heiberg, was the most risk-willing of the two firms. Heiberg himself stated that, "We were a little bolder than Dyno, a little more 'trigger-happy', to use that word, in a lot of what we were doing".[40] Norcem's views on risk and their decision-makers' perceptions of them are reflected in their chosen investment countries. The countries were distant from Norway, both geographically and culturally. Notable examples of this include Norcem's investments in Ghana, Liberia, and Ras al-Khaimah. Dyno was more focused on keeping the company and its investments secure, and its investments were both in countries that were geographically close to and distant from Norway. The firm took some risks in regard to its investments, though not as many as Norcem. Dyno was more willing to accept risks in situations where they were affected by increased competition, however, for instance in the case of Singapore, where increasing local production put pressure on Dyno to invest if it wanted to maintain its market share.

Research on risk and FDI has primarily focused on the risks involved in the investment itself. However, for Dyno, and partly for Norcem, the risk of not investing also played a role in the risk assessment and investment decision. One of the main arguments in support of Dyno's investment in Singapore was that, "If our company does not establish local production, we must run the risk of losing our present position".[41] It was likewise argued in regard to its Finnish investment that it was, "probably the last possibility for keeping an interesting share of adhesives deliveries to Fin-

39 Interview with Heiberg, August 2015.

40 Interview with Heiberg, August 2015.

41 Styremøte 5. 6. Lim- og formalinfabrikk i Singapore. 1969. (RA, Dyno: nr. 32. 114).

land".[42] Thus, without the FDIs, Dyno risked losing the market share that it had established through export.[43] Norcem, though to a lesser degree, came to a similar conclusion with regard to its investments in the Philippines and Liberia. Norcem argued that the FDI in the Philippines was necessary for the survival of Fjord Plast boat production because "large transport costs have proven it impossible to deliver the smaller boats from Fjord to this market".[44] In addition, the investment in Liberia was intended to ensure deliveries of clinker from Norway.[45] The risk of not investing and potentially losing their existing market share was an important aspect of their risk assessments and investment decisions, and it affected how the two firms viewed and assessed the investments.

In some of the potential investments that were discussed by the two firms, the risks were deemed to be too high compared to what the firms expected to gain from them. In those cases, the firms decided to avoid the risk by not investing. Examples of this include a discussion which took place at Dyno about acquiring a firm in Sweden which was decided against because the cost was seen as too high compared to the firm's worth.[46] Norcem also decided against direct investments in cement factories in the US, and instead relied on exports. The reason given for this was that the risks and investment costs involved were too high and could thus have had a significant impact on the firm as a whole if the investment was not a success.[47] The size of the other investments varied, but none were large enough to pose a threat to the whole firm if they failed. Deciding against investing was thus a risk-mitigation strategy used by two firms that otherwise were relatively willing to take risks. This shows that there was a limit to how large a risk these firms were willing to take, and that avoidance was used as a risk-mitigation strategy. Keeping the firm secure was considered as more important than taking this risk. This fits with March and Shapira's findings, where managers perceived risk as something that should be avoided when the survival of the firm is under threat.[48]

---

42 Formalin- og Limfabrikk i Finland. 1971. (RA, Dyno: nr. 34, 114 Styret).

43 Styremøte 5. 6. Lim- og formalinfabrikk i Singapore. 1969. (RA, Dyno: nr. 32. 114).

44 "Fjord plast", *Nytt i Norcem:* 2/3-75.

45 "Klinkereksport sikret ved kjøp av cement-mølle", *Nytt i Norcem:* 2-77.

46 Handels- og Fabriksaktiebolaget Petunia. Styremøte 4.9. 1967. (RA, Dyno: nr. 31, 114).

47 Interview Heiberg, August 2015.

48 *March/Shapira,* Managerial Perspectives, 1404–1418.

Political risk

The most significant risk associated with the investments outside of Europe are political risks. Included in this category of risk are political instability, government policy instability, and social risk.[49] Norcem was the only company that had to deal with political risk throughout its investments, while for Dyno this was mainly a concern ahead of its investment in Singapore.[50] Political risks were a crucial consideration in regard to Norcem's investments in Ghana and Liberia, but also in its investments in the Philippines and in Ras al-Khaimah. Some research on political risk had been conducted before the firms invested abroad, but it was a relatively new research field until the 1980s.[51] Political risk was clearly a concept that both firms were aware of and concerned about before their investments abroad in the 1960s and 1970s. Political risks are referenced several times in the data, and the GIEK provided a separate insurance policy to cover political risk in developing countries. The term 'political risk' was used by the firms to describe both political instability and government policy changes, such as the confiscation of subsidiaries and *coup d'états*.

Several strategies were implemented to manage or mitigate political risks by the two firms. One of those strategies, the selection of what they considered to be less risk-prone countries, was used both to avoid political risk and to limit risk in general. For instance, Dyno chose to establish an FDI in Singapore rather than in nearby countries as a part of its risk-management strategy, with Singapore being preferred over other countries because it was seen as having a more stable economic and political environment.[52] Dyno's knowledge about the political and investment environment in Singapore was greater than it was for other nearby countries, and this further contributed to the firm considering this a less risky choice.

One of the other significant risk-management strategies that was used to mitigate political risk was insurance from the GIEK. Both firms had previous experience with the GIEK's guarantee scheme, as they had used it to insure their exports. The guarantees against political risks were used for the FDIs that were outside of Europe. The guarantees from the GIEK against political risk in regard to their investment could have contributed to this, as 90% of both of their investments was guaranteed against political risk at

49 *Miller*, Framework, 311–331.
50 Styremøte 5. 6. 1969. (RA, Dyno: nr. 32. 114).
51 *Kobrin*, Political Risk: A review, 67–80.
52 Styremøte 5. 6. 1969. (RA, Dyno: nr. 32. 114).

the time of the investment.[53] Norcem used the insurance for several of its investments while Dyno used it for the investment in Singapore. For Dyno, the guarantees were set as a condition before it would commence with the FDI in Singapore.[54] The investment in Singapore was a large financial investment for NSI, but the political risk of investing in Singapore was, to a large degree, offset by the guarantees from the GIEK. The guarantees thus made the investment feel more secure for Dyno.

Another important risk-management strategy implemented against political risk was maintaining personal relationships and trust. This helped to ensure the firms' position in the relevant country, and it granted access to new investment opportunities. Networks and trust can be used to mitigate opportunistic behaviour of partners, and can also promote and increase information transfer.[55] Forming relationships with government officials in particular can provide useful information about governmental processes.[56] This strategy was utilised by Norcem and, although to a lesser degree, also by Dyno. Halvorsen, the former manager of Dyno, said,

> In general, you made friends – that is what you did. Friends whom you could trust and, if it went wrong, that one could talk to. Thus, as part of the internationalisation process this is, I think, a main point. Especially for a Norwegian firm with little capital and a small business, that only has to offer specialities within adhesives that one can buy from elsewhere.[57]

One of the reasons this was seen as a useful risk-management strategy for Dyno was due to the firm's size. From an international perspective, both Norcem and Dyno were small firms with limited resources. Maintaining a close relationship with the people it invested with and the leadership in the country it was invested in was therefore an important strategy. Norcem, for example, did not have the resources required to bribe officials at the same scale as larger firms. Close cooperation and relationship cultivation with government actors were therefore used in order to retain the monopolistic position it had gained in Ghana and Liberia against financially stronger competitors. For Norcem, this risk-mitigation strategy was also useful in its investment in Ras al-Khaimah, where its relationship with

53 St. prp. Nr. 66 (1964–1965). Om Garanti-Instituttet for Eksportkreditts virksomhet i 1964.

54 Styremøte 22.12 - Singaporeprosjektet. 1969. (RA, Dyno: 32. 114 styret).

55 *Rousseau/Sitkin/Burt/Camerer*, Trust, 393–404.

56 *Doh/Lawton/Rajwani*, Nonmarket Strategy, 22–39.

57 Interview Halvorsen, August 2015.

the government in relation to the management of the cement factory contributed to making its first FDI in the country in 1977 a possibility. The previous involvement in the country also ensured that Norcem knew its investment partner before becoming financially involved. Heiberg argued, "We found that we could rely on them and they found that they could rely on us, which made it easier to say 'yes, let us invest together'".[58]

However, relying on networks, friendships and trust is a complex risk-management strategy. In particular, this was the case for Norcem in Ghana, Liberia, and Ras al-Khaimah, as it is difficult to maintain a friendship with the political leadership in a country with frequent regime or leadership changes. It was therefore also crucial not to be too closely associated with a former government, so as to be able to build a relationship with a new government without being linked inextricably with its predecessor.[59] The complexity of this strategy was emphasised in Norcem's application for guarantees from the GIEK. The application was sent without the Sheikh's knowledge, and Norcem requested that the application be kept a secret, stating that

> Since Sheikh Saqr is both the political leader of the Emirate and a part of this project, it will be very unfortunate for both this project and later cooperation if it becomes known to him that we seek guarantee coverage for political risks. We therefore request confidentiality regarding the case, and that it must not be made public in statistics or in other public information that can be traced back to this project.[60]

Based on the above, it is evident that political risk was a known and even an essential aspect of the firms' international investments, and that it played a significant role in the firms' investments outside of Europe. Both Norcem and Dyno used guarantees from the GIEK to insure against political risk, and Dyno even established this as a requirement before commencing with the investment in Singapore.[61] It is possible, however, that Norcem would have commenced with the investments regardless of the insurance. Insurance via the GIEK was thus seen by Norcem as helpful, but not as a necessary strategy to mitigate political risks. The two companies both also highlighted the importance of a close relationship with the elites of the countries in which they invested. In Norcem's case, corruption and

---

58 Interview Heiberg, August 2015.
59 Interview Heiberg, August 2015.
60 Søknad om investeringsgaranti. 1976. (RA, GIEK: Da-L0021).
61 Styremøte 22.12 - Singaporeprosjektet. 1969. (RA, Dyno: 32, 114 styret).

bribery was a risk it had to manage. Corruption is here defined as bribes paid to government officials to gain 'favours'; something which research shows can increase the cost of investing by up to 20%. It can, however, also contribute to securing certain advantages, such as obtaining a monopoly in a given market.[62] This issue was similarly managed by maintaining close relationships with the leadership in the two countries, together with ensuring a high and consistent quality of production and making a social contribution to the countries.[63] In general, it can therefore be said that maintaining a high and consistent quality product and establishing a reputation as a firm that could be trusted was essential for the success of the firms in their investments.

Entry mode

The selection of entry mode and, with it, the selection of ownership structure are essential aspects of risk management in FDIs. Research by Benito on the ownership structures used by Norwegian manufacturing firms found that firms that invested in politically-unstable countries were more likely to select shared ownership.[64] Dyno and Norcem considered sharing the risk with other participants as a risk management strategy in almost all of their investments. A majority of the investments established by the two firms were joint ventures in which the other partner or partners were locals. This contributed to limiting the risks involved by sharing them with the other participants, but also by obtaining local knowledge about the country. Halvorsen from Dyno argued that the preference for joint ventures was intended to limit risk and because of a need to "know our limits".[65] Heiberg from Norcem emphasised the importance of the ability to be flexible in regard to ownership: "We had no clear policy ... we had to be flexible depending on the political situation we found in the nations where we were".[66] The only investment that was wholly owned was the in-

62 *Barassi/Zhou*, Corruption, 302–312.
63 Interview Heiberg, August 2015.
64 *Benito*, Ownership Structures, 157–198.
65 Interview Halvorsen, August 2015.
66 Interview Heiberg, August 2015.

vestment in the UK by Grubernes (Dyno). Grubernes chose to acquire the whole company in England primarily for tax reasons.[67]

The two firms were the majority owners in most of their investments. In two of Dyno's investments, the company had shared ownership equally with one or several other participants, while Norcem was the minority owner in two of its investments. In the investments where the Norwegian firms were the minority owner or where ownership was shared equally, the Norwegian firm contributed know-how and management experience. The exception to this rule was Dyno's first investment in West Germany, where the local partner was responsible for management and sales, while Dyno provided the know-how. Table 1 below shows the ownership structures used in the two firms' investments.

Table 1: Ownership structure of the FDIs

Company	Investment	Year	Ownership	Other participant
Dyno	Germany	1967	Joint venture	German company 50%
Dyno	England	1969	Acquisition	
Dyno	Singapore	1970	Joint venture	Local investors 35%
Dyno	Denmark	1972	Joint venture	Consumers of adhesives 66%
Dyno	Finland	1972	Joint venture	Consumers of adhesives 50%
Norcem	Ghana	1967	Joint venture	Ghanaian State 85%
Norcem	Philippines	1976	Joint venture	Local investor 49%
Norcem	Ras al-Khaimah	1977	Joint venture	Sheikh Saqr bin Mohammed al-Qasimi 60%
Norcem	Liberia	1977	Joint venture	Liberian State 25%

One crucial aspect of how risk is managed within a shared ownership structure is through the selection of the other partner or partners. Dyno and Norcem used this strategy extensively. In Dyno's investments in Denmark and Finland, for example, the other partners in the joint venture were the consumers of the product, and thus some of the risks were mitigated through ensuring sales due before the factory had begun operating. On this strategy, the former manager of Dyno stated, "It reduced our risk and our chances".[68] This strategy is closely connected to the use of net-

67 Cooper, Pegler & Co. Ltd from Ildal, Waaler & co. 1970 (RA, Dyno: Grubernes Sprængstoffabriker A/S. Bilag til styreprotokoller 1969–1970. Nr 3/24: 150.212:114.31.).

68 Interview Halvorsen, August 2015.

works, friendships and trusts as forms of risk-mitigation, as mentioned above.

For Norcem, its partner in joint ventures was often the local government. Norcem used this strategy in several of its investments, with the aim of managing risks. According to James and Vaaler, this can function as an effective risk-management strategy, though this is mainly the case when the local government holds less than 50% of the ownership, and it works best when the local government holds between 21% and 30% of the equity.[69] In Norcem's investments in both Ghana and Ras al-Khaimah, the government was the majority owner with an ownership share of 75% and 60% respectively. Heiberg, the manager of Norcem, found the strategy useful, explaining that, "In Africa, we were partners with the government, I saw this as an advantage because they also had a responsibility in this, so if they broke us down, it would affect them as well".[70] It was only in Norcem's investment in Liberia that the government held the minority share, with 25% ownership.

It is clear that the firms implemented several strategies with the aim of managing the risks involved in their foreign investments, and several of the strategies used are aligned with modern research on risk management in FDIs. As this research has shown, entry mode was one of the most actively used strategies by the two firms, both in their investments in Europe and the rest of the world. An important aspect of this was a focus on the other partner(s) in the joint ventures. Partners were specifically selected because they could contribute to limiting risks, either through having local knowledge, through being a guaranteed purchaser in the future, or through their being local government actors. Consequently, one of the most used and discussed risk strategies was sharing the risk with partners in joint ventures. Besides this, the two most used strategies to mitigate risks were guarantees from the GIEK and maintaining a close relationship with the government and the cooperating partners.

Summary and Conclusions

This paper has shown that risk and risk management was a consideration in both firms' foreign investment activities, even though they invested abroad before the majority of the scientific research on the topic had been

69 *James/Vaaler,* State Ownership.
70 Interview Heiberg, August 2015.

conducted. The two firms also implemented various risk-management and mitigation strategies, such as the selection of an entry mode, the selection of participants in joint ventures, the selection of countries, and the use of guarantees against risks. For instance, the firms chose to avoid risks by deciding not to start or continue with the investment, they took risks in order to pursue opportunities, and they shared risk with other parties.

A majority of the investments made by the two firms in the 1960s and 1970s were successful, both financially and in establishing the firms in the relevant country or region. Several of the subsidiaries that were invested in or established still exist today, under new owners. Two of the investments can be identified as failures, due to the lack of profit and the firms' decision to divest after a few years' involvement, including Dyno's first investment in West Germany in 1966 and Norcem's investment in the Philippines in 1976. Dyno withdrew from its investment in West Germany in 1971, only five years after production had started. The subsidiary struggled financially and Dyno suffered a financial loss.[71] Norcem's investment in the plastic boat factory in the Philippines in 1976 also only lasted for a few years before the company decided to divest.[72]

In general, very few of the risk mitigation strategies that were implemented by the two firms in their FDIs were decided upon following a process whereby components of risk were defined and methodologically addressed. This was particularly the case for the investments that did not succeed. One of the primary issues in all of the failed investments appears to have been a lack of research in general, in particular regarding their competitors. There was a large increase in research carried out by Dyno between its first investment, in West Germany, and its second, in Singapore. If Dyno had carried out further research on the competition in West Germany, it might have been better prepared for the competition it met from German companies.

Some of the risks were assessed, planned for and mitigated in advance, but in several of the investments, the risks were only addressed, and the problems were only solved when they arose. Nevertheless, a majority of the investments by the two firms were successful, and this inspired the firms to continue investing internationally. Risk assessment and risk management contributed to the success of the investments, even though they were established prior to the increase in scientific interest in the field. It is

71 Protokoll fra styremøtet 28.9.1971 i Norsk Sprængstofindustri A/S. 1971. (RA, Dyno: 34. 114 styret).

72 Interview Heiberg, August 2017.

therefore unlikely that increased scientific knowledge on risk and risk management in relation to FDI would have had a significant impact on the way in which a majority of the investments would have been conducted, yet it could have had some more or less negligible implications in the cases of the investments that did not perform as well as expected. Several of the investments could have benefited from further research on the competition, from a higher focus on risk assessment, and from earlier-laid plans as to how to manage the risks involved in the investments. The firms were, however, willing to take the risks involved with their investments because the two firms had identified international expansion as a future aim. Both firms continued to undertake FDIs all around the world and they grew into international organisations with subsidiaries in several different countries before they were themselves acquired by other firms.

Bibliography

Aharoni, Yair/Tihanyi, Laszlo/Connelly, Brian L.: Managerial decision-making in international business: A forty-five-year retrospective, in: Journal of World Business 46 (2), p. 135–142

Anonymous: Norcem vokser internasjonalt, in Aftenposten, 12. Mai. 1978

Amdam, Rolv Petter: The internationalisation process theory and the internationalisation of Norwegian firms, 1945 to 1980, in: Business History 51 (2009), p. 445–461

Aven, Terje: The risk concept — historical and recent development trends, in: Reliability Engineering & System Safety 33 (2012), 3, p. 33–44

Barassi, Marco R./Zhou, Ying: The effect of corruption on FDI: A parametric and non-parametric analysis, in: European Journal of Political Economy 28 (2012), 3, p. 302–312

Benito, Gabriel R.: Ownership structures of Norwegian foreign subsidiaries in manufacturing, in: The International Trade Journal 10 (1996), 2, p. 157–198

Björkman, Ingmar/Forsgren, Mats: Nordic international business research: a review of its development, in: International Studies of Management & Organization 30 (2000), p. 6–25

Brouthers, Keith D./Hennart, Jean-Francois: Boundaries of the firm: Insights from international entry mode research, in: Journal of Management 33 (2007), 3, p. 395–425

Casson, Marc/Da Silva Lopes, Teresa: Foreign direct investment in high-risk environments: an historical perspective, in: Business History 55 (2013), 3, p. 375–404

Cohrssen, John J./Covello, Vincent T.: Risk analysis: a guide to principles and methods for analyzing health and environmental risks. Springfield (VA) 1999

Das, T. K./Teng, Bing-Sheng: Trust, control, and risk in strategic alliances: An integrated framework, in: Organization studies 22 (2001), 2, p. 251–283

Doh, Jonathan P./Lawton, Thomas C./Rajwani, Tazeeb.: Advancing nonmarket strategy research: Institutional perspectives in a changing world, in: The Academy of Management Perspectives 26 (2012), 3, p. 22–39

Eduardsen, Joans S./Marinova, Svetla T.: Decision-makers' risk Perception in the Internationalisation of Small and Medium-Sized Firms, in: International Journal of Export Marketing 1 (2016), 1, p. 4–26

Gartmann, Frithjof: Sement i Norge 100 år. Oslo 1990

Inhaber, H./Norman, S.: The increase in risk interest, in: Risk Analysis 2, (1982), 3, p. 119–120

Jensen, Nathan: Political risk, democratic institutions, and foreign direct investment, in: The Journal of Politics 70 (2008), 4, p. 1040–1052

James, Barclay E/Vaaler, Paul M.: Minority rules: State ownership and foreign direct investment risk mitigation strategy. New York 2013

John, Anna/Lawton, Thomas C.: International political risk management: Perspectives, approaches and emerging agendas, in: International Journal of Management Reviews 20 (2018), 4, p. 847–879

Knight, Frank H.: Risk, Uncertainty and Profit. (1921) New York 2012

Kobrin, Stephen J.: Political risk: A review and reconsideration, in: Journal of International Business Studies 10 (1979), 1, p. 67–80

March, James G./Shapira, Zur: Managerial perspectives on risk and risk taking, in: Management science 33 (1987), 11, p. 1404–1418

Miller, Kent D.: A framework for integrated risk management in international business, in: Journal of international business studies 23 (1992), 2, p. 311–331

Norwegian Official Report: 35. Strukturproblemer og vekstmuligheter i norsk industri, Oslo 1979

Norwegian Official Report: 47. Behovet for internasjonalisering av norsk næringsliv, Oslo 1981

Norwegian Official Report: 54. Om revisjon av valutareguleringen, Oslo 1983

Nytt i Norcem, Norcem's internal magazine, 1-1969 "Norcem eksporterer i år 1,1 million tonn cement"

Nytt i Norcem, Norcem's internal magazine, 2/3-1975. "Fjord's plast etablering på Filippinene et faktum"

Nytt i Norcem, Norcem's internal magazine 3-1976. "Internasjonalisering"

Nytt i Norcem, Norcem's internal magazine 2-1977. "Klinkereksport sikret ved kjøp av cement-mølle"

Renn, Ortein: Three decades of risk research: accomplishments and new challenges, in: Journal of risk research 1 (1998), 1, p. 49–71

Rosa, Eugene A.: Metatheoretical foundations for post-normal risk, in: Journal of risk research, 1 (1998), 1, p. 15–44

Rousseau, Denise M./Sitkin, Sim. B./Burt, Ronald S./Camerer, Colin F.: Not so different after all: A cross-discipline view of trust, in: Academy of management review 23 (1998), 3, p. 393–404

St. prp. Nr. 66 (1964–1965). Om Garanti-Instituttet for Eksportkreditts virksomhet i 1964

Security in a Globalizing World: the Debate on Foreign Capital in West Germany in the 1970s

Christian Marx

Introduction

With the end of the post-war boom, economic crises put an end to high growth figures in Western Europe. The institutional status quo with its system of fixed exchange rates collapsed, while unemployment figures rose and industrial structural change accelerated. The industrial world changed fundamentally as a result of the completion of reconstruction, the end of exchange rate protectionism, and the opening of international commodity, financial, and capital markets. International competition intensified, while at the same time labour-intensive industries were relocated from Europe to other regions of the world, shifting the global economic balance.[1] In particular, foreign direct investment increased rapidly during that period. The number and size of multinational companies reached a new level, heralding the start of the latest globalisation process. In this respect, the 1970s can be seen as a period of accelerated structural change and a worldwide caesura in the history of multinational companies.[2]

These liberalisation processes broke with many familiar routines, challenged the experience of a generation marked by constant economic growth, and, not least, triggered uncertainty about how to respond to such changes. Growing world trade and increasing quotas of foreign direct investments were an expression of an intensifying global economic division of labour, which was perceived as a threat by many contemporaries.[3] Not only the repeatedly escalating East-West conflict and the development of new high-risk technologies such as nuclear power were recognised as threats, but also the loss of jobs due to the deindustrialisation of some West European regions and the appearance of foreign competitors on do-

1 *Chassaigne*, Années; *Doering-Manteuffel/Raphael*, Nach dem Boom; *Plumpe/Steiner*, Mythos.
2 *Chandler/Mazlish*, Introduction, 2; *Dunning/Lundan*, Multinational Enterprises, 189–196, 738–740; *Jones*, Multinationals from the 1930s to the 1980s, 88.
3 *Conze*, Suche, 15-18, 550-552.

mestic markets. The threat scenario and the awareness of security began to expand significantly.[4]

As early as the 1960s, high levels of foreign direct investment by US companies in Western Europe led to widespread defensive reactions.[5] By the 1970s, West German companies ranked among the largest investors abroad and in this respect they had caught up with their Western European competitors. At the same time, the oil price shock of 1973 revealed the vulnerability of Western economies.[6] The oil embargo imposed by the Arab oil-producing countries on the US and the Netherlands, as well as the general production restrictions and price increases imposed by OPEC, destroyed the complex communication and interaction routines of the global oil economy and challenged the sovereignty of Western industrialised countries, while the major oil companies largely succeeded in maintaining their market power.[7]

It was precisely this mixture of industrial structural change, internationalisation, and the shift in the world economy that caused deep uncertainty in Western European societies. At the same time, the increasing importance of oil as both a raw material and an energy resource in Western European countries was obvious.[8] Companies had to find answers to these challenges by converting their production processes and energy base. The political actors were confronted with the task of guaranteeing their country's energy security and implemented, for example, extensive research projects to revitalise coal as a source of energy and to expand nuclear power.[9] In addition to the challenges which faced the industrial sectors affected by structural change, it was the state that ran the risk of losing competence in its traditional terrain – namely the guarantee of national sovereignty.[10] In spite of accelerating globalisation, however, the nation state remained a significant actor in numerous historical dimensions, most importantly with regard to the classic areas of foreign and social policy, in which security functioned as a socio-cultural orientation point.[11]

4 *Conze*, Geschichte, 19; *Raphael*, Gesellschaftsgeschichte; *Wehner*, Versicherung.

5 *Servan-Schreiber*, Défi Américain. See also the contributions of Sabine Pitteloud and Kristin Stanwick Bårnås to this volume.

6 *Conze*, Geschichte, 114-118.

7 *Graf*, Oil; *Glässer*, Marktmacht.

8 *Galambos/Hikino/Zamagni*, Global Chemical Industry; *Stokes*, Technology Transfer.

9 *Marx*, Failed Solutions; *Marx*, Atomzeitalter.

10 *Grande*, Globalisierung; *Habermas*, Jenseits des Nationalstaats?; *Zürn*, Regieren.

11 *Conze*, Kultur.

Furthermore, exploding oil revenues at the hands of Middle Eastern states prompted them to search for new and attractive investment opportunities, with recycled petrodollars, for instance, finding a market in industrialised Western European countries. This is the starting point of the present article, which examines the reactions of West German politicians and entrepreneurs to the increasing investment activities of states from the Middle East in the 1970s, analyses the interactions between politics and economics, and discusses some of the long-term implications of this debate. In the context of security discourse, some actors have called for far-reaching restrictions of property rights, while others have defended the free movement of capital as a central component of a liberal economic order, thus revealing a fundamental tension between freedom and security, which is crucial to the history of security in its various conceptions.[12] The freedom of ownership and the sovereignty of the national economy, which had long gone hand in hand during the twentieth century, came into conflict.[13] Internationalisation and de-territorialisation had consequences which blurred the boundaries between internal and external security.[14]

Against this background, the following section first discusses the nationality of investments in the context of economic liberalism and economic nationalism, before focusing on the German debate on restricting foreign direct investment from Middle Eastern states. The sale of a block of shares of the German automobile manufacturer Daimler-Benz to Iran was the trigger for intensive debate, and one which was deeply embedded in an international context, since the German government expected countermeasures from other governments in the event of legal restrictions.

On the nationality of investments under economic liberalism and economic nationalism

When in 1968 Jean-Jacques Servan-Schreiber warned against the American challenge (*Le Défi américain*), he was less concerned about the organisational or technological superiority of US companies (the so-called "technological gap") than about the conquest of central European industrial structures by US corporations. According to Servan-Schreiber, there was a danger

12 *Conze*, Art. Sicherheit/Schutz.

13 On the importance of foreign direct investment in the Eastern European transformation processes after 1989–90, cf. *Šćepanović*, National Interests; *Ther*, Ordnung, 114–116; and the contribution of Eva Schäffler in this volume.

14 *Conze*, Geschichte, 37–42.

that in the ranking of the world's industrial powers, American companies in Europe would soon take third place below the US itself and the Soviet Union instead of European states themselves. Discussions about the pros and cons of American direct investment in Western Europe were not new, but the fact that the volume of such investment had increased so considerably since the founding of the European Economic Community (EEC) in 1958 placed the issue at the top of the agenda.[15] In some key areas of technological and industrial progress, US companies already took a dominant position in Europe by the mid-1960s. For example, US companies accounted for 80% of production of electronic data processing equipment and 95% of production of integrated circuits. In this context, Gerhard Stoltenberg warned that the expansion of US firms in Europe could be achieved with very little capital expenditure, and this at a time when of the four billion dollars newly invested in 1965, 55% came from bonds on the European capital market, 35% from profits in Europe and subsidies from European countries, and only 10% from direct transfers from the US. "We pay them to buy us."[16]

Servan-Schreiber reached a wide audience with his book. The high level of attention that it received can be explained by a mixture of topicality in daily politics, latent anti-Americanism, and concerns about the power of multinational corporations. In his arguments, he implicitly included the idea of being able readily to determine the nationality of companies, and he based this in particular on the nationality of the owners. Nonetheless, the question of how to determine the nationality of a company has never been an easy one to answer. It is certain, however, that the nationality of companies in cross-border transactions and investments has become relevant and is something that has been assessed differently in different places and at different times – sometimes by the company itself, sometimes by third parties.[17]

---

15 Even before the discussion on foreign direct investment, a securitisation of technology transfers had begun in the 1950s, when West German chemical companies demanded a policy of national protection of private sector know-how, while the federal government placed more emphasis on liberal market relations than on national security interests. Cf. *Daniels*, Brain Drain.

16 "Gerhard Stoltenberg über Servan-Schreiber: ‚Die amerikanische Herausforderung'. Abendlands Untergang (II)?", in: Der Spiegel 11/1968, 11.03.1968, p. 154–157. At that time Stoltenberg was Federal Minister for Research; previously he was *Privatdozent* for Modern History at the University of Kiel and Director of the Department for Economic Policy at Krupp. [Quote: "Wir bezahlen sie dafür, daß sie uns kaufen."]

17 *Gehlen/Marx/Reckendrees*, Ambivalences.

Many observers have argued that national prosperity in the emerging global economy depended on the competitiveness of their domestic companies. The objective of French industrial policy to create competitive "national champions", as proclaimed by Charles de Gaulle in the 1950s, was a very early example of this,[18] with the later debate on Germany as production location (*Standort Deutschland*) in the 1990s being another.[19] Since the 1960s the attempt to increase national wealth has accelerated enormously; "national champions" were selected and promoted by governments to carry their countries' flags into the arena of international competition.[20]

The nationality of a company did not become relevant for the first time in the 1960s (examples can be found in the nineteenth century), but it became noticeably more relevant after the First World War and has remained important ever since.[21] German companies had already built up foreign distribution and production capacities in the nineteenth century and had had to learn what it meant to be classified as an "enemy" company. According to the British Trading with the Enemy Act of 1914, ownership of enemy assets had been put in trust and business activities of German companies were monitored by the Board of Trade. Similarly, in 1917 an Office of Alien Property Custodian was established within the US government that served as a custodian for enemy-owned property in the United States.[22]

When Great Britain and the US were once again at war with the German Reich during the Second World War, these institutions were revived. As a result, German companies twice lost large parts of their foreign ownership and patents in the first half of the century. This hostility towards foreigners in their own society and the spreading atmosphere of suspicion towards enemy foreigners characterised numerous wartime societies.[23] The confiscation of property was not part of the separation of territories due to the war; rather, governments intervened greatly in property rights within their own countries. The freedom to invest abroad suddenly had to be balanced against national interests, which were also used to eliminate or at least weaken unwelcome competitors.[24]

---

18 *Hayward*, State Imperative.

19 *Handschuhmacher*, Privatisierung; *Meteling*, Konkurrenz.

20 *Hayward*, Industrial Enterprise.

21 *Etges*, Wirtschaftsnationalismus.

22 *Caglioti*, Property rights.

23 *Leonhard*, Büchse.

24 During the Second World War, Swiss companies put restrictions of transferability on registered shares to reject undesirable shareholders on the basis of their nation-

After 1945, in times of increasing economic interdependence, national categories played a central role in economic processes. This corresponds to the view that economic nationalism and liberalism might go hand in hand with each other and that the former is not a genuinely anti-liberal concept. Rather, economic nationalism often arises from the congruent interests of companies and nation states and is thus the result of a multitude of individual decisions. While classical protectionist economic nationalism is fundamentally opposed to takeovers from abroad and focuses on the domestic economy, liberal economic nationalism sometimes brings in nationalistic motives to justify cross-border transactions. Contrary to the traditional view, (neo-)liberalism and economic nationalism do not have to be understood as antagonists in the field of political economy, but rather as compatible with each other.[25]

Against the background of the increasing importance of market-liberal concepts in the last third of the twentieth century, it is necessary to assess restrictions on foreign direct investments in the context of economic nationalism. With the surprising liberal turnaround of Germany and the implementation of the so-called "social market economy" after the Second World War – when France, Great Britain, and the US were using stronger forms of market control – economic liberalism henceforward acted as a nationalising mechanism and a regulatory framework for West Germany. The fixation on exports and a stable currency became the two main pillars of West German economic nationalism during the economic miracle. As currency competition increased with the end of the Bretton Woods system, the DM advanced to an international reserve currency under the leadership of the Bundesbank.[26] Against this background West Germany became a net capital exporter. While foreign direct investments into West Germany exceeded those of German companies abroad by about one billion DM in 1974, almost two billion net DM were being exported one year later.[27]

---

ality. This selective protectionism continued after 1945 and was supplemented by self-regulation of the companies in 1961. Cf. *David/Mach*, Corporate Governance, 847–854.

25 *Helleiner*, Economic Nationalism; *Pickel*, Introduction. See also *Berger*, Historians.

26 *Müller*, Nationalist Undercurrents.

27 *Deutsche Bundesbank*, Umschwung; *Deutsche Bundesbank*, Stand; „Industrie. Auslandsinvestitionen: Überall Deutschland", in: Der Spiegel 51/1969, 15.12.1969, p. 54–68; „Unternehmen. Run nach USA", in: Der Spiegel 28/1973, 09.07.1973, p. 78–80; „Ausverkauf der USA", in: Der Spiegel 6/1974, 04.02.1975, p. 69; „Die meisten zieht es in die gleichen Ecken", in: Der Spiegel 46/1975, 10.11.1975, p. 97–108.

Nevertheless, it was precisely at this time that an intensive debate on restrictions on foreign direct investment developed. In principle, the Foreign Trade and Payments Act (FTPA) (*Außenwirtschaftsgesetz*) of 1961 regulated the foreign exchange of goods, services, and capital. The foreign exchange control laws enacted after the Second World War, which provided a ban on foreign trade unless with permission (*Erlaubnisvorbehalt*), had been overtaken by the economic development of the 1950s. Exemptions from the general ban on foreign trade had been successively granted to such an extent that the principle had been reversed and the West German government had therefore to submit a draft for a new law in 1959.[28] After negotiations in several parliamentary committees the FTPA was announced in April 1961.[29]

From this point onwards foreign trade was characterised by the principle of freedom. The FTPA effectively contained – with exception of the import of goods – no specific restrictions. Legal transactions in foreign trade could only be restricted if harmful consequences for the economy or individual branches were to be expected or if the security of West Germany or its foreign interests were endangered. The law repeatedly attracted public attention, particularly due to its export controls which applied to armaments. Concerning capital investments, restrictions on the acquisition of land, companies, or securities could be imposed on non-resident foreigners, but the principle of freedom prevailed, with interventions into private property or against the freedom of contract only made possible in exceptional circumstances.

Even though increasing US direct investment led to public criticism almost immediately after the enactment of the FTPA, this did not change the liberal policy of the West German government in the 1960s. This changed only in conjunction with the slowdown in economic growth, with the introduction of new threats to national resource security (and thus to national sovereignty, most notably in the context of the first oil price crisis), and with the appearance of foreign investors outside the transatlantic alliance bloc.

---

28 „Erster Schriftlicher Bericht des Außenhandelsausschusses (17. Ausschuss) über den von der Bundesregierung eingebrachten Entwurf eines Außenwirtschaftsgesetzes“, in: Bundestagsdrucksache 3/2386, 13.01.1961, 1–23.

29 „Außenwirtschaftsgesetz vom 28. April 1961“, in: Bundesgesetzblatt, Teil I, 1961, No. 29, 05.05.1961, p. 481–495.

Breaking the taboo – Krupp, Daimler-Benz, and the Iran deal

The circle of owners of German companies only internationalised to a limited extent in the 1970s, but a powerful alliance of political and economic agents wanted to restrict the sale of German company shares to foreigners, or at least to limit the exercise of their ownership rights. These initiatives were concentrated upon oil-producing countries, whose capital stock had grown enormously as a result of oil price increases. While the US was seen as an ally in the context of the Cold War, whose increasing investments were generally accepted, a wide range of public actors, including politicians and businessmen, were sceptical about investments from the Middle East. In their view, Arab investors threatened the existence of the domestic economy. This scepticism reflected the prevailing picture of a hierarchical divide between the highly-developed Western European states on the one hand and the emerging countries of the Middle East on the other. It may be argued that the perception of the relationship between Western Europe and the Middle East was shaped more by the powerful desert epic *Lawrence of Arabia* (1962) than by the economic dependencies of both regions.

The sale of a blocking minority of 25.04% of the share capital in late summer 1974 of the largest subsidiary of the Krupp Group, Fried. Krupp Hüttenwerke AG, to the Iranian state via the National Iranian Steel Industries was the first landslide. Although Iran and West Germany were close trading partners, Iranian investment in a long-established German company met with reservations.[30] Through this means, the Krupp Group was able to strengthen its equity base – especially as the sale yielded proceeds which were twice as high as that which German banks considered to be the true value of the Krupp shareholding. The transaction was therefore perceived less as a sell-off of the West German economy and more as a welcome return of oil money. This perception was related to the fact that Krupp was in a weak earnings phase and that it was no longer one of the key companies of technical and industrial progress. On the German side, Berthold Beitz, the long-time chief representative and grey eminence of the Krupp Group, was the central figure in the sales negotiations; Jürgen Ponto, the deputy chairman of the Krupp supervisory board and spokesman of the executive board of Dresdner Bank – who strongly advocated the internationalisation of the German economy and the liberalisation of capital movements (and whom some initially suspected was behind the deal) –

30 *Bösch*, Schah.

had less influence. Neither Beitz nor Ponto feared the influence of the Iranians and the security of the national economy did not seem at risk to them.[31]

As early as January 1974, the Quandt family had offered their participation to Iran, but those negotiations had broken down. A few months later, in November 1974, it was Ponto who arranged the sale of a 14% block of Daimler-Benz shares belonging to the industrialist family Quandt for DM one billion to the Sheikh of Kuwait. In so doing, he broke a taboo for many German politicians and entrepreneurs. After the Quandt-Kuwait-transaction Ponto was confronted with a lot of criticism since it was a mega-deal that was unprecedented in German business history. While some newspapers praised the sale as Ponto's "masterpiece", the former German Minister of Finance Franz Josef Strauß was shocked by the shift in ownership. Above all, the secrecy surrounding the buyer attracted considerable criticism, signalling the highly controversial nature of Middle Eastern investment in Germany. Only Ponto and a few confidants knew the name of the investor, with neither the Board of Management nor the Supervisory Board of Daimler-Benz or the German government being informed of their identity. It was only in December 1974, when Dresdner Bank released a press statement about the investor, that this information came to light.[32]

In contrast to the case of Krupp, where the company itself had been involved in the selection of the investor, the covert sale of the Quandt shareholding triggered great public outrage and an intense debate about sell-offs of the German economy. The German public was shocked to discover that the OPEC countries had accumulated gigantic petrodollar reserves and that their surpluses in a single year were sufficient to take over all listed West German companies. For large parts of German society it was a common practice to work with administrations and companies with exclusively German staff, directors, and shareholders. With the immigration of foreign workers, this picture had altered somewhat, but its firms were still perceived as "German" companies. Owing to the threat of foreign capital,

31 *Ahrens/Bähr*, Ponto, 155–156; „Perser bei Krupp", in: Die Zeit, 26.07.1974. A sale of shares of the Krupp holding was refused in 1974, even though the Iranian government had already been granted a corresponding right of pre-emption at that time. In October 1976, Iran also acquired a 25.01% stake in the holding Fried. Krupp GmbH. Cf. „Perser-Geld bei Krupp: ‚Einiges ändert sich'", in: Der Spiegel 44/1976, 25.10.1976, p. 30–33.

32 *Ahrens/Bähr*, Ponto, 181-182; Gamerdinger an Pöhl, 02.12.1974; Ausführungen von Jürgen Ponto, 03.12.1974, Bundesarchiv Koblenz (BArch) B126/65672.

there was the danger that foreign investors and directors would determine the strategy of such companies in the future and that highly relevant knowledge about advanced technologies would ebb away.[33] Hence, against the backdrop of the economic turbulences of the 1970s, perceptions of insecurity spread beyond the classic dimensions of military and defence policy and the ownership structure of the companies became a security problem that needed to be addressed. In particular it was believed that Daimler-Benz was too much of a star of the German economy to be lost to Middle Eastern sheikhs. Although Kuwait was only interested in a financial investment and did not want to exercise any entrepreneurial influence, the public mood was boiling and soon reached the highest political level.[34]

The political debate on foreign investment and the international dimension of investment restrictions

In the late 1960s, in reaction to increasing direct investments flowing into West Germany, the Ministry of Economic Affairs considered granting a right of pre-emption to the state in the case of sales of shares to foreigners. Since such a pre-emptive right would not have constituted expropriation, such a restriction would have been permissible, but the draft violated the EEC Treaty and was therefore not pursued any further.[35] In the latter half of 1974, when events came thick and fast with the sale of shares in Krupp and Daimler-Benz, the Ministry of Economic Affairs and the Ministry of Finance again discussed the possibility of restricting property rights in order to protect the national economy.

According to contemporary law, the FTPA stipulated that remunerations received by Germans for services to foreigners were subject to reporting requirements. The acquisition of a share itself was not, however, subject to reporting requirements. There were no restrictions on foreign interests in West Germany and the same applied to German interests abroad. Here, the freedom of the FTPA prevailed. Nevertheless, there was scope for the introduction of reporting obligations and also for additional restrictions – either to protect the security of West Germany, to maintain purchasing power, or to secure a balance of payments. As Helga Steeg, Head of Department V (Foreign Economic Policy and Development Aid) at the

33 On the 1950s, cf. *Daniels*, Brain Drain.

34 *Ahrens/Bähr*, Ponto, 182–188; *Conze*, Geschichte, 47–68, 82–101.

35 Vermerk Dr. Walter, 07.06.1967, BArch B102/241651.

Ministry of Economic Affairs, made clear, the protection of foreign relations or monetary reasons hardly justified intervention. According to her, intervention was possible at best by referring to the broad concept of security. Steeg emphasized economic policy arguments and referred to possible counter-reactions abroad which could severely impede the flow of investment in other countries. Here, an aspect of liberal economic nationalism became visible, which relied on maintaining or increasing economic power by promoting the free movement of capital.[36] Furthermore, Steeg pointed to the fact that the majority of foreign direct investment in West Germany originated from other industrialised countries (97% in 1974), and this was rather desirable in the view of the German government. Even taking into account the Daimler-Benz transaction, the share of so-called developing countries (including the Middle East) increased to a maximum of only 6%. With this in mind, the likelihood of a massive intervention into property rights appeared doubtful.[37]

Despite public criticism in the context of the Quandt-Kuwait deal, the German government maintained its positive assessment of intensive international capital integration and the free movement of capital and it recommended that individual cases such as Krupp or Daimler-Benz should not be dramatised.[38] On the one hand, the German government did not believe that national security would be endangered by such individual investments; on the other hand, it could not ignore publicly-articulated security concerns, but it had no ready solution for foreign trade reasons. The high degree of foreign integration of the West German economy was not only evident in the export and investment of German companies abroad, but also in the import dependency of the raw materials sector. For this reason, the German government was wary about any new restrictions.[39] This wariness was based in particular on figures from the German central bank (*Deutsche Bundesbank*), according to which German direct investments abroad and foreign direct investments in West Germany were roughly

36 *Helleiner*, Conclusion.

37 Steeg an Minister, 29.11.1974, BArch B102/241650. As a lawyer and former Deputy German Director at the World Bank in Washington (1965–1967), Steeg was a proven expert in the field of international payment transactions.

38 Martin Grüner (Staatssekretär beim Bundesminister für Wirtschaft) an Karl-Heinz Hansen (SPD), 11.12.1974, BArch B102/241650; Botschaft der BRD in Kuwait an das Auswärtige Amt, 04.01.1975, BArch B102/241652; „Industrie-Familien: Der große Ausverkauf", in: Der Spiegel 4/1975, 20.01.1975, p. 22–32.

39 Stellungnahme zu der Frage des Abgeordneten Matthias Engelsberger (CDU/CSU-Fraktion), 16.12.1974, BArch B102/241650.

equal in mid-1974, and the fact that West Germany was slowly turning into a capital exporter. Furthermore, the government was supported in its liberal economic policy by the Foreign Trade Advisory Council (*Außenwirtschaftsbeirat*), which considered foreign direct investments as an important contribution to the growth of the world economy.[40]

Nevertheless, the German government considered that the requirement for early and full disclosure of sales transactions was justified and therefore examined different models. Three approaches were discussed: 1) an approval requirement (*Genehmigungsvorbehalt*); 2) an obligation to notify in advance (*Vorausmeldepflicht*); and 3) a form of self-regulation of companies (*Selbstbindung*). While the first two proposals were based on the FTPA, the third variant provided for a voluntary regulatory mechanism, which was in line with the tradition of liberal corporatism and would have limited state influence in the economy. The approval requirement was the most comprehensive and effective measure to prevent "undesirable" investments, but it represented the clearest departure from the German policy of free movement of capital and would also have sent an undesired signal in the international arena. The obligation to give notice in advance would have avoided this signal effect, but it was a blunt sword, because infringements did not affect the effectiveness of the investment.[41] With regard to advanced notification, Deutsche Bundesbank also questioned whether sales via third parties, such as a bank in the Daimler-Benz case, would be covered by the planned scheme.[42]

This was followed by a meeting in the Federal Ministry of Economic Affairs on 18 December 1974, which was attended by representatives of the Federal Ministry of Finance, the Federal Ministry of Justice, the Federal Ministry of Defense and the Bundesbank. The participation of the Ministry of Defence in particular points to the fact that the actors detected a security problem here. Simultaneously, a change in security perceptions took place, resulting in security being extended to the field of foreign trade and capital

---

40 Resolution des Außenwirtschaftsbeirates am 10. Dezember 1974, 12.12.1974, BArch B126/65672.

41 Stellungnahme zu der Frage des Abgeordneten Matthias Engelsberger (CDU/CSU-Fraktion), 16.12.1974, BArch B102/241650; Kriterien für die Genehmigung ausländischer Beteiligungen an deutschen Unternehmen, 09.01.1975; Kontrolle der Auslandsinvestitionen in der BRD, 14.01.1975, BArch B102/241651; Bundesminister der Finanzen: Kontrolle der Auslandsinvestitionen in der BRD, 16.01.1975, BArch B102/241652; Albrecht und Gamerdinger an Staatssekretär Pöhl, 10.12.1974; Tietmeyer an Steeg, 11.12.1974, BArch B126/65672.

42 Bürger und Lüke (Deutsche Bundesbank) an Haase (BMWi), 12.12.1974, BArch B102/241650.

transfers. The participants concluded that it would hardly be possible to issue a regulation which could not be circumvented in any way. They therefore agreed to produce various drafts and to wait for the self-restriction agreement to be announced by the German economy, as they preferred such a solution.[43] The political actors warned against an overhasty reaction by the state. In contrast, in January 1975 the Central Bank Council (*Zentralbankrat*) pleaded for the introduction of an approval requirement for foreign direct investments for monetary reasons, but this appeal remained unheard, with the Federal Ministry of Economic Affairs giving preference to a form of voluntary self-restriction.[44]

Both the feared signal effect in the international arena and the simultaneous effects of the oil price shock illustrated the international dimension of the debate. Although globalisation was still in its infancy, the global economic interdependencies became clearly evident and this was not limited to West Germany. The debate on foreign investment and economic securitisation was also held in many other industrialised countries. In view of the growing number of US takeovers, the British Parliament made foreign takeovers a topic of discussion as early as the late 1950s and early 1960s, whereas the political discourse on this subject declined somewhat in Great Britain during the 1970s.[45] In France, the same debate reached its peak at the end of the 1960s.[46]

Although foreign takeovers of British companies did not play a major role in the 1970s, either numerically or as a subject of discussion in the British Parliament, certain foreign investments were nevertheless classified as a threat or undesirable influence. With the Industry Act, enacted on 11 November 1975, the United Kingdom established new criteria – in addition to the exchange control rules which were already in place, which allowed the state to intervene in property rights when a change in control of a major industrial company was imminent and was contrary to the interests of the country. The law was deliberately vague in this respect and ultimately left the responsibility to the discretion of the Minister of Industry, who could prohibit a proposed takeover by a non-resident (prohibition or-

43 Vermerk betr. Erwerb deutscher Unternehmen und Unternehmensbeteiligungen durch Ausländer, 19.12.1974, BArch B126/65672.

44 426. Sitzung des Zentralbankrats der Deutschen Bundesbank, 05.12.1974, Historisches Archiv der Deutschen Bundesbank (HA-BBK) B330/7499/1; 428. Sitzung des Zentralbankrats der Deutschen Bundesbank, 09.01.1975, HA-BBK B330/7884/1.

45 *Callaghan/Hees*, Wirtschaftsnationalismus; *Callaghan/Hees*, Nation.

46 *Servan-Schreiber*, Défi Américain.

der) or exercise a state pre-emption right in favour of the National Enterprise Board (vesting order).[47]

In the United States, the Foreign Investment Study Act of 1974 launched a foreign direct investment investigation in the same direction. In principle, the US – similar to West Germany – adopted a liberal position on international capital movements and treated foreign and domestic investors more or less equally. The only exceptions were in the context of national defence, the preservation of natural resources, or special fiduciary considerations. In the 1970s, however, foreign direct investment into the US also increased and with it came reservations. Security also gained importance as a topic in the United States and was no longer limited to defence; the expansion of the understanding of security and the political discussion about it were international phenomena. In the case of defence companies, defence policy reasons may also have played a role, but the securitisation of companies in the face of takeovers by foreign investors reached far beyond this sphere.[48]

While the US had become the world's largest exporter of capital after the Second World War, it was now increasingly faced with takeovers of domestic companies by foreign investors. As a consequence, similar argumentation patterns developed here: „While foreign investments do not yet constitute a significant percentage of total U.S. investment, the rapid increase has caused some fears that control over certain industries may be passing to foreign investors."[49] Hence, the fear of losing control over the "national" economy was also evident in the US. In the end, the Foreign Investment Study came to the conclusion „that the United States did not maintain an adequate mechanism for monitoring foreign investments". In response to these concerns President Ford created the Committee on Foreign Investment in the United States (CFIUS) in 1975. The CFIUS had no substantial authority to regulate or prohibit foreign investments that raised

47 Deutsche Botschaft London an Auswärtiges Amt, 15.12.1975; Industry Act 1975, BArch B102/273459; Viele Staaten schützen sich vor Überfremdung ihrer Industrie, in: Handelsblatt, 04.02.1975, BArch B126/65673.

48 *Conze*, Geschichte, 47-49.

49 White House: Statement by the President, 28.10.1974; Restrictions on Foreign Direct Investment in the United States, o.D., BArch B102/241650; Memorandum for the President, 23.10.1974, Gerald R. Ford Presidential Library, White House Records Office: Legislation Case Files, Box 11, folder "1974/10/26 S2840 Foreign Investment Study Act of 1974" [quotation].

national security concerns, but only the power to monitor investments and request foreign governments to file preliminary reports.[50]

Even though the US regulatory framework was not appropriated by West Germany, restrictions abroad formed an important reference point for West German decision-makers. A synopsis prepared by the Federal Ministry of Economic Affairs showed the full scope of possible measures, ranging from complete freedom of capital movement to reporting requirements and exchange controls. While France and Italy, with their interventionist industrial policies, had numerous options for intervention, US companies could be encouraged to behave in line with the state with the threat of the withdrawal of government and arms contracts. The comparison showed that there were no regulations to keep certain foreign investors out. It was precisely this lack of regulation with regard to Middle Eastern investments that was a driving force behind German efforts to control capital movements. Foreign regulations protected the domestic capital market and shareholders or prevented monopolies. In contrast, the Federal Ministry of Economic Affairs had no information about forms of self-regulation by companies.[51]

An international comparison showed that foreign countries had better instruments than West Germany to prevent the undesirable foreign ownership of corporations. Corporate law options would not be an effective substitute for public law provisions. The degree of liberalisation of the German capital market was unrivalled in the Western world, with exception of Luxembourg and Switzerland. The scale ranged from the impossibility of any participation in certain branches of industry (US, Japan), to the impossibility of participation beyond a certain quota (France, Italy, US, Japan), to approval and reporting requirements in many countries. In most cases, these defensive measures were anchored in foreign exchange laws and regulations concerning the right of establishment and investment. Often there was a wide gulf between legal regulations and investment realities. In

50 Travalini, Foreign Direct Investment [quotation p. 783]. See also „Auch in den USA wächst die Furcht vor Überfremdung“, in: General-Anzeiger, 10.04.1975, BArch B126/65673.
The situation in the US was confusing due to numerous federal and state regulations and various institutions (the Pentagon, the Anti-Trust Authority, etc.). According to the Securities Exchange Act, every participation of more than 5% of domestic and foreigners in a public company had to be reported. Cf. Abwehrmöglichkeiten gegen eine Überfremdung von Kapitalgesellschaften im Ausland und in der BRD, 30.01.1975, BArch B102/241652.

51 Synopse über die Regelung zur Kontrolle von ausländischen Beteiligungen an inländischen Gesellschaften, 28.01.1975, BArch B102/241652.

France, for example, major shareholdings in armaments, heavy and electronics industries were completely closed to foreigners. At the same time, the French government also considered intensifying regulations to protect against foreign infiltration.[52]

Within the OECD Committee on International Investment and Multinational Enterprises, West Germany, the US, Switzerland, and Japan regarded the massive influx of petrodollars from the Middle East as a problem, while a second group (including Great Britain, Canada, France, Italy, Austria, Sweden, Finland, Norway, Denmark, Portugal, the Netherlands, and Belgium) classified such investments as relatively unproblematic – not least because some of these countries already had stricter regulations in place. Nevertheless, Japan wanted to maintain its friendly relations with oil-producing countries because of its dependence on foreign oil imports, and the US and Switzerland did not want to deviate from their liberal positions either. Here, to a certain extent, security aspects had to be balanced against each other (i.e. security of supply versus security from foreign investors). There was general agreement that new measures should not create restrictions between OECD countries and that open discrimination against oil countries should be avoided as well. The rejection of major investments from the Middle East was thus by no means limited to Germany. In the context of the Cold War and in view of their existing dependence on raw materials, however, Western states did not want to open up an insurmountable front against oil-producing states.[53]

The ministerial drafting of restriction options

The first oil price crisis and the subsequent global economic crisis made entrepreneurs, politicians and the public aware of the interdependencies of the global economy. Not only did industrialised countries such as West Germany compete with other industrialised countries for raw materials, but the relationship with many emerging and developing countries supplying raw materials also became increasingly conflicted against the background of economic turbulence and the growing self-confidence of former colonial areas.[54] When the heads of state of the six most important indus-

52 Abwehrmöglichkeiten gegen eine Überfremdung von Kapitalgesellschaften im Ausland und in der BRD, 30.01.1975, BArch B102/241652. See also Reich, Roads.

53 Vermerk betr. OECD-Ausschuss, 05.03.1975, BArch B102/273459.

54 On the security of supply of West Germany of important import-dependent metal raw materials in the 1970s, see Ole Sparenberg's contribution in this volume.

trial nations met for the first time in Rambouillet on 15 November 1975 to discuss economic issues, the agenda included not only the functional principles of global interdependence but also possible mechanisms for international economic cooperation. From then on, high unemployment, persistent inflation, and serious energy problems were to be overcome together. The first meeting of the leading economic nations did not mean to turn away from world trade and the global division of labour, but it was rather to commit to them.[55]

This also reflected the position of large parts of the West German business community, and it was also true with regard to capital movements one year before; in this respect, a general prevention or restriction of all incoming foreign direct investments was no longer an issue by the end of 1974. This is quite remarkable, because at the same time the oil crisis once again showed its full political impact, as it was impressively demonstrated by the decision of the German Bundestag on 5 December 1974 to transfer a five-year "carte blanche" to the government to take countermeasures in the event of a new energy crisis.[56]

In contrast to a general prevention strategy, a voluntary self-control of the economy or a state requirement for approval was still discussed within the Federal Ministry of Economic Affairs. The Krupp and Daimler-Benz deals had attracted too much public attention for the issue of security from foreign investors to be ignored. As a result, at the beginning of January 1975, the Federal Ministry of Economic Affairs developed new criteria for classifying foreign investments – by country (Arab countries, developing countries, OECD countries, EEC countries), by factual criteria (size of capital investment, security risks, sectors, direct or portfolio investment), or a combination of both. It determined that investments from the EEC or OECD countries should not be subject to any approval requirement and that they ought to conform to both the EEC Treaty and the OECD Code of Liberalisation. These countries were not considered as dangerous. In the case of Arab and developing countries, it was planned to suspend an approval requirement if cooperation agreements existed – for example, in the case of existing investment agreements with Iran, Egypt, Morocco, Tunisia, Jordan, Yemen or Sudan, with similar agreements offered to Saudi Arabia

55 *James*, Rambouillet.

56 „Bericht und Antrag des Ausschusses für Wirtschaft (9. Ausschuss) zu dem von der Bundesregierung eingebrachten Entwurf eines Gesetzes zur Sicherung der Energieversorgung bei Gefährdung oder Störung der Einfuhren von Erdöl, Erdölerzeugnissen oder Erdgas (Energiesicherungsgesetz 1975)", in: Bundestagsdrucksache 7/2898, 04.12.74.

and Lebanon. The Ministry of Economic Affairs was aware of the difficulty of discrimination against certain countries, and it was hardly comprehensible why some countries represented a danger from which German companies had to be protected, while others did not. From the point of view of foreign trade and with regard to raw materials and energy supply policy, such differentiation was considered extremely problematic. Nor did factual criteria offer a magic bullet. A distinction between direct and portfolio investments was doubted even by experts. Only in the case of restrictions that directly affected the security of West Germany, such as in the armaments or nuclear energy sectors, did restrictions seem fully feasible.[57] Beyond that narrowly-defined field, the questions as to what security against the sell-off of the German economy meant and with what measures this could be achieved remained open.[58]

Moreover, the Federal Ministry of Economic Affairs considered two other aspects: Firstly, the ministry pointed out the interactions between capital movements and foreign trade. Foreign investment could certainly include production, and especially the growing volume of direct investments in the 1970s pointed to the growing importance of productive investment, but often they served as bridgeheads for trade. Against the background of Germany's export orientation, politicians and entrepreneurs therefore voted in favour of maintaining a liberal position on capital movements. Secondly, a structural change in the relationship between industrialised, newly industrialising, and developing countries became apparent – and was unstoppable by West Germany; trade in goods therefore changed into multilateral collaborations with reciprocal investments. Especially from the

57 Aufzeichnung betr. Kriterien für Genehmigung ausländischer Beteiligungen an deutschen Unternehmen, 09.01.1975, BArch B102/241651.

58 For security policy reasons, participations in all "secrecy-protected" (*geheimschutzbetreut*) companies, energy supply companies, banks and insurance companies, intelligence and transport companies were to be avoided; for technological reasons, foreign participations in companies supported by state funds was rejected; the draft also rejected foreign participations in major banks (Deutsche Bank, Dresdner Bank, Commerzbank), shipyards (Howaldt, Blohm & Voß) as well as in the automotive (Mercedes, VW, BMW), steel (Krupp, Thyssen, Mannesmann), and chemical industry (BASF, Bayer, Hoechst), in engineering (GHH) and electrical companies (Siemens, AEG-Telefunken). Cf. Vermerk betr. Kontrolle von Auslandsinvestitionen. Konkretisierung der neuralgischen Industriebereiche, 17.01.1975, BArch B102/241652.

perspective of Germany's import dependence in the raw materials sector, it was an argument against new restrictions on capital movements.[59]

As a consequence, the negotiating partners themselves increasingly came to the fore. The threat of a legal regulation compelled the President of the German Banking Association, Alwin Münchmeyer, to inform the Federal Ministry of Economic Affairs Hans Friderichs in mid-December 1974 that the Banking Association preferred a voluntary solution and that it wanted to draft a code of conduct with the industry by January 1975. According to this code of conduct, restrictions upon foreign shareholdings should only be implemented after a careful consideration of the macroeconomic arguments.[60]

Ponto proposed concrete measures in this regard to Hans Friderichs on 19 December 1974. The German banks wanted to commit themselves to notify German companies and state agencies if a certain percentage of their capital was bought or ordered by a foreign investor, and to make agreements with foreign banks for this purpose. The Ministry of Economic Affairs supported such a solution in view of the disadvantages of state regulation, but there were still concerns, largely because companies were not subject to any obligation in this respect. Conversely, Ponto made it clear that companies should be free to draw any conclusions from the banks' communications. The draft only envisaged a kind of standstill obligation (*Stillhalteverpflichtung*) on the part of companies. Here Ponto's fundamental liberal position became apparent once again. At the same time, the ministry elaborated plans for investment agreements with the oil-producing countries. The German government had already held talks on this with Saudi Arabia and Iran; other potential investors were Kuwait and the United Arab Emirates.[61]

Finally, a solution under company law was discussed in which voting rights and shareholding were to be separated. Under the German Stock Corporation Act (*Aktiengesetz*) of 1965, for example, the introduction of multiple voting rights for German nationals was possible in order to safe-

---

59 Vermerk betr. Kontrolle der Auslandsinvestitionen in der Bundesrepublik Deutschland, 14.01.1975, BArch B102/241651.

60 Steeg an Minister, 16.12.1974, BArch B102/241650.

61 Vermerk betr. Kontrolle der Auslandsinvestitionen in der Bundesrepublik Deutschland, 14.01.1975, BArch B102/241651. In June 1975 Saudi Arabia confirmed its willingness to pursue a stable and long-term investment policy in Germany. Cf. Apel an Friderichs, 18.06.1975; Schmidt an Friderichs, 19.06.1975; Sohl an Friderichs, 30.06.1975, BArch B102/273459; Friderichs an Schmidt, 05.06.1975, BArch B126/65673.

guard macroeconomic interests. The Volkswagenwerk Act of 1960 even went beyond this provision. However, a fundamental splitting of share ownership into shares with preferential voting rights and voting disadvantages would have required an amendment to the German Corporation Act – and would also have necessitated parallel measures for other forms of company. Moreover, unequal treatment of nationals and foreigners was difficult to reconcile with international agreements. A restriction of voting rights up to a certain percentage of shareholding was also possible. The Ministry of Economic Affairs appreciated this idea because this regulation aimed at the core of the problem and offered the fewest opportunities for circumvention, yet at the same time making it more difficult for companies to raise capital.[62]

Table 1: Possible forms of control in capital movements

FTPA	Commitment of the parties	Other possibilities
Reporting obligations (*Meldepflichten*) Approval requirement (*Genehmigungsvorbehalt*)	Self-commitment of the German economy Investment agreements with producing countries	Company law (*Gesellschaftsrecht*) Antitrust law (*Kartellrecht*) Public pre-emption

Table 1 presents the various possibilities for restricting capital movements, which were discussed in Bonn in early 1975. There were also concerns about foreign investors before the 1970s, however – and as a result of contemporary experience of crises in West Germany – this situation developed into a concrete security problem that could not be ignored by political actors any longer. Here the expansion of the concept of security became obvious.[63] On the one hand, the external threat from unwelcome investors had to be fended off; on the other hand, German entrepreneurs and politicians recognised the vulnerability in the energy and raw materials sector and did not want to endanger the supply of vital resources. The state remained an important point of reference in this respect, but voluntary self-restrictions transferred a large part of the security responsibility to private companies. For reasons of foreign trade and regulatory policy, the ministry had little interest in state regulation in the context of the FTPA and

62 Vermerk betr. Kontrolle der Auslandsinvestitionen in der Bundesrepublik Deutschland, 14.01.1975, BArch B102/241651.

63 *Conze*, Geschichte, 47–49.

favoured voluntary control of the parties, something which was also in line with the suggestions of the German business community.[64]

Diverging ideas within the German economy

In January 1975, the Association of the German Industry (*Bundesverband der Deutschen Industrie*, BDI) and the Association of German Banks (*Bundesverband Deutscher Banken*, BDB) recommended that banks and companies inform each other as well as the German government about foreign investment intentions. The security of the national economy should not be endangered from outside. As Sohl (BDI) and Münchmeyer (BDB) pointed out, however, such recommendations should not jeopardise the importance of the free movement of capital, undermine the inalienable principle of private property, or hinder the positive effects of influxes of foreign capital in preserving jobs and broadening the financial base of German enterprises.[65] On 29 January a further meeting with several representatives of the industry was held at the Ministry of Economic Affairs, in which the voluntary protective measures envisaged by industry and the possibilities for state intervention were discussed.[66]

Although the West German economy had agreed on a joint declaration in line with the corporate market economy, fractures within the group of entrepreneurs soon became apparent. In particular Deutsche Bank was heavily critical of the sale of the Quandt package. Franz-Heinrich Ulrich (Deutsche Bank) feared that the Flick family could also sell its 37.9% Daimler-Benz shareholding to the Iranian Shah Mohammad Reza Pahlavi, giving the Middle East a capital majority of 53% of the German carmaker. Since the Flick Group was prepared to sell its entire Daimler-Benz package to Iran, Ulrich became alarmed and informed the German government in January 1975. Deutsche Bank wanted to counteract this form of recycling of petrodollars. Thereupon Ulrich played the national card, convincing Flick to sell only a 29% package, and bought that block of shares in the name of Deutsche Bank for almost two billion DM – earning the praise of both Finance Minister Hans Apel and Chancellor Helmut Schmidt. The

64 Steeg an Minister, 14.01.1975, BArch B102/241651.

65 BDI/BDB an Helmut Schmidt, 22.01.1975, BArch B102/241652 u. BArch B126/65672.

66 Sohl an BDI, 11.02.1975, BArch B102/241652; Aufzeichnung über das Gespräch zwischen Bundesminister Dr. Friderichs und dem Beratungsgremium am 29.1.1975, 30.01.1975, BArch B126/65672.

media and the public unanimously welcomed the deal. Furthermore, Ulrich pleaded for a limitation of voting rights in order to prevent foreign shareholders from exerting too much influence on West German industrial companies. Deutsche Bank consistently claimed to be the protector of the German economy.[67]

A voluntary self-restriction of voting rights was in the interest of the political decision-makers, since it did not affect the liberal position of the government on capital movements. There were several ways of doing this: the first option involved a restriction of voting rights which remained in line with the government's objective of democratising share ownership; the second involved the possibility of placing reserve shares in the hands of the management, which could be distributed if necessary; while the third involved issuing shares with multiple voting rights, but this was in contradiction to the principle of equality of shareholders. As a consequence, a restriction of voting rights turned out to be the ideal way to limit undesirable capital investments.[68]

Several industrial groups for which Deutsche Bank acted as the principal bank (*Hausbank*) – such as Mannesmann and BASF – followed Ulrich's plan, whereas Ponto (Dresdner Bank) considered the idea of a voting right restrictions to be inappropriate. Although a foreign capital majority in Daimler-Benz was not desirable for Ponto either, he defended the deal and referred repeatedly to the importance of the free movement of capital. In February 1975, in a programmatic article entitled "No fear of foreign capital", he explained the dependence of the export-oriented West German economy on open markets and the free movement of capital. In fact, in the following years Kuwait was not interested in controlling central corporate

67 *Ahrens/Bähr*, Ponto, 188–190; „Industrie-Familien: Der große Ausverkauf", in: Der Spiegel 4/1975, 20.01.1975, p. 22–32; Bundeskartellamt an Deutsche Bank betr. Anteilserwerb an der Daimler-Benz AG, 14.01.1975; Martin Grüner (BMWi) an Hermann Höcherl (MdB), 28.01.1975, BArch B102/241652; „Deutsche Bank erwirbt Daimler-Paket", in: FAZ, 15.01.1975; Kurzprotokoll der 94. Kabinettsitzung der Bundesregierung, 15.01.1975, BArch B126/65672.
The possible restrictions under company law for limiting foreign influence (registered shares, shares of a special kind, shares with multiple voting rights, shares with maximum voting rights) were discussed in detail within the Ministry of Economic Affairs. Cf. Gesellschaftsrechtliche Möglichkeiten, 21.01.1975, BArch B102/241652.

68 Vermerk von Stoller betr. Stimmrechtsbegrenzung, 07.03.1975, BArch B102/273459.

decisions at Daimler-Benz, but treated its involvement as a portfolio investment.[69]

During that discussion, the news suddenly broke that Iran intended to acquire a 25.02% share in Babcock & Wilcox AG in Oberhausen in the spring of 1975, equating to approximately 178 million DM or 75 million US dollars. The seller of this deal was the British parent company Babcock & Wilcox Ltd. The German Babcock Group mainly produced machinery and steam boiler plants. In return for the takeover of shares, the Iranian state placed the largest order in the 78-year history of the company. The London Group managers had previously tried to sell their shares to German banks and industrial companies or to the second major shareholder, Berliner Handels-Gesellschaft–Frankfurter Bank, but without success. Unlike the Daimler-Benz deal, however, this transaction attracted far less public attention. One reason for this was that the Oberhausen-based company was less well-known; another was that in the case of the seller it was a British group – and not a German industrialist family. Neither politicians nor the Federal Cartel Office (*Bundeskartellamt*) prevented the sale, as it was not assumed that it – even in combination with the Krupp shareholding – would lead to a dominant position for Iran on the market.[70] The German government still held a positive view of international capital movements and also took this position *vis-à-vis* Iran, whose oil revenues rose less than expected anyway. Against the background of growing foreign direct investments by German companies, the flow of capital could not be a one-way street. In addition, the German government concluded an agreement with the Iranian government according to which consultations had to take place before Iranian investments in West Germany became reality in order to prevent emotional public reactions.[71]

Nevertheless, the demand for a restriction of voting rights remained. In the summer of 1975, for example, BASF introduced a limit on voting rights at a nominal DM 50 million. At its Annual Stockholders' Meeting in June 1975, the Bayer Board of Management also advocated the introduction of a maximum voting right in order to ward off hostile foreign takeovers. Although the German Association for the Protection of Share-

69 *Ahrens/Bähr*, Ponto, 191-192.

70 Telegramm Bundeskartellamt an Bundeswirtschaftsministerium, 23.07.1975, BArch B102/273459; „Industrie. Paket-Diplomaten", in: Der Spiegel 16/1975, 14.04.1975, p. 94; US Department of Commerce, Foreign Direct Investment in the United States. Volume 5: Appendices G-I, April 1976, p. G315–G316.

71 Vermerk betr. Iranische Kapitalbeteiligung in der BRD, 13.10.1975, BArch B102/273459.

holdings (*Deutsche Schutzvereinigung für Wertpapierbesitz*) opposed the proposal, the majority of those at the meeting voted in favour of it. The German economy was thus divided into two groups on this issue.[72] The Bayer Board of Management welcomed the idea of restricting voting rights, not least because it was supported by the government, namely the German Chancellor, the Finance Minister, and the Minister of Economic Affairs.[73] On the opposite side, Ponto referred to property rights as a cornerstone of the German market economy and he did not want to discourage foreign investors.[74]

Voluntary self-restriction was opportune for the German government, since this solution did not require a new legal framework, but politicians nevertheless wanted to be prepared in case it did not function as intended. Against this background, the federal ministries, under the leadership of the Federal Ministry of Economic Affairs, agreed in the summer of 1975 to draft a law to amend the FTPA, which could be enacted at short notice. According to this draft, the acquisition of shareholdings in German companies could be prohibited or restricted in order to ward off damaging effects to the economy as a whole – in terms of the security of the state, research and technology, or economic infrastructure. If the companies did

72 „HV-Barriere soll die Ölgelder bremsen", in: Handelsblatt, 31.01.1975; „Barriere gegen Überfremdung", in: Rheinischer Merkur, 30.05.1975, BArch B126/65673; Bayer Vorstandssitzung, 04.03.1975 u. 06.05.1975, Bayer AG: Corporate History & Archives, Leverkusen (BAL) 387-1-15; BASF Vorstandssitzung, 14.01.1975 u. 11.02.1975; Einführung des Höchststimmrechts, 05.02.1975, Anlage 1 zu 5/75; BASF Vorstandssitzung, 08.04.1975; Einführung eines Höchststimmrechts, 08.04.1975, Anlage 1 zu 10/75, BASF Unternehmensarchiv (UA); Ausführungen von Overbeck, 26.03.1975, Historisches Archiv Commerzbank AG (HAC) 500/7902-2002 Band 1; BASF an ihre Aktionäre, 09.05.1975; Dresdner Bank an Depotkunden mit BASF-Aktien, 23.05.1975; Deutsche Bank an Depotkunden mit BASF-Aktien, 12.06.1975; Gedanken zum Thema Stimmrechtsbeschränkung, HAC 500/7902-2002 Band 2; „Die Perser kommen. Öl-Geld in der deutschen Industrie", in: Der Spiegel 30/1974, 22.07.1974; „Anonymer Verkehr", in: Der Spiegel 6/1975, 03.02.1975, p. 64–66; „Stimmrechtsbeschränkung: Zwei Lager", in: Der Spiegel 7/1975, 10.02.1975, p. 72; „Völlig ungewöhnlich", in: Der Spiegel 13/1975, p. 79–80; Reinert, Bayer, 213; Roth, Höchststimmrecht.

73 Bayer Vorstandssitzung, 21.01.1975, BAL 387-1-15.

74 *Ahrens/Bähr*, Ponto, 191–192; Ponto an Sohl, 19.12.1974, BArch B126/65672; Ausführungen von Ponto, 16.06.1975, HAC 500/7902-2002 Band 2.

not succeed in solving the security problem through voluntary self-restriction, the state should intervene.[75]

Throughout 1975, the issue of Middle Eastern investments in German companies remained on the political agenda. However, Ponto proved to be capable of adapting. When the German electrical engineering group AEG-Telefunken slipped deeper and deeper into crisis in the mid-1970s and was faced with a mountain of short-term debt, it soon became clear that a lasting recovery could only be achieved by selling loss-making subsidiaries. In the end, the executive and the supervisory board agreed to withdraw from power plant construction, which was concentrated in a joint subsidiary of AEG and Siemens (Kraftwerk Union, KWU). As a consequence, Siemens was the main potential buyer, but the company was not willing to accept the conditions imposed by AEG and the banks, which included taking over inherited liabilities. At the same time, the sale of the KWU shareholding had a political dimension since KWU was the only German manufacturer of nuclear power plants and thus had a prominent position in terms of the national security of supply. In contrast to the Daimler-Benz deal, Ponto – at the same time chairman of the AEG supervisory board – informed Chancellor Schmidt during the negotiations about the reticence of the Siemens group as well as about a potential foreign buyer. In addition to the US electrical company General Electric and the French conglomerate Saint-Gobain, the Shah of Persia appeared on the scene as a potential buyer.[76] While there was increased public debate about the risks of nuclear technology at that time, the German government saw the danger of losing touch with international developments in the nuclear sector.[77] In this situation, at the beginning of 1975, Chancellor Schmidt spoke out explicitly against the takeover of the KWU by Arab investors and threatened to impose legislative measures.[78]

In addition, the official agreement with other main suppliers of nuclear materials recommended taking special precautions when exporting sensi-

---

75 Haase (BMWi) an Gamerdinger (BMF), 25.06.1975; Entwurf zur Änderung des AWG, 20.06.1975; Vermerk des BMF zum Entwurf eines Gesetzes zur Abwehr unerwünschter Auslandsinvestitionen, 25.07.1975, BArch B126/65673.

76 *Ahrens/Bähr*, Ponto, 169–174; „Unternehmen. Wacher Verstand" in: Der Spiegel 50/1975, 08.12.1975, p. 85–86.

77 On the risk perception in the nuclear power industry, see the contribution of Sascha Brünig in this volume.

78 ARD-Sendung „Im Brennpunkt: Mekka für Ölmilliarden. Bericht über die Investitionen der arabischen Ölstaaten in der westlichen Welt", 15.01.1975, BArch B126/65672.

tive nuclear facilities and transferring technology and opposed a deal with Iran. Furthermore, the Ministry of Education and Research referred to the promotion of nuclear power technology by the public sector and feared problems with Brazil, which had ordered several plants from KWU. While Schmidt pressed for a German solution, the Minister of Economic Affairs Friderichs, who travelled to Tehran with Ponto in July 1975, could imagine Iranian participation in the KWU, even if he preferred German involvement as well. There thus existed divergent positions within the government. Ultimately, AEG, which was under financial pressure, offered Siemens the entire KWU package in 1976, leaving aside the inherited liabilities, and sold the stake for DM 618 million in November 1976. Hence, in contrast to Krupp and Daimler-Benz, a national solution finally prevailed in the case of KWU – and the German government appeared to be quite satisfied.[79]

In a question-and-answer session of the German Bundestag in late 1976, the government again made clear that it was in favour of a liberal foreign trade policy that included the free movement of capital. According to the government, this was a prerequisite for an increased international division of labour, technological progress, and economic growth. Against the background of increasing West German foreign direct investment abroad, it rejected legal restrictions on foreign investors and was extremely satisfied with the voluntary commitment of the German economy.[80]

Conclusion and outlook

The sale of the Krupp and Daimler-Benz shareholdings, combined with the first oil price crisis and the feeling of a loss of sovereignty, led to a public outcry and warnings against a sell-off of the German economy. While a whole range of security measures were discussed in the political arena at the end of 1974, entrepreneurs called for voluntary self-regulation to cope with security problems – far away from laws and legal directives. In January 1975, it was obvious that the majority of politicians and businessmen involved favoured voluntary self-restriction. This was due to the international integration of West Germany and the corresponding internationali-

79 *Abelshauser/Kopper*, Ordnungspolitik, 75–76; *Ahrens/Bähr*, Ponto, 174–176; Würzen (Abteilung IV) an Minister, 03.12.1975; Schmidt an Friderichs, 21.01.1976, BArch 102/273459.

80 Grüner (BMWi) an Dollinger (MdB), 19.11.1976, BArch 102/273459.

sation of German companies. The West German government did not want to violate the economically-liberal OECD guidelines or provoke restrictive countermeasures by other states.[81] This demonstrated the vulnerability of the German economy in the energy and raw materials sectors. Voluntary self-restriction thus offered a solution that was in line with the tradition of German corporatism and made the economy more resilient by circumventing countermeasures.[82]

Moreover, the efforts to restrict foreign investments were directed one-sidedly against oil-producing countries from the Middle East. Although there had been an intense debate about the expansion of US multinationals in Western Europe in the 1960s, German politicians and entrepreneurs agreed that foreign direct investments from Western countries were welcome. While the sale of the Babcock and KWU shareholdings fuelled the debate about foreign investors – particularly because of the special security interests in the case of KWU – the principal guideline of the German government was clear: it did not want to accept every investor, but neither did it want to intervene legally. The sales of shares by certain actors from the Middle East was to be securitised, since the industrialised countries were already dependent upon their oil reserves and those states were not among the Western allies in the context of the Cold War. The Federal Ministry of Economic Affairs and the Federal Ministry of Finance therefore drafted a law which might be enacted at short notice if necessary. In this way, the government was able to maintain its official liberal position in foreign trade and to protect the domestic economy. The commitment to the freedom of world trade and capital movements, in combination with the protection from foreign investors, cannot be described as a form of classic protectionist economic nationalism; rather, it is a perfect example of how economic nationalism and liberalism could go hand in hand.[83]

Not all entrepreneurs followed this policy. While Franz-Heinrich Ulrich and Deutsche Bank took the position of protecting German economic interests – especially in the case of Daimler-Benz – Jürgen Ponto and Dresdner Bank held a much more liberal position, assuming that German companies would benefit far more from the free movement of capital in both directions than from restrictions imposed by the private sector or even the state. In his view, the German economy needed foreign capital, so there

81 Similar arguments for market openness with reference to possible protectionist countermeasures by other countries were emphasized by Callaghan/Hees for Great Britain. See *Callaghan/Hees*, Nation, 290–293.

82 *Conze*, Geschichte, 114–118.

83 *Helleiner/Pickel*, Economic Nationalism.

was no security against foreign direct investment, only with it. Ponto described the fear of foreign infiltration in 1975 as a passing mirage that would soon dissipate.[84] The discussion about Middle Eastern investments in the event slowed down significantly from 1976 onwards. This was due to the fact that the real price of oil fell and the revenues of the oil-producing countries provoked fewer concerns.[85]

During the second oil price crisis in 1979–80, security-based arguments gained importance once again, especially once Kuwait's entry into the German chemical company Hoechst became a reality in 1982. The involvement of Arab states in German companies remained suspect to many entrepreneurs and politicians. In the minds of most Germans, Daimler-Benz, Krupp or BASF were German companies and their future ought to be restricted in order to guarantee the security of the German economy as a whole. Despite increasing global economic interdependence, economic nationalism still had a high impact at the beginning of the 1980s. A 1981 study of the sociological stratification of Bayer stockholders explicitly examined the acquisition of shares by OPEC countries. Qatar, Kuwait, Bahrain, Dubai, and Oman held 660,000 Bayer shares at that time, and Deutsche Bank held a further 1,500,000 shares on behalf of OPEC countries. Furthermore, Bayer management suspected that some of the newly-acquired shares in the United Kingdom, France, and Switzerland were held by OPEC countries. This internal company analysis shows that the concept of security – which was expanded to foreign trade in the wake of the oil price and energy crises of the 1970s – was still valid in the early 1980s, and that the sale of shares to foreign investors from the Middle East was still perceived as a problem that needed to be securitised. In spite of this, Bayer's top management showed a relaxed attitude, as none of the shareholders came close to the maximum voting rights of five percent of the share capital.[86]

While BASF limited the voting rights of its shareholders more closely than Bayer to a maximum of three percent of the share capital, Hoechst followed the policy of its main bank, Dresdner Bank, and waived a voting right restriction. The three West German chemical groups thus took different positions with respect to the potential danger of undesired foreign influence in the early 1980s. Speculation in the West German press at the

84 „Fata Morgana", in: Die Zeit Nr. 18, 25.04.1975, p. 26.

85 *Göbel*, Ölpreiskrisen, 31–39.

86 Weitkemper an Bayer-Vorstand, 29.12.1981, BAL 380-7-63; „Ölpotentaten mit dem Fuß in der Tür der Großchemie", in: Frankfurter Neue Presse, 02.12.1981, Hoechst-Archiv (HA), Hoe 33 C/2/1/c.

end of 1981 about a possible entry of Qatar into BASF and Kuwait into Hoechst therefore took place under different conditions.[87] Indeed, in the autumn of 1982, it became public knowledge that Kuwait held a 24.9% stake in the share capital of Hoechst, for which it had to raise around DM 1.4 billion.[88] Nevertheless, among the Western European chemical companies, Hoechst, with its major shareholder Kuwait, was an exception. Although the proportion of foreign shareholders increased from the 1970s onwards, this was mainly due to higher ownership shares from Western European, American, and Japanese investors.

Until the 1990s, it was hardly possible to take over a major German company against the will of the German banks. When the major German banks withdrew from financing industrial companies and consequently gave up some of their supervisory board mandates, the German corporate network dissolved and the protection against (hostile and foreign) takeovers ended. Ultimately, in 2010 the mutual interdependence of companies was only about one-fifth of the level of 1976.[89] Moreover, foreign capital had far more positive connotations in the 1990s than in the 1970s. Many German companies sought their way into foreign stock exchanges, and as a result, the share of foreign shareholders in German companies increased significantly. Once again, the threat scenario and the perception of security had changed.

Germany was transformed into an attractive financial market in the 1990s. Conversely, these steps towards liberalisation soon required new regulations. In this context, binding insider rules, provisions for the publication of facts that influence the share price, and a reporting obligation when a certain participation limit was reached, were issued in summer 1994. In anticipation of these new regulations, the Bayer Annual Stockholders' Meeting in April 1994 voted to suspend the voting rights restriction introduced in 1975 (including the 5% clause).[90] In 1997, the executive and the supervisory board of BASF proposed to abolish the maximum voting rights which had been introduced on 12 June 1975.[91] While German companies had reacted to the threat from foreign investors with restrictions in the mid-1970s, by the mid-1990s a far-reaching form of openness

87 „Ölpotentaten mit dem Fuß in der Tür der Großchemie", in: Frankfurter Neue Presse, 02.12.1981, HA Hoe 33 C/2/1/c.

88 „Kuwait Petroleum Corporation – breite Struktur und vorsichtige Politik", in: Chemische Industrie 7/1983, HA Hoe 33 C/2/1/c.

89 *Berghoff*, Epochenschwelle; *Windolf*, Corporate Network.

90 Geschäftsbericht Bayer 1994, p. 23.

91 Geschäftsbericht BASF 1996, p. 2.

towards investors of almost any nationality had become the norm. This did not mean that economic nationalism and security concerns came to an end at the beginning of the twenty-first century, as present reservations about Chinese investment make clear, but the global threat scenario has shifted noticeably.

Bibliography

Ahrens, Ralf/Bähr, Johannes: Jürgen Ponto. Bankier und Bürger. Eine Biografie. München 2013

Berger, Stefan: Historians, Nationalism Studies, and the Economy, in: Berger, Stefan/Fetzer, Thomas (eds.): Nationalism and the Economy. Explorations into a Neglected Relationship. Budapest / New York 2019, p. 23–41

Berghoff, Hartmut: Die 1990er Jahre als Epochenschwelle? Der Umbau der Deutschland AG zwischen Traditionsbruch und Kontinuitätswahrung, in: Historische Zeitschrift 308 (2019), p. 364–400

Bösch, Frank: Zwischen Schah und Khomeini. Die Bundesrepublik Deutschland und die islamische Revolution im Iran, in: Vierteljahrshefte für Zeitgeschichte 63 (3) (2015), p. 319–349

Caglioti, Daniela Luigia: Property rights in time of war. Sequestration and liquidation of enemy aliens' assets in Western Europe during the First World War, in: Journal of Modern European History 12 (4) (2014), p. 523–545

Callaghan, Helen/Hees, Alexandra: Wirtschaftsnationalismus im Wandel der Zeit. Der politische Diskurs um ausländische Unternehmensübernahmen in Großbritannien seit den 1950er–Jahren. Köln 2013

Callaghan, Helen/Hees, Alexandra: "Nation" und "Markt" als Legitimationsgrundlagen im politischen Diskurs. Parlamentarische Debatten um ausländische Unternehmensübernahmen in Großbritannien seit den 1950er Jahren, in: Sachweh, Patrick/Münnich, Sascha (eds.): Kapitalismus als Lebensform? Deutungsmuster, Legitimation und Kritik in der Marktgesellschaft. Wiesbaden 2017, p. 275–302

Chandler, Alfred D./Mazlish, Bruce: Introduction, in: Chandler, Alfred D./Mazlish, Bruce (eds.): Leviathans. Multinational Corporations and the New Global History. Cambridge 2005, p. 1–15

Chassaigne, Philippe: Les années 1970. Une décienne révolutionnaire. 3. Auflage. Paris 2018

Conze, Eckart: Sicherheit als Kultur. Überlegungen zu einer "modernen Politikgeschichte" der Bundesrepublik Deutschland, in: Vierteljahrshefte für Zeitgeschichte 53 (3) (2005), p. 357–380

Conze, Eckart: Die Suche nach Sicherheit. Eine Geschichte der Bundesrepublik Deutschland von 1949 bis in die Gegenwart. München 2009

Conze, Eckart: Geschichte der Sicherheit. Entwicklung – Themen – Perspektiven. Göttingen 2018

Conze, Werner: Art. Sicherheit/Schutz, in: Brunner, Otto/Conze, Werner/Koselleck, Reinhart (eds.): Geschichtliche Grundbegriffe. Historisches Lexikon zur politisch-sozialen Sprache in Deutschland. Bd. 5. Stuttgart 1984, p. 831–862

Daniels, Mario: Brain Drain, innerwestliche Weltmarktkonkurrenz und nationale Sicherheit. Die Kampagne der westdeutschen Chemieindustrie gegen Wissenstransfers in die USA in den 1950er Jahren, in: Vierteljahrshefte für Zeitgeschichte 64 (2016), 3, p. 491—515

David, Thomas / Mach, André: Corporate Governance, in: Halbeisen, Patrick / Müller, Margrit / Veyrassat, Béatrice (eds.): Wirtschaftsgeschichte der Schweiz im 20. Jahrhundert. Basel 2012, p. 831–872

Deutsche Bundesbank: Umschwung in der Bilanz der Direktinvestitionen, in: Monatsberichte der Deutschen Bundesbank 30 (10) (1978), p. 31–36

Deutsche Bundesbank: Stand der Direktinvestitionen Ende 1976, in: Monatsberichte der Deutschen Bundesbank 31 (4) (1979), p. 26–40

Doering-Manteuffel, Anselm/Raphael, Lutz: Nach dem Boom. Perspektiven auf die Zeitgeschichte seit 1970. 3., ergänzte Auflage. Göttingen 2012

Dunning, John H./Lundan, Sarianna M.: Multinational Enterprises and the Global Economy. 2. Auflage. Cheltenham 2008

Etges, Andreas: Wirtschaftsnationalismus. USA und Deutschland im Vergleich (1815–1914). Frankfurt am Main / New York 1999

Galambos, Louis/ Hikino, Takashi/Zamagni, Vera (eds.): The Global Chemical Industry in the Age of the Petrochemical Revolution. New York 2007

Gehlen, Boris/ Marx, Christian/Reckendrees, Alfred: Ambivalences of nationality. Economic nationalism, nationality of the company, nationalism as strategy: An introduction in: Journal of Modern European History 18 (1) (2020), p. 16–27

Glässer, Wiebke: Marktmacht und Politik. Das internationale Kartell der Ölgesellschaften 1960–1975. Berlin 2019

Göbel, Stefan: Die Ölpreiskrisen der 1970er Jahre. Auswirkungen auf die Wirtschaft von Industriestaaten am Beispiel der Bundesrepublik Deutschland, der Vereinigten Staaten, Japans, Großbritanniens und Frankreichs. Berlin 2013

Graf, Rüdiger: Oil and Sovereignty. Petro-Knowledge and Energy Policy in the United States and Western Europe in the 1970s. New York / Oxford 2018

Grande, Edgar: Globalisierung und die Zukunft des Nationalstaats, in: Beck, Ulrich/Bonß, Wolfgang (eds.): Die Modernisierung der Moderne. Frankfurt am Main 2001, p. 261–275

Habermas, Jürgen: Jenseits des Nationalstaats? Bemerkungen zu Folgeproblemen der wirtschaftlichen Globalisierung, in: Beck, Ulrich (ed.): Politik der Globalisierung. Frankfurt am Main 1998, p. 67–84

Handschuhmacher, Thomas: "Was soll und kann der Staat noch leisten?" Eine politische Geschichte der Privatisierung in der Bundesrepublik 1949–1989. Göttingen 2018

Hayward, Jack Ernest Shalom: Industrial Enterprise and European Integration. From National to International Champions in Western Europe. Oxford et al. 1995

Hayward, Jack Ernest Shalom: The State Imperative, in: Elgie, Robert/Grossman, Emiliano/Mazur, Amy G. (eds.): The Oxford Handbook of French Politics. Oxford 2016, p. 44–59

Helleiner, Eric: Economic Nationalism as a Challenge to Economic Liberalism? Lessons from the 19th Century, in: International Studies Quarterly 46 (2002), p. 307–329

Helleiner, Eric: Conclusion. The Meaning and Contemporary Significance of Economic Nationalism, in: Helleiner, Eric/Pickel, Andreas (eds.): Economic Nationalism in a Globalizing World. Ithaca / London 2005, p. 220–234

Helleiner, Eric/Pickel, Andreas (eds.): Economic Nationalism in a Globalizing World. Ithaca / London 2005

James, Harold: Rambouillet, 15. November 1975. Die Globalisierung der Wirtschaft. München 1997

Jones, Geoffrey: Multinationals from the 1930s to the 1980s, in: Chandler, Alfred D./Mazlish, Bruce (eds.): Leviathans. Multinational Corporations and the New Global History. Cambridge 2005, p. 81–104

Leonhard, Jörn: Die Büchse der Pandora. Geschichte des Ersten Weltkrieges. München 2014

Marx, Christian: Failed Solutions to the Energy Crises. Nuclear Power, Coal Conversion, and the Chemical Industry in West Germany since the 1960s, in: Bösch, Frank/Graf, Rüdiger (eds.): The Energy Crises of the 1970s. Anticipations and Reactions in the Industrialized World. Köln 2014, p. 251–271

Marx, Christian: Der zerplatzte Traum vom industriellen Atomzeitalter: Der misslungene Einstieg westdeutscher Chemiekonzerne in die Kernenergie während der 1960er und 70er Jahre, in: Zeitschrift für Unternehmensgeschichte 60 (1) (2015), p. 3–28

Meteling, Wencke: Internationale Konkurrenz als nationale Bedrohung – Zur politischen Maxime der "Standortsicherung" in den neunziger Jahren, in: Jessen, Ralph (ed.): Konkurrenz in der Geschichte. Praktiken – Werte – Institutionalisierungen. Frankfurt am Main 2014, p. 289–316

Müller, Klaus: Nationalist Undercurrents in German Economic Liberalism, in: Helleiner, Eric/Pickel, Andreas (eds.): Economic Nationalism in a Globalizing World. Ithaca / London 2005, p. 141–163

Pickel, Andreas: Introduction: False Oppostions. Recontextualizing Economic Nationalism in a Globalizing World, in: Helleiner, Eric/Pickel, Andreas (eds.): Economic Nationalism in a Globalizing World. Ithaca / London 2005, p. 1–17

Plumpe, Werner/Steiner, André (eds.): Der Mythos von der postindustriellen Welt. Wirtschaftlicher Strukturwandel in Deutschland 1960 bis 1990. Göttingen 2016

Raphael, Lutz: Jenseits von Kohle und Stahl. Eine Gesellschaftsgeschichte Westeuropas nach dem Boom. Berlin 2019

Reich, Simon: Roads to follow: regulating direct foreign investment, in: International Organization 43 (3) (1989), p. 543–584.

Reinert, Thomas: Begegnung mit Bayer. Historische Facetten eines innovativen Unternehmens. Frankfurt am Main 2014

Roth, Günter H.: Höchststimmrecht. Furcht vor den Ölscheichs oder Verselbständigung des Managements, in: Zeitschrift für Rechtspolitik 8 (9) (1975), p. 204–206

Šćepanović, Vera: National Interests and Foreign Direct Investment in East-Central Europe after 1989, in: Berger, Stefan/Fetzer, Thomas (eds.): Nationalism and the Economy. Explorations into a Neglected Relationship. Budapest / New York 2019, p. 209–236

Servan-Schreiber, Jean-Jacques: Le Défi Américain. Paris 1968.

Stokes, Raymond G.: Technology Transfer and the Emergence of the West German Petrochemical Industry, 1945–1955, in: Diefendorf, Jeffry M. (ed.): American Policy and the Reconstruction of West Germany. Washington, D.C. 1993, p. 217–236

Ther, Philipp: Die neue Ordnung auf dem alten Kontinent – Eine Geschichte des neoliberalen Europa. Berlin 2014

Travalini, Joanna Rubin: Foreign Direct Investment in the United States. Achieving a Balance between National Economy Benefits and National Security Interests, in: Northwestern Journal of International Law & Business 29 (3) (2009), p. 779–799

Wehner, Christoph: Die Versicherung der Atomgefahr. Risikopolitik, Sicherheitsproduktion und Expertise in der Bundesrepublik Deutschland und den USA 1945–1986. Göttingen 2017.

Windolf, Paul: The Corporate Network in Germany, 1896–2010, in: David, Thomas/Westerhuis, Gerarda (eds.): The Power of Corporate Networks. A Comparative and Historical Perspective. New York / London 2014, p. 66–85

Zürn, Michael: Regieren jenseits des Nationalstaates. Globalisierung und Denationalisierung als Chance. Frankfurt am Main 1998

Security of Supply: West Germany and the Global Markets for Base Metals, 1965–80

Ole Sparenberg

Introduction

Security constitutes an anthropological basic need and has long been an aim of policy as well as an expectation placed upon the state. At the same time, security is a historical concept that changes across political, social, and economic contexts. As such, debates on security offer insights into the historical changes of a society.[1] The 1970s, in particular the period following the first oil price shock of 1973, is widely regarded as a time of crisis, indeed as one of three systemic crises of the twentieth century alongside 1905–14 and 1929–39.[2] Within this period, the notion of international security, as opposed to internal security in the face of domestic terrorism, changed from a mostly military concept to an extended one that included many economic aspects.[3] Few would dispute that oil supply posed the main external challenge to economic security in the Western world following the first oil price shock.[4] Energy experts realised this well before October 1973, when oil became a dominant topic in public debate,[5] and the oil price shock is still present in the public memory today.

While some threats to security were as obvious to contemporary actors as they were to later generations, it is difficult to say what it is that transforms a given phenomenon into a threat to security, or indeed why and at what moment these historical actors came to perceive it as a threat. Historian Mario Daniels has asked how the legal and illegal transfer of industrial knowledge came to be construed, at different times, as a serious threat to state and society that called for dedicated counter measures, rather than a concern for individual enterprises. He described this process, with a term

1 *Conze*, Suche, 17–18.
2 *Maier*, Malaise, 27, 44.
3 *Böhm*, Sicherheit, 19.
4 *Dietrich*, Oil Revolution; *Venn*, Oil.
5 *Graf*, Security; *id.*, Öl.

from international relations theory, as "securitization".[6] In a similar vein, this chapter looks at the supply of base metals like copper, nickel and aluminium and its "securitization" from the mid-1960s to the early 1980s. These are metals which were (and still are) critical resources for any highly industrialised economy and the dependence upon their supply increased markedly over the course of the twentieth century. This chapter asks when, why and by whom the supply of these metals was perceived as a security issue and which responses were contemplated or taken to improve security of supply. Furthermore, the chapter examines when the worries about the security of supply ebbed away again and how serious the threat in this field was in retrospect. The chapter then analyses the rise and fall of a security concern that occupied the state and the business sector with varying intensity for more than ten years, even though it became largely overshadowed in public memory by the oil crisis.

Taking West Germany as a case study of a highly industrialised Western state, based upon published sources, documents from German state archives and commodity price data, this chapter first analyses how concerns about the security of base metal supply emerged in West Germany and how the perceived threat evolved in the wake of the oil price shock. Next follows an examination of the measures taken by West Germany to safeguard its security of supply, in particular its repeated attempts to establish a national stockpile for critical commodities. Finally, and with the benefit of hindsight, the actual extent of the threat to West German security of supply is discussed based on commodity price series.

The chapter argues that the "securitization" of base metals began prior to and independently of the oil price shock, but that the successes of OPEC (Organization of the Petroleum Exporting Countries) added another dimension to this process and changed the nature of the threat to the West German supply. While security of supply was at first seen in the context of the competition between industrialised states for scarce resources, after October 1973 the confrontation between raw material producers (in the Global South) and raw material consumers (in the Global North) took centre stage. The critical question became whether or not ore-exporting countries would be able to follow OPEC's example. This chapter further argues that the threat of base metal scarcity was mainly an anticipated crisis rather than an actualized one, and that the security of their supply was never seriously compromised during the 1970s.

---

6 *Daniels*, Landesverrat; *id.*, Brain Drain.

Increased competition for metals (1966–73)

The availability of raw materials, in particular metals, was a crucial issue in Germany during the First World War and again during the Nazi era, especially when the Allied blockade in wartime and the autarkic policy in the 1930s impeded imports. In each of these two periods Germany made strides towards substitution and recycling, but in ways which resulted in increased costs and losses of quality in its final products.[7] After the Second World War, however, West Germany soon became re-integrated in the global economy. By importing food and raw materials while exporting manufactured goods, West Germany resumed its tradition of free trade from the late nineteenth century. Its trade relations with newly-independent former colonies were also unburdened of their (recent) colonial past. In this way, West Germany profited from decolonisation.[8]

By the 1970s, West Germany represented the world's fourth-largest consumer of metals, and most of these metals were imported.[9] Import dependency amounted to 56% for zinc ore, 80% for lead ore, 90% for iron ore, 97% for copper ore and 100% for everything else, including economically important metals like aluminium, nickel, chrome, tin, manganese and cobalt. Import dependency in West Germany was somewhat higher than the average of the European Economic Community (EEC) but very similar to that of Japan.[10] The United States, in comparison, benefitted from a broader domestic mining sector, even though its dependency on imported metal had also grown since the 1920s.[11] While such a high import dependency could be seen as part and parcel of the international division of labour, it also involved risks to economic security. Such risks became apparent during the 1960s, when the West German state and those in its business sector began to worry that a steady flow of resources from abroad at reasonable prices was not guaranteed.

The West German industry experienced shortages of nickel – a crucial ingredient of stainless steel, among other things – that started in 1966 and lasted until 1970. In January 1967, the Trade Association of Foundries, sent to the Ministry of the Economy copies of letters from various members who drew attention to the severe shortage of nickel. A similar letter from

7 *Scherner*, Lernen; *Luxbacher*, Anwendungsgebiete; *Maier*, Ideologie.
8 *Kleinschmidt/Ziegler*, Wirtschaftsinteressen, 3.
9 *Saßmannshausen*, Bergbau, 15.
10 Antwort der Bundesregierung auf die Kleine Anfrage: Rohstoffsicherung, Deutscher Bundestag Drucksache (BT Drs.) 7/4479, 15.12.1975, 8–17, 22.
11 *Wade*, Raw Materials, 185–186.

the Guild Association of Engravers and Galvanisers followed in April of the same year. While these trades were most likely not of great importance to the Ministry, engineering company Krauss-Maffei also wrote in April to complain about the shortage. It stressed that it needed nickel for the Federal Army's new Leopard tanks that it was building.[12]

In March 1968, the Association of Stainless Steel-Producers submitted a lengthy memorandum describing the nickel shortage and urging the Ministry to take action. The memo explained that the shortage was mainly caused by the dramatic worldwide increase in nickel demand during the previous years, partly owing to the war in Vietnam. The mining companies were not only incapable of expanding their production, but they were also temporally paralysed by labour disputes. Only three companies dominated nickel supply in the Western world at this time: INCO and Falconbridge from Canada and Le Nickel from France. Despite the shortage, they did not raise the prices but instead rationed supply to their customers. To compensate for this, customers could only resort to the so-called "grey market" and buy nickel at elevated prices from smaller exporters like the Soviet Union and South Africa. According to German stainless steel-producers, this caused them additional costs of 28 million DM in 1967. Furthermore, they saw their international competitiveness under threat, with Le Nickel allegedly supplying the French industry on a preferential basis, and British nickel consumers having close ties to the two Canadian mining companies.[13]

The Ministry of the Economy shared this assessment of the shortage's causes, and it also saw the West Germany industry at a disadvantage when compared to its competitors.[14] Nickel, however, was not only scarce in West Germany, but the shortage was felt throughout the Western world.[15] *The Financial Times* reported that the "free market" price of nickel – or what the German companies referred to as its "grey market" price – had

12 Wirtschaftsverband Giesserei-Industrie, betr, Versorgung der Eisen- und Stahlgießereien mit Nickel, 20.1.1967; Bundesinnungsverband der Graveure, Galvaniseure, Gürtler und verwandter Berufe, betr. Nickelanoden-Engpaß, 4.4.1967; Krauss-Maffei Aktiengesellschaft, betr. Nickelbedarf, 21.4.1967, Bundesarchiv Koblenz (BArch) B 102/127601.

13 Edelstahlvereinigung e. V., Sicherung der Legierungsversorgung unter besonderer Berücksichtigung des Nickelbedarfs, 8. März 1968, BArch B 102/127601. See also: *Pasdach/Sames*, Vorausschau, 165f.

14 Referat III C 4, Aufzeichnung zur Eingabe der Edelstahlvereinigung e. V., 17.10.1968 p. 1; Referat III C 4, Vermerk: Grundlinien einer Rohstoffversorgungspolitik für Nickel, 10.1.1969, 3, BArch B 102/258836.

15 *Newman*, Nickel.

soared to £7,000 per ton by November 1969, as opposed to the "fixed price" of only £986 per ton charged by INCO and the other two leading producers. The FT expected the "fixed price" to rise to at least £1,250, however, as a result of a very costly settlement between INCO and its workers following a 128-day strike in 1969.[16] Despite the spread between the two prices and their dominating market position, the three main producers, led by INCO, did not raise their prices considerably but instead resorted to rationing because they pursued a cautious price strategy to foster consumption and keep consumers from substituting nickel with other metals.[17] Also under oligopolistic conditions, the aluminium industry pursued a similar strategy of price stability in the 1960s to increase the market share of aluminium over other metals.[18] By late 1969, the so-called *Nickelkrise* (nickel crisis) was also discussed in the West German press,[19] before the supply situation relaxed again sooner than expected and the crisis came to an end in 1970.[20]

The nickel shortage of the late 1960s served as a warning shot that drew attention to the overarching problem of security of supply. The memorandum of stainless steel producers from 1968 contained an outlook that regarded nickel as an example for base metals in general.[21] Several press articles and speeches followed in 1969 and 1970, which highlighted the threats posed to oil and metal supply. When Willy Brandt became Chancellor in October 1969, he alluded to the need to safeguard the industry's raw material and energy supply in his first policy statement.[22] The annual economic reports published by the Federal government in 1970 expressed concerns about the security of supply regarding commodities like nickel, chrome, manganese, molybdenum and tungsten for the first time.[23] The Federation of German Industries (*Bundesverband der Deutschen Industrie*) shared this assessment in their annual report 1970, which also referred to high import dependency and the increased international competition for

16 *Edwards*, Free-market nickel; *id.*, Nickel supplies.

17 Referat IV A 5 an IV B 6, betr. 2. Welthandelskonferenz, hier: Vorbereitung der Grundstofferörterungen. Beitrag für Nickel, 15.1.1968, 5, BArch B 102/258836; *Anon.*, Absolut hilflos.

18 *Barclay/Girvan*, Restructuring, 240.

19 *Anon.*, Nickelmarkt; *Anon.*, Absolut hilflos; *Diekhof*, Anschlag.

20 *Newman*, Nickel; Referat III C 4, Vermerk betr. Rohstoffversorgung der Bundesrepublik Deutschland, insbesondere Nickel, 20.1.1971, 1, BArch B 102/258836.

21 Edelstahlvereinigung e. V., Sicherung der Legierungsversorgung unter besonderer Berücksichtigung des Nickelbedarfs, 8. März 1968, 13, BA B 102/127601.

22 *Deutscher Bundestag*, Stenographischer Bericht, 28.10.1969, 28.

23 Jahreswirtschaftsbericht 1970 der Bundesregierung, BT Drs. 6/281, 27.1.1970, 28.

resources.[24] To initiate a discussion between the state and the business sector, the Federation of German Industries launched a dedicated task force on resource supply in October 1970.[25] In the following years, the topic stayed on the agenda, but it was not yet seen as urgent. The government's economic report published in February 1973 even saw an upside to higher commodity prices, namely that the growing purchasing power of raw material-exporting developing countries would also increase their demand for German manufactured goods.[26]

By 1969, there developed a consensus that high import dependency and the increased competition for resources between the industrialised states represented a threat to West Germany's economic security. A lecture on 23 November 1970 by Ulf Lantzke, a high-ranking official from the Ministry of the Economy, stressed that West Germany's high import dependency was a logical consequence of the international division of labour. As such, it did not represent a problem *per se* as long as an unobstructed supply on equal terms was guaranteed. This, however, had become highly dubious.

Apart from short-term shocks like the closing of the Suez Canal in 1956 and 1967, Lantzke and others were mainly concerned about the competition for raw materials among industrialised states in a market that had recently seen a surge in demand. Besides, from the German point of view, there was no level playing field. Competitors from Western Europe and the US enjoyed an advantage over the West German industry because they held stakes in mining companies operating abroad and had preferential access to their products, and the recent problems with nickel supply were considered a case in point. As a result, West Germany would lose its competitiveness against other industrialised states. While West Germans critically stressed their own inactivity, Japan, the long-underestimated competitor,[27] was perceived as the counter-example; a nation whose state and industries had already tackled the problem by engaging in mining projects overseas.[28]

---

24 *Bundesverband der Deutschen Industrie*, Jahresbericht 1969/70, 100, 106.
25 *Bundesverband der Deutschen Industrie*, Jahresbericht 1970/71, 95.
26 Jahreswirtschaftsbericht 1973 der Bundesregierung, BT Drs. 7/225, 21.2.1973, 26.
27 *Ziegler*, Deutschland, 45.
28 *Lantzke*, Sicherung; *Anon.*, Rohstoff-Versorgung; *Freyberg*, Rohstoffversorgung; *Pasdach/Sames*, Vorausschau, 165.

Metals, Cartels and the Global North-South divide (1973–80)

Metal prices started to soar dramatically well before the Arab-Israeli War and the oil price-shock in October 1973. Nevertheless, OPEC's price hike and boycott had a profound influence on how states like West Germany perceived the security of their metal supply in the following years.

The price hike for metals like copper, aluminium and nickel, but many other commodities as well, continued throughout 1973 and reached fever pitch in spring 1974. In November 1973, British magazine *The Economist* spoke of "metal madness" at the London Metal Exchange.[29] Several factors led to this development. Economic growth in the industrialised world up to 1973 had significantly strengthened the demand for all classes of commodities. Rising prices then led to panic buying and speculation, pushing prices up further. Supply, on the other hand, could not keep pace with demand. External circumstances such as bad weather, labour disputes and transport problems in some markets added to this. In the early 1970s, price hikes also reflected the weakness of the US dollar and British pound, the currencies in which most commodities were traded. The rising oil prices from October 1973 onwards only added to the problem.[30]

The inability of production to keep up with demand in the United States and Great Britain in 1973-74 also led to temporary shortages of various manufactured goods like steel, glass, printing paper and building materials, but not in West Germany.[31] Gasoline was already in short supply in the United States during the summer of 1973.[32] American consumers even experienced a shortage of toilet paper in the winter of 1973–74 which – not unlike the similar shortage in Germany in early 2020 – was basically a self-fulfilling prophecy due to hoarding.[33] Consequently, commodities were already in the limelight, independently of the Arab oil boycott.

Nevertheless, OPEC's use of oil as a political tool changed the way Western societies thought about commodities and prompted a shift in their attention towards commodity-exporting states and their potential power. Soon after the oil price-shock, there was a widespread impression that oil was just the beginning and that other commodity exporters would soon follow OPEC's example. On 19 November, magazine *Der Spiegel* anx-

---

29 *Anon.*, Key Indicators.
30 *Anon.*, Handel; *Anon.*, Commodity Rich; *Radetzki*, Anatomy, 59.
31 *Anon.*, Running short; *Anon.*, Zeitungspapier; *Anon.*, What is short.
32 *Lifset*, Energy Crisis, 29.
33 *Anon.*, Knappheit; *Malcolm*, Shortage; cf. https://coronarchiv.geschichte.uni-hamburg.de/projector/s/coronarchiv/item/2739 (accessed 30.5.2020).

iously wondered whether copper producers from Zambia or tin miners from Malaysia could do this.[34] One week later, the newly-established *Interministerieller Staatssekretär-Ausschuss für Rohstoff-Fragen* (State Secretary Committee on Commodities) with representatives from the Ministries of Economy, Finance, Defence, Economic Cooperation, Research and Technology as well as the Foreign Office, met for the first time. The committee was tasked with improving West German security of supply with critical regard to commodities in general and to metals in particular. It focussed explicitly upon those commodities where developments parallel to those in the energy market could be expected due to the supply being concentrated in a few countries.[35] Promoting a dialogue between state and business, the Federal President Gustav Heinemann invited around 30 representatives of raw material-consuming trades to a discussion in the chancellor's bungalow in Bonn on 21 January 1974 in the presence of the Minister for the Economy, Hans Friederichs, and the Minister for Research and Technology, Horst Ehmke. The invitation to this discussion posed the question of how West Germany could prepare itself for future events similar to the current oil crisis, and the conversation of that evening revolved around various commodities including metals and the respective roles of the state and the private sector.[36] At around the same time, the Minister of Finance (and soon-to-be Chancellor) Helmut Schmidt penned a memorandum on the state of the global economy for the leadership of the Social Democratic Party in which he anticipated the rise of further commodity cartels following the example of OPEC.[37]

In early 1974, the annual economic reports of both the Federal Government and the Federation of German Industries stressed the differences between oil and other commodities. Nevertheless, both reports were cautious not to rule out the possibility that other commodity markets might develop similar to the oil market because drastic price increases and high import dependency also characterised the supply of many other commodities.[38] Looking back from early 1975, the next of the government's economic reports noted that developing countries had intensified their efforts in

34 *Anon.*, Vorräten, 29.

35 Protokoll, BArch B 102/156838.

36 Vermerk betr. Kurzprotokoll über den Verlauf des Gesprächs über Rohstoffversorgung am 21. Januar 1974 im Kanzlerbungalow, 29.1.1974, BArch B 102/156838.

37 *Schmidt*, Politiker, 41.

38 Jahreswirtschaftsbericht 1974 der Bundesregierung, BT Drs. 7/1684, 6.2.1974, 17; *Bundesverband der Deutschen Industrie*, Jahresbericht 1973/74, 34.

using commodity exports to increase their political leverage. Commodity supply, the report concluded, had thus assumed an increasingly political dimension.[39]

In this way, the topic of commodity supply became part of the Global North-South Divide, the political and economic conflict between the industrialised North and the underdeveloped South. Evidently, the link between the Third World and commodities did not just emerge in 1974.[40] The often heavy dependence of these states on exports of mineral and agricultural commodities was a relic from the period of colonial rule when the colonies' role was to act as a convenient source of raw materials, while at the same time providing an assured market for manufactured goods.[41] As Julius Nyerere, the first President of Tanzania, stated, political independence was only the first step towards liberation as long as these structures of international trade and the control of former colonial economies by their colonisers persisted.[42] As more and more African and Asian states gained their independence in the post-war decades, they became the majority in the United Nations. The Group of 77 (G77), as they became known, used the UN General Assembly and forums like the UN Conference on Trade and Development (UNCTAD) to make their demands heard and to push for a reform of international economic relations.[43]

Nevertheless, the relationship to the Third World did not feature prominently in the discourse on commodity supply before 1973–74, even though the speech by Lantzke in 1970 referred to the increasingly self-confident developing countries as one actor that West German commodity policy had to take into account.[44] Perhaps the first time that the Third World moved to the centre of attention in the context of commodity supply was in the summer of 1973, when the American analyst and former adviser to Henry Kissinger, C. Fred Bergsten, published an article entitled "The threat from the Third World". Here he pointed out the increasing vulnerability of the United States and other industrialised nations to developing

39 Jahreswirtschaftsbericht 1975 der Bundesregierung, BT Drs. 7/3197, 30.1.1975, 19.

40 The term Third World is used here as a historical term that was also used as a self-designation and is in no way meant to be derogatory. The term was originally coined in direct reference to the Third Estate during the French Revolution and stresses those states' ambitions to rise against the established order, just like the Third Estate had done, cf. *Tomlinson*, Third World; *Venn*, Oil, 174–175.

41 *Maizels*, Commodities, 7.

42 *Nyerere*, Third World, 21.

43 *Sluga*, Transformation, 224–225; *Garavini*, Empires, 30–44.

44 *Lantzke*, Sicherung, 8.

countries due, *inter alia*, to their growing dependence on commodities from the Global South. As Bergsten pointed out, the Third World had acquired considerable market power that it could use by withholding supplies or by price gouging.[45] Bergsten had been called an alarmist at first, but his views seemed to be confirmed after October 1973. He then became the the leading authority on this topic and was frequently quoted in the international press, including in West Germany.[46]

By 1974, there were a number of developments that seemed to confirm Bergsten's views. Several producer associations or commodity cartels were trying to follow OPEC's example. Among these "mini-Opecs"[47] or "little OPECs"[48] the Council of Copper Exporting Countries, CIPEC (*Conseil Intergouvernemental de Pays Exportateurs de Cuivre*) – whose name even echoed that of OPEC itself – was the best known. Chile, Zambia, Zaire and Peru, who represented 40% of global copper production (but 80% of copper exports) had founded CIPEC in 1967, but the cartel only attracted international attention after 1973.[49] In contrast, the IBA (International Bauxite Association) only came into being in March 1974. Its founding members included Jamaica, Guyana, Surinam, Guinea, Sierra Leone, Yugoslavia and Australia which accounted for 70% of global production of aluminium ore. Remarkably, Australia was neither a Third World country nor a member of the Non-Aligned Movement but joined IBA to appease other Commonwealth states by supporting the cause of the Third World. The foundation of IBA was a direct response to the oil price shock, as OPEC had demonstrated that collusion was possible. At the same time, producers were compelled to fix bauxite prices at their current levels in order to offset their much-increased oil bills.[50] Iron ore-exporting states created the APEF (*Association des Pays Exportateurs de Mineral de Fer*) in 1975.[51] Still, owing to the ubiquity of iron ore in the world, this was never an effective cartel and it received far less attention than CIPEC and IBA. Finally, producer states of commodities as diverse as phosphate, bananas and coffee tried to coordinate prices and production in some way at this time.[52]

45 *Bergsten*, Threat, 107–109.
46 *Dicks*, Nightmare; *Anon.*, Supply cartels; *Jürgensen*, Dutzend; *Anon.*, Ordnung, 101.
47 *Anon.*, Cartels.
48 *Dicks*, Nightmare.
49 *Culver*, Council; *Mingst*, Cooperation; *Radmann*, CIPEC.
50 *Culver*, Bauxite; *Bergsten*, Bauxite; *Litvak/Maule*, Bauxite.
51 *Culver*, Iron; *Anon.*, Ordnung, 98.
52 *Anon.*, Supply cartels.

Observers in industrialised states were not only worried about the impact of these cartels on their respective markets, but were haunted by the prospect of their entering into an alliance with one another, possibly financed by OPEC.[53] Joint action by several cartels would have made substitution far more complicated, thereby increasing pressure on consumers. In the end, this threat never materialised although CIPEC, IBA and OPEC did liaise with each other.[54] While these commodity cartels received considerable attention in the Global North following 1973, their prospects of success and the question of whether oil was an exception or not were discussed extensively and not without controversy. Bergsten was the main point of reference for the view that "oil [was] not unique" and that cartels like the IBA would succeed in emulating OPEC.[55] Others argued that "petroleum [was] the exception, not the rule", however, and that critical conditions for successful collusion were not present in the case of other commodity producers.[56] This referred in particular to the ability of oil producers to adopt a long-term perspective due to their vast financial reserves, as well as the existence of a shared national objective, like that of their common fight against Israel. In response to a parliamentary inquiry led by the opposition in 1978, the West German government declared that these cartels had so far failed to control prices and production volumes and that this was unlikely to change.[57] Most analysts and journalists seemed sceptical of the possibility that other commodity producers could recreate OPEC's success, but whether they could or not was extensively discussed throughout the 1970s.

The nationalisation of foreign-owned companies represented another way for Third World countries to gain greater sovereignty over their economies. This had also been an essential mechanism for OPEC members before 1973.[58] In the context of metals, Chile's gradual nationalisation of US-owned copper mines is a well-known example.[59] For industrialised countries, this was worrying and not just because any compensations that were paid to owners – if there were any – were generally regarded as insufficient. It was expected that nationalisations would reduce overall metal

53 *Jürgensen*, Dutzend; *Bergsten*, World.
54 *Mingst*, Cooperation, 274.
55 *Bergsten*, Bauxite, 20.
56 *Krasner*, Oil.
57 Antwort der Bundesregierung auf die Große Anfrage: Rohstoffpolitik, BT Drs. 8/1981, 7.7.1978, 2.
58 *Venn*, Oil, 38–39; *Garavini*, Decolonization, 477–479.
59 *Culver*, Council, 501; *Mingst*, Cooperation, 277–279.

supply for two reasons: first, because the new owners might lack the capital and experience necessary to keep up or increase production; and second, because mining companies from the Global North often became reluctant to make any further investments abroad if their property was at risk from expropriation.[60] In a statement to the State Secretary Committee on Commodities on 13 July 1976 three German companies – Preussag, Metallgesellschaft and Vereinigte Aluminiumwerke – explained that governments' actions in the Global South typically fell short of the outright expropriation of foreign-owned mining companies and their assets. Instead, governments allegedly resorted to means such as provoking riots, imposing excessive taxation, or by placing obligations on companies to buy overpriced local products or to hire unqualified local managers.[61]

The New International Economic Order (NIEO) and the Sixth Special Session of the UN General Assembly

Tensions between the Global North and South reached a climax during the Sixth Special Session of the UN General Assembly on the Question of Raw Materials and Development (9 April to 2 May 1974). During this event, the Third World demonstrated a remarkable unity and radically brought into question the established global economic order. The initiative for this Special Session came from the Algerian leader Houari Boumédiène following US and French proposals for a conference on energy. Algeria, as a leading OPEC member, tried to avoid such a conference where oil consumers from the North and South alike might pillorise oil-exporters.[62] By shifting the focus to the topic of commodities in general, OPEC could instead portray itself as a model for other raw material-producing countries in their struggle for full sovereignty over natural resources and for economic decolonisation.[63]

After the Special Session, the General Assembly, dominated by Third World states, adopted a resolution entitled the Declaration on the Estab-

60 *Anon.*, Ordnung, 106; Der interministerielle Staatssekretär-Ausschuß für Rohstoff-Fragen, Zwischenbericht zur Rohstoffpolitik, März 1976, 17, BArch B 102/248665.

61 Stellungnahme, 13.7.1976, BArch B 102/248665.

62 Vermerk betr.: Algerische Initiative zur Einberufung einer Sondersitzung der Generalversammlung der Vereinten Nationen über Rohstoff-Fragen, 12.2.1974, Politisches Archiv Auswärtiges Amt (PA), B 30(ZA) 113294.

63 *Dietrich*, Oil Revolution, 264, 275.

lishment of a New International Economic Order, which addressed the questions of development and global economic inequality and put commodities at the centre.[64] The New International Economic Order (NIEO) outlined by the (non-binding) declaration was to be based on the sovereignty of states over their own natural resources, including the right to nationalisation. The declaration also called for a just and equitable relationship between the prices of raw materials and manufactured goods as well as for support for producers' associations or commodity cartels. Given the fact that many of the developments which industrialised states found alarming were effectively declared to be the fundamentals of this new international order, the reaction of the Global North was mostly one of aversion.[65]

By 1974, the outlook for industrialised states and their security of supply were gloomy. Following the Sixth Special Session, *The Economist* summarised: "For the first time the developing countries of the world are flexing their muscles at the rich industrialised nations, wielding what they hope will be a new economic weapon: commodity power."[66] In West Germany, the Foreign Office noted a global shift of power to the disadvantage of Western industrialised states. This was seen as a long-term, non-reversible development based not only on the Third World's numerical strength in the UN but also its growing political, military and economic potential. As a result, the Foreign Office saw the East-West confrontation in a less serious light when compared to the increasing threat of North-South polarisation, especially in an economic sense.[67] The State Secretary Committee on Commodities retrospectively described the Special Session as a "turning point in the relations between industrialised and developing states" and admitted that the self-assurance of the latter had taken the industrialised states by surprise.[68] The Third World's demands for the NIEO were also noted with alarm by the Federation of German Industries, which warned against making any tactical concessions. The industry saw the NIEO as an attempt at a radical transformation of the global economy to-

64 UN General Assembly Resolution Nr. 3201 (S-VI), Declaration on the Establishment of a New International Economic Order, 1.5.1974.

65 *Natorp*, Konsens; *Anon.*, Questions, 320.

66 *Anon.*, Commodity Rich, 76.

67 Dok. 340: Aufzeichnung des Ministerialdirektors van Well, 22. November 1974, in: Institut für Zeitgeschichte (ed.): Akten zur Auswärtigen Politik der Bundesrepublik Deutschland 1974, Vol. 2. München 2005, 1508–1511.

68 Der interministerielle Staatssekretär-Ausschuß für Rohstoff-Fragen, Zwischenbericht zur Rohstoffpolitik, März 1976, 2, BArch B 102/248665.

wards a planned economy complete with price and production controls, nationalisations and commodity cartels. Such dirigism, the Federation of German Industries claimed, would only lead to a loss of income and growth for all parties.[69]

Following these developments in 1973–74, there was a persistent sense of threat in West Germany regarding the security of the base metal supply. This was even though actual supply was never interrupted and prices dropped again after 1974 before they rose again later in the decade. In 1975, Günther Saßmannshausen, the CEO of the Preussag group, admitted that ore-exporting states had failed to replicate OPEC's success and that producers were hard hit when demand collapsed in the economic downturn following the oil price shock. He stated that it was too early to give the all-clear, however, as supply problems would re-emerge when growth and demand recovered. Industrialised states thus should not reduce their efforts to secure their commodity supply, Saßmannshausen stressed.[70] Despite the fact that a favourable supply situation had returned after 1973–74, the Federation of German Industries noted in 1976 that there were still considerable risks of politically-motivated interruptions in the supply of critical commodities.[71] Trust in the security of supply had been shaken and the topic remained on the political agenda – if not in the headlines – throughout the 1970s. In 1975 and 1978 the Christian-Democratic opposition launched two parliamentary enquiries directed at the government's commodity policy (*Rohstoffpolitik*) – or, as they saw it, the lack thereof.[72] The Christian-Democrats accused the Social-Liberal coalition of neglecting the vital economic interests of West Germany, but both sides largely agreed in their perception of the threat. The government's State Secretary Committee on Commodities, which had been established in November 1973, continued to operate until at least 1978.[73] Concerns about commodity supply even experienced a revival in 1978-79. As in 1973-74, price hikes and worries on the metal markets were not only a "Chomeini-Hausse" following the revolution in Iran where other commodities followed oil.[74] Preexisting and unrelated factors were also extant, like the situation in South-

69 *Bundesverband der Deutschen Industrie*, Jahresbericht 1974/75, 15, 149–150.

70 *Saßmannshausen*, Bergbau, 7, 40.

71 *Bundesverband der Deutschen Industrie*, Jahresbericht 1975/76, 153.

72 Kleine Anfrage: Rohstoffsicherung, BT Drs. 7/4366, 28.11.1975; Große Anfrage: Rohstoffpolitik der Bundesregierung, BT Drs. 8/1681, 4.4.1978.

73 Fünfte Sitzung des interministeriellen Staatssekretärausschusses für Rohstoff-Fragen, 12.5.1978, BArch B 102/248666.

74 *Anon.*, Währungsreserven.

ern Africa where the White minority regimes in the Republic of South Africa and Rhodesia – traditionally reliable suppliers of base metals to the Western world – came under increasing political and military pressure.[75] Soon afterwards, however, concerns about base metal supply ebbed away.

The perceived threat to West Germany's security of supply throughout the rest of the 1970s followed the pattern established in 1973–74. In contrast, concerns about the physical depletion of resources, as popularised by the Club of Rome in its publication "Limits to Growth" (1972) found a large audience but were regularly dispelled by experts from the government as well as from the industry. They insisted instead that, given West Germany's high import dependency, the political conflict between producer and consumer states – including the cartelisation of commodity markets – represented a critical problem.[76] From the opposition's point of view, nothing less was at stake than the competitiveness of the German industry, employment and economic growth.[77] The government was reluctant to draw bleak pictures of the situation, yet in 1978 its annual economic report it stated that the rise of energy and raw material prices added to various problems burdening growth and employment.[78]

While the international tensions were seen as a confrontation between two large groups of states – the Global North and the Global South – the main point of reference in West Germany was still the nation-state. The State Secretary Committee on Commodities noted an "increasing economic nationalism" among developing states, but also among some commodity-exporting countries in the Global North.[79] A "newly awakened national resource consciousness" was observed by Saßmannshausen following the oil price shock, something which had pushed all states towards a more nationally-orientated resource policy regardless of whether or not they were part of a supranational economic community. He did not expect

75 Fünfte Sitzung des interministeriellen Staatssekretärausschusses für Rohstoff-Fragen, 12.5.1978, BArch B 102/248666; Antwort der Bundesregierung auf die Große Anfrage: Rohstoffpolitik, BT Drs. 8/1981, 7.7.1978, 3. Imports from Rhodesia were officially impossible due to an embargo imposed by the UN. West German sources, therefore, mostly spoke vaguely about mineral imports from "Southern Africa" which tacitly included Rhodesia.

76 *Saßmannshausen*, Bergbau, 40; Antwort der Bundesregierung auf die Große Anfrage: Rohstoffpolitik, BT Drs. 8/1981, 7.7.1978, 2.

77 Kleine Anfrage: Rohstoffsicherung, BT Drs. 7/4366, 28.11.1975, 1; Große Anfrage: Rohstoffpolitik der Bundesregierung, BT Drs. 8/1681, 4.4.1978, 1.

78 Jahreswirtschaftsbericht 1978 der Bundesregierung, BT Drs. 8/1471, 26.1.1978, 16.

79 Der interministerielle Staatssekretär-Ausschuß für Rohstoff-Fragen, Zwischenbericht zur Rohstoffpolitik, März 1976, 8, BArch B 102/248665.

a common commodity policy within the EEC because its members' interests and circumstances were too diverse.[80]

Responses

West Germany, like other states in the Global North, responded in multiple ways to safeguard its supply of base metals. Most of the steps contemplated or taken were intended to improve or diversify supply rather than to change or reduce demand. Similar to the case of oil where steps had already been made before October 1973,[81] West Germany initiated measures to enhance metal supply in the late 1960s. While doing so, in spite of serious concerns about security of supply, the West German actors generally maintained a sense of proportion. Already in 1970, Lantzke outlined the limits of security: since 100% security would be too expensive, the aim was instead to achieve a relative improvement.[82]

As mentioned above, autarky and the substitution of imports with domestic resources played a significant role in Germany during the First World War and under National Socialism. There was no path dependency of this kind in the 1970s, however. The topic of autarky was occasionally raised only to be disregarded immediately. Lantzke in 1970 and the Christian Democrat Ferdinand Breidbach in parliament in 1978 both stressed that Germany's insufficient domestic resource base and the export orientation of its industry ruled out any kind of autarkic policy.[83] A retreat from the global economy, the *Frankfurter Allgemeine Zeitung* warned in an article entitled "Flirting with autarky?" (1973), would spell the end of everything that had been accomplished in West Germany since 1948.[84]

West Germany nevertheless did take a second look at its domestic mineral deposits during the 1970s. Subsidies helped to prolong the lifespan of several fluorite and barite as well as lead and zinc mines, but these were not critical resources.[85] Besides, a Federal Drilling Programme (*Bundesbohrprogramm*) was launched in 1979 to test the deep subsoil and discover

80 *Saßmannshausen*, Bergbau, 10, 18.

81 *Graf*, Öl, 51, 65; Die Energiepolitik der Bundesregierung, BT Drs. 7/1057, 3.10.1973, 8.

82 *Lantzke*, Sicherung, 6.

83 Ibid., 6; *Deutscher Bundestag*, Stenographischer Bericht, 16.11.1978, 9081.

84 *Eick*, Autarkie.

85 Der interministerielle Staatssekretär-Ausschuß für Rohstoff-Fragen, Zwischenbericht zur Rohstoffpolitik, März 1976, 31, BArch B 102/248665.

new ore deposits.[86] There were no doubts, however, that the key to the security of supply did not lie in the Harz Mountains or the Black Forest.

The key was instead seen in broadening and diversifying supply from abroad in order to be less dependent on a limited number of potentially unstable or hostile producer states. The West German government considered financial guarantees for companies engaged in exploration and mining to be the most important element of its commodity policy.[87] A central part of this was the Exploration Support Programme (*Explorations-Förderprogramm*), which had started in November 1970. Its origins can be traced back to the nickel crisis when it was modelled on an earlier subsidy for uranium exploration.[88] Under this programme, companies received grants of up to 50% of the total costs of finding new mineral deposits which they only had to repay if the projects led to commercially-exploitable outcomes.[89] The programme encouraged the business sector to invest in new mining projects by reducing the financial risk. By 1977, 54 mining projects outside of Germany as well as 20 within Germany were supported in this way. Of the projects abroad, 63% were located in industrialised countries like Canada, the United States, Europe and Australia, where property rights were considered secure. Annual expenditure started at DM 4.7 million in 1971, increasing to DM 30 million by 1977, with the most significant increase taking place between 1973 and 1974.[90] The programme ran until 1990, and a total of 410 projects had been supported with DM 603 million over the years.[91]

In general, Western mining companies reacted by orientating their investments according to the political risk and began to withdraw from the

---

86 Fünfte Sitzung des interministeriellen Staatssekretärausschusses für Rohstoff-Fragen, 12.5.1978, BArch B 102/248666. Interestingly, the „Bundesbohrprogramm“ was conceived as a continuation of the „Reichsbohrprogramm" 1934–45.

87 Der interministerielle Staatssekretär-Ausschuß für Rohstoff-Fragen, Zwischenbericht zur Rohstoffpolitik, März 1976, 27, BArch B 102/248665.

88 Referat III C 4, Aufzeichnung zur Eingabe der Edelstahlvereinigung e.V., 17.10.1968, 3, 6, BArch B 102/258836.

89 Der Bundesminister für Wirtschaft, Richtlinien über die Gewährung von Zuschüssen zur Verbesserung der Versorgung der Bundesregierung Deutschland mit mineralischen Rohstoffen. Vom 6. November 1970, Bundesanzeiger Nr. 210 (10.11.1970), 1–2.

90 Antwort der Bundesregierung auf die Große Anfrage: Rohstoffpolitik, BT Drs. 8/1981, 7.7.1978, 18, 20.

91 Antwort der Bundesregierung auf die Kleine Anfrage: Rohstoffsicherung der Bundesrepublik Deutschland, BT Drs. 12/342, 9.4.1991, 2.

Third World.[92] Despite a worsening investment climate, West German foreign investment (not only resource extraction) in developing countries was still growing in 1975, but it grew predominantly in those countries that protected foreign property.[93]

The 1970s were characterised by an easing of tensions between East and West when compared to the increasing tensions between North and South.[94] Consequently, increased cooperation with the Eastern Bloc represented another way to diversify supply. In the case of natural gas, such cooperation became very important in this decade.[95] According to the State Secretary Committee on Commodities, communist states were interested in collaborating in the field of metals to obtain know-how and capital, but such projects depended upon political developments between the two blocs. Furthermore, new forms of collaboration had to be found since the different economic systems ruled out direct investments. The committee therefore saw metal supplies from the East only as a medium- to long-term contribution to the security of supply.[96]

The concerns about commodity supply provided a strong incentive for research into new and unconventional resources in places where no mining had taken place so far like on the deep-sea floor and in Antarctica. West German companies and those from other industrialised states had worked on deep-sea mining since the late 1960s,[97] but the West German Antarctic research programme only started in the late 1970s.[98] These were no short-term solutions, however, since the government expected that the first commercial deep-sea mining operations would begin in the mid-1980 and that metals from the ocean floor would only have a real impact on the market around the year 2000. Mineral extraction from Antarctica was assumed to be still further in the future.[99] In 2020, neither of these two projects has yet come to fruition.

Apart from the diversification and expansion of supply, there were also prospects of ensuring base metal security on the demand side. Changes in

92 *Anon.*, Commodity Rich, 77.

93 *Bundesverband der Deutschen Industrie*, Jahresbericht 1975/76, 154–156.

94 *Graf*, Security, 331; *Venn*, Oil, 177.

95 *Högselius*, Gas.

96 Der interministerielle Staatssekretär-Ausschuß für Rohstoff-Fragen, Zwischenbericht zur Rohstoffpolitik, März 1976, 32, BArch B 102/248665.

97 *Sparenberg*, Perspective.

98 *Kehrt*, Gondwana.

99 Fünfte Sitzung des interministeriellen Staatssekretärausschusses für Rohstoff-Fragen, 12.5.1978, BArch B 102/248666; *Deutscher Bundestag*, Stenographischer Bericht, 16.11.1978, 9094.

the lifestyle of Western societies to reduce consumption were rarely discussed and would have been challenging to implement in any case.[100] The West German government nevertheless contemplated research and development in the field of recycling and the effective use of raw materials. Such measures were considered to be a contribution to both the security of supply and overall environmental protection.[101] As Saßmannshausen pointed out in 1975, recycling already played a significant role in the West German metal supply: recycling contributed to 44% of iron and steel, 40% of lead, 31% of aluminium and 22% of copper.[102] Recycling, however, was not a magic bullet because in times of high demand scrap metal likewise became a scarce resource. During the nickel crisis of the 1960s, the US had temporally banned the export of scrap metal containing nickel, and the EEC had discussed similar export restrictions.[103] Furthermore, scrap metal supply often lags behind demand in times of increased consumption because much of the metals go into durable goods and only becomes available for recycling when these goods reach the end of their lifespan. In West Germany, the widespread use of stainless steel containing nickel was still a relatively new phenomenon in the 1960s. For this reason, scrap metal did not represent a significant source of nickel at that time.[104]

Recycling was one of the few cases where reference to raw material supplies under National Socialism was made when the West German environment agency, the *Umweltbundesamt*, commissioned a study on recycling in the Nazi era. The agency explicitly cited the need to learn from historical methods of recycling due to the currently increasing political weight of commodity-exporting countries and the resulting susceptibility of industrialised nations to blackmail.[105]

The industrialised states' commodity policy also included political responses to the producer states in the Global South. A military retaliation was obviously never on the table for West Germany, but the US shied

100 *Wade*, Raw materials, 186; *Swansbrough*, Crisis, 22-24.

101 Der interministerielle Staatssekretär-Ausschuß für Rohstoff-Fragen, Zwischenbericht zur Rohstoffpolitik, März 1976, 38–40, BArch B 102/248665; Bundesbericht Forschung VI, 28.6.1979, 50, BT Drs. 8/3024.

102 *Saßmannshausen*, Bergbau, 24.

103 Edelstahl-Vereinigung e.V. an den Herrn Bundesminister für Wirtschaft betr. Verbot der Ausfuhr von nickelhaltigem Schrott in den USA, 28.6.1967, BArch B 102/127601; Referat III C 4, Aufzeichnung zur Eingabe der Edelstahlvereinigung e.V., 17.10.1968, 1; Referat III C 4, Vermerk: Grundlinien einer Rohstoffversorgungspolitik für Nickel, 10.1.1969, 2, BArch B 102/258836.

104 *Pasdach/Sames*, Vorausschau, 170.

105 *Huchting*, Abfallwirtschaft, 252.

away from such a measure even though there had been precedents in the past. After the Vietnam War another military intervention would have met with considerable resistance at home and was likely to provoke violent reactions throughout the Third World.[106] But the United States also had other options because it was an important commodity exporter in its own right, controlling a major part of the global exports of wheat, other grains and soybeans. The United States thus had considerable clout to put pressure on developing countries that were in need of food imports.[107]

In general, however, a more conciliatory approach towards the Third World dominated among the industrialised states. This was also what Bergsten recommended would be in America's best interest when he had first identified the "threat from the Third World".[108] In 1970, when competition among consumer states was still considered to be the main challenge, Lantzke paid attention to the needs of resource-exporting developing countries. He suggested looking for ways of cooperation that would suit both sides' economic interest and would take into account the developing countries' desire to participate in resource extraction and processing.[109] Later, in 1976, the State Secretary Committee on Commodities also stressed that economic growth and social progress could only be achieved through cooperation between industrialised and developing countries: both depended on the exchange of natural resources and capital as well as technical know-how. According to the committee, direct investments in certain developing countries like Brazil and Sierra Leone were still possible. The actual behaviour of these countries was different from the radical stance of the Third World as a whole in the UN.[110] With this in mind, the Foreign Office distinguished between the legitimate demands of developing countries like equal relations and stable, fair export prices on the one hand and excessive measures like nationalisations without compensation and demands for free access to private technology on the other.[111] At least parts of the West German press showed understanding for the demands of the Global South, acknowledging that the industrialised states were in a

106 *Bergsten*, Threat, 115; *Swansbrough*, Crisis, 16–18.
107 *Dicks*, Nightmare; *Anon.*, Commodity Rich, 77.
108 *Bergsten*, Threat, 121.
109 *Lantzke*, Sicherung, 8.
110 Der interministerielle Staatssekretär-Ausschuß für Rohstoff-Fragen, Zwischenbericht zur Rohstoffpolitik, März 1976, 38–40, BArch B 102/248665.
111 Tischvorlage betr. Gesamtkonzept für die Nord-Süd-Verhandlungen, 30.4.1976, 3, PA B 1(ZA) 178639.

weak position from a moral point of view.[112] In Canada, even government officials felt that the Canadian Aluminium producer Alcan was largely the author of its own misfortunes after the company's interests had been nationalized in Guinea (1961) and Guyana (1971) because the company had failed to develop a sense of corporate responsibility.[113]

The Lomé Convention and the Common Fund for Commodities were results of this conciliatory approach. Signed in February 1975 and reflecting the events of 1973–74, the first Lomé Convention – concluded between the EEC and 46 African, Caribbean and Pacific states – included trade preferences in favour of the latter group as well as compensatory finance for adverse fluctuations in commodity prices and provisions for aid and investment.[114] Contemporary press reports, however, criticised the convention for Europe's small financial commitment when compared to the agricultural subsidies within the EEC.[115] The Common Fund was a commodity-related agreement at the global level signed in June 1980. Ideas for a comprehensive programme to support commodity-exporting states, including a central fund to finance buffer stocks as well as measures to couple the prices of commodities and manufactured goods had been discussed within UNCTAD since 1968. Industrialised states resisted and only became more cooperative in the wake of the oil price shock. Still, they dragged their feet and, to the extent that the threat from the Third World diminished over the decade, the idea had been watered down considerably, resulting in an organisation distributing aid instead of the fundamental restructuring of the global commodity trade as it had originally been envisaged.[116]

West Germany also considered developmental aid payments as a way to improve security of supply through cooperation with the Global South, although at this juncture mining projects had not been a focus of West German aid.[117] Saßmannshausen claimed in 1975 that the hitherto more altruistic orientation of development policy provided a sound basis for trust to pursue the West German resource interests.[118]

112 *Herlt*, Tribunal; *Anon.*, Ordnung, 97.

113 *Gendron*, Canada, 228–231.

114 *Frøland/Ingulstad*, Europe, 313; *Migani*, EEC, 271–273.

115 *Anon.*, Ordnung, 106.

116 *Maizels*, Commodities, 112–124.

117 Der interministerielle Staatssekretär-Ausschuß für Rohstoff-Fragen, Zwischenbericht zur Rohstoffpolitik, März 1976, 29-30, BArch B 102/248665.

118 *Saßmannshausen*, Bergbau, 37.

Stockpiling of critical commodities

The responses discussed so far aimed at expanding and diversifying resource supply in the medium and long term. The obvious way to alleviate short-term interruptions of supply was the stockpiling of strategic materials. While several states, including the United States, followed this path, West Germany never launched such a programme. Still, stockpiling was intensively discussed in West Germany from the late 1960s to at least 1980. The United States maintained (and still maintains) the most extensive stockpile of a large number of commodities – mainly metals – that were considered critical for the nation's security. Following the Strategic Materials Act of 1939 and America's subsequent wartime experience, the post-war US programme was based on the Strategic and Critical Materials Stock Piling Act of 1946.[119] Switzerland and Sweden also started stockpiles before the Second World War while Japan and France began their programmes only in the 1970s.[120] In the field of energy, the West German government obliged the oil industry from 1965 to maintain stocks and decided to build up a state-owned oil stock in 1970.[121]

The idea of a state-owned or state-supported stockpile for critical metals seems to have emerged twice independently in West Germany in 1968. On the one hand, the association of stainless steel producers proposed such a measure during the nickel shortage.[122] On the other hand, the project emerged on the initiative of state secretary Klaus Dieter Arndt from the Ministry of Economics. For financial and legal reasons the resulting draft by the Ministry of Economics did not provide for a state-owned stockpile nor did it oblige the private sector to hold additional stocks. Instead, the draft envisaged that companies would conclude contracts with the state whereby the company would build up stocks and the state would subsidise the capital costs and offset any risks in exchange for certain rights over the commodities. The draft referred to a large variety of commodities like base metals but also chemicals, natural rubber and fibres for which the supply was heavily import-dependent.[123]

---

119 *Paley*, Resources, 162–164; *Radetzki*, Handbook, 139–141.

120 Antwort der Bundesregierung auf die Kleine Anfrage: Rohstoffsicherung der Bundesrepublik Deutschland, BT Drs. 12/342, 9.4.1991, 6.

121 *Illing*, Energiepolitik, 143.

122 Referat III C 4, Aufzeichnung zur Eingabe der Edelstahlvereinigung e.V., 17.10.1968, 4-5, BArch B 102/258836.

123 Referat W/IV A 2, Vermerk betr. Bevorratung volkswirtschaftlich wichtiger Rohstoffe, 26.9.1972, BArch B 102/156838. While this document explicitly ruled

Early on the idea met with resistance from the Ministry of Finance as well as from within the Ministry of Economics. Critics doubted its necessity and anticipated that it would entail higher than expected costs.[124] Finally, the notion of stockpiling based on contracts with the private sector was terminated in a Cabinet meeting on 9 July 1970 for financial reasons.[125] This was a point in time when the nickel crisis had just passed, however, and when metal markets were calm, during which the topic had lost its urgency. The Ministry of Economics nevertheless did not rule out reviving the idea later when the build-up of the oil reserve would be complete, which until then enjoyed priority.[126]

Even though voices from the business sector that preferred less bureaucratic support for companies holding stocks were pleased with the termination or postponement of the government's plans,[127] the idea remained alive. In 1971, representatives of stainless steel producers even urged the Ministry of Economics to start stockpiling now because metal prices were low. State secretary Carsten Rohwedder agreed but had no funds available.[128] The Christian-Democratic opposition used a parliamentary debate in 1978 to demand that the government start a stockpiling programme immediately instead of waiting to shut the stable door after the horse had bolted. Members of the Social-Liberal government coalition responded by

---

out the possibility that the stockpiling project had any root in West German defence policy, an earlier note from 1968 mentioned NATO's switch to a "Flexible Response" and the resulting need to prepare for crises below the threshold of a full-scale military attack: Referat IV A 2, Vermerk betr. Bevorratung mit wichtigen Waren der gewerblichen Wirtschaft, 7.3.1968, BArch B 102/156832.

124 Der Leiter der Abteilung V an Herrn Staatssekretär Dr. von Dohnanyi betr. Bevorratung wichtiger Grundstoffe, 11.6.1969; MinRat Moehrke, Referat IV A 2, Vermerk betr. Bevorratung wichtiger Importwaren; hier Referentengespräch mit dem BMF am 12.6.1969, 13.6.1969, BArch B 102/156835.

125 Referat IV A 2, betr. Bevorratung volkswirtschaftlich wichtiger Importwaren, 20.7.1970, BArch B 102/203767; 34. Kabinettssitzung am Donnerstag, dem 9. Juli 1970, in: Bundesarchiv (ed.): Die Kabinettsprotokolle der Bundesregierung, www.bundesarchiv.de/cocoon/barch/000/k/index.html (accessed 26.5.2020).

126 Referat W/IV A 2, Vermerk betr. Bevorratung volkswirtschaftlich wichtiger Rohstoffe, 26.9.1972, 3, BArch B 102/156838. The annual cost of building up the oil reserve was DM 150 million compared to expected annual costs of DM 50-150 million to the government for the commodity stockpile (depending on the number of commodities and the scale of the stockpile).

127 *Anon.*, Blütenträume; *Anon.*, Beschaffung.

128 Referat III C 4, Ergebnisvermerk über die Besprechung der Edelstahlindustrie am 24. Juni 1971 mit Herrn Staatssekretär Dr. Rohwedder, 14.7.1971, BArch B 102/203767.

stressing the responsibility of the companies to hold their own raw material inventories but also agreed that the state should assist in the case of commodities that were highly critical for the economy as a whole.[129] The government's annual economic reports of 1970, 1975 and 1980 also mentioned its intention to look into the possibility of stockpiling.[130] There was thus a broad consensus in West Germany that some kind of state stockpiling programme would be a positive contribution to economic security.

In the end, it boiled down to a question of cost. What was needed was a creative way to finance a stockpile without straining the federal budget or overburdening the private sector. In the summer of 1970, the Foreign Office and the Ministry of Finance proposed to buy commodities for the stockpile programme then under discussion within the framework of the German-American offset agreement. In this agreement, Bonn had committed itself to purchase goods in the United States to offset the costs of the American military presence in West Germany.[131] The Ministry of Economics was sceptical, however: the only metal that could be considered for purchase in the United States was copper, but given the demand of the US economy it was doubtful if large amounts would become available for export to West Germany.[132]

Herbert Ehrenberg, a prominent Social-Democratic member of parliament, made another proposition in 1975 that would shape the discussion until the end of 1980. After first bemoaning the fact that the lessons of the oil crisis were quickly forgotten and that the Federal budget allowed little financial leeway, Ehrenberg suggested using the substantial currency reserves of the Bundesbank to finance stockpiles of oil and other critical raw materials. According to his proposal, the Bundesbank would not buy commodities itself, but rather grant an interest-free credit line to Kreditanstalt für Wiederaufbau, a state-owned bank, which would then lend to companies for the purchase of commodities. Ehrenberg saw hardly any addi-

---

129 *Deutscher Bundestag*, Stenographischer Bericht, 16.11.1978, 9082, 9085, 9093.

130 Jahreswirtschaftsbericht 1970 der Bundesregierung, BT Drs. 6/281, 27.1.1970, 28; Jahreswirtschaftsbericht 1975 der Bundesregierung, BT Drs. 7/3197, 30.1.1975, 20; Jahreswirtschaftsbericht 1980 der Bundesregierung, BT Drs. 8/3628, 30.1.1980, 12.

131 *Abelshauser*, Wirtschaftsgeschichte, 184.

132 Referat IV A 5 an die Referate III C 4, IV A 2 betr. Bevorratungsprogramm des BMWi und deutsch-amerikanischer Devisenausgleich, 10.6.1970, BArch B 102/203767.

tional costs for the Bundesbank compared to its usual investments in foreign sovereign debt. He also ruled out any threat to monetary stability.[133]

In March 1979, following the Iranian revolution and in times of rising metal prices, the Minister of Finance, Hans Matthöfer, took up Ehrenberg's proposal after Chancellor Helmut Schmidt also had suggested such a measure.[134] Later that October, the Ministry of Economics had already worked out a concept along these lines and submitted it to the parliament's Committee on Budgets. The concept placed the primary responsibility upon the private sector but acknowledged that the state had to step in in case of highly import-dependent commodities like chromium, manganese, vanadium, cobalt and various types of asbestos. In case of these commodities, additional stocks with a range of up to one year were considered to be necessary to prevent adverse effects on industrial production and employment. According to the concept, individual companies or a consortium would build up stocks and also would share part of the costs. The stockpile, however, would have been mainly financed by a DM 600 million credit of the Bundesbank. The state's budget would pay only the interest rates, which were estimated at DM 54 million for the whole period until 1984.[135]

The project soon attracted criticism. Across the political spectrum, the press saw the project as setting a worrying precedent by giving the government access to the Bundesbank's currency reserves, thus endangering the bank's independence. Besides, the Bundesbank's loan was considered as a threat to monetary stability, amounting to money creation. Disputes between industry and government about the rights of disposal over the stockpiled materials were another problem. The administration even suspected that companies would covertly draw from such stocks when prices were high but outside any emergency. Also, the conservative press insinuated the existence of a hidden agenda against South Africa, a major supplier of all the specific commodities included in the stockpile plans except cobalt. Such a stockpile made it easier for West Germany to heed the calls of the UN towards an economic embargo against the Apartheid regime, or so the *Frankfurter Allgemeine Zeitung* suspected.[136]

---

133 *Ehrenberg*, Öl.

134 *Anon.*, Währungsreserven.

135 Übersicht über die Aufzeichnungen zu den Titeln des Kapitels 0902 des Entwurfs des Bundeshaushaltsplanes 1980, 1–3, BArch B 102/247820.

136 *Anon.*, Währungsreserven; *Anon.*, Ärger; *Anon.*, Vorrat; *Kg.*, Weg; *Anon.*, Puffer; *Anon.*, Beschluß.

Topics like these were also included in a note that the Ministry of Economics drafted for their minister to prepare him for expected questions during the discussion in the budgetary committee. The ministry even foresaw that critical voices would liken the creative way of financing via the Bundesbank's currency reserves to the infamous *Mefo-Wechsel* that were used by the National Socialists.[137] Ultimately, nothing came of it, since the government dropped the policy in November 1980, thus marking the end of the plans for a national stockpile of metals in West Germany.[138]

In 1991, the government declared unequivocally: "State-owned or state-supported stockpiles for mineral commodities are not a suitable instrument for the German commodity policy."[139] The discussions about stockpiling illustrated a fundamental problem in dealing with scarcity: when supply is sufficient, actors shy away from the costs of stockpiling. When there are shortages and price hikes, however, it is usually too late and building up a stockpile becomes difficult and expensive. West Germany at least avoided the mistake of buying when prices were at their highest.

Security of supply in retrospect

In retrospect, the question arises how great the threat to the security of supply really was in the 1970s. There were no boycotts and no acute shortages such as those in the case of nickel in the late 1960s. The government made it clear in the mid-1970s that present risks to the commodity supply of the West German industry did not exist, but that medium- and long-term risks did exist.[140] Even more so than in the case of energy policy,[141] West German commodity policy was a reaction to the anticipation of future crises. It is therefore hard to evaluate the efficiency of the West German commodity policy as it was never really put to the test.

---

137 Referat IV A 2, Notiz betr. Rohstoffbevorratungsprogramm im Parlament; Haushaltsdebatte, 12.9.1979, BArch B 102/247820.

138 *Anon.*, Beschluß.

139 Antwort der Bundesregierung auf die Kleine Anfrage: Rohstoffsicherung der Bundesrepublik Deutschland, BT Drs. 12/342, 9.4.1991, 3.

140 Antwort der Bundesregierung auf die Kleine Anfrage: Rohstoffsicherung, BT Drs. 7/4479, 15.12.1975, 1; Der interministerielle Staatssekretär-Ausschuß für Rohstoff-Fragen, Zwischenbericht zur Rohstoffpolitik, März 1976, 1, BArch B 102/248665.

141 *Bösch/Graf*, Anticipations, 10.

The best yardstick for measuring scarcity and risks on the markets for metals and other commodities is price. A look at monthly indexed US dollar prices for a selection of base metals including copper, aluminium and nickel in the period from 1960 to 1985 shows rising and increasingly volatile prices from 1964 onwards followed by an extreme surge that started in early 1973 (before the oil price shock), reaching a peak in April 1974 amidst the height of the tensions between the industrialised countries and the Third World, including worries about the spread of "mini-OPECs". Prices collapsed afterwards but moved upwards again in the second half of the decade, with another extreme peak in the wake of the second oil price shock. Another downwards trend followed, and nominal prices did not reach the level of early 1980 again before 1988.[142]

Figure 1. Base metals (excl. iron ore), monthly prices in nominal USD, 1960-85 (2010=100)

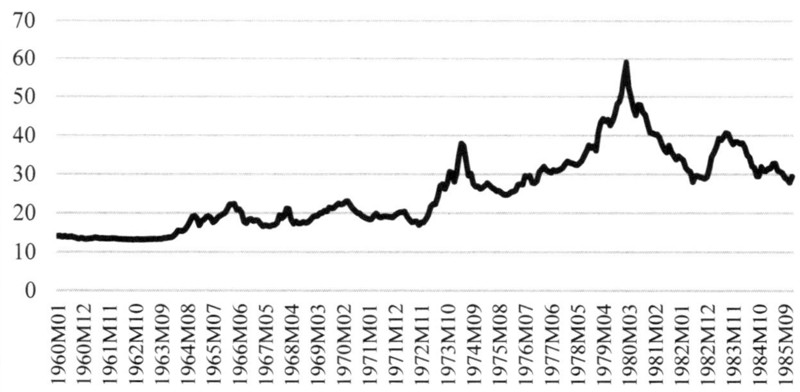

At first glance, Figure 1 seems to confirm the idea that metals were increasingly scarce and that security of supply was endangered between the mid-1960s and 1980. The picture changes, however, when looking at annual inflation-adjusted real prices.[143] The deflator used here is the Manufac-

142 World Bank Commodity Price Data (The Pink Sheet), www.worldbank.org/en/research/commodity-markets#1 (accessed 27.5.2020). The weights used in the index of base metals is based on developing countries' export values (47% copper, 33% aluminium, 10% nickel, 5% zinc, 3% tin and 2% lead).

143 Ibidem.

turing Unit Value Index (MUV), which is a trade-weighted index of major industrialised countries' exports of manufactured goods.[144] The use of annual data compensates for the sometimes extreme short-term fluctuations of nominal prices like those seen in 1974. Looking at the real prices of base metals reveals that the highest levels had been reached in 1966 and 1969, while the peaks of 1974 and 1979 were less pronounced. Above all, a long downward trend becomes evident, beginning in 1969. In direct proportion to the fall in the real prices of raw materials, the bargaining power of ore-exporting states also decreased and, conversely, the situation for consumers like those in West Germany improved.

Figure 2. Base metals (excl. iron ore), annual prices in real 2010 USD, 1960-85 (2010=100)

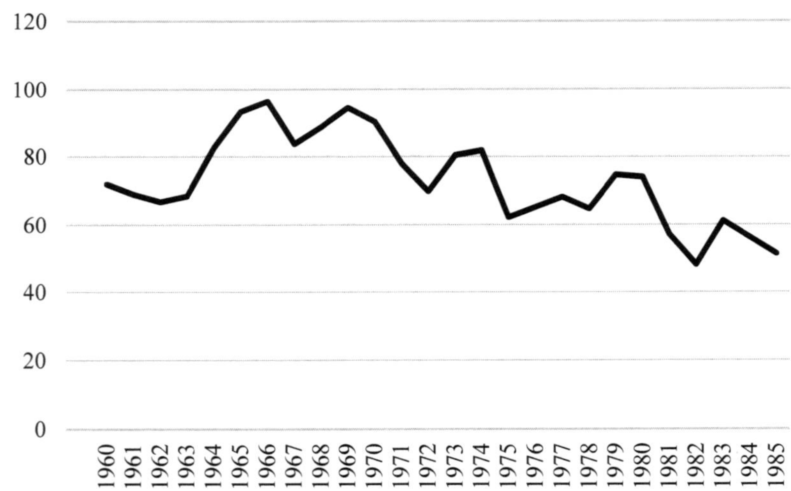

The fact that the terms of trade were improving from the consumer states' standpoint obviously did not rule out short-term interruptions of supply due to wars, natural disasters and so forth that could pose a threat to the

144 Using the MUV overcomes the problem of exchange rate changes that would arise with the use of a national price index. As the MUV expresses the size of a basket of manufactured exports that could be obtained for one US dollar at different times, it provides an appropriate counterpoint for measuring the purchasing power of commodity-exporting countries; *Radetzki*, Handbook, 72.

security of supply. Declining real prices did not bode well for any attempts of cartelisation by the ore-exporting states in the Global South, however. It also meant that the commodity cartels had not been able to reverse the downward trend of real prices. Widespread "cartel paranoia" – as one analyst called it in 1976 – turned out to be unfounded.[145] The same was true regarding the Global North's worries about the New International Economic Order declared by the UN General Assembly in 1974. Trusting in a false belief in their commodity power and their numerical strength, the Third World had overplayed its hand in the confrontation with the industrialised states as UN officials and diplomats from the Global South acknowledged in retrospect.[146] OPEC had stylised itself as a role model and champion of the Third World, but – contrary to what the North had feared and the South had hoped for – the alliance between OPEC and other commodity exporters never came to fruition. Instead, high oil prices caused a grave economic crisis for most Third World countries, who were drowning in national debt. At the same time, Arab oil producers preferred to accumulate their money in Western banks rather than practising solidarity with the Global South.[147]

Several factors contributed to the decline in real commodity prices. On the demand side, the economic downturn in the industrialised countries following the oil price shocks substantially slowed down demand for all kinds of commodities. Besides, there was a longer-term trend of declining consumption of natural raw materials per unit of GDP. This trend was caused by the increasing displacement of natural materials by synthetics – affecting mainly agricultural commodities like fibres, but also metals like tin, copper and lead – as well as by technological innovations and changes in the economic structures in industrialised (or increasingly post-industrial) countries. Supply, on the other hand, continued to expand as developing countries – facing falling prices, high energy costs and rising debts – had little choice but to increase exports, thus driving down prices still further. Moreover, new capacities in mining were coming on stream as the result of investments that were made when metals were scarce and prices were high.[148]

In 1974, metal prices were further depressed by large sales from the US government stockpile and from excessive commercial stocks in Japan that

145 *Fried*, Trade, 644.
146 *Weiss/Carayannis/Emmerij/Jolly*, UN Voices, 227–231.
147 *Dietrich*, Oil Revolution, 295, 299, 306.
148 *Maizels*, Commodities, 14–20; *Wengenroth*, Eiffelturm.

were the result of panic buying when prices were rising. In retrospect, it is clear that the events of 1973–74 were not the harbinger of a new era of commodity power, but merely one of three commodity booms in recent history together with 1950–51 and most recently 2004–10.[149]

Finally, the importance of the metal trade and the role of developing countries must be put into perspective. In general, the volume of international trade in non-fuel minerals was much smaller than that of oil. Also, the major share of trade in non-fuel commodities took place between industrialised countries (including the Eastern Bloc) and not between the North and the South.[150] Contrary to the expectations of the early 1970s, a look at the relative importance of West Germany's foreign trade partners does not support the idea of growing market power and political weight of commodity exporters. Rather, in the last third of the twentieth century, the exchange among industrialised countries dominated and the relative importance of commodity exporters as trade partners declined. Only oil-exporting states played a more significant role as trade partners for West Germany, but their importance decreased in the 1980s.[151] The leverage possessed by metal-exporting countries on West Germany and similar states was therefore fairly weak.

In this context, it is important to note that the security of one can be the insecurity of another. While industrialised states enjoyed secure supplies in the 1980s and political, economic and academic interest in commodities dwindled in the Global North, developing countries which depended on commodity exports experienced hardships comparable to the Great Depression of the 1930s.[152]

Conclusion

Economic security assumed increasing importance in the post-war decades as the military threat of the Cold War receded somewhat into the background. From the late 1960s, possible shortages and interruptions of the supply of base metals like copper, nickel and aluminium were perceived as a threat to companies, economic growth and employment in West Germany, as they were in other Western industrialised states. These concerns

---

149 *Radetzki*, Handbook, 66–72.
150 *Fried*, Trade, 643.
151 *Ziegler*, Deutschland, 54–55.
152 *Maizels*, Commodities, 9–10; *Radetzki*, Handbook, 1–2.

were triggered by widespread nickel shortages between 1966 and 1970, which were caused by the preceding rapid growth of demand combined with labour disputes in the Canadian mining industry. In retrospect, this would remain the only real metal shortage in this period, and this was somewhat ironic because Canada was in no way a politically unstable or hostile Third World state. Based on the experience with nickel, the state and private businesses began to "securitize" metal supply and increasingly perceived import-dependency as a vulnerability.

At first, the issue was seen in the light of competition for commodities between industrialised states and this fundamentally shaped the discussion which took place in 1969. This perceived threat changed after the first oil price shock in November 1973, however, against the background of sky-rocketing commodity prices. There then arose widespread concerns that the case of oil marked only the beginning of a broader confrontation between raw material-consuming industrialised states and raw material-producing Third World states wielding their new-found "commodity power". The threat to the security of supply was seen in the context of economic decolonisation and the Global North-South divide. Even though it soon became apparent that the "mini-OPECs" in the field of metals stood little chance to repeat the oil-producers' success, the discussion went on until the end of the decade. Following to the revolution in Iran, tensions in Southern Africa and a resulting second peak in commodity prices, the discussion surrounding the security of metal supply reached another high point in 1978–79 but ceased again soon afterwards.

West Germany responded in several ways to this challenge, including by implementing measures designed to expand and diversify metal supply as well as diplomacy and aid directed to states in the Global South. Unlike other industrialised nations where strategic stockpiles already existed or were newly created, actors in West Germany discussed a state-supported stockpiling scheme for more than a decade, but finally never launched such a programme. It is important to note that while public attention for commodity policy was at its highest in the wake of the 1973 oil price shock, several measures to improve commodity supply like subsidies for mineral exploration and research into deep-sea mining had started well before this. In hindsight, West Germany was well-advised not to start a stockpiling programme given the long-term downwards trend of commodity prices and the absence of interruptions of supply. This also meant that the effectiveness of the West German commodity policy was never really put to the test.

Even though it is easy in retrospect to dismiss the concerns about metal supply as alarmist, events from the late 1960s onwards fell outside of the actors' purview and were inevitably a cause for concern. Likewise, it was a false but obvious analogy to expect further successful commodity cartels in the wake of the first oil price shock. The rapidly increasing demand for metals and growing global interdependence, as well as a radically changed international community – in which post-colonial states outnumbered Western countries in the UN – were new and unfamiliar developments. Actors from all sides struggled to find their way in this reshaped political and economic landscape. Miscalculations by the actors in both the state and in the business sectors in the Global North and South were the result. Analysing the perceived threat that led to the "securitization" of base metal supplies thus offers an insight into the economic and political challenges that faced West Germany in the 1970s, such as increasing global interdependence and an international community that had been transformed by decolonisation and the broader repercussions of the oil price shock.

Regarding these challenges, there are evident parallels between the debate on base metal supplies and the contemporary debate on the influence of foreign capital in West Germany, as examined in the contribution of Christian Marx in this volume. Another parallel is the revival of these concerns in the twenty-first century and the role played by China. Commodities in general and metals in particular experienced another boom between 2004 and 2011, which – notwithstanding its longer duration – resembled the boom which took place in 1973–74 in several ways. This time Rare Earth Elements (REE) stood in the spotlight when China cut its exports and boycotted Japan in 2010. Prices for REEs skyrocketed, and fears of China's commodity power and expectations of a global race for scarce raw materials ran rampant.[153] Again, states and businesses in the Western world "securitized" metal supplies and initiated various measures to protect their access to these resources, and the boom was a transitory phenomenon. Remarkably, there was hardly any reference to the 1970s in the public debate on commodities around 2010. At the time of writing, in spring 2020, prices of commodities including metals are falling again, reflecting a sharp slowdown in global manufacturing activity due to the COVID-19 pandemic.[154] The security of metal supply is currently the least of the concerns of companies and states, yet this will most likely change again in the future as the boom-and-bust cycle continues.

153 *Jung/Wagner*, Rohstofflücke; *Normile*, Specter; *Mildner/Lauster*, Machtressource; *Klare*, Race, 152–182.

154 *World Bank*, Commodity, 37.

Bibliography

Anonymous: Absolut hilflos, in: Der Spiegel, 17.11.1969, p. 173
Anonymous: Ärger über Matthöfer, in: Der Spiegel, 23.4.1979, p. 123
Anonymous: Auf Vorrat: Chrom statt Dollar, in: Der Spiegel, 7.5.1979, p. 116
Anonymous: Ein vernünftiger Beschluß, in: Frankfurter Allgemeine Zeitung, 15.11.1980, p. 13
Anonymous: Forget those cartels, in: The Economist, 15.2.1975, p. 85
Anonymous: Gegen staatliche Beschaffung, in: Frankfurter Allgemeine Zeitung, 27.5.1974, p. 9
Anonymous: Handel mit Dynamit, in: Der Spiegel, 30.7.1973, p. 70–71
Anonymous: Kein Puffer, in: Der Spiegel, 10.3.1980, p. 79–81
Anonymous: Key Indicators: World Commodity Prices, in: The Economist, 17.11.1973, p. 128
Anonymous: Knappes Zeitungspapier, in: Der Spiegel, 22.10.1973, p. 111
Anonymous: Mit knappen Vorräten sorglos geaast, Der Spiegel, in: 19.11.1973, p. 25–30
Anonymous: Nicht alle Blütenträume reifen…, in: Der Metallmarkt. Wochenbericht Verein deutscher Metallhändler, 18.9.1970
Anonymous: Noch eine Knappheit, in: Frankfurter Allgemeine Zeitung, 4.1.1974, p. 7
Anonymous: Questions concerning establishment of a New International Economic Order, in: Yearbook of the United Nations 1974. New York 1977, p. 305–357
Anonymous: Rohstoff-Versorgung. Ärmste der Welt, in: Der Spiegel, 27.1.1969, p. 38–40
Anonymous: Running short, in: The Economist, 29.9.1973, p. 84
Anonymous: Supply cartels may spur inflation, in: The Guardian, 13.12.1974, p. 13
Anonymous: The new commodity rich, in: The Economist, 11.5.1974, p. 76–77
Anonymus: Währungsreserven für Rohstofflager?, in: Frankfurter Allgemeine Zeitung, 1.3.1979, p. 11
Anonymous: What is short and why, in: The Economist, 8.12.1973, p. 108
Anonymous: Wir erzwingen die neue Ordnung, in: Der Spiegel, 1.9.1975, p. 96–106
Anonymous: Nickelmarkt. Wenn Kanadier streiken, in: DIE ZEIT, Nr. 43, 24.10.1969, p. 39
Abelshauser, Werner: Deutsche Wirtschaftsgeschichte. Von 1945 bis zur Gegenwart. München 2011
Barclay, Lou Anne/Girvan, Norman: Transnational restructuring and the Jamaican bauxite industry. The swinging pendulum of bargaining power, in: Gendron, Robin S./Ingulstad, Mats/Storli, Espen (eds.): Aluminum Ore. The Political Economy of the Global Bauxite Industry. Vancouver 2013, p. 238–267

Bergsten, C. Fred: The threat from the Third World, in: Foreign Policy 11 (Summer 1973), p. 102–124

Bergsten, C. Fred: The world may have to live with shortages, in: The New York Times, 27.1.1974, p. 3

Böhm, Enrico: Die Sicherheit des Westens. Entstehung und Funktion der G7-Gipfel (1975-1981). München 2014

Bösch, Frank/Graf, Rüdiger: Reacting to anticipations: Energy crises and energy policy in the 1970s. An Introduction, in: Historical Social Research 39 (2014), 4, p. 7–21

Conze, Eckart: Die Suche nach Sicherheit. Eine Geschichte der Bundesrepublik Deutschland von 1949 bis in die Gegenwart. München 2009

Culver, William W.: Intergovernmental Council of Copper Exporting Countries, in: Leonard, Thomas M. et al. (eds.): Encyclopedia of U.S.-Latin American Relations Vol. 2. Los Angeles 2012, p. 500–501

Culver, William W.: International Bauxite Association (IBA), in: Leonard, Thomas M. et al. (eds.): Encyclopedia of U.S.-Latin American Relations Vol. 2. Los Angeles 2012, p. 501–502

Culver, William W.: Iron Exporting Countries, Association of (APEF), in: Leonard, Thomas M. et al. (eds.): Encyclopedia of U.S.-Latin American Relations Vol. 2. Los Angeles 2012, p. 510–511

Daniels, Mario: "Wirtschaftlicher Landesverrat" im „Wirtschaftskampf gegen Deutschland". Die deutsche Chemieindustrie und die Bekämpfung ausländischer Industriespionage in den 1920er Jahren, in: Historische Zeitschrift 299 (2014), 2, p. 352–383

Daniels, Mario: Brain Drain, innerwestliche Weltmarktkonkurrenz und nationale Sicherheit. Die Kampagne der westdeutschen Chemieindustrie gegen Wissenstransfer in die USA in den 1950er Jahren, in: Vierteljahrshefte für Zeitgeschichte 64 (2016), 3, p. 491–515

Dicks, Adrian: Recurrent nightmare for U.S., in: Financial Times, 14.3.1974, p. 31

Diekhof, Rolf: Anschlag auf ein Monopol: Das Preisdiktat für Nickel soll gebrochen werden, in: DIE ZEIT, 7.8.1970, p. 21

Dietrich, Christopher R. W.: Oil Revolution. Anticolonial Elites, Sovereign Rights, and the Economic Culture of Decolonization. Cambridge 2017

Edwards, John: Free-market nickel price soars as INCO strike starts, in: Financial Times, 11.7.1969, p. 4

Edwards, John: Nickel supplies below normal for 5 month, in: Financial Times, 17.11.1969, p. 1

Ehrenberg, Herbert: Öl statt Gold. Ein Vorschlag zur Rohstoffbevorratung, in: DIE ZEIT, 14.2.1975, p. 42

Eick, Jürgen: Liebäugeln mit der Autarkie?, in: Frankfurter Allgemeine Zeitung, 3.11.1973, p. 1

Freyberg, Werner: Rohstoffversorgung für Deutschland muß langfristig gesichert werden, in: Handelsblatt, 21./22.11.1969, p. 29

Fried, Edward R.: International trade in raw materials: myths and realities, in: Science, Vol. 191, No. 4228, p. 641–646

Frøland, Hans-Otto/Ingulstad, Mats: "Europe cannot engage in autarchical policies." European raw materials strategy from 1945 to the present, in: Sanders, Andreas R. D./Sandvik, Pål Thonstad/Storli, Espen (eds.): The Political Economy of Resource Regulation. An International and Comparative History, 1850–2015. Vancouver 2019, p. 302–326

Gendron, Robin S.: Canada and the nationalization of Alcan's bauxite operations in Guinea and Guyana, in: Gendron, Robin S./Ingulstad, Mats/Storli, Espen (eds.): Aluminum Ore. The Political Economy of the Global Bauxite Industry. Vancouver 2013, p. 211–237

Graf, Rüdiger: Between national and human security: Energy security in the United States and Western Europe in the 1970s, in: Historical Social Research 35 (2010), 4, p. 329–348

Graf, Rüdiger: Öl und Souveränität. Petroknowledge und Energiepolitik in den USA und Westeuropa in den 1970er Jahren. Berlin 2014

Garavini, Giuliano: Completing decolonisation. The 1973 "oil shock" and the struggle for economic rights, in: The International History Review 33 (2011), 3, p. 473–487

Garavini, Giuliano: After Empires. European Integration, Decolonization, and the Challenge from the Global South. Oxford 2012

Herlt, Rudolf: Das Tribunal der Zornigen, in: DIE ZEIT, 19.4.1974, p. 1

Högselius, Per: Red Gas. Russia and the Origins of the European Energy Dependence. New York 2013

Huchting, Friedrich: Abfallwirtschaft im Dritten Reich, in: Technikgeschichte 48 (1981), 3, p. 252–273

Illing, Falk: Energiepolitik in Deutschland. Die energiepolitischen Maßnahmen der Bundesregierung 1949–2015. Baden-Baden 2016

Jürgensen, Hans: Ein Dutzend Rohstoffkartelle?, in: Frankfurter Allgemeine Zeitung, 10.4.1974, p. 13

Jung, Alexander/Wagner, Wieland: Die Rohstofflücke, in: Der Spiegel, 2.11.2009, p. 85–86

Kehrt, Christian: Gondwana's promises. German geologists in Antarctica between basic science and resource exploration in the late 1970s, in: Historical Social Research 40 (2015), 2, p. 202–221

Kg.: Falscher Weg, in: Frankfurter Allgemeine Zeitung, 7.5.1979, p. 11

Klare, Michael T.: The Race for What's Left. The Global Scramble for the World's Last Resources. New York 2012

Kleinschmidt, Christian/Ziegler, Dieter: Deutsche Wirtschaftsinteressen zwischen Entwicklungshilfe und Dekolonisierung: eine Einleitung, in: Kleinschmidt, Christian/Ziegler, Dieter (eds.): Dekolonisierungsgewinner. Deutsche Außenpolitik und Außenwirtschaftsbeziehungen im Zeitalter des Kalten Krieges. Berlin/Boston 2018, p. 1–17

Krasner, Stephen D.: Oil is the exception, in: Foreign Policy 14 (Spring 1974), p. 68–84

Lantzke, Ulf: Sicherung der Rohstoffversorgung in der Bundesrepublik Deutschland. Referat anläßlich eines internationalen Fachkongresses der Friedrich-Ebert-Stiftung am 23. November 1970 in Leverkusen (BMWi-Texte; 118). Bonn 1970

Lifset, Robert D.: A new understanding of the American energy crisis of the 1970s, in: Historical Social Research 39, 4 (2014), p. 22–42

Litvak, Isaiah A./Maule, Christopher J.: The International Bauxite Agreement: A commodity cartel in action, in: International Affairs 56 (1980), 2, p. 296–314

Luxbacher, Günther: „Für bestimmte Anwendungen best geeignete Werkstoffe finden." Zur Praxis der Forschung an Ersatzstoffen für Metalle in den deutschen Autarkie-Phasen des 20. Jahrhunderts, in: NTM. Zeitschrift für Geschichte der Wissenschaften, Technik und Medizin 19 (2011), 1, p. 41–68

Maier, Charles S.: "Malaise." The crisis of capitalism in the 1970s, in: Ferguson, Niall et al. (eds.): The Shock of the Global. The 1970s in Perspective. Cambridge, Mass./London 2010, S. 25–48

Maier, Helmut: Ideologie, Rüstung und Ressourcen. Das Kaiser-Wilhelm-Institut für Metallforschung und die „Deutschen Metalle" 1933-1945, in: id. (ed.): Rüstungsforschung im Nationalsozialismus. Organisation, Mobilisierung und Entgrenzung der Technikwissenschaften. Göttingen 2002, p. 357–388

Maizels, Alfred: Commodities in Crisis. The Commodity Crisis of the 1980s and the Political Economy of International Commodity Policies. Oxford 1992

Malcolm, Andrew H.: The "shortage" of bathroom tissue. A classic study in rumor, in: New York Times, 3.2.1974, p. 29

Migani, Guia: The EEC and the challenge of the ACP states' industrialisation, 1972–1975, in: Grabas, Christian/Nützenadel, Alexander (eds.): Industrial Policy in Europe after 1945. Wealth, Power and Economic Development in the Cold War. Basingstoke 2014, p. 256–276

Mildner, Stormy-Annika/Lauster, Gitta: Machtressource Metalle. Achillesferse der alten Wirtschaftsnationen?, in: Internationale Politik 66 (2011), 3, p. 53–59

Mingst, Karen A.: Cooperation or illusion. An examination of the Intergovernmental Council of Copper Exporting Countries, in: International Organization 30 (1976), 2, p. 263–287

Natorp, Klaus: Vorgetäuschter Konsens, in: Frankfurter Allgemeine Zeitung, 3.5.1974, p. 1

Newman, Barry: Nickel rationing ends but surplus unlikely, in: The Guardian, 30.12.1970, p. 14

Normile, Dennis: Haunted by "specter of unavailability", experts huddle over critical materials, in: Science, Vol. 330, No. 6011 (17.12.2010), p. 1598

Nyerere, Julius: Third World Negotiating Strategy, in: Third World Quarterly 1 (1979), 2, p. 20–23

Paley, William S. (ed.): Resources for Freedom. Vol. 1: Foundations for Growth and Security. Washington, DC 1952

Pasdach, Uwe Jens/Sames, Carl-Wolfgang: Die langfristige Vorausschau von Angebot und Nachfrage bei mineralischen Rohstoffen, dargestellt am Beispiel Nickel, in: Erzmetall 22 (1969), 4, p. 165–174

Radetzki, Marian: The anatomy of three commodity booms, in: Resources Policy 31 (2006), p. 56–64

Radetzki, Marian: A Handbook of Primary Commodities in the Global Economy. Cambridge 2008

Radmann, Wolf: CIPEC – The copper exporting countries, in: INTERECONOMICS 8 (1973), 8, p. 245–249

Saßmannshausen, Günther: Bergbau und Rohstoffe: Schlüssel zum Fortschritt. Perspektiven der Rohstoffversorgung der Bundesrepublik Deutschland nach der Energiekrise 1973/74, in: Jahrbuch für Bergbau, Energie, Mineralöl und Chemie 83 (1975), p. 1–43

Scherner, Jonas: Lernen und Lernversagen. Die „Metallmobilisierung“ im Deutschen Reich 1939 bis 1945, in: Vierteljahrshefte für Zeitgeschichte 66 (2018), 2, p. 233–266

Schmidt, Helmut: Der Politiker als Ökonom, in: id.: Kontinuität und Konzentration, 2. ed. 1976, p. 36–52

Sluga, Glenda: The Transformation of International Institutions. Global Shock as Cultural Shock, in: Ferguson, Niall et al. (eds.): The Shock of the Global. The 1970s in Perspective. Cambridge, Mass./London 2010, p. 223–236

Sparenberg, Ole: A historical perspective on deep-sea mining for manganese nodules, 1965–2019, in: The Extractive Industries and Society 6 (2019), 3, p. 842–854

Swansbrough, Robert H.: The mineral crisis and U.S. interests in Latin America, in: The Journal of Politics 38 (1976), 1, p. 2–24

Tomlinson, Brian Roger: What was the Third World?, in: Journal of Contemporary History 38 (2003), p. 307–321

Venn, Fiona: The Oil Crisis. London et al. 2002

Wade, Nicholas: Raw materials. U.S. grows more vulnerable to Third World cartels, in: Science, Vol. 183, No. 4121 (18.1.1974), p. 185–186

Weiss, Thomas G./Carayannis, Tatiana/Emmerij, Louis/Jolly, Richard: UN Voices. The Struggle for Development and Social Justice. Bloomington 2005

Wengenroth, Ulrich: Eiffelturm und Coladose. Über den Zusammenhang von Wirtschaftswachstum und Metallverbrauch, in: Kultur & Technik 19 (1995), 3, p. 11–15

World Bank: Commodity Markets Outlook. April 2020. Implications of COVID-19 for Commodities. Washington, DC 2020

Ziegler, Dieter: Deutschland und der Weltmarkt, in: Kleinschmidt, Christian/Ziegler, Dieter (eds.): Dekolonisierungsgewinner. Deutsche Außenpolitik und Außenwirtschaftsbeziehungen im Zeitalter des Kalten Krieges. Berlin/Boston 2018, p. 19–55

Performing Diligence: Nuclear Labour, Reactor Safety, and Public Relations in the West German Nuclear Industry in the 1980s

Sascha Brünig

On 28 March 1979, a partial meltdown occurred at the Three Mile Island nuclear power plant near Harrisburg, Pennsylvania.[1] Through a combination of technical malfunctions and failure to correctly assess the scope of the accident, a small dose of radioactivity was released into the environment. With parts of the local population preparing to evacuate the surrounding towns and villages, public confidence in nuclear power decreased considerably.[2] Three Mile Island's ramifications were not felt solely in the US. In West Germany, too, the accident provided a severe challenge to nuclear power advocates, as opposition to the building of new nuclear plants reached a new high.[3] In no small part, this aggravated anti-nuclear activism in the wake of Three Mile Island was an outcome of the conflict over nuclear power that had been raging in the Federal Republic since the mid-1970s. Nevertheless, the accident at Three Mile Island and the way the event captivated the public for days on end functioned as a focal point that allowed for a (re)unification of different (and sometimes contradictory) strands of nuclear critique.[4]

Confronted with mass manifestations of nuclear anxiety (most importantly in the West German capital of Bonn, where nearly 150,000 demonstrators gathered on 14 October 1979), nuclear industry leaders and state authorities found themselves struggling to dispel concerns that a similar accident could occur in the Federal Republic. Against the background of Three Mile Island's emblematic representation of nuclear power's suppos-

---

1 Previous versions of this chapter were discussed at the Integrated Graduate School of SFB/TRR 138 'Dynamics of Security' and at the Oberseminar of Prof. Eckart Conze, Philipps University Marburg. I extend my sincere gratitude to everyone involved.

2 *Walker*, Three Mile Island.

3 *Bösch*, Power; *Bösch*, Zeitenwende, 333–362.

4 This argument, albeit with a focus on the U.S. in the 1980s, is provided by *Zaretsky*, Radiation.

edly fatal risks, however, the reassurance that West German plants were built differently and possessed more elaborate safety systems than their American counterparts proved largely ineffective. Instead, the industry became involved in what many nuclear power advocates considered an uphill battle against an emotionally-charged discussion of Three Mile Island and its lessons for West German nuclear safety.[5]

This article argues that the accident – which many contemporaries perceived as an existential threat to the West German nuclear industry and nuclear power in general – provided the incentive for a substantial transformation of industry public relations. Having been invisible for decades, the "hidden specialists of nuclear power"[6] (i.e. engineers, technicians, and nuclear plant workers) increasingly took centre stage. This transformation from public invisibility to technological standard-bearers played out through a number of public relations measures. In unprecedented numbers, visitors were informed about the everyday material practices of nuclear work, either on-site at power plants (many of which possessed designated visitors' centres) or at trade fairs and expositions around the country. Utility companies such as Rheinisch-Westfälisches Elektrizitätswerk (RWE) offered lotteries in which entrants could win guided tours through one of their plants. Providing the public with insights into the material practices of operating nuclear technology drew upon and furthered a discourse of German '*Ingenieurskunst*' (art of engineering) that posited an unparalleled national prowess in all things technical. Adverting campaigns commissioned by Kraftwerk Union (KWU), West Germany's largest nuclear technology manufacturer, featured photographs of nuclear personnel at work in a section of a plant or in an office, turning to the camera as if having been momentarily pulled away for a picture. As '*Ingenieurskunst*' and the national legacy it represented became personalised, material practices also became entangled with notions of a specifically German safety culture that dated back to the formation of the engineering profession.[7]

The history of nuclear power in the Federal Republic has been extensively researched and forms an impressive body of scholarship. A large number of contributions have focussed on the social and political discours-

5 For nuclear power and fear in the Federal Republic see *Weisker*, Emotion; *Weisker*, Expertenvertrauen; also *Biess*, Angst, 359–412.

6 *Johnston*, Children, preface; *Johnston*, Engineer.

7 For an examplary venture into the German engineering notion of 'Arbeitsschutz' see *Kleinöder*, Unternehmen.

es in which nuclear power became entangled.[8] On the other hand, studies on the development of nuclear technology (often researched by current or former industry engineers and managers or by pro-nuclear politicians) have provided rich, albeit somewhat technicist histories of nuclear power, which often pushed public discourse to the background.[9] Only recently, attempts have been made at developing analytical pathways which integrate both strands of research. Most notably, Helmuth Trischler and Robert Bud have called for greater attention to the "gadgets, devices, machines and systems that become individual brands within the public sphere", thus forming "public technologies".[10] This article embraces their proposal. It rests on a theoretical framework that implores the cultural history of technology to take seriously the materiality of technical artefacts and practices. To a large degree, this framework is informed by the growing importance that anthropologists, sociologists, and historians have attributed to the fact that "social processes of representation ... are embedded in the material world of things".[11] In this perspective, rather than as disconnected entities that can be analysed separately, technical materiality and the cultural representation of technology emerge as inherently constitutive of one another.

Departing from this observation, this article traces how the insistence on an unparalleled diligence in nuclear safety was enacted within the material practices of nuclear work and how, in turn, the utilisation of nuclear work for public relations purposes fed back into the professional identities of nuclear personnel.[12] I argue that the transformation of industry public relations towards showcasing material practices possessed a dual dimension: While the principal aim of the nuclear industry lay with more effectively communicating its engineering and operational thoroughness to a West German public that was perceived to be increasingly anti-nuclear, turning engineers and technicians into figureheads of the nuclear industry also provided professional identification to a workforce that felt increasingly beleaguered by growing public scrutiny of the 'nuclear state' (R. Jungk)

8 *Engels*, Naturpolitik, 344–375; *Arndt*, Tschernobyl; *Hasenöhrl*, Zivilgesellschaft, 200–234 and 405–471; *Kirchhof/Meyer*, Protest; *Hillengaß*, Atomkraft; *Schüring*, Atomstaat; *Tompkins*, Protest; *Milder*, Democracy; *Wehner*, Versicherung; *Gaumer*, Wackersdorf, *Augustine*, Technocracy; *Jordan*, Ausgestrahlt; *Schramm*, Kirche; *Pohl*, Atomprotest; *Kirchhof*, Pathways.

9 *Müller*, Kernenergie; *Laufs*, Reaktorsicherheit.

10 *Trischler/Bud*, Public Technology, 188 and passim.

11 *Pinch*, SCOT, 45.

12 For an excellent inquiry into the French nuclear workplace and the production of professional identities see *Hecht*, Identity.

and the supposedly authoritarian, even proto-fascist inclinations of a technology in which they were (economically as well as symbolically) invested.[13] In showing how both communicative dimensions were intricately connected, this article can be read as a contribution to the history of technology as well as to the cultural history of labour and business history.

Empirically, the article's argument is based on a close reading of nuclear industry public relations material from the 1980s. The selection of eligible sources follows an augmented definition of the term 'nuclear industry', which is broadened to include all companies that either built or operated nuclear technology.[14] Similarly wide is the definition of 'public relations' material: advertisements and brochures aimed explicitly at a public audience are included, as well as trade journals and periodicals widely received within the Federal Republic. While this augmented scope provides the article with a broad empirical base, there is one crucial caveat to be disclosed: the fact that, regrettably, the archival tradition of the West German nuclear industry is sketchy, if sources are (made) accessible at all.[15] A number of important questions thus cannot be addressed. These include who was responsible for strategising company public relations, whether the material was designed in-house or whether this task was delegated to public relations agencies, and so forth. Because sources for researching these questions are hard to attain, the article profits considerably from an extensive interview conducted with physicist Ulrich Waas, a former staff member of KWU's public relations department.

In what follows, I will examine the changing role played by the material practices of nuclear work in public relations and the way that these practices were discursively represented. Before doing so, however, it is warranted to situate these transformations against the background of Three Mile Island. The next section will therefore provide an overview of the vigorous debates on nuclear safety and human failure in the aftermath of the accident and contextualise the growing unease of engineers and power plant workers with the nuclear controversy in the Federal Republic.

---

13 *Jungk*, Atomstaat; for the pressures on nuclear workers in the debate on the 'nuclear state' and beyond see *Wendland*, Reaktorsicherheit, 317ff.; a concise history of the debate in the late 1970s Federal Republic is provided by *Dannenbaum*, "Atom-Staat".

14 For a similar approach see *Radkau*, Aufstieg; *Radkau/Hahn*, Aufstieg.

15 This holds especially true for the case of KWU. While significant portions of the company's archives in Erlangen have allegedly been destroyed in the early 2000s, their mother corporation Siemens have regrettably never created a systematic archive of KWU business proceedings, c.f. *Schüring*, Advertising, fn. 24.

Three Mile Island and the Debate on Human Failure in Nuclear Safety

In the Federal Republic, Three Mile Island functioned as an accelerant for the opposition to nuclear power as well as for the ever-growing anti-nuclear movement.[16] As news broadcasts and TV commentators relayed images of terrified Harrisburg residents directly into the living rooms of the Federal Republic, the narrowly-avoided meltdown of the reactor's core seemed to confirm that the nuclear industry had grossly misrepresented nuclear power's supposedly fatal flaws.[17] Photographs of Three Mile Island's cooling towers quickly established themselves as potent images of nuclear catastrophe, with the public having no political say over the threat literally looming large on the horizon.

Unease was growing among proponents of nuclear power as well. At the opening ceremony of the European Nuclear Conference in May 1979, chairman of the Jülich nuclear research centre Karl Heinz Beckurts condemned the "sensationalism and hysterical fear-mongering in the West German public that renders impossible a responsible discussion of the important and complex topic of nuclear safety".[18] Similarly, a contributor at a workshop organised by RWE and held a few weeks after the accident, diagnosed a "vicious cycle of fear" within which the West German public was supposedly caught.[19]

For many within the nuclear industry, Three Mile Island was the writing on the wall that pointed to a potentially irreversible upheaval of nuclear policy. Not only were approval procedures for scheduled nuclear plants affected, which significantly hampered the nuclear industry's business outlook; all the more challenging for the long-term future of the nuclear business was the perception that guiding principles of industrial modernity were in the process of being undermined. With the threat of nuclear catastrophe greater than ever before, Three Mile Island and the ensuing discussions on the future of nuclear power constituted more than a debate on a supposed runaway technology. Rather, as conceptions of techno-scientific rationality that had formed the bedrock of post-war modernisation were politicised, the nuclear debate "exposed a rift that ran straight through the

16 *Augustine*, Technocracy, 145–150.
17 *Bösch*, Power, 71; *Radkau/Hahn*, Aufstieg, 333.
18 *Beckurts*, Kernenergie.
19 *Zischka*, Teufelskreis.

core of twentieth-century society".[20] One victim of this development were Probabilistic Risk Assessment (PRA) studies, which many nuclear industry leaders had previously regarded as an effective tool in winning over nuclear sceptics.[21]

The politicisation of techno-scientific rationality provided a particular challenge to the nuclear community as it conflicted with the traditional self-image of the engineering profession. As the sociographic research of Eugen Kogon and Gert Hortleder from the early 1970s illustrates, engineers and technicians largely embraced a Weberian professionalism and considered themselves above the fray of political conflict.[22] With this self-perception corresponded a heavy idealisation of the political sphere in which confrontations of interest were supposed to be overcome by rational and dispassionate assessment.[23] Even if the engineering profession somewhat departed from this idealisation and took on a more pragmatic stance,[24] nuclear engineers in particular largely upheld a strong division between the political and technological spheres.[25]

Pressure on nuclear workers also increased from a different angle. Against the backdrop of negligent and erroneous accident management by the Three Mile Island operating crew, discussion turned to the fallibility of humans in a reactor safety regime that was becoming consistently more complicated as more and more technical components were integrated.[26] To many technicians, these discussions amounted to a public withdrawal of confidence. Their disenchantment was exacerbated as the political fallout of Three Mile Island induced a reorganisation of safety responsibilities mandated by the Minister of the Interior Gerhart Baum (FDP). Baum's ministry introduced regulation detailing the mandatory presence of nuclear engineers in the control room at all times.[27] For the veteran '*Kraftwerksmeister*' (plant foremen), who often possessed significantly longer operational experience than engineers, this was taken as an affront: first, the spectre of computerisation had threatened to make a growing

20 *Weart*, Fear, 203; for a constructivist perspective on emotionality and rationality in the nuclear conflict and the use of emotions as an argument see *Götter*, Emotionen.

21 *Esselborn/Zachmann*, Safety.

22 *Kogon*, Stunde; *Hortleder*, Ingenieure; see also *Hänseroth*, Fortschritt.

23 *Hortleder*, Gesellschaftsbild.

24 Cf. *Engels/Hertzog*, Macht; *Hertzog*, Politisierung.

25 *Johnston*, Children.

26 *Herzog*, Versagen; *Radkau/Hahn*, Aufstieg, 334; cf. *Augustine*, Technocracy, 68.

27 *Bösch*, Power; for the discussion of this step within the nuclear industry see *Fechner*, Schutzbarriere.

number of jobs superfluous;[28] now, the status of non-academic plant personnel was further weakened as they were perceived as the frailest link in a safety regime narrowly taming the primordial forces of nuclear power.[29]

Hollywood, meanwhile, translated the growing public unease with nuclear power into products of popular culture. A prime example for the cinematic depiction of nuclear-engineers-turned-villains is the movie *The China Syndrome* (1979). Incidentally, the all-star cast film was released just twelve days prior to the accident at Three Mile Island and – with fiction seemingly becoming reality – attracted considerable numbers of viewers in the US. In the movie, a television crew (played by Jane Fonda and Michael Douglas), filming in the control room of a nuclear plant, witnesses a narrowly-averted accident that hints at serious deficiencies in the reactor's design. The rattled shift supervisor subsequently finds numeruous technical irregularities, all of which are downplayed by plant management and withheld from the public. While the filmmakers especially vilify the irresponsible behaviour of plant management, the main storyline of the movie is undoubtedly "the quandary of an ethically minded nuclear engineer vacillating between company loyalty, on the one hand, and concerns about engineering safety on the other".[30] To many viewers, the attempted cover-up of a severe danger to the public seemed to hint at a loss of professional ideals within the engineering community. Admittedly, *The China Syndrome's* success remained largely confined to the US, but the West German nuclear industry initially perceived it as a potentially substantial threat and even organised a film screening with a specially-assembled audience made up of technicians, public relations specialists, psychologists, and film critics to assess its possible harm on public trust in nuclear experts.[31]

Against this background, engineers and technicians within the nuclear industry increasingly constituted a professional community under threat. At the same time, motivation was high to recapture public trust. As the example of one KWU engineer demonstrates, the desire to engage in discussion with nuclear sceptics and persuade them of one's diligence and trustworthiness made some go to somewhat extreme lengths:

> Then there was one engineer, who was responsible for designing and testing valve fittings. And he wrote a letter to the editor of the local

---

28 *Fränz*, Techniker; *Heßler*, Obsoleszenz.

29 *Bösch*, Power; for the history of professional status struggles between engineers and 'Meister' see *Radkau*, Technik, 204.

30 *Johnston*, Children, 254.

31 Informationskreis Kernenergie, China Syndrome, BArch B 196/20644.

> newspaper, ten pages long, detailing the norms for these valves and the thoroughness with which he went about his work. Now, the editorial staff, they said: is he completely out of his mind? Let him submit his doctoral thesis elsewhere![32]

The initiative of company staff to enlist in public relations did not go unnoticed by KWU management. In fact, the company attempted to further a sense of public involvement within its workforce. As the physicist Werner Rudloff, who headed KWU's public relations department at the time, observed a few years later,

> we tried to convey that the public discussion of nuclear power as well as on energy in general could not be delegated but was a matter in which everyone should be invested. For this insight to take hold among company staff, we utilized every information channel available – talks and presentations at staff meetings, reports in the staff newspaper and circular letters to special groups within the company.[33]

Following Three Mile Island, these attempts by Rudloff's department sparked considerable interest among KWU staff; a development that was not met with universal acclaim. For years, union representatives had criticised that KWU supposedly used its workers as "hostages" in the stand-off against nuclear critics by tying the job security of its employees to the condition of the nuclear business.[34] To them, calls for a greater involvement of workers in public relations merely represented the latest attempt to save nuclear capital from its demise. Union criticism notwithstanding, over the following months and years, a substantial number of engineers and technicians became active protagonists in the gradual transformation of their companys' public relations strategies, as the material practices of nuclear work were brought to the fore.

Engineers, Technicians, and the Personification of Diligence

Joachim Radkau has ranked the conflict over nuclear power among "the largest and most prolific discourses in the history of the Federal Repub-

32 Interview Waas, transcript.

33 *Rudloff*, Fallbeispiel, 296.

34 *Griewat*, KWU, 180 and passim; also *Rot/Grün*, Kernenergie; a history of the varied stance of unions towards nuclear power is provided by *Mohr*, Gewerkschaften.

lic".[35] Despite this fact, the technical artefacts of nuclear power had remained conspicuously absent from public relations material throughout the 1970s. Some KWU and Deutsches Atomforum (DAtF) information brochures supplied to mass audiences had occasionally used photographs from inside nuclear plants in an illustrative function. Rarely, however, did these brochures convey the materiality of nuclear technology:

> The construction materials, the nuts, bolts, weld seams, the backup systems, the computers and instruments, let alone barbed wire fences around the power plant and security installations [were] not seen.[36]

Instead, most information material had featured simplified sketches of the technical plant system. Many brochures had been explicitly designed to portray nuclear power as a benevolent technology.[37] At trade fairs such as at the large Hannover Messe, a striking feature had been the nearly complete absence of technical models. KWU and DAtF had instead attempted to attract passers-by with large billboards that elaborately argued for the economic indispensability of nuclear power; a point that was reiterated at discussion events held with managers at exhibition stands.[38] Just as nuclear technology had remained largely absent from the public eye, so had nuclear engineers, technicians, and workers – a professional vacancy even more striking considering that increasing expert trust had formed the dominant strategy of the nuclear industry in dealing with anti-nuclear activism.[39]

In large part, this public absence of nuclear workers is attributable to the widespread apprehension within nuclear industry management when it came to publicise technological specificities. During the "experimental phase" (J. Radkau) of nuclear power in the 1960s, there had been numerous reactor malfunctions and even a few small accidents. As a result, public scrutiny had increased. Even if large scale protests were still a decade away, a number of nuclear industry managers as well as pro-nuclear politicians had subsequently argued for reticence in public briefings.[40] Not least because of industry export interests, strong public accountability was regarded as a potential liability, as news of even the smallest and negligible malfunction brought into question the engineering soundness of West

35 *Radkau*, Kernkraft-Kontroverse, 307.
36 *Schüring*, Advertising, 380.
37 *Schüring*, Advertising, 380.
38 *Intern*, Messe; for the importance of trade fairs as venues of industry self-assurance see *Schüring*, Advertising.
39 *Weisker*, Expertenvertrauen; *Kupper*, Expertise.
40 *Radkau*, Aufstieg, 411–418.

German reactor technology as a whole. Public uptake of nuclear work had been further hindered by the conviction among industry leaders that communicating the intricacies of nuclear power was a lost cause because of the inherent complexities of nuclear technology.[41]

Three Mile Island ushered in a departure from this scepticism. After the accident, conventional industry communication strategies *vis-à-vis* the public were subjected to harsh criticism. The editor of the industry journal *Atomwirtschaft*, for instance, lamented the "information catastrophe of Harrisburg" and denounced the response to the nuclear anxieties that had proliferated in the wake of the accident as "lethargic". In the future, "not only should plant staff know which measures to take in case of an accident; so, too, should the public".[42] Most importantly, this required highlighting time and again the qualifications of nuclear personnel and how diligently they practiced the everyday tasks of nuclear plant operation.

Crucial media for this transformation were customer magazines. Circulars such as *Strom* (which was supplied to households by RWE) provided distinctive benefits. On the one hand, they possessed a particularly high circulation volume and allowed the nuclear industry to engage directly with its customers. On the other hand, they enabled the industry to dispense with journalists and other multipliers who, accurately or not, were often regarded as espousing anti-nuclear sentiments.[43]

Strom and other customer magazines also allowed for a more personable approach to nuclear technology. In 1981, for instance, the magazine featured a portrait of a foreman at the Biblis nuclear power plant located in the south of Hesse (Fig. 1). The plant, whose technical configuration bore some resemblance to the totalled reactor at Three Mile Island, had been one of the hot spots of the nuclear controversy, with local anti-nuclear groups coining the phrase "Harrisburg liegt in Biblis" (Harrisburg is located in Biblis).[44] Even after having been employed at the plant for more than ten years, the article informed, Biblis plant personnel regularly had to attend the 'Kraftwerksschule' (plant school) in Essen to refresh their command of every procedure necessary for an emergency shutdown of the reactor. As the foreman pointed out, they had even attempted simulating the Three Mile Island accident there, but had had to realise that it was impossible to recreate the accident conditions "if only because our reactor is built

41 *Ehrhardt*, Stromkonflikte, 219f.; *Schüring*, Advertising, 378.

42 *Müller*, Harrisburg.

43 *Augustine*, Technocracy, 105–111, 144f. and 151f.; for a broad assessment of the interaction between nuclear experts and the news media see *Jordan*, Ausgestrahlt.

44 *Umwelt Akut*, cover.

differently than the one at TMI".[45] Furthermore, while the operation of nuclear plants undoubtedly presented specific risks, "these dangers are not greater than in any conventional power plant. ... One has to know how to deal with these risks. And for this, we are specialitsts".[46] In this and in numerous other portrayals, the figure of the confident 'specialist' functioned as a particularly effective communicative device: it conveyed the profound nature of one's competences and at the same time highlighted the meticulous and ongoing training efforts required to bear such a designation.

Der Kraftmann

Kraftwerksmeister Karl Jezek über Biblis: „Heute so selbstverständlich wie jede Fabrik."

Früher, da haben sie Witze gemacht, wenn Karl Jezek in Biblis in seine Stammkneipe kam. Makabre Witze: „Karl, Du strahlst ja heute wieder so. Kommst wohl gerade von der Schicht in Deinem Kraftwerk ..."
„Aber heute", sagt Karl Jezek, „heute gibt es diese blöden Witze nicht mehr. Es wird überhaupt nicht mehr über das Kernkraftwerk gesprochen. Alle wissen, daß es sicher ist. Deswegen ist die Anlage so selbstverständlich wie irgendeine andere Fabrik."
Kraftwerksmeister Jezek, 51 Jahre alt, ist von Anfang an in Biblis dabei. Er ist einer der 50 ersten, die voll Stolz ihre silbernen Schutzhelme tragen. „Bis 1971 war ich im Braunkohlekraftwerk im Rheinland beschäftigt", sagt Karl.

Man hört ihm noch deutlich [illegible] ner Herkunft an. „Ich hatte damals [illegible] ne Ahnung von Atomen. Aber das [illegible] Kraftwerk hat mich interessiert." [illegible] also nicht der Verdienst, der [illegible] „Der ist hier genauso wie in der [illegible] kohle, obwohl die Arbeit anstrengender ist."
Warum anstrengender? „Wegen der dauernden Schulung." Karl Jezek [illegible] zur Kraftwerk-Schule, seit er im [illegible] ber '71 nach Biblis gekommen ist [illegible] seiner 51 Jahre.
„Wir spielen hier dauernd [illegible] denkbaren Ereignisse in [illegible] Reaktor durch, lernen jeden [illegible] kleinen Handgriff, bis wir [illegible] Schlaf beherrschen. Wir haben [illegible] sucht, den Störfall Harrisburg [illegible]

konstruieren. Aber wir haben gemerkt, daß so etwas bei uns nicht möglich ist: schon von der Reaktorbauart gar nicht."
Jedes Jahr einmal ist Prüfungszeit am Simulator. Dann muß Herr Jezek zeigen, daß er noch alles kann, daß er auch im unwahrscheinlichsten Ernstfall richtig reagiert. Ist seine Arbeit gefährlich?
„Nicht gefährlicher als in einem anderen Kraftwerk. Natürlich birgt die Kernenergie in sich ein Risiko. Aber diese Gefahr ist bekannt und gebannt. Man muß eben richtig damit umgehen. Und das können wir."
Herr Jezek und seine Kollegen laufen ständig mit Strahlenmeßgeräten am Körper herum. „Alle halbe Jahr wird kontrolliert. Ich habe bisher im ganzen Jahr weniger Strahlung abgekriegt als eine erlaubte Tagesdosis."
Kein anderer Industriezweig auf der Welt unterliegt so strengen Vorschriften wie die Kernenergie. In keinem Bereich gibt es ein vergleichbares Sicherheitsdenken.
Durch die friedliche Nutzung der Kernkraft ist in Deutschland eine völlig neue Sicherheitsphilosophie entstanden. Ihr sichtbarster Ausdruck: die „Reaktorsicherheitsstudie".
Weder Straßenverkehr, Schiffbau und Stahlerzeugung noch Chemieindustrie oder Bergbau wurden einer ähnlichen „gedanklichen" Sicherheitsprüfung unterworfen.
Das Ergebnis: Der von den Kernkraftgegnern in theoretischen Überlegungen so häufig beschworene Superunfall, die nukleare Katastrophe, wird nicht stattfinden. Denn bereits die hochgerechnete Wahrscheinlichkeit eines solchen Unglücks liegt außerhalb des für uns Vorstellbaren, nämlich in einem Zeitraum von Milliarden Jahren.
Zum Vergleich: Unsere Erde ist noch nicht einmal fünf Milliarden Jahre alt.
Bis heute ist auf der Welt kein Fall bekannt, bei dem ein Mensch in der Umgebung eines der 250 Kernkraftwerke auf der ganzen Welt durch Radioaktivität ums Leben gekommen wäre. Bei einem Zwischenfall im deutschen Kernkraftwerk Gundremmingen starben zwei Arbeiter – aber nicht durch Strahlung, sondern durch austretenden Dampf. Ein Unfall, der auch in herkömmlichen Kraftwerken leider vorkommen könnte.

Fig. 1: Der Kraftmann, courtesy of RWE Group Corporate Archives, Essen

Nuclear specialists not only featured in customer magazines; the public was also increasingly brought in contact with them at guided tours through nuclear plants. Often, the plants chosen for these visits were cur-

45 *Strom*, Kraftmann.
46 *Strom*, Kraftmann.

rent hot-spots of the nuclear controversy. In the immediate aftermath of the accident at Three Mile Island, for instance, two winners of an RWE lottery were invited to the Mülheim-Kärlich plant in the vicinity of Koblenz. Showcasing Mülheim-Kärlich's specialists was by no means a coincidence: its reactor had been engineered by German Babcock together with Brown, Boveri & Cie. and exhibited the most similarities of any German reactor to the technology that had so catastrophically failed at Three Mile Island.[47] After the visit had concluded, a large article in *Strom* acquainted RWE customers with the two winners: "Mrs. Schneider from Lübbecke and Mr. Kasper from Meppen gave their opinion: this trip had been informative as well as reassuring".[48] Most of the guided tour had been spent discussing with plant personnel the lessons of Three Mile Island for West German reactor safety. Subsequently, participants were interviewed and concluded that "in the Federal Republic, there is substantially more being done to ensure reactor safety than perhaps in other countries".[49]

Assurances of an unparalleled thoroughness in safety matters were a familiar phenomenon throughout the decade, as the nuclear industry was occupied with translating the material practices of nuclear work in the Federal Republic into a universal role model – to entice prospective buyers from abroad, but also, and more importantly, to win over domestic nuclear sceptics. By making nuclear workers the standard-bearers of their business, however, industry public relations spoke to multiple audiences. In addition to convincing the public of the justifiability of nuclear risk, putting engineers, technicians, and workers front and centre also provided an opportunity to affirm professional identities.

Nuclear 'Ingenieurskunst' and the Enactment of Professional Identities

As described in the previous section, the nuclear industry went to considerable lengths to get its staff involved in public relations. Starting in 1980, for instance, KWU's newly-expanded public relations department organised weekend retreats (so-called media seminars), in which journalists and newspaper editors mingled with company personnel. Because of their multifaceted nature, media seminars constituted a communicative context that

47 For a summary of the post-TMI debate about Mülheim-Kärlich within the nuclear industry see *Laufs*, Reaktorsicherheit, 131.

48 *Strom*, Reise.

49 *Strom*, Reise.

extended outwards to the public as well as inwards to company staff. Both dimensions were intricately connected. A representative sample of staff was invited to the seminars and asked freely to communicate their unease with the conflict over nuclear power; a welcome opportunity to discharge accumulated frustration. The primary aim behind this measure was to contribute to a better mutual understanding between the nuclear industry and the media. From the perspective of a former staff member of KWU's public relations department, gatherings such as these were deemed particularly effective, as

> these journalists that came to the seminars understood for the first time how the nuclear controversy affected Otto Müller [John Doe, S.B.] who manufactured reactor technology for our company.[50]

Confrontation with the pressures felt by the specialists of nuclear technology often created a sense of profound concern on the part of the media representatives present.[51] Of course, industry-media dialogue such as this also offered a chance for company management to socialise with influential journalists, often resulting in a significant amelioration of the strained relationship between the media and the nuclear industry.

While media seminars were discontinued in the mid-1980s, public visibility of nuclear workers sharply increased in the aftermath of the catastrophic accident at Chernobyl in April 1986. As even formerly adamant supporters of nuclear power pondered the economic viability of an immediate decommisioning of the Federal Republic's nuclear plants,[52] KWU commissioned a large advertising campaign under the title "*Sicherheit ist unser Grundgesetz*" (Safety is our basic law). Appearing in large newspapers, it featured technicians and engineers involved in designing or operating reactor safety systems. Every page-sized ad featured a worker, foreman, or manager in the middle of attending to a plant component, turning towards the camera. Arranged beneath the photograph was an information box in which the person portrayed addressed the reader directly.

50 Interview Waas, transcript.
51 Interview Waas, transcript.
52 *Augustine*, Technocracy, 163–167.

Fig. 2: Sicherheit an jedem Punkt, courtesy of Siemens Historical Institute, Berlin

Admittedly, in face of the existential challenge posed by the Chernobyl catastrophe, ads such as these were pricipally geared towards the West German public. KWU's main intention certainly lay with bending public fear of nuclear power back in their favour and securing the future of the nuclear business. Nevertheless, their advertisement campaign has to be recognised as a form of communication tailored to speak to multiple audiences. In this vein, it is not difficult to grasp that passages such as the following also carried an identificatory message to a professional community that felt the pressures of public scrutiny like never before (Fig. 2):

> Here, I [a nuclear plant technician, S.B.] am pictured during an ultrasound examination of a pipeline. Nothing escapes my view. ... Until a pipeline system such as this is authorised, we will have filled over 1,500 file folders with our examination protocols. ... This diligence has made the safety of our nuclear installations famous throughout the world. We will continue to abide by it.[53]

Another ad featured an engineer tasked with designing safety systems. Extraordinarily high costs notwithstanding, he and his colleagues viewed it as imperative that every component of plant safety systems be checked and double checked. Particularly noteworthy is the cultural matrix in which he embedded the significance of their technical task:

> As an engineer, I find that my colleagues and I have the moral obligation to ensure the success of an indispensable technical progress with every measure at our disposal. As a father of two children, ... I will continue to abide by the principle of safety first.[54]

Revealing himself as a father of two provided a personable and relatable message. At the same time, the engineer demonstratively (re)instated his professional community as "selfless guarantors"[55] of technical progress. In doing so, he affirmed a conviction staunchly defended within his profession: the faith that technology enabled societies to tackle the pressing challenges of mankind; an idea that had come under renewed attack not least in sociologist Ulrich Beck's influential essay *Risk Society* that was published shortly after Chernobyl.[56]

Even as the pressures of the immediate post-Chernobyl debates had alleviated, the late 1980s remained a strenuous time for nuclear industry public relations departments. With the future of the nuclear business appear-

53 *Zeit*, Sicherheit (KWU ad).
54 *Zeit*, Mark (KWU ad).
55 *Hänseroth*, Fortschritt.
56 *Beck*, Risikogesellschaft.

ing far from certain, a print ad commissioned by the Vereinigung Deutscher Elektrizitätswerke (VDEW) maintained that German reactor safety was exemplary throughout the world. Under the caption "Security. Made in Germany", an information box informed: "Our nuclear plant operations are so safe that we can justify the application of domestic nuclear power production anywhere, anytime."[57] The rationale behind this line of argument was as obvious as it was overcompensating: professional accountability amounted to nothing less than a universal safety guarantee for domestic nuclear installations. With the demonstrative adoption of 'Made in Germany' as its title, the ad ceremoniously arranged power plant workers as contemporary incarnations of a national legacy, evoking a collective *lieu de mémoire* of German industry and the precision that made their workforces and their products renowned throughout the world.[58]

Testimonials to this nuclear variant of '*Ingenieurskunst*' were publicised throughout the decade. To demonstrate the international demand for nuclear technology 'Made in Germany', visits by foreign delegations to domestic nuclear installations were deemed particularly effective. RWE, for instance, made sure to report extensively on a Japanese delegation that had visited the Biblis nuclear plant. As purported in *Strom* after the visit, a Japanese engineer belonging to the delegation had alleged that, because of their technical configuration and the professionalism espoused by plant staff, "German nuclear installations are the safest in the world". Apparently, the leader of the delegation had even grandiosely compared the West German nuclear industry's technological prowess to the accomplishments of the US space program.[59] *Strom* ran other articles that informed about the visits of Soviet, Chinese, Egyptian, and Kenyan delegations to the nuclear plants in Biblis, Kahl, and Kalkar,[60] while KWU reported prospective Saudi-Arabian and Moroccan buying interests.[61]

Foreign interest in West German reactor technology and operational expertise demonstrated to nuclear workers that their craft and professionalism was in high demand. Perhaps best suited to illustrate the intricate entanglement of the material practices of nuclear work with German '*Ingenieurskunst*' is the example of *Camerata Nucleare*, the nuclear industry's chamber orchestra which recruited its members from the workforces of

57 *Merian*, Sicherheit (VDEW ad).

58 *Umbach*, Germany.

59 *Strom*, Reaktoren.

60 *Strom*, Wer.

61 *KWU-Report*, Interesse; for a history of West German nuclear exports in the 1970s see *Romberg*, Atomgeschäfte.

nuclear plants. Founded by Reinhardt Ettemeyer, at the time the technical manager of the nuclear plant at Grundremmingen, its purpose was to "convey that nuclear technicians not only possess a sober technical mind but also a musical and sensitive side", as the KWU company staff magazine *Intern* observed in 1987.[62] Due to the fact that the orchestra's musicians were scattered all over the Federal Republic, performances were limited. Traditionally, *Camerata Nucleare* took the stage at the opening ceremony of the annual "Jahrestagung Kerntechnik" (annual nuclear technology conference) that was organised jointly by DAtF and Kerntechnische Gesellschaft (KTG).

Musical high culture, however, was not the only allusion to engineering prowess evoked by nuclear industry public relations departments. Sometimes, the specialists of nuclear power were introduced on a very different note. An article in the illustrated magazine *Bunte* (which was especially aimed at a female readership), for instance, sung the praises of one nuclear worker in a markedly gendered tonality:

> This blonde, muscular giant with over ten years of practical experience in nuclear power belongs to the most treasured workforce in the Federal Republic. Because the health of these 'supermen' is such a precious commodity, it is vigorously watched over by a large medical staff.[63]

The fact that the article portrayed nuclear workers as larger-than-life characters should not be confused for irony. As nuclear personnel were transformed into literal incarnations of '*Ingenieurskunst*', nuclear safety was painted as entirely dependent on (the well-being of) male bodies.[64] As Gabrielle Hecht has observed, entangling nuclear power with images of "heroic masculinity" provided a particularly effective identificatory message as it "simultaneously reasserted and constructed the pioneering nature of nuclear work"[65] and instilled the (predominantly male) nuclear industry workforce with a sense of sorely missed pride. Against this background, it comes as no surprise that the KWU staff magazine *Intern* made sure to reprint the piece in full.[66]

62 *Intern*, Kammerorchester.
63 *Bunte*, Angst (KWU ad), reprinted in *Intern*, Angst.
64 *Wajcman*, Feminism; *Oldenziel*, Technology.
65 *Hecht*, Identity, 502.
66 *Intern*, Angst.

Conclusion

In reaction to growing anti-nuclear sentiment in the wake of the accident at Three Mile Island in March 1979, the public relations strategies of the West German nuclear industry transformed profoundly. Advertising campaigns that had previously featured highly abstract depictions of nuclear technology now became substantially more multifaceted both in view of their messages as well as their audiences. At a time of proliferating nuclear anxieties, companies such as KWU and RWE increasingly aimed at personifying diligence and reliability. The result was a growing visibility of nuclear work within public relations material.

Up until the early 1980s, the materiality of nuclear power had been obscured from view, as educating the public about technical specificities had been perceived as a potential liability. This scepticism faded in large part due to the realisation by industry management that public relations were in need of a substantial overhaul after Three Mile Island. Through multiple advertising campaigns, technical components of nuclear power increasingly developed into "brands within the public sphere".[67] In the process, they took on the qualities of "political artefacts"[68] in the sense that they became entangled within a powerful narrative of German '*Ingenieurskunst*' that posited a national legacy in all things technical.

At the managerial level, it became increasingly clear that the future of the nuclear business would be decided by the effectiveness of trust and identity production, both outward as well as inward.[69] After the intense debates on nuclear safety and human failure in nuclear power operations after Three Mile Island, the often incomprehensible and opaque concept of nuclear safety was grafted onto ideals of (male) workmanship and material diligence. Taking part in a task that was deemed singularly important for the survival of the nuclear business, engineers, technicians, and workers were turned into stakeholders of the successes (and failures) of their industry.

The resulting visibilisation of nuclear work constituted a "de-securitizing move",[70] as it was designed to (re)instill the West German public with confidence that the risks of nuclear power were technically manageable. However, the introduction of engineers, technicians, and workers and the

67 *Trischler/Bud*, Public Technology, 188.
68 *Winner*, Artifacts.
69 Interview Waas, transcript.
70 *Buzan/Waever/de Wilde*, Security.

appropriation of their labour for industry public relations also fed back into the workplace experience of nuclear personnel. With their new visibility, the material practices of nuclear plant operations were "transformed from a collection of technical manoeuvres into a set of culturally meaningful actions".[71] As nuclear engineers and technicians enacted '*Ingenieurskunst*' for the camera, everyday workplace practices – be it in factory halls or in the control room of a nuclear power plant – were charged with new meaning.

Sources

Angst Nein Danke. Wie Atomkraftwerker mit ihrem Job fertig werden und wie gefährlich er ist, in: Bunte, reprinted in Intern. Zeitschrift für die Mitarbeiter der Kraftwerk Union Aktiengesellschaft 12 (1980), 5, p. 20–21

Beckurts, Karl Heinz: Kernenergie im Schatten von Harrisburg und Gorleben. Eröffnungsansprache des Präsidenten der ENC 79, in: Atomwirtschaft 24 (1979), 6, p. 325–327

Beim Kammerorchester der Kerntechniker Deutschlands stimmt jeder Ton, in: Intern. Zeitschrift für die Mitarbeiter der Kraftwerk Union Aktiengesellschaft 19 (1987), 3, p. 24

Die sichersten Reaktoren der Welt, in: Strom. RWE-Information 11 (1979), 3

Der Kraftmann, in: Strom. RWE-Information 13 (1981), 4

Eine Reise nach Mülheim-Kärlich, in: Strom. RWE-Information 11 (1979), 3

Fechner, J. B.: Schutzbarriere Mensch im Kernkraftwerk. Anforderungen aus der Sicht des Bundesministers des Innern, in: Atomwirtschaft 25 (1980), 6, p. 299–302

Fränz, Kurt: Können Techniker eine Besserung des Verhältnisses der Gesellschaft zur Technik herbeiführen?, in: Atom + Strom 29 (1983), 6, p. 147–149

Griewat, Frank-Kuno: KWU intern – ein Kollege berichtet, in: Mez, Lutz/Wilke, Manfred (eds.): Der Atomfilz. Gewerkschaften und Atomkraft. Berlin 1977, p. 177–186

Harrisburg liegt in Biblis, in: Umwelt Akut. Zeitschrift der Bürgerinitiativen des Rhein-Main-Neckar-Raums 29 (1979), cover

Informationskreis Kernenergie, China Syndrome, Federal Archives BArch B 196/20644

Interesse an Kernenergie bekundet. Marokkos Energieminister besuchte Bundesrepublik, in: KWU-Report 6 (1979), 5, p. 13

71 *Hecht*, Identity, 502.

Interview with Ulrich Waas (staff member of KWU public relations department), August 29, 2019, Frankfurt am Main. Transcript

Jede dritte Mark für die Sicherheit (KWU ad), in: DIE ZEIT, April 17, 1987, p. 21

Müller, Wolfgang D.: Harrisburg – eine Informations-Katastrophe, in: Atomwirtschaft 24 (1979), 6, p. 311–312

Rot, Peter/Grün, Wilhelm: Kernenergie oder Die Atomisierung der Gewerkschaften?, in: Jacobi, Otto/Müller-Jentsch, Walther/Schmidt, Eberhard (eds.): Arbeiterinteressen gegen Sozialpartnerschaft. Kritisches Gewerkschaftsjahrbuch 1978/79. Berlin 1979, p. 177–190

Rudloff, Werner: Fallbeispiel VI: Öffentlichkeitsarbeit in der Investitionsgüterindustrie am Beispiel der Kraftwerk Union AG, in: Haedrich, Günther/Barthenheier, Günter/Kleinert, Horst (eds.): Öffentlichkeitsarbeit. Dialog zwischen Unternehmen und Gesellschaft. Ein Handbuch. Berlin/New York 1982, p. 287–298

Sicherheit an jedem Punkt (KWU ad), in: DIE ZEIT, April 10, 1987, p. 19

Sicherheit. Made in Germany (VDEW ad), in: Merian 44 (1991) 8, p. 63

Wer Wann Wo War, in: Strom. RWE-Information 13 (1981), 4

Zischka, Anton: Im Teufelskreis der Angst. Nach einem Vortrag, gehalten auf dem 7. Workshop „Energie" des RWE am 6. November 1979 in St. Englmar, in: Atom + Strom 26 (1980), 1, p. 12–16

Bibliography

Arndt, Melanie: Tschernobyl. Auswirkungen des Reaktorunfalls auf die Bundesrepublik Deutschland und die DDR. Erfurt 2011

Augustine, Dolores L.: Taking on Technocracy. Nuclear Power in Germany, 1945 to the Present. New York 2018

Beck, Ulrich: Risikogesellschaft. Auf dem Weg in eine andere Moderne. Frankfurt am Main 1986

Biess, Frank: Republik der Angst. Eine andere Geschichte der Bundesrepublik. Reinbek 2019

Bösch, Frank: Taming Nuclear Power: The Accident near Harrisburg and the Change in West German and International Nuclear Policy in the 1970s and early 1980s, in: German History 35 (2017), 1, p. 71–95

Bösch, Frank: Zeitenwende 1979. Als die Welt von heute begann. München 2019

Buzan, Barry/Waever, Ole/de Wilde, Jaap: Security: A New Framework for Analysis, Boulder/London 1998

Dannenbaum, Thomas: "Atom-Staat" oder "Unregierbarkeit." Wahrnehmungsmuster im westdeutschen Atomkonflikt der siebziger Jahre, in: Brüggemeier, Franz-Josef/Engels, Jens Ivo (eds.): Natur- und Umweltschutz nach 1945. Konzepte, Konflikte, Kompetenzen. Frankfurt am Main/New York 2005, p. 268–286

Engels, Jens Ivo: Gender roles and German anti-nuclear protest. The women of Wyhl, in: Bernhardt, Christoph/Massard-Guilbaud, Geneviève (eds.): Le démon moderne. La pollution dans les sociétés urbaines et industrielles d'Europe. Clermont-Ferrand 2002, p. 407–424

Engels, Jens Ivo: Naturpolitik in der Bundesrepublik. Ideenwelt und politischer Verhaltensstil in Naturschutz und Umweltbewegung. Paderborn 2006

Engels, Jens Ivo/Hertzog, Peter: Die Macht der Ingenieure. Zum Wandel ihres politischen Selbstverständnisses in den 1970er Jahren, in: Revue d'Allemagne et des pays de langue allemande 43 (2011), 1, p. 19–38

Esselborn, Stefan/Zachmann, Karin: Nuclear safety by numbers. Probabilistic risk analysis as an evidence practice for technical safety in the German debate on nuclear energy, in: History and Technology 36 (2020), 1, p. 129–164

Gaumer, Janine: Wackersdorf. Atomkraft und Demokratie in der Bundesrepublik 1980–1989. München 2018

Götter, Christian: Emotionen als Argument – Die Debatte um die Kernenergie im Biblis der 1970er Jahre, in: Smeddinck, Ulrich (ed.): Emotionen bei der Realisierung eines Endlagers. Interdisziplinäre Perspektiven. Braunschweig 2016, p. 35–47

Hänseroth, Thomas: Technischer Fortschritt als Heilsversprechen und seine selbstlosen Bürgen. Zur Konstitutierung einer Pathosformel der technokratischen Hochmoderne in Deutschland, in: Vorländer, Hans (ed.): Transzendenz und die Konstitution von Ordnungen, Berlin/Boston 2013, p. 267–288

Hasenöhrl, Ulrike: Zivilgesellschaft und Protest. Eine Geschichte der Naturschutz- und Umweltbewegung in Bayern 1945–1980. Göttingen 2011

Hecht, Gabrielle: Enacting Cultural Identity: Risk and Ritual in the French Nuclear Workplace, in: Journal of Contemporary History 32 (1997), 4, p. 483–507

Hertzog, Philipp: Pragmatische Politisierung. Verkehrsplaner und die Grenzen der Machbarkeit um 1980, in: Archiv für Sozialgeschichte 52 (2012), p. 379–401

Herzog, Benjamin: "Menschliches Versagen" in der Kernenergie. Der Rollenwandel des Menschen in den Präventionskonzepten einer Hochrisikotechnologie, in: Hannig, Nicolai/Thießen, Malte (eds.): Vorsorgen in der Moderne: Akteure, Räume und Praktiken. München 2017, p. 105–126

Heßler, Martina: Obsoleszenz der Menschen? Interpretationen des Mensch-Maschinen-Verhältnisses in der Moderne, in: Boschung, Dietrich/Kaerlein, Timo/Udelhofen, Stefan (eds.): Kulturelle Figurationen der Obsoleszenz. Würzburg 2019, p. 99–114

Hillengaß, Christian: Atomkraft und Protest. Die politische Wirkung der Anti-AKW-Bewegung in Deutschland, Frankreich und Schweden. München 2011

Hortleder, Gerd: Das Gesellschaftsbild des Ingenieurs. Zum politischen Verhalten der Technischen Intelligenz in Deutschland. Frankfurt am Main 1970

Hortleder, Gerd: Ingenieure in der Industriegesellschaft. Zur Soziologie der Technik und der naturwissenschaftlichen Intelligenz im öffentlichen Dienst und in der Industrie. Frankfurt am Main 1973

Johnston, Sean F.: Making the Invisible Engineer Visible. DuPont and the Personification of Nuclear Expertise, in: Technology and Culture 52 (2011), 3, p. 548–573

Johnston, Sean F.: The Neutron's Children: Nuclear Engineering and the Shaping of Identity. Oxford 2012

Jordan, Katrin: Ausgestrahlt. Die mediale Debatte um "Tschernobyl" in der Bundesrepublik und in Frankreich 1986/87. Göttingen 2018

Jungk, Robert: Der Atomstaat. Vom Fortschritt in die Unmenschlichkeit. Reinbek 1977

Kirchhof, Astrid M./Meyer, Jan-Henrik: Global Protest against Nuclear Power. Transfer and Transnational Exchange in the 1970s and 1980s, in: Historical Social Research 39 (2014), 1, p. 165-190

Kirchhof, Astrid M. (ed.): Pathways into and out of Nuclear Power in Western Europe. Austria, Denmark, Federal Republic of Germany, Italy, and Sweden. Munich 2020

Kleinöder, Nina: Unternehmen und Sicherheit. Strukturen, Akteure und Verflechtungen im betrieblichen Arbeitsschutz der westdeutschen Eisen- und Stahlindustrie nach 1945. Stuttgart 2015

Kogon, Eugen: Die Stunde der Ingenieure. Technologische Intelligenz und Politik. Düsseldorf 1976

Kupper, Patrick: Expertise und Risiko, Vertrauen und Macht. Gesellschaftliche Ursachen erodierender Autorität von Kernenergie-Experten in den 1970er Jahren, in: Schweizerische Zeitschrift für Geschichte 55 (2005), 1, p. 60–69

Laufs, Paul: Reaktorsicherheit für Leistungskraftwerke. Entwicklung im politischen und technischen Umfeld der Bundesrepublik Deutschland. Berlin/Heidelberg 2013

Milder, Stephen: Greening Democracy. The Anti-Nuclear Movement and Political Environmentalism in West Germany and Beyond, 1968–1983. Cambridge 2017

Mohr, Markus: Die Gewerkschaften und der Atomkonflikt. Münster 2001

Müller, Wolfgang D.: Geschichte der Kernenergie in der Bundesrepublik Deutschland. 2 vol. Stuttgart 1990 and 1996

Oldenziel, Ruth: Making Technology Masculine: Men, Women, and Modern Machines in America, 1870–1945. Amsterdam 1999

Pinch, Trevor: The Social Construction of Technology (SCOT): The Old, the New, and the Nonhuman, in: Vannini, Phillip (ed.): Material Culture and Technology in Everyday Life: Ethnographic Approaches. New York et. al. 2009, p. 45–58

Pohl, Natalie: Atomprotest am Oberrhein. Die Auseinandersetzung um den Bau von Atomkraftwerken in Baden und im Elsass (1970–1985). Stuttgart 2019

Radkau, Joachim: Aufstieg und Krise der deutschen Atomwirtschaft 1945–1975. Verdrängte Alternativen in der Kerntechnik und der Ursprung der nuklearen Kontroverse. Reinbek 1983

Radkau, Joachim: Die Kernkraft-Kontroverse im Spiegel der Literatur – Phasen und Dimensionen einer neuen Aufklärung, in: Herrmann, Armin/Schumacher, Rolf (eds): Das Ende des Atomzeitalters? Eine sachlich-kritische Dokumentation. München 1987, p. 307–334

Radkau, Joachim: Technik in Deutschland. Vom 18. Jahrhundert bis heute. Frankfurt am Main/New York 2008

Radkau, Joachim/Hahn, Lothar: Aufstieg und Fall der deutschen Atomwirtschaft. München 2013

Romberg, Dennis: Atomgeschäfte. Die Nuklearexportpolitik der Bundesrepublik Deutschland 1970–1979. Paderborn 2020

Schramm, Luise: Evangelische Kirche und Anti-AKW-Bewegung. Das Beispiel der Hamburger Initiative kirchlicher Mitarbeiter und Gewaltfreie Aktion im Konflikt um das AKW Brokdorf 1976–1981. Göttingen 2017

Schüring, Michael: Advertising the nuclear venture: the rethorical and visual public relation strategies of the German nuclear industry in the 1970s and 1980s, in: History and Technology 29 (2013), 4, p. 369–398

Schüring, Michael: "Bekennen gegen den Atomstaat." Die evangelischen Kirchen in der Bundesrepublik Deutschland und die Konflikte um die Atomenergie 1970–1990. Göttingen 2015

Tompkins, Andrew S.: Better Active than Radioactive! Anti-Nuclear Protest in 1970s France and West Germany. New York 2017

Trischler, Helmuth/Bud, Robert: Public technology: nuclear energy in Europe, in: History and Technology 34 (2018), 3–4, p. 187–212

Umbach, Maiken: Made in Germany, in: Schulze, Hagen/François, Etienne (eds.): Deutsche Erinnerungsorte, vol. 2. München 2001, p. 405–418

Wajcman, Judy: Feminism Confronts Technology. University Park, PA 1991

Walker, J. Samuel: Three Mile Island: A Nuclear Crisis in Historical Perspective. Berkeley/Los Angeles/London 2004

Weart, Spencer R.: The Rise of Nuclear Fear. Cambridge, MA/London 2012

Wehner, Christoph: Die Versicherung der Atomgefahr. Risikopolitik, Sicherheitsproduktion und Expertise in der Bundesrepublik Deutschland und den USA 1945–1986. Göttingen 2017

Wendland, Anna Veronika: Reaktorsicherheit als Zukunftskommunikation: Nuklearpolitik, Atomdebatten und kerntechnische Entwicklungen in Westdeutschland und Osteuropa 1970–2015, in: Kampmann, Christoph/Marciniak, Angela/Meteling, Wencke (eds.): "Security turns its eye exclusively to the future." Zum Verhältnis von Sicherheit und Zukunft in der Geschichte. Baden-Baden 2018, p. 305–352

Weisker, Albrecht: Expertenvertrauen gegen Zukunftsangst. Zur Risikowahrnehmung der Kernenergie, in: Frevert, Ute (ed.): Vertrauen. Historischen Annäherungen. Göttingen 2003, p. 394–421

Weisker, Albrecht: Powered by Emotion? Affektive Aspekte in der westdeutschen Kernenergiekontroverse zwischen Technikvertrauen und Apokalypseangst, in: Brüggemeier, Franz-Josef/Engels, Jens Ivo (eds.): Natur- und Umweltschutz nach 1945. Konzepte, Konflikte, Kompetenzen. Frankfurt am Main/New York 2005, p. 203–221

Winner, Langdon: Do Artifacts Have Politics?, in: Daedalus 109 (1980), 1, p. 121–136

Zaretsky, Natasha: Radiation Nation: Three Mile Island and the Political Transformation of the 1970s. New York 2018

Illustration Credits

Fig. 1: Der Kraftmann, in: Strom. RWE-Information 13 (1981), 4

Fig. 2: Sicherheit an jedem Punkt, in: Die Zeit, April 10, 1987, p. 19

The Threat of Insolvency: Czech Enterprises Searching for Financial Security in the Early 1990s

Eva Schäffler

After the end of state socialism, Czech enterprises[1] faced insecure times. What affected them most directly was the transformation from a planned to a market economy. This transformation was carried out by reforms following three main objectives.[2] First, minimising state intervention and deregulating the market. Second, liberalising trade and prices. Third, privatising enterprises, which with only very few exceptions were in the hands of the state.[3] While these economic reforms were implemented, enterprises were confronted with a lot of new challenges, including how they should keep up their output and sales figures without state controlled trade, both on a national and on an international level, and how they should pay their bills and their workers when they did not have enough turnover. Not being able to tackle all of these challenges at once, the search for financial security and attempts to obviate the threat of insolvency became of vital importance.

This paper takes a closer look at both the threat of insolvency the enterprises experienced and the search for financial security on which they embarked. In doing so, it focuses on the time before as well as during the very early phase of the privatisation process,[4] that is around the years 1991 and 1992. The paper aims to contribute to answering the question as to how

---

1 The paper only deals with enterprises located in the Czech Republic (today's borders) even though it mostly covers the very early 1990s during which the ČSFR (Czech and Slovak Federative Republic) still existed.

2 On the origins of the "triad of liberalization, deregulation, and privatization" and on its general significance for East European transformations, see, for example: *Ther*, Europe.

3 Compared to its neighboring countries Poland and Hungary, where private ownership had already played a more important role during the 1980s, the ČSSR had an extremely small private sector until 1989–90 (*Žídek*, Central, 11f.).

4 Generally, Czech privatisation can be divided into three steps. First, restitution took place. Under certain conditions, citizens could be compensated for private property taken from them after the Communist coup in 1948, or they could have their property returned to them. Second, the so-called small privatisation began, during which small and medium-sized enterprises were sold directly or via auc-

concepts of security, particularly the change of these concepts, should be analysed from a historical point of view. Another objective is to take a share in the historisation of the Czech economic transformation process.[5] In doing so, it suggests that telling the history of this process as a history of (in)security is a valuable option – though definitively not the only one.[6]

The first section commences with some general remarks on the role and the concept of (in)security in post-socialist economic transformations and in historical research. Then, the second section gives some basic information on company magazines, which are the predominant source used in this paper. The third and main section examines the overall role of debt during and after state socialism before dealing with five Czech industrial enterprises and their fight against insolvency. We will see what the reasons for their financial problems were and which countermeasures were taken in order to regain financial security. Moreover, the companies' discourse on insolvency will be analysed, taking into account inter- as well as intra-enterprise perspectives.

1. *(In)security in post-socialist economic transformation and in historical research*

In all post-socialist countries, economic transformations opened up new possibilities while at the same time leading to new insecurities. For example, enterprises had to deal with less predictability and stability as well as with an overall change in values (e.g. competitiveness became far more important than before). As the vast majority of companies only slowly became familiar with new market conditions, their existence became endangered. One common phenomenon was a lack of financial security, which meant that companies had severe solvency issues to the extent that they were threatened with complete shutdown. Of course, this threat did not

---

tions. Third came the so-called big privatisation, in which larger enterprises were privatised. Roughly, this last phase was prepared during the years of 1990 and 1991 and implemented from 1992 to 1994. For an English-language overview of Czech privatisation, see, for example: *Žídek*, Central, 211–262.

5 While economic, political, and social sciences have covered the Czech economic transformation already quite extensively, this subject is still fairly new to historians. Pioneering studies in this field are: *Krátká*, Letos; *Kopeček*, Architekti.

6 For example, another valuable perspective on post-socialist history opens up when looking at path dependencies from state socialist times (continuities in expert cultures are analysed in: *Kopeček*, Architekti). Also, it makes sense to examine the influence of negotiation processes (*Schäffler*, Transformation).

only affect the businesses as such but also their employees: many workers feared for their jobs and, in most cases for the first time in their lives, they experienced unemployment.[7] Even though the collapse of the old political and economic system had been mostly welcomed, nostalgia for lost securities soon became a widespread symptom.[8]

However, an increase of insecurity is not only a phenomenon that is associated with systems transforming from a planned to a market economy. Also, on a more general level, capitalist societies are said to have a rather high level of insecurity. In the nineteenth century, Karl Marx and Friedrich Engels predicted that the new bourgeois age would come with continuous changes and thus continuous insecurity, not only in the economic but also in the social sphere.[9] Nowadays, some sociologists speak of insecurity as a strategic element of capitalism: making individuals feel insecure assures that they permanently work harder than they actually want to.[10] A more positive perspective can be found in economic science, where some scholars argue that economic uncertainty generates flexibility and causes societies to develop further.[11]

Historians have written about the productive effects of insecurity, too – for example Eric Hobsbawm with regard to revolutions.[12] In fact, (in)security is not only a common concept in social, political, and economic science but also in all fields of historical research. While this concept is probably most popular in political history,[13] there is no historical subdiscipline that exclusively deals with the history of security.[14] Still, there is one principle that is essential for all 'historians of security': namely that security is

---

7 For example, a survey carried out by the Czech Centre for Empirical Research (STEM/Středisko empirických výzkumů) in 1991 revealed that, over the previous ten years, only 4.6% of the respondents had been unemployed and experienced a job search lasting longer than one month. (http://nesstar.soc.cas.cz/webview/index/en/nesstar/-SDA.c.nesstar/-esky.d.1/V-zkumy-transformace.d.19/Soci-ln-spravedlnost-91.s.CSDA00118/Partner-respondenta-pr-ce-respondenta-a-jeho-partnera.h.3/byl-nezamestnany-/fVariable/CSDA00118_V50, last retrieved on 29.04.2020).

8 More general information on post-socialist transformations, insecurities, and so forth, can be found in, for example: *Orenstein*, Out; *Ther*, Europe.

9 *Bonß*, (Un-)Sicherheit, 43.

10 E.g., *Rosa*, Beschleunigung.

11 E.g. *Heiner*, Uncertainty (this example is given in: *Bonß*, (Un-)Sicherheit, 56).

12 *Hobsbawm*, Europäische.

13 One well-known example from German historiography is: *Conze*, Sicherheit.

14 *Zwierlein*, Sicherheitsgeschichte, 365.

neither a universal nor an ahistorical concept and thus needs to be historicised.

For example, when talking about security in the modern era, a paradox is usually pointed out. On the one hand, modernity is defined as a project the aim of which is to overcome contingency, which means reducing life risks, creating more security, and so forth. On the other hand, the emergence of new insecurities is seen as a typical trait of this period.[15] But can this paradox also be detected in post-socialist transformation societies? From a theoretical point of view, it is definitively obsolete to classify post-socialist transformation as a modernisation process.[16]

This is also the case from an empirical point of view, as this paper shows. In analysing how Czech enterprises dealt with financial (in)security, the aforementioned paradox can hardly be detected. From the point of view of such companies, the transformation process almost exclusively brought about new insecurities. However, getting back the old securities provided by a planned economy was simply not possible. Therefore, the main challenge for companies was to tackle the problems and uncertainties at hand, including regarding their solvency. Eventually, many enterprises were able to regain financial security – albeit only from the perspective of a capitalist and not from the perspective of a socialist system. The fact that Czech companies were confronted with altering definitions of (financial) security makes their case particularly interesting from the perspective of historical security research, which focuses on how security concepts changed over the course of time.[17]

2. *Company magazines as sources*

In order to shed light on the role of financial insecurity in post-socialist transformations, this paper is based on the evaluation of the company

---

15 *Tönsmeyer/Vowinckel*, Sicherheit, 163f.

16 Classical modernisation theory was applied to the transformation process right after the collapse of state socialism (e.g. *Huntington*, Third). Post-socialist transformation processes were thus interpreted as developments towards western political and economic standards. However, modernisation theory approaches were soon criticised and replaced by alternatives which focused more on the historical context, on the role of actors, and so forth (for an overview of transformation theory approaches, see section II in: *Merkel*, Handbook.).

17 *Conze*, Securitization, 455.

magazines[18] of five Czech industrial enterprises (Barum, Fatra, MEZ Mohelnice, Rudné Doly Příbram and ZVU Strojírny).[19] These were chosen after evaluating approximately twenty-five company magazines at the archives of ČMKOS (Českomoravská konfederace odborových svazů, i.e. the Bohemian-Moravian Confederation of Trade Unions) in Prague, at the Regional Archives in Opava and at the company archives of Continental in Hannover. In addition, press articles were used in order to depict the positions of other contemporary stakeholders.[20]

Company journals have existed since the nineteenth century and are used as sources in various historical subdisciplines, for instance in business and media history.[21] When these journals are examined, two main tendencies are exhibited: either they are primarily a study subject of their own,[22] or – as they are in this paper – they serve to reveal more about certain aspects of a company's development. Even though we do not know whether every figure and every piece of information which was published in these magazines are reliable, we can be sure that the magazines represent the companies' perspective on what was going on. They thus allow us to assess how certain effects of the transformation from a planned to a market economy – the continuous threat of insolvency, for example – were perceived and dealt with 'from below'. At the same time, the magazines' representation of the threat of insolvency reveals how the companies defined (in)security and how they communicated their respective definitions.

Generally, the company journals in question provide a broad range of information covering financial, economic, and technological issues, while at the same time providing insights into the everyday working lives of their employees. For example, there are articles honoring long-serving workers and articles on company soccer matches. What can be also found are articles addressing the overall political or economic situation as well as standard entertainment features such as crosswords or jokes. Usually, the ma-

18 There are several terms for magazines published by companies, e.g. company magazine, company journal, employee magazine, house organ, and so forth. The two first terms are used synonymously throughout the paper.

19 For more information on these enterprises (industrial branch, location, and so forth) and why they were selected, see chapter 3.2.

20 All press articles are cited herein with the name of the newspaper, the title of the article, and the publication date. Volumes, issues and page numbers are mostly impossible to specify as the articles were researched with the help of a newspaper clipping service available at the Czech National Archives (Centrum kupónové privatizace, Monitoring Tisku), which does not contain this kind of information.

21 *Heller*, Company, 179.

22 See, for example: *Esbester*, Organizing.

gazines were authored by a small editorial team and their main audiences were the enterprises' employees themselves.

In order to understand what kind of source Czech company journals from the 1990s are, it makes sense to look back at the state's socialist period. During this time, the journals had a mostly propagandistic character, both on a political and on an economic level. This meant, for example, that party decisions were praised and workers were encouraged to produce more. Popular text genres were articles or printed speeches by managerial staff. These texts also remained popular after the end of state socialism, but after this point they were increasingly used to discuss the problems which the companies were confronted with,[23] for example the problem of financial insecurity or, more specifically, the threat of insolvency.

3. Czech enterprises fighting insolvency in the early 1990s

3.1. Debt in Czechoslovakia before and after the end of state socialism

Before examining how Czech enterprises dealt with the insolvency problem, some basic information on the role of debt in Czechoslovakia is needed. Czechoslovakia did not suffer from high external debt neither before nor after 1989–90. At the end of 1989, the Czechoslovak external debt *per capita* amounted to approximately 400 US Dollars, while in Poland it was more than twice and in Hungary more as four times as high.[24] One year later, the ČSFR owed 8.1 billion US Dollars and in mid-1992 it owed 9.8 billion US Dollars to foreign creditors.[25] In 1999, the external debt level in the Czech Republic had decreased to approximately 590 million US Dollars.[26]

In contrast, internal debt had been a central feature during state socialism and became even more prevalent after its end. One substantial part of internal debt consisted of bank loans taken out by state-owned enterprises.

23 The tendency towards a more truthful and critical way of reporting was also detected in the case of Soviet company magazines, see: *Hass*, Rethinking, 69f.

24 Figures according to United Nations Economic Commission for Europe (UNECE), cited in: *Begg*, Economic, 248.

25 Figures according to Federal Statistical Office, Czech Statistical Office, and Czechoslovak State Bank, cited in: *Dyba/Švejnar*, Stabilization, 102f.

26 Figure according to Czech Ministry of Finance (https://www.mfcr.cz/cs/verejny-sektor/rizeni-statniho-dluhu/dluhova-statistika/struktura-a-vyvoj-statniho-dluhu, last retrieved on: 26.03.2020).

In 1989, this debt roughly amounted to 90% of GDP.[27] Quantitatively less significant types of internal debt were private credits as well as outstanding payments between companies. Between 1985 and 1989, private households had taken out loans to a total of 42 billion crowns, equaling around 7% of GDP in 1989. During the same period, intra-enterprise debt piled up to approximately 25 billion crowns, which was a little more than 4% of GDP in 1989.[28]

After the end of state socialism, the number of bank loans greatly increased.[29] For example, from February 1991 to May 1991, the amount the Czech State Savings Bank (Česka státní spořitelna) lent to its customers grew more than hundredfold: from 5 million CZK to 508.3 million CZK.[30] In 1992, 80% of all Czech enterprises and 90% of all Slovak enterprises had taken out bank loans.[31] Intra-enterprise debt also started to increase significantly. It reached roughly 45 billion CZK at the end of 1990 and roughly 145 billion CZK at the end of 1991.[32]

Politicians and the media, and – as we will see later, the enterprises themselves – were well aware of this development. For example, a representative of the left wing party Strana demokratické levice (SDL) noted: "The situation is such that everyone owes something to everyone."[33] A similar remark was made by the business newspaper *Hospodářské noviny*: "Nobody pays nobody, everybody is indebted to everybody."[34] The weekly journal *Ekonom* described the Czech economy as a "vicious circle in which

---

27 Figure according to Federal Statistical Office, Czech Statistical Office, and Czechoslovak State Bank, cited in: *Dyba/Švejnar*, Stabilization, 101; *Vltavská/Sixta*, Historical, 121.

28 Figures according to Federal Statistical Office, Czech Statistical Office, and Czechoslovak State Bank, cited in: *Dyba/Švejnar*, Stabilization, 101; *Vltavská/Sixta*, Historical, 121.

29 There were several reasons for this increase, many of them resulting from extremely high state influence on the banking sector. In fact, a thorough bank privatisation was not reached until the late 1990s and early 2000s. For more information on the Czech banking sector and on its credit policy see: *Holman*, Transformace, 67f.; *Mejstřík*, Restructuring.

30 Matějka, Petr/Fašanková, Zuzana: Účást České státní spořitelny v privatizaci, in: Československé banky (1991) 17, 7.

31 Kučera, Jiří: Vlastníkem je stát, in: Práce, 11.09.1992.

32 Figures according to Federal Statistical Office, Czech Statistical Office, and Czechoslovak State Bank, cited in: *Dyba/Švejnar*, Stabilization, 101.

33 "Situace je taková, že dnes jsou všichni všem něco dlužní." (Ján Zán cited in: N. N.: Lavina bankrotů v pobyhu, in: Hálo Noviny, 24.09.1992).

34 "Nikdo nikomu neplatí, každý každému je dlužen." (Dolečková, Marcela: Stát se stará, in: Hospodářské Noviny, 26.05.1993).

many individuals are to some extent debtors as well as they are to some extent creditors."[35]

Even though at the start of the 1990s, many big Czech enterprises were highly indebted, bankruptcies and specifically shutdowns were not a very imminent threat. This was owing to the government's wish to get as many enterprises as possible through the privatisation process and to prevent – at least during the next few years – unemployment[36] and other negative socioeconomic consequences.[37] For example, high ranking officials such as Jindřich Vodička, Minister for Work and Social Affairs, and Vladimír Dlouhý, Minister for the Economy, pointed out that a large number of bankruptcies had to be avoided at all costs, and that the state had to be more active in order to deal with the insolvency problem.[38]

Accordingly, the road towards fully-fledged bankruptcy legislation was lengthy and controversial.[39] Only in October 1991 was a provisional regulation set up (Zákon č. 328/1991 Sb.). However, it granted enterprises that were not privatised – which was the case for almost all larger enterprises – a special status. For them, it was completely impossible to initiate bankruptcy proceedings. In April 1993, a new and final version of the law was put into effect (Zákon č. 122/1993 Sb.). This regulation increased the risk of actual bankruptcies, but still contained protective mechanisms in order to keep the number of bankruptcies as low as possible.

In fact, the law's immediate effect on the Czech economy remained insignificant. For example, in the first three weeks after the law had come into

35 „[B]ludný kruh, ve kterém jsou mnohé subjekty tak trochu dlužniky, a tak trochu věřiteli." (N.N.: Anketa Bankroty za dveřmi, in: Ekonom, 22.04.1993).

36 In fact, until in the late 1990s an economic crisis emerged, the level of unemployment remained extremely low (particularly in comparison to other post-socialist countries): in 1991 it was at 4.1%, in 1993 at 3.5%, and in 1995 at 2.9% (figures according to Czech(oslovak) Ministry of Labor and Social Affairs, cited in: *Večerník/Matějů*, Ten, 31). For an overview on the economic crisis in the late 1990s, see, for example: *Hodulák/Krpec*, Hospodářská, 201–203.

37 Superficially, the wish to prevent bankruptcies did not match the government's general proposition to build a "market without adjectives" ("trh bez přívlastků"), that is, a 'real' market economy in which state interventions were (almost) nonexistent. However, also in other regards, a gap between the government's market liberal rhetoric and its actual reform policies can be detected. This gap has been observed and further analysed by several authors, including: *Orenstein*, Out, 62f. and 71f.; *Myant*, Rise, 264.

38 N.N.: Bankroty pod kontrolu?, in: Prostor, 02.10.1992; Marek, Tomáš: (Ne)cesta pro bankrotáře, in: Mladá Fronta Dnes, 10.09.1992.

39 For a detailed analysis of the legislative process and its associated controversies, see: *Schäffler*, Transformation.

effect, seventeen bankruptcy applications were filed at the commercial court in Prague. After six weeks, thirty-four applications had been received.[40] Most companies that actually went bankrupt were either small or medium-sized companies, while big companies were consistently viewed and treated as 'too big to fail'.[41]

3.2. *Reasons for and countermeasures against insolvency*

Nevertheless, in 1991 and 1992, the threat of insolvency was a pressing issue for big industrial enterprises. Generally, insolvency was perceived as a problem that could have a negative impact upon the privatisation process of companies and, ultimately, on their very survival. In order to improve their financial situation, enterprises were eager to identify the reasons for their solvency problems and to take measures in order to tackle them.

In the present paper, both reasons and countermeasures are examined with reference to five industrial enterprises. Considering that the insolvency issue was widespread in the early 1990s and had its roots in more general economic developments, these finding certainly have a more universal relevance. The selected enterprises were located all over the Czech Republic and represent important Czech industrial branches, including engineering and the chemical and mining industries.[42] Today, four of the five enterprises still exist after several ownership changes, but with each having – with one exception – considerably fewer employees than they had under state socialism.

The first company is Barum, a manufacturer of rubber tires located in the South Moravian town of Otrokovice. Barum had approximately 3,700 employees in 1989 and became part of the Continental Group in 1993. Today, it still belongs to Continental and as of 2017 it had around 4,800 employees.[43] The second example is Fatra, a plastic processing company in the

40 N.N.: Ostrava bez bankrotů, v Praze zatím 34 bankrotů, in: Český Deník, 02.06.1993.

41 *Holman*, Transformace, 68.

42 From the mid-nineteenth century onwards, the Czech lands had evolved into a highly industrialised region. In 1990, 36.6% of Czech GDP was generated in industrial enterprises (*Slaný*, Makroekonomická, 353). Defining mines as industrial enterprises is justifiable given that mining is sometimes assigned to the primary and sometimes to the secondary sector (*Cezanne*, Allgemeine, 268).

43 Employee figures according to: *Pavlínek*, Successful, 235; Barum Homepage: https://www.barum.cz/nakladni/znacka (last retrieved on 27.04.2020).

South Moravian town of Napajedla, which had around 3,000 employees in 1989. In 2015, around 1,100 people worked for Fatra, which had become a part of Agrofert Holding in 2000.[44] Moravské elektrotechnické závody Mohelnice (MEZ Mohelnice), an electrical equipment manufacturer located in the North Moravian town of Mohelnice, is the third company. By the start of 1991, it had around 3,000 employees and approximately 2,000 in 2014.[45] As of 1994, its owner is Siemens. The fourth example is Rudné doly Příbram, an ore mine in the Central Bohemian town of Příbram, which had roughly 2,900 employees in 1991.[46] It ceased to exist in 2001 and is thus the only of the five case companies that has not survived. ZVU Strojírny, an engineering company in the chemical industry (specifically coal gasification) in the East Bohemian city of Hradec Králové, is the fifth company. At the start of 1991 it had around 5,000 employees, but this number had declined to 500 by 2015.[47] Currently, ZVU Strojírny belongs to Safichem, a Switzerland-based holding company of approximately twenty Czech enterprises.

During the early 1990s, all five companies were in a financially insecure situation. Barum, for instance, had been insolvent since the fall of 1990, only regaining its solvency in mid-March 1991.[48] Shortly afterwards, the tire manufacturer returned to being insolvent once more, before regaining its solvency in June 1991. Given its financial instability, Barum's managing director Pavel Pravec was sure that the survival of the company was at stake.[49] Whether it would be able to make it through the transformation process was also a question for MEZ Mohelnice. After approximately 1,000

44 Employee figures according to: N. N./Sileš, Petr: Fatra se zaměřuje na export, in: Zlínský Deník, 19.04.2007 (https://zlinsky.denik.cz/podnikani/fatra-se-zameruje-na-export-20.html, last retrieved on 27.04.2020); Wicherek, Jaroslav/Dokulilová, Karla: Fatra 80. 1935/2015. Napajedla 2015, https://www.fatra.cz//wp-content/uploads/2015/11/FATRA-publikace-80-let.pdf (last retrieved on 27.04.2020).

45 Employee figures according to: N. N.: Pravidla dnešních dnů, in: Hlas MEZU 42 (1991), 17, 04.09.1991, 3; Siemens, s. r. o., odštěpný závod Elektromotory Mohelnice: Podnik podporující zdraví. Mohelnice 2014, http://www.szu.cz/uploads/Vzdelavaci_akce/CHPPL/KD_141204/Siemens_s.r.o.pdf (last retrieved on 27.04.2020), 4.

46 Employee figure according to: *Bricault*, Major, 236.

47 Employee figures according to: Lněnička, Jaroslav: Zvu a trh, in: Hradecký Kovák 42 (1991), 6, 15.02.1991, 1–2, at 2; ZVU Strojírny Homepage: https://www.zvus-trojirny.cz/cz/detail-novinky?aid=36 (last retrieved on 27.04.2020).

48 Bačák, Milan: Platební neschopnost minulostí, in: Barum 39 (1991), 7, 05.04.1991, 1–4, at 1.

49 Mikulčíková, Hana/Pravec, Pavel: Jde o přežítí, in: Barum 39 (1991), 14, 28.06.1991, 1.

employees had lost their jobs in 1991,[50] its fortunes improved: in October 1992, its debts and outstanding payments had dropped by 60% compared to the previous year.[51] Within the same timeframe, however, the company's output had decreased by almost 50%.[52]

The reasons to which Barum and MEZ Mohelnice and the three other case enterprises ascribed their solvency issues were quite similar and can be divided into macro- and microeconomic factors. From a macroeconomic point of view, price increases, the dissolution of the Council for Mutual Economic Assistance (COMECON),[53] currency devaluation, and changes in the banking sector were identified. For each company, these developments led to an increase in production costs predominantly because resource and supplier prices had gone up. The companies also had problems in finding buyers and were earning less when selling their products. Particularly, currency devaluation led to less revenue from exports. However, the companies had also trouble compensating revenue losses by taking out bank loans. After 1989–90, credit checks had become stricter and interest rates had increased. From a microeconomic point of view, arguments centred on poor payment practices[54] – a phenomenon that had been also omnipresent during state socialist times.[55]

50 N. N.: Pravidla dnešních dnů, in: Hlas MEZU 42 (1991), 17, 04.09.1991, 3.

51 *Volek, Karel et al*: Dluhy se daří umazávat jen pomalu, in: Hlas MEZU 43 (1992), 15, 07.10.1992, 1–2, at 2.

52 Hodina, Jiří: Platební neschopnost snížená, in: Hlas MEZU 43 (1992), 13, 26.08.1992, 1.

53 The Council for Mutual Economic Assistance (COMECON), an economic organisation led by the Soviet Union, existed from 1949 to 1991. Its members included the countries from the Eastern Bloc as well as some other socialist states (such as Cuba and Vietnam). COMECON aimed at creating an independent 'socialist world market' by coordinating its members' economic plans.

54 Articles mentioning one or the other of these reasons include, for example: Lněnička, Jaroslav: Start do tržního hospodaření, in: Hradecký Kovák 42 (1991), 1, 11.01.1991, 1–2; Surma, Jaroslav: Fatra je–není solventní, in: Fatra 41 (1991), 2, 01.02.1991, 1–2, at 1; Kocourková, B.: Jak řešit platební schopnost podniku, in: Hornický Kahan 35 (1991), 9, 08.05.1991, 1–2, at 1; Bačák, Milan: Platební neschopnost minulostí, in: Barum 39 (1991), 7, 05.04.1991, 1–4, at 1; Klimša, Drahomír: Můžeme naším zákazníkům ještě něco nabídnout?, in: Hlas MEZU 42 (1991), 14/15, 1–2, at 1.

55 Generally, poor payment practices can be characterised as a specific manifestation of the "soft budget constraint" defined as typical trait of a socialist economy by János Kornai (*Kornai*, Economics). The term "soft budget constraint" points to the fact that in a socialist economy, loss-making enterprises receive subsidies to compensate deficits, while in an ideal market economy, permanently loss-making companies must exit the market. Therefore, unpaid bills, both from the creditor's

Given the variety of factors leading to solvency problems, the five case enterprises adopted three types of countermeasures in order to gain more financial security: first, the companies tried to improve their liquidity by canvassing new customers and attracting foreign investors,[56] preferably from Western European countries; second, they made efforts to lower their debt levels through write-offs and through taking out new loans; and third, they tried to tackle the problem of outstanding payments. They noticed that outstanding payments mostly existed because customers were unable or unwilling to pay. However, they also realised that, to a certain extent, this problem was self-inflicted through sloppy invoicing practices. In the following, these three types of countermeasures will be analysed more closely.

Finding customers from abroad was, for example, one of ZVU Strojírny's strategies to improve its solvency. To this end, the company resorted to external experts, mainly from marketing and consulting agencies.[57] A similar strategy was used by MEZ Mohelnice, which tried to increase its revenue by paying more attention to customer satisfaction and product marketing.[58] In fact, the electrical equipment manufacturer was able to build a large sales network. In 1991–92, companies from thirty-six countries, including neighboring countries such as Germany or Austria but also those further afield, such as Taiwan or Argentina, had developed business relations with MEZ Mohelnice.[59]

MEZ Mohelnice's quest for financial security also resulted in a search for an international investor. In March 1992, the Siemens group first approached MEZ Mohelnice in order to discuss a possible joint venture.[60] However, after almost two years of negotiations, the original plan was not put into practice. Instead, the German company and the Czech Ministry of

---

and the debtor's point of view, are perceived as less problematic in a socialist than they are in a market economy.

56 Generally, the role of foreign investment in the Czech transformation process was rather small. About $0.7 billion flowed into the country in 1991. In 1992, investments amounted to $1.1 billion and in 1995 a peak of $2.5 billion was reached (*Kosta*, Transformation, 167; *Pesendorfer*, Restaurationsprozess, 163.).

57 Lněnička, Jaroslav: Zvu a trh, in: Hradecký Kovák 42 (1991), 6, 15.02.1991, 1–2, at 2.

58 N. N.: Co nám může pomoci? Marketing!, in: Hlas MEZU 42 (1991), 4, 26.02.1991, 1–2, at 1.

59 N. N.: Cílem spokojenost všech obchodních partnerů, in: Hlas MEZU 44 (1993), 12, 17.06.1993, 1.

60 Šafářová, Dana/Simon, Rudi P.: Zájem o joint venture trvá, in: Hlas MEZU 44 (1993), 5, 11.03.1993, 1.

Privatisation came to an agreement that Siemens would buy MEZ Mohelnice as a whole, along with two other electrical equipment manufacturers from Moravia, namely MEZ Frenštát and MEZ Drásov.[61]

In Barum's case, the search for an investor only resulted in a partial takeover. In early 1991, the tire manufacturer started to reach out to international investors, among them the German Continental group.[62] After almost two year of negotiations, a German-Czech joint venture[63] was formed with Continental to purchase 76% of Barum.[64] In the following years, the company was able to reach a considerably higher level of financial security. At the end of 1994, Barum's management announced that it had no debts or loans and was therefore very well prepared for the future.[65]

In 1991, ZVU Strojírny, Rudné doly Příbram as well as MEZ Mohelnice tried better to prepare for their future by applying to the state for a debt write-off. Their hope was that having to spend less money for repaying loans would allow them to spend more money on other purposes, including for resources or for marketing purposes. The companies also expected to benefit indirectly from the debt write-off because it would improve their customers' solvency. At the end of 1991, however, none of the three enterprises were selected to take part in the write-off process, which was perceived as harsh setback in their endeavors to arrive at a more financially stable situation.[66]

Despite this, indebted enterprises still had the opportunity to negotiate directly with the banks. For example, Fatra was trying to get new loans from Komerční banka, mostly for buying resources.[67] Later, the plastic processing company managed to agree on an 11.5 million CZK debt write-

61 Skalová, Olga: Siemens kupuje za 1,3 milliardy korun tři české výrobce elektromotorů MEZ, in: Hospodářské noviny, 05.01.1994.

62 Delegáti konference ZO FOS prac. Chemického průmyslu a. s. Barum Otrokovice: Dopis ministrovi, in: Barum 39 (1991), 1, 22.02.1991, 1.

63 German-Czech joint ventures were a quite frequent phenomenon: Very well-known is the joint venture of Volkswagen and Škoda, but there are also other examples such as Continental – Barum or Linde – Technoplyn.

64 N. N.: Conti hält 76 Prozent und will Produktion verdoppeln, in: Conti Intern, April/May 1993, 3.

65 Mikulčíková, Hana: Bez dluhů a úvěrů, in: Barum 41 (1994), 25.11.1994, 1.

66 N.N.: Jak je to s oddlužením, in: Hlas MEZU 42 (1991), 21, 20.10.1991, 1; Bulíček, Miloslav: Stojíme před závažnými úkoly, in: Hradecký Kovák 43 (1992), 1, 17.01.1992, 1–2, at 1; Oktábcová, V.: Jak se bránit rostoucí platební neschopnosti, in: Hornický Kahan 36 (1992), 2, 12.01.1992, 1; Miler, Karel: Náš podnik bez oddlužení, in: Hlas MEZU 43 (1992), 1, 15.01.1992, 1.

67 Surma, Jaroslav: Fatra je–není solventní, in: Fatra 41 (1991), 2, 01.02.1991, 1–2, at 2.

off with the same bank.[68] Similarly, MEZ Mohelnice tried to obtain new bank loans even though, by early 1991, twelve of its negotiations to this end had not brought positive results.[69] Later on, however, the electrical equipment manufacturer was able to obtain at least some short-term loans.[70]

While the first and second type of countermeasures against insolvency focused either upon getting money from customers and investors from abroad or from banks, the third type of countermeasures were mainly focused upon getting money from domestic customers. In fact, outstanding payments were a significant threat to the companies' financial security. In mid-1991, for instance, Rudné doly Příbram was waiting for around 108 million CZK from their business partners.[71] Fatra was in a similar situation: In mid-May 1992, its customers' outstanding payments amounted to approximately 208 million CZK.[72]

Given this situation, the enterprises took various measures not to further increase the amount of their outstanding payments. The companies therefore resolved to check more thoroughly their customers' solvency before concluding a contract. Moreover, they tried to draft better contracts, for example by being more precise about payment periods and installments, or by introducing obligatory prepayment and shorter payment periods, as well as by implementing higher late payment fees. Another strategy was not to accept new orders from buyers who had not paid outstanding debts. The enterprises started working on their own invoicing practices, such as by send invoices as quickly as possible and only after carefully checking whether the customer's name, address, and so forth, were correct.[73]

---

68 Surma, Jaroslav: Kolik nás vlastně je, in: Fatra 42 (1992), 1, 17.01.1992, 1.

69 Musil, Jan: Jak obtížná je situace podniku, in: Hlas MEZU 42 (1991), 4, 26.02.1991, 1.

70 Hodina, Jiří: Platební neschopnost snížená, in: Hlas MEZU 43 (1992), 13, 26.08.1992, 1.

71 Kocourková, B: Jak řešit platební schopnost podniku, in: Hornický Kahan 35 (1991), 9, 08.05.1991, 1–2, at 1.

72 Maňasová, A.: Má dáti – dal, in: Fatra 42 (1992), 9, 25.05.1992, 1.

73 Lněnička, Jaroslav: Zvu a trh, in: Hradecký Kovák 42 (1991), 6, 15.02.1991, 1–2, 2; Bačák, Milan: Platební neschopnost minulostí, in: Barum 39 (1991), 7, 05.04.1991, 1–4, at 1; Kocourková, B: Jak řešit platební schopnost podniku, in Hornický Kahan 35 (1991), 9, 08.05.1991, p. 1–2, at 2; Oktábcová, V: Jak se bránit rostoucí platební neschopnosti, in: Hornický Kahan 36 (1992), 2, 12.01.1992, 1; Bulíček, Miloslav: Stojíme před závažnými úkoly, in: Hradecký Kovák 43 (1992), 1, 17.01.1992, 1–2, at 1; Maňasová, A.: Má dáti – dal, in: Fatra 42 (1992), 9,

The companies also tried to collect already existing debt, with the most common strategy to this end being actively to demand outstanding payments. Most of the time, however, the companies were willing to negotiate with debtors and often agreed on extended payment periods. Even if customers were notoriously in default, the companies usually did not want to cut ties as new customers were hard to come by. At the same time, the companies were aware of the fact that some of their customers' debts would turn out to be irrecoverable.[74]

One company which put a lot of effort into collecting outstanding payments was Rudné doly Příbram. Generally, the ore mine's strategy was to talk to its debtors in person and strenuously to ask them to pay their debt as soon as possible. A more specific means to settle payment conflicts were arbitrations: while in the first quarter of 1990 Rudné doly Příbram had initiated 100 arbitrations, by the first quarter of 1991 this number had more than doubled.[75] In September 1991, the ore mine decided to exert public pressure on their defaulting business partners: the enterprise's magazine featured a list of fourteen enterprises that were its biggest debtors.[76] Eventually, Rudné doly Příbram's strategy to appeal to and to exert pressure upon its debtors seemed to work in some cases. For example, in December 1991, compromises with two overdue customers had been negotiated.[77]

Rudné doly Příbram's determination to retrieve outstanding payments was also the theme of a caricature in the enterprise's magazine. The picture shows an employee of the ore mine talking to one of its debtors: "Good day, director! We are from Rudné doly and came to ask, how the situation is regarding your inability to pay our company!" The employee's politeness only exists on a verbal level, however – behind him stands a very tall and

25.05.1992, 1; Volek, Karel et al.: Dluhy se daří umazávat jen pomalu, in: Hlas MEZU 43 (1992), 15, 07.10.1992, 1–2, at 1.

74 Bulíček, Miloslav: Stojíme před závažnými úkoly, in: Hradecký Kovák 43 (1992) 1, 17.01.1992, 1–2, at 1; Musil, Jan: Jak obtížná je situace podniku, in: Hlas MEZU 42 (1991), 4, 26.02.1991, 1; Bačák, Milan: Platební neschopnost minulostí, in: Barum 39 (1991), 7, 05.04.1991, 1–4, at 1; Volek, Karel/Konečná Hana/Luňák, Jiří: Dluhy se daří umazávat jen pomalu, in: Hlas MEZU 43 (1992), 15, 07.10.1992, 1–2, at 2; Lněnička, Jaroslav: Start do tržního hospodaření, in: Hradecký Kovák 42 (1991), 1, 11.01.1991, 1–2; Kocourková, B.: Jak řešit platební schopnost podniku, in Hornický Kahan 35 (1991), 9, 08.05.1991, 1–2.

75 Kocourková, B.: Jak řešit platební schopnost podniku, in: Hornický Kahan 35 (1991), 9, 08.05.1991, 1–2.

76 N. N.: Naši dlužníci. Seznam největších ‚neplatičů faktur' v srpnu, in: Hornický Kahan 35 (1991), 17, 25.09.1991, 3.

77 N. N.: Kompromisní jednání, in: Hornický Kahan 35 (1991), 23, 18.12.1991, 1.

muscular boxer. Frightened by this situation, the debtor is trying to hide behind his desk.[78]

3.3. Discourse on insolvency and financial security

As we have seen, the companies in question took various measures in order to deal with the threat of insolvency. These measures aside, however, company magazines reveal a great deal about how financial security issues were perceived and discussed. In the present section, the discourse on insolvency will be evaluated from both an inter-enterprise and an intra-enterprise perspective.

Regarding inter-enterprise debt, the companies were eager to present themselves as creditors and not as debtors. For this purpose, they emphasised that there was a difference between primary and secondary insolvency: primary insolvency being constituted by the company's own debt, and secondary insolvency being comprised of other companies' outstanding

78 Voříšek, P.: Caricature, in: Hornický Kahan 35 (1991), 22, 04.12.1991, 1.

payments.[79] For example, Fatra pointed out that its financial security issues were mostly temporary and not self-inflicted.[80] According to the plastic processing company's own account, its payment practices were better than those of their business partners. Even though the company sometimes had problems in paying its bills, it always settled its dues as soon as it had the means to do so.[81] Its debt to other companies was consequently twenty-six times lower than what other companies owed to Fatra.[82] A similar calculation was made by Barum: the tire manufacturer declared that the amount it owed to other enterprises was about one-third of its business partners' debts.[83]

Rudné doly Příbram also held critical views on its debtors. One assumption was that many of the ore mine's customers were 'robbing Peter to pay Paul', that is they eliminated debts by incurring new ones.[84] Moreover, a caricature in Rudné doly Příbram's company magazine suggested that business partners kept making orders and at the same time did little or nothing to improve their financial situation. In the caricature, a carelessly dressed and unkempt man sits in a restaurant and tells the waiter: "Unfortunately, I have sad news for you! My attorney has recently notified me that I find myself in deep insolvency."[85]

---

79 This differentiation was also common in the contemporary press, e. g. Málek, Radek: Kdy spadne na podniky Damoklův meč?, in: Prostor, 22.09.1992; Šimeček, Alexej: Čas bankrotů neuzrál, in: Hospodářské noviny, 29.09.1992.

80 Surma, Jaroslav: Fatra je–není solventní, in: Fatra 41 (1991), 2, 01.02.1991, 1–2, at 2.

81 Maňasová, A.: Má dáti – dal, in: Fatra 42 (1992), 9, 25.05.1992, 1.

82 N. N.: Jak nám plati, in: Fatra 42 (1992), 21, 06.11.1992, 1.

83 Delegáti konference ZO FOS prac. Chemického průmyslu a. s. Barum Otrokovice: Dopis ministrovi, in: Barum 39 (1991), 1, 22.02.1991, 1.

84 In the Czech original, the phase "vytloukat klín klínem" is used, which means "to knock out a wedge with a wedge" (N. N.: Naši dlužníci. Seznam největších ‚neplatičů faktur' v srpnu, in: Hornický Kahan 35 (1991), 17, 25.09.1991, 3).

85 Voříšek, P.: Caricature, in: Hornický Kahan 35 (1991), 16, 11.09.1991, 1.

In fact, the threat of insolvency – regardless of whether it was 'primary' or 'secondary' insolvency – was an issue not only on an inter-enterprise but also on an intra-enterprise level. With regard to the latter, solvency issues were mostly discussed concerning job cuts and shutdowns, a topic that, after more than four decades of state socialism, was fairly new for Czech society. Generally, surveys from the early 1990s show that unemployment and precarious life conditions were perceived as threats, even though many Czechs were confident that they would not have to face them personally.[86] For example, a large study in 1991 featured the following question: 'Do you think that, during the next five years, the percentage of poor people in Czechoslovakia will increase, decrease or stay more or less the same?' Almost two-thirds of the respondents believed that it would increase.[87] Two years later, a survey revealed a more optimistic attitude. When asked about

86 In fact, unemployment numbers remained very low (see footnote 36).

87 Survey by Center for Empirical Research (STEM/Středisko empirických výzkumů), http://nesstar.soc.cas.cz/webview/index/en/nesstar/-SDA.c.nesstar/-esky.d.1/V-zkumy-transformace.d.19/Soci-ln-spravedlnost-91.s.CSDA00118/Chudoba-a-bohatstv-.h.4/zmena-chudych/fVariable/CSDA00118_V82 (last retrieved on 29.04.2020).

their own future as employees, 70% expected to keep their jobs, while only 26% were uncertain and 4% were certain of actually losing them.[88]

Nevertheless, the threat of job cuts – and closely connected to it the issue of insolvency – was frequently mentioned on an enterprise level. Mostly, managements pointed out the companies' insecure situation and noted that employees needed to work harder and better adapt to market conditions if they wanted to keep their jobs. For example, in early 1991, Jaroslav Lněnička, managing director of ZVU Strojírny, appealed to his staff: "If we want to keep this enterprise in a somewhat acceptable economic situation and if we don't want layoffs ... it is necessary that we start playing the market game. If we don't manage to do this, someone else will play it instead of us and without us."[89] Very similar arguments were used about one year later when the management of ZVU Strojírny urged its employees more actively to take part in improving the company's situation. It was made clear that they could not continue to carry out their work as they had under state socialism.[90]

Similarly, Barum's management pointed out that the company's future was insecure and that various long-term measures had to be taken in order to improve its financial situation. Eventually, the quality of its tires would decide whether the company would be able to continue its existence under the conditions of a market economy. Barum's management also stressed that doing business in a market economy meant being permanently threatened with solvency problems and even with bankruptcy.[91]

A more optimistic view was held by MEZ Mohelnice's representatives, but only at first. In July 1991, Drahomír Klimša, manager of the sales department, stated: "The fact that we are able to sell our products on very discerning international markets and that our customers are willing to pay for them means in my opinion that we are still an interesting and promising

---

88 Survey by Public Opinion Research Institute (IVVM/*Institut pro výzkum veřejného mínění*) at the Czech Statistical Office, cited in: N.N.: Bankroty odběratelů odhrožují třetinu podniků, in: Český deník, 04.05.1993.

89 "Pokud chceme zachovat podnik v nějaké ekonomický přijatelné poloze a nepropouštět ... je nutno začít hrát tržní hru. Jestliže to neuděláme, bude ji hrát někdo jiný za nás a bez nás. " (Lněnička, Jaroslav: Zvu a trh, in: Hradecký Kovák 42 (1991), 6, 15.02.1991, 1–2, at 2).

90 Bulíček, Miloslav: Stojíme před závažnými úkoly, in: Hradecký Kovák 43 (1992), 1, 17.01.1992, 1–2, 1.

91 Bačák, Milan: Platební neschopnost minulostí, in: Barum 39 (1991), 7, 05.04.1991, 1–4, at 4.

supplier from a customers' perspective."[92] However, after severe job cuts in 1991, managing director Jiří Kuchář explained early the following year that the state of the company was, "after a difficult operation", suffering from high debt, low solvency, and decreasing sales figures.[93]

Overall, we can say that these managerial appeals had a rather pessimistic or alarming undertone, and that 'sticks' rather than 'carrots' were frequently used in intra-enterprise communication. Nevertheless, caricatures published in the Rudné doly Příbram's company magazine suggest that the threat of insolvency, and thus the threat of earning less or losing one's job, were faced with a grim sense of humor. For example, a caricature published in March 1992 shows an executive employee talking to his associates: "I have two announcements for you, guys – First, the good one: There will be enough work! And now the bad one: Even though there is enough work, there is not enough money for your salaries!"[94]

---

92 "To, že jsme schopni naše výrobky realizovat na nejnáročnějších zahraničních trzích, že jsou zákazníci ochotni za ně zaplatit, znamená podle mého názoru, že jsme pro zákazníky pořád zajímavým a perspektivním dodavatelem." Klimša, Drahomír: Můžeme naším zákazníkům ještě něco nabídnout?, in: Hlas MEZU 42 (1991), 14/15, 03.07.1991, at 1–2, 2.

93 Kuchář, Jiří: Podnik jako po těžké operaci, in: Hlas MEZU 43 (1992), 1, 15.01.1992, 1–2, at 1.

94 Voříšek, P.: Caricature, in: Hornický Kahan 36 (1992), 3, 11.03.1992, 1.

4. *Summary and Conclusion*

By evaluating the company newspapers of five Czech industrial enterprises, this paper has shown that the fight against insolvency as well as the search for financial security were important issues during the early 1990s. Just like for other stakeholders – from politicians to private individuals – the first years of the transformation period were a highly insecure time, both from the perspective of the companies' management as well as from that of their employees. Working conditions started to change and so did every employee's personal responsibility to contribute to the enterprises' future success. Even though foreign direct investment was often not readily available,[95] Czech companies were afraid of being unable to preserve their own (brand) identity. A common fear was that they would end up as an 'extended workbench' for a competitor from the West.

However, both for the employers and the employees, the most important question was whether the companies would be able to survive until the privatisation process and beyond it – something which four of the five analysed enterprises managed to do. In the early 1990s, this had not been certain as several problems posed serious threats to the companies' survival. From a financial point of view, insecurity increased for both macro- and microeconomic reasons. The companies could not resort to most securities the old economic system had provided, such as fixed resource prices and regulated domestic and international markets. They were therefore earning less, while at the same time their need for capital was growing. Filling this gap with bank loans was only possible to a certain extent, and paying back these loans turned out to be difficult because the companies had problems not only in selling but also in getting paid for their products. In fact, outstanding payments from their respective business partners continued to threaten the companies' solvency.

The companies knew about these problems and tried to find countermeasures to tackle their solvency issues. Apart from taking out credits, they made efforts to attract new customers and also investors from abroad, most notably from Western Europe. Another strategy was to reduce inter-enterprise debt: on the one hand, the companies aimed to prevent outstanding payments in the first place, for example by drafting more precise contracts; on the other hand, they tried to collect already existing debt, for example by appealing directly to their debtors or by initiating arbitration proceedings.

---

95 See footnote 56.

The companies' solvency issues were not only addressed through the implementation of concrete measures, but were also hotly debated in corporate discourse. Concerning inter-enterprise debt, it was more common to point out other companies' failures than to recognise one's own shortcomings. Even though 'everyone was indebted to everyone', the companies were eager to present themselves as creditors and not as debtors. Moreover, financial insecurity and its potential consequences, particularly job cuts, were a relevant topic in intra-enterprise communications. Managers mainly emphasised the responsibility of employees actively to contribute to improving the company's situation. It was made clear that they had to work harder and adapt quickly to the new market conditions – otherwise their jobs would be in danger.

Overall, both the factual and the discursive ways of dealing with insolvency issues show that the companies were determined to survive the privatisation process. Their behavior also indicates that they were well aware that there was no way back to a financially secure situation like the one that they had experienced during the days of state socialism. At the same time, the enterprises seem to have recognised that they needed to look for some new sort of financial security. In order to achieve this aim they adopted a variety of measures – some of them more and some of them less useful than others.

The examples discussed above of their fight against insolvency and their quest for financial security thus show that, for Czech industry, the transformation was a learning-by-doing process. It is very likely that similar observations could be also made when examining other stakeholders in the transformation process: for example, politicians had to deal with multiple insecurities as well. However, their determination to get back to a more secure situation did not always lead directly to successful results but was often hit-and-miss.

Another important observation is that, under certain historical conditions, security concepts can lose their relevance quite quickly. The example of Czech enterprises demonstrates that this is especially true in the context of significant political and economic upheavals. However, if one definition of financial security disappears, a new definition does not automatically manifest itself. For example, financial security was more or less a prerequisite during state socialism, but during the early 1990s there was no fixed new concept to which the enterprises could turn. Rather, they had to find ways out of their solvency issues, for example by adapting their everyday business practices to the requirements of a market economy. By creating new strategies to overcome solvency problems, they were – at least implicitly – contributing to finding a new definition of financial security.

They thus took part in a securitisation process:[96] before 1989–90, both the actual relevance of and the discourse surrounding financial (in)security were rather marginal. However, with the introduction of a market economy, being in a financially stable situation was increasingly perceived as vital aspect of a company's security and its ability to 'survive'. At the same time, the maximum level of financial security which a company could reach began to decrease. What would have been considered as totally insecure in a socialist economy – for example, the continuous threat of an actual shutdown – slowly became a normality. Altogether, the example of Czech companies during the early 1990s shows that, when dealing with concepts of security from a historical point of view, it is particularly important to not perceive them as fixed. Instead, we need to analyse how these concepts were continuously shaped by the affected stakeholders' attitudes and behavior.

Bibliography

Begg, David: Economic Reform in Czechoslovakia: Should We Believe in Santa Klaus?, in: Economic Policy 6 (1991), 13, p. 243–286

Bonß, Wolfgang: (Un-)Sicherheit in der Moderne, in: Zoche, Peter et al. (eds.), Zivile Sicherheit. Gesellschaftliche Dimensionen gegenwärtiger Sicherheitspolitiken. Bielefeld 2014, p. 43–70

Bricault, Giselle et al. (eds.): Major Business Organizations of Eastern Europe and the Commonwealth of Independent States 1992–93. London 1992

Cezanne, Wolfgang: Allgemeine Volkswirtschaftslehre. München 2005

Conze, Eckart: Die Suche nach Sicherheit. Eine Geschichte der Bundesrepublik Deutschland von 1949 bis in die Gegenwart. München 2009

Conze, Eckart: Securitization. Gegenwartsdiagnose oder historischer Analyseansatz?, in: Geschichte und Gesellschaft 38 (2012), 3, p. 453–467

Daniels, Mario: „Wirtschaftlicher Landesverrat" im „Wirtschaftskampf gegen Deutschland". Die deutsche Chemieindustrie und die Bekämpfung ausländischer Industriespionage in den 1920er Jahren, in: Historische Zeitschrift 299 (2014), 2, p. 352–383

96 Originally, the term securitisation mainly referred to state and political contexts. However, in historical research, securitisation can be applied more broadly (*Conze*, Securitization, 457f.), for example, in order to analyse the behaviour of economic stakeholders such as companies (as has been done in: *Daniels*, Landesverrat).

Dyba, Karel/Švejnar, Jan: Stabilization and Transition in Czechoslovakia, in: Blanchard, Oliver Jean et al. (eds.): The Transition in Eastern Europe. Volume 1. Chicago 1994, p. 93–122

Esbester, Mike: Organizing work. Company magazines and the discipline of safety, in: Management & Organizational History 3 (2013), 3-4, p. 217–237

Hass, Jeffrey K.: Rethinking the post-Soviet experience. The market meets the moral economy. New York 2012

Heiner, Ronald A.: The Origin of Predictable Behaviour, in: The American Economic Review 73 (1983), 4, p. 560–595

Heller, Michael: Company magazines 1880–1940. An overview, in: Management & Organizational History 3 (2013), 3–4, p. 179–196

Hobsbawm, Eric: Europäische Revolutionen. 1789 bis 1848. Zürich 1962

Hodulák, Vladan/Krpec, Oldřich: Hospodářská politika, in: Balík, Stanislav et al. (eds.): Veřejné politiky v České republice v letech 1989-2009. Brno 2010, p. 169–221

Holman, Robert: Transformace české ekonomiky v komparaci s dalšími zeměmi střední Evropy. Prague 2000

Huntington, Samuel P.: The Third Wave. Democratization in the Late Twentieth Century. Norman 1991

Kosta, Jiří: Die Transformation des Wirtschaftssystems in der Tschechoslowakei und den beiden Nachfolgestaaten, in: Pradetto, August (ed.): Die Rekonstruktion Ostmitteleuropas. Politik, Wirtschaft und Gesellschaft im Umbruch. Opladen 1994, p. 157–187

Kornai, János: Economics of shortage. Amsterdam 1980

Kopeček, Michal (ed.): Architekti dlouhé změny. Expertní kořeny postsocialismu v Československu (1980–1995). Prague 2019

Krátká, Lenka: Letos musíme být spokojenější než loni! Proměny české firemní kultury po roce 1989. Prague 2019

Mejstřík, Michal et al.: Restructuring and Development of the Banking Sector in Advanced Transition Country: The Czech Republic, in: Mejstřík, Michal (ed.), Cultivation of financial markets in the Czech Republic. Prague 2004, p. 19–113

Merkel, Wolfgang et al (eds.): The handbook of political, social, and economic transformation. Oxford 2019

Myant, Martin: The Rise and Fall of Czech Capitalism. Economic Development in the Czech Republic since 1989, Cheltenham 2003

Orenstein, Mitchell A.: Out of the Red. Building Capitalism and Democracy in Postcommunist Europe. Ann Arbor 2001

Pavlínek, Petr: A Successful Transformation? Restructuring of the Czech Automobile Industry. Heidelberg 2008

Pesendorfer, Dieter: Der Restaurationsprozeß des Kapitalismus in der ehemaligen Tschechoslowakei, Probleme des Übergangs. Frankfurt/New York 1998

Rosa, Hartmut: Beschleunigung. Die Veränderung der Zeitstrukturen in der Moderne. Frankfurt am Main 2005

Schäffler, Eva: Transformation als Aushandlungsprozess: Die Entstehung eines Konkursgesetzes in der Tschechischen Republik der 1990er Jahre, in: Rechtskultur. Zeitschrift für europäische Rechtsgeschichte 7 (2018), 1, p. 32–47

Slaný, Antonín: Makroekonomická analýza a hospodářská politika. Prag 2003

Ther, Philipp: Europe since 1989. A history. Princeton/Oxford 2016

Večerník, Jiří/Matějů, Petr (eds.): Ten years of rebuilding capitalism. Prague 1999

Vltavská, Kristýna/Sixta, Jaroslav: A Historical View on the Development of Czech Economy from 1970, in: Prague Economic Papers 24 (2015), 1, p. 105–122

Zwierlein, Cornel: Sicherheitsgeschichte. Ein neues Feld der Geschichtswissenschaften, in: Geschichte und Gesellschaft 38 (2012), 3, p. 365–386

Žídek, Libor: From Central Planning to the Market Transformation of the Czech Economy 1989–2004. Budapest 2017

Author information

Kristin Stanwick Bårnås

Kristin Stanwick Bårnås currently works as a consultant and researcher in Norway, primarily focusing on business and industry development. She obtained her PhD in Management from University of Strathclyde in Glasgow in 2018 with a thesis on the management of Foreign Direct Investment Risk by three Norwegian Firms in the 1960s and 1970s. She holds a master's degree in history where she did research on the history of ISO 14001, the environmental management standard. Her research interests therefore involve international standardization and environmental management systems, together with internationalization, business promotion, and export.

Marcus Böick

Marcus Böick is PostDoc researcher and lecturer in the field of Contemporary History at the Historical Institute of the Ruhr-University Bochum. His current project analysis the history of German private security business since the late nineteenth-century in its transnational contexts. He obtained his PhD in history in 2016 from University Bochum. His thesis dealt with the transformation of the socialist planned economy in Eastern Germany after 1990 operated by the Treuhandanstalt. Previously, he was awarded with a PhD scholarship by the Federal Foundation for the Reappraisal of the SED Dictatorship in Berlin. Besides his interest in different European and American security regimes, his research is focused on the history of post-socialist transformations, the history of organizations as well as the histories of privatization and marketisation.

Sascha Brünig

Sascha Brünig is a research associate at the collaborative research group 'Dynamics of Security. Types of Securitization from a Historical Perspective' at Philipps University Marburg, Germany. He is working on a dissertation on the history of nuclear power in the 1980s and early 1990s Federal Republic. He holds a Master's Degree from Philipps University Marburg, having obtained his Bachelor's Degree at the Universities of Marburg and

Strasbourg. His research interests cover the cultural history of technology, environmental history, and the history of knowledge.

Mark Jakob

Mark Jakob currently is a PostDoc researcher with the collaborative research group 'Dynamics of Security. Types of Securitization from a Historical Perspective' at the Philipps University in Marburg, Germany. There, he is working on a comparative study of German and British export credit insurance until the Second World War. He obtained his PhD in history in 2009 from the Goethe University in Frankfurt am Main with a thesis on the change of social and economic conceptions of the family in West German family policy and its academic advisors between 1954 and 1982. He taught at the universities of Göttingen, Marburg, and the Jacobs University, Bremen, and worked as co-ordinator's assistant at the DFG Priority Programme 'Experience and expectation'. His research interests, apart from business history, are regional economic and social history, the history of family and youth policies, and history of the bourgeoisie.

Nina Kleinöder

Nina Kleinöder is a Postdoc research assistant at the Department of History and Cultural Studies, Economic and Social History, at the Philipps-University of Marburg, Germany. Her research is interested in Business History, History of working environments and colonial history. Her PhD thesis (2015) and her work as a Postdoc researcher at the University of Düsseldorf, Germany, focussed on the History of Labour (Occupational Health and Safety) and the change of working environments ("Humanisation of Work") in 20th century Germany. Her current project on colonial railway building aims to link German colonial history in Africa with modern Business History approaches.

Christian Kleinschmidt

Christian Kleinschmidt has been Professor of Economic and Social History at Philipps-Universität Marburg since 2009. Within the SFB 138 ("Dynamics of Security") he is head of the sub-project "External Economic Securitization". His research focuses on the history of business, the history of international economic relations, and the history of consumption.

Christian Marx

Christian Marx currently is a researcher at the Leibniz Institute for Contemporary History in Munich, Germany. There, he is working on a collective biography of the top management of the German central bank (Deutsche Bundesbank) in the two postwar decades (1948-1969). He obtained his PhD in history in 2011 from the University of Trier with a thesis on the corporate governance of a large German iron and steel company in the first half of the 20th century, and worked on corporate networks in Germany, France and the United States. In 2020, he finished his habilitation on the multinationalisation of European companies from the chemical industry since the 1970s. He taught at the universities of Trier and Saarbrücken. His research interests, apart from business history, are environmental and social history as well as the history of networks and elites.

Sabine Pitteloud

Sabine Pitteloud is a lecturer at the Paul Bairoch Institute of Economic and Social History of the University of Geneva. Thanks to a Doc.Mobility Fellowship from the Swiss National Science Foundation, she was a visiting scholar at the Humboldt Universität Berlin and at the Robert L. Heilbroner Center for Capitalism Studies of the New School for Social Research in 2017. Her research investigates the political and institutional role of multinationals, their coordination efforts within business interest associations, and their ability to deal with political risks in historical perspective. Her new project focuses on the role of business interests in the implementation of environmental norms.

Eva Schäffler

Eva Schäffler is a researcher at the Leibniz Institute for Contemporary History (IfZ) in Munich, where she is writing a study on the Czech economic transformation in the 1990s. In 2019, she received the Dobrovský Fellowship of the Czech Academy of Sciences. Her latest publications focus on transnational as well as on legal-historical aspects of the Czech privatization process. Generally, her research focus is on economic, social and gender history of Central Eastern Europe in the second half of the 20th century (including the GDR/eastern Germany). She studied History, European and Czech Studies in Germany, Austria, Spain and the Czech Republic and wrote her PhD thesis on "Partner relationships in the GDR/eastern Germany between late and post-socialism" (book published by Harrassowitz in 2017). She worked as research assistant and lecturer at the University of Salzburg, but also as project manager at a German-Czech Euroregion.

Ole Sparenberg

Ole Sparenberg holds a post-doctoral scholarship from the Gerda Henkel Foundation in 2019 and 2020 and teaches at the Karlsruhe Institute of Technology. He is currently working on the environmental and economic history of deep-sea mining projects from the 1960s to the present. After obtaining his PhD in history in 2010 from Göttingen University with a thesis on fisheries and whaling under the Nazi autarky economy, he worked as a research assistant at Saarbrücken University from 2011 to 2018. His research interests include the economic and environmental history of the 20th century, in particular mineral and living resources.